子連れ狼

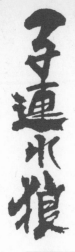

LONE
WOLF
AND
CUB

story
KAZUO KOIKE

art
GOSEKI KOJIMA

DARK HORSE MANGA™

translation
DANA LEWIS

lettering & retouch
DIGITAL CHAMELEON

cover illustration
FRANK MILLER with **LYNN VARLEY**

publisher
MIKE RICHARDSON

editor
MIKE HANSEN

assistant editor
TIM ERVIN

consulting editor
TOREN SMITH for **STUDIO PROTEUS**

book design
DARIN FABRICK

art director
MARK COX

Published by Dark Horse Manga, a division of Dark Horse Comics, Inc., in association with Kabushiki Kaisha Live Works and Koike Shoin Publishing Company, Ltd.

Dark Horse Manga
10956 SE Main Street, Milwaukie, OR 97222
www.darkhorse.com

First edition: April 2001
ISBN 978-1-56971-509-3

5 7 9 10 8 6

Printed in Canada

Lone Wolf and Cub Vol. 8: Chains of Death

To find a comics shop in your area, call the
Comic Shop Locator Service toll-free at 1-888-266-4226

CHAINS OF DEATH

子連れ狼

By KAZUO KOIKE
& GOSEKI KOJIMA

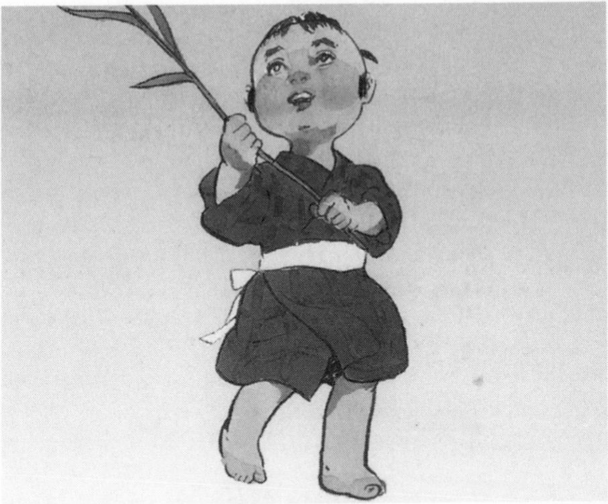

VOLUME

8

A NOTE TO READERS

Lone Wolf and Cub is famous for its carefully researched re-creation of Edo-Period Japan. To preserve the flavor of the work, we have chosen to retain many Edo-Period terms that have no direct equivalents in English. Japanese is written in a mix of Chinese ideograms and a syllabic writing system, resulting in numerous synonyms. In the glossary, you may encounter words with multiple meanings. These are words written with Chinese ideograms that are pronounced the same but carry different meanings. A Japanese reader seeing the different ideograms would know instantly which meaning it is, but these synonyms can cause confusion when Japanese is spelled out in our alphabet. *O-yurushi o* (please forgive us)!

LONE WOLF AND CUB

TABLE OF CONTENTS

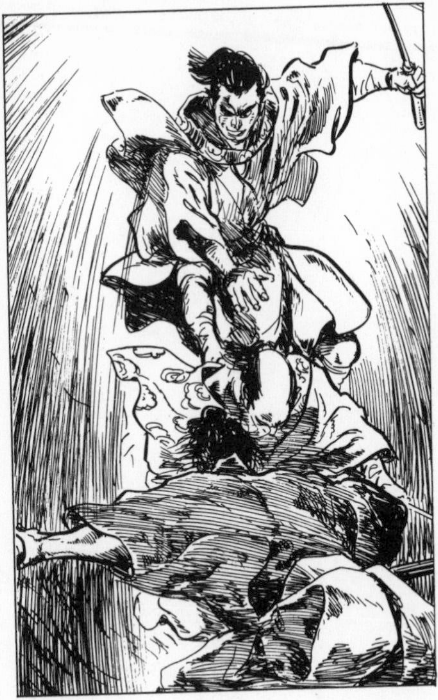

the thirty-ninth

Tidings of the Geese

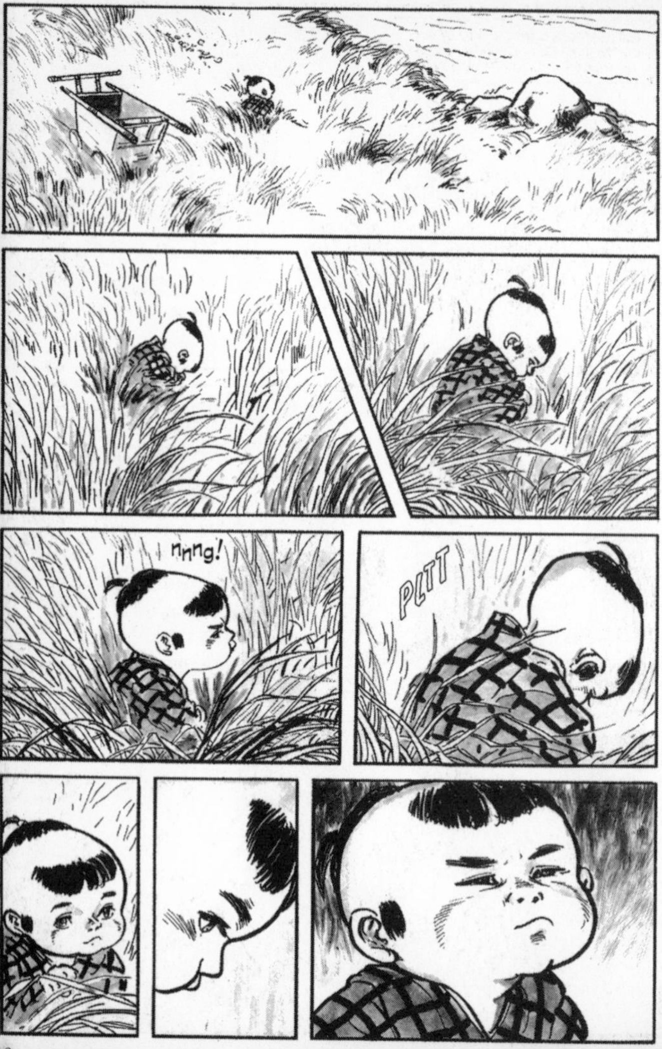
PLTT
nnng!

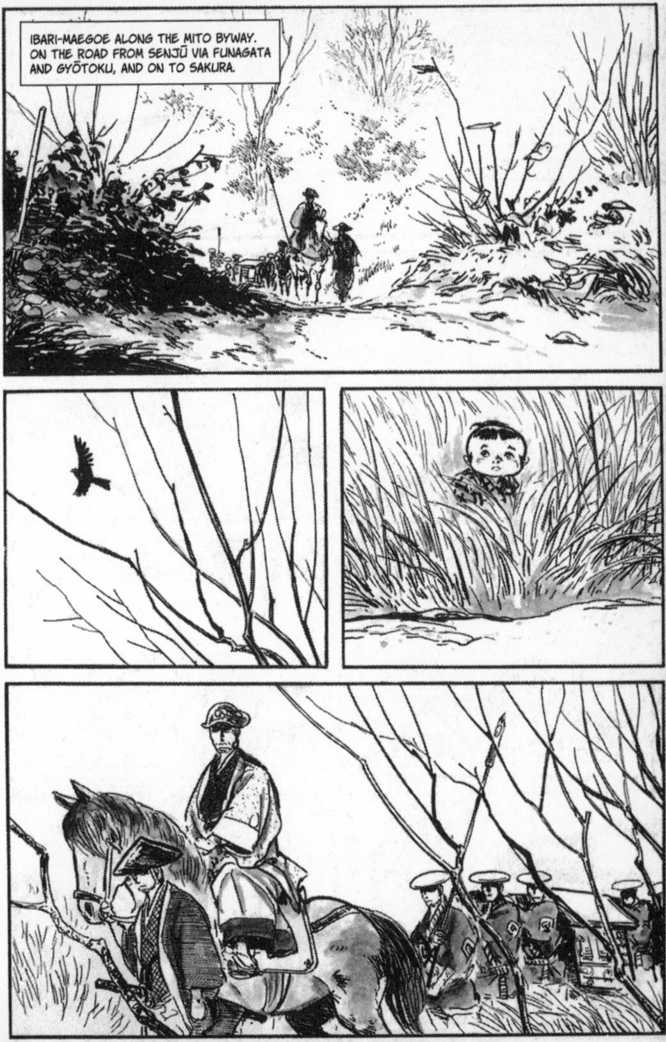
IBARI-MAEGOE ALONG THE MITO BYWAY.
ON THE ROAD FROM SENJŪ VIA FUNAGATA
AND GYŌTOKU, AND ON TO SAKURA.

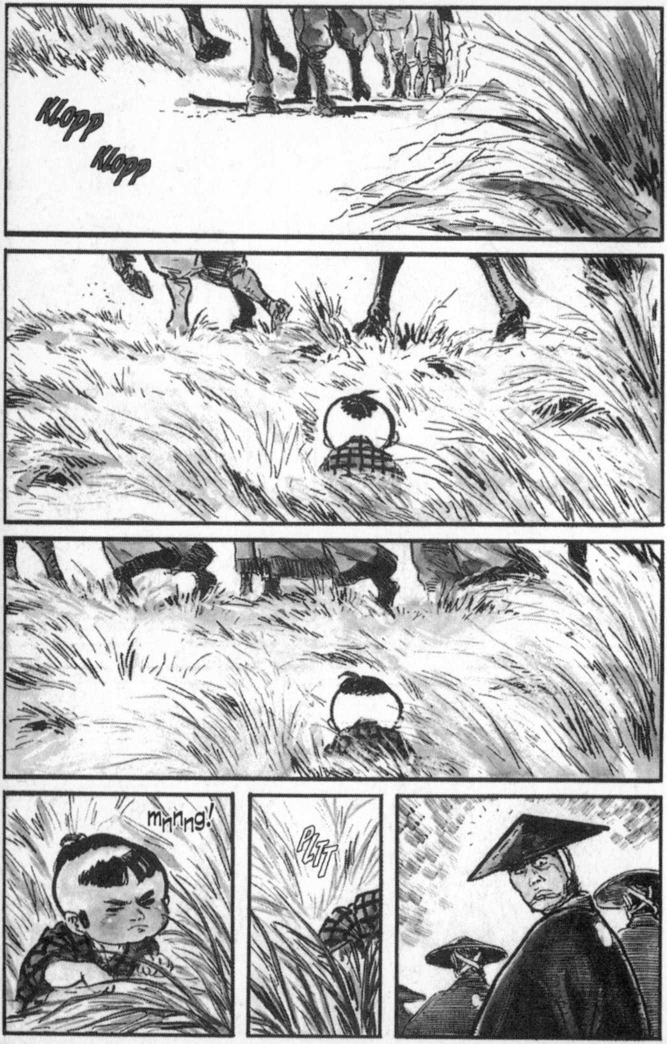
KLOPP
KLOPP
mnnng!
PLTT

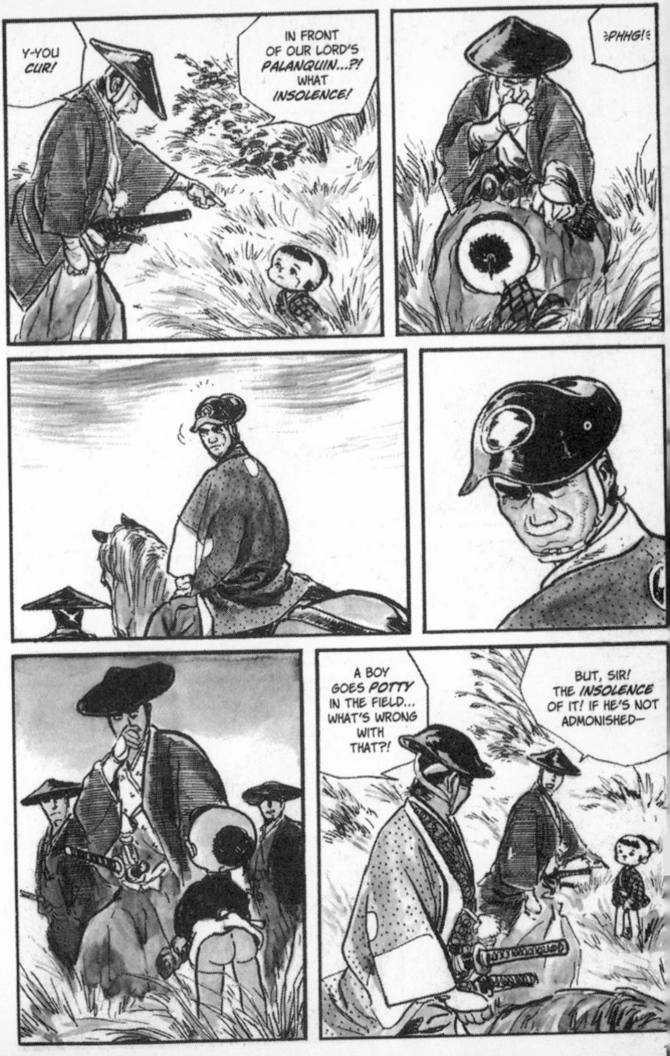
Y-YOU CUR!
IN FRONT OF OUR LORD'S PALANQUIN...?! WHAT INSOLENCE!
PHHG!
A BOY GOES POTTY IN THE FIELD... WHAT'S WRONG WITH THAT?!
BUT, SIR! THE INSOLENCE OF IT! IF HE'S NOT ADMONISHED—

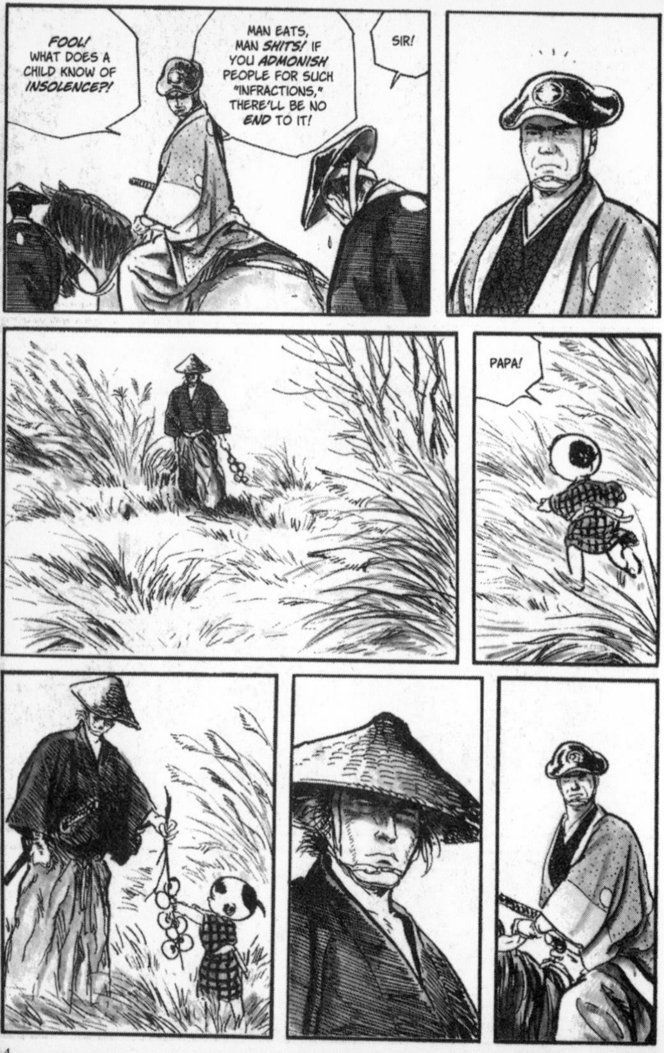
FOOL! WHAT DOES A CHILD KNOW OF INSOLENCE?!
MAN EATS, MAN SHITS! IF YOU ADMONISH PEOPLE FOR SUCH "INFRACTIONS," THERE'LL BE NO END TO IT!
SIR!
PAPA!

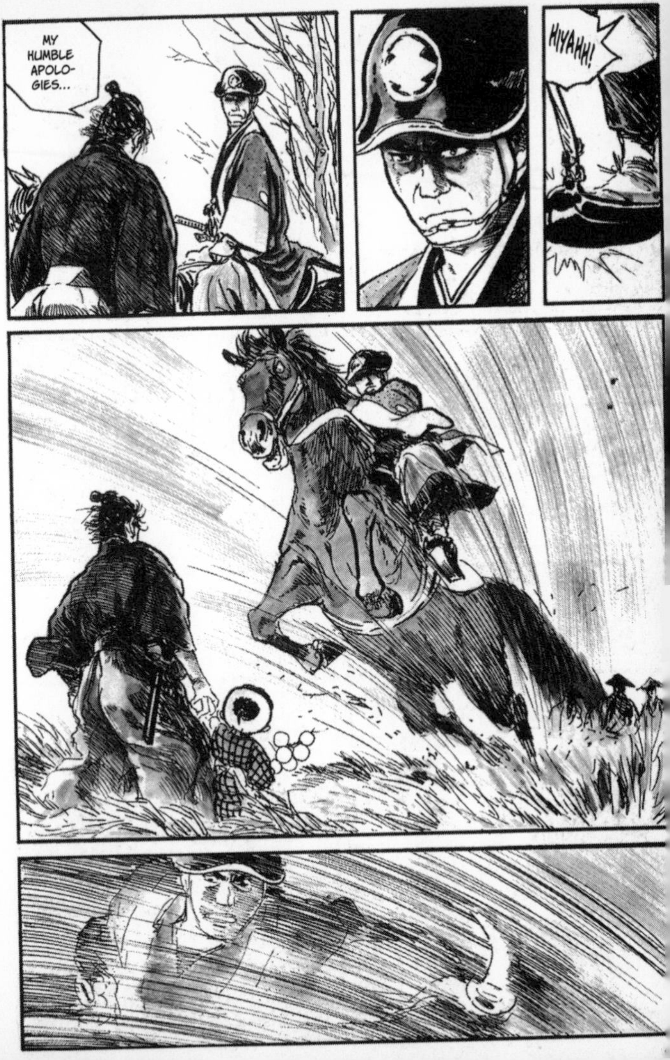
MY HUMBLE APOLOGIES...
HIYAHH!

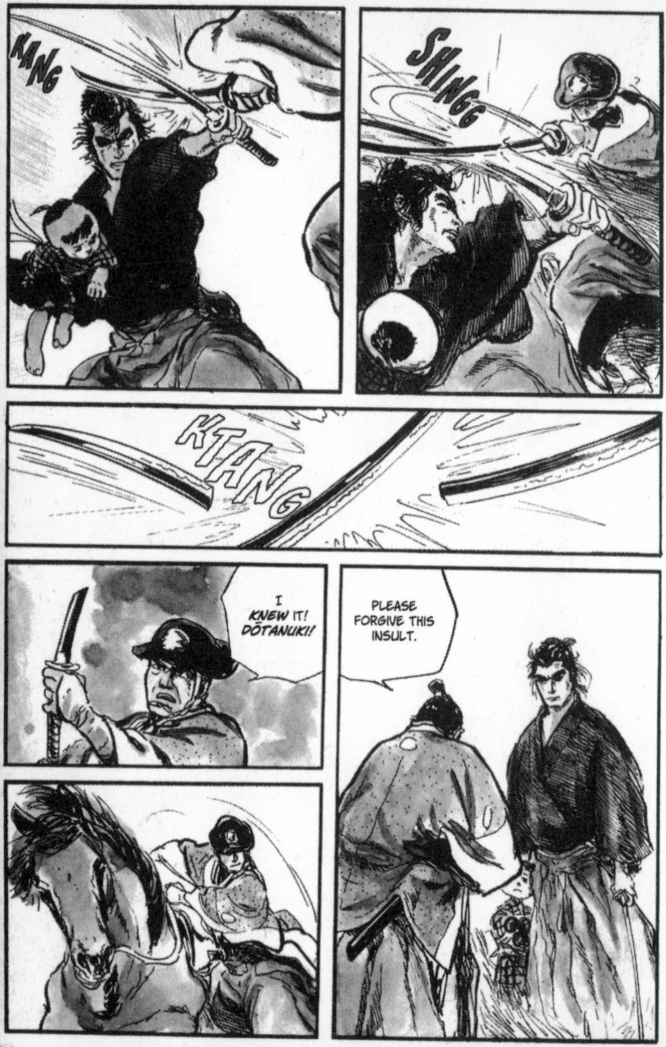
KANG
SHINGG
KTANG
I KNEW IT! DŌTANUKI!
PLEASE FORGIVE THIS INSULT.

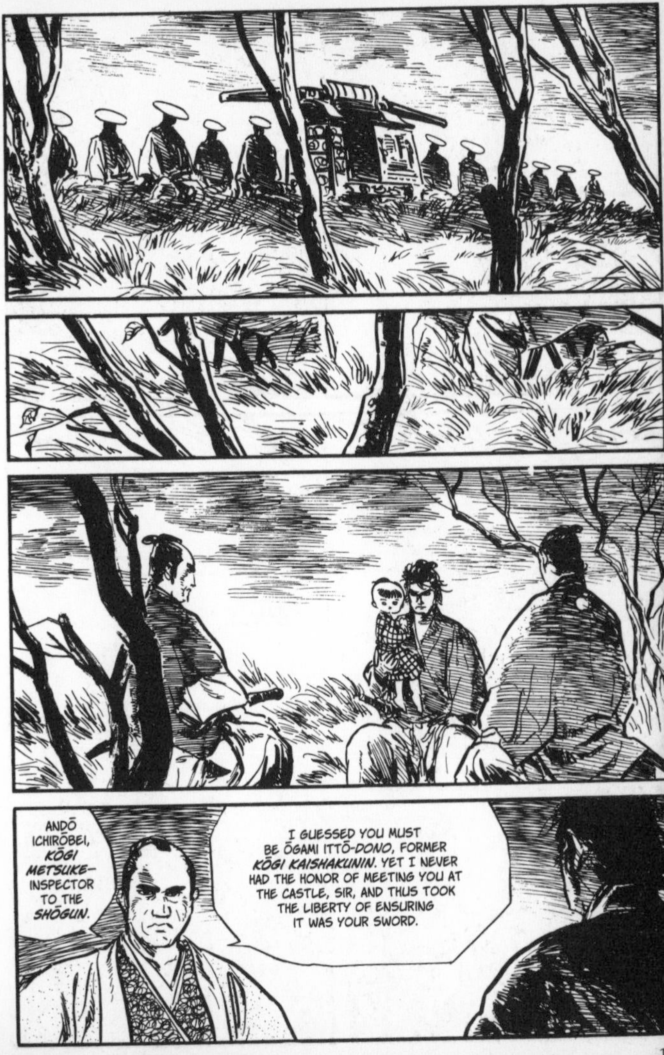
I GUESSED YOU MUST BE ŌGAMI ITTŌ-*DONO*, FORMER *KŌGI KAISHAKUNIN*. YET I NEVER HAD THE HONOR OF MEETING YOU AT THE CASTLE, SIR, AND THUS TOOK THE LIBERTY OF ENSURING IT WAS YOUR SWORD.
ANDŌ ICHIRŌBEI, *KŌGI METSUKE*—INSPECTOR TO THE *SHŌGUN*.

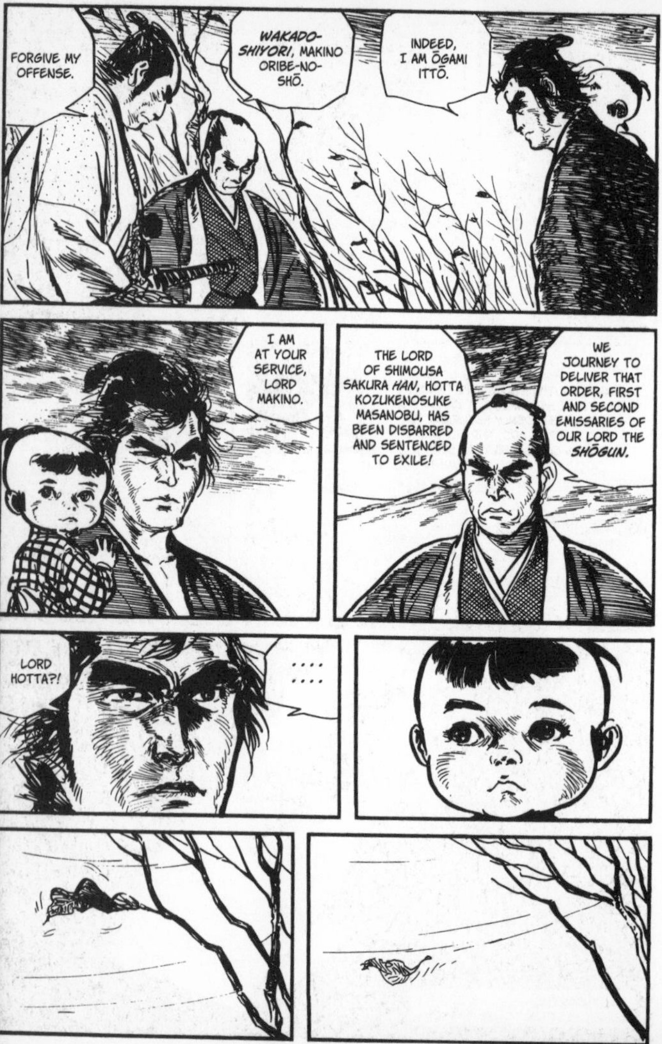
FORGIVE MY OFFENSE.
WAKADO-SHIYORI, MAKINO ORIBE-NO-SHŌ.
INDEED, I AM ŌGAMI ITTŌ.
I AM AT YOUR SERVICE, LORD MAKINO.
THE LORD OF SHIMOUSA SAKURA *HAN*, HOTTA KOZUKENOSUKE MASANOBU, HAS BEEN DISBARRED AND SENTENCED TO EXILE!
WE JOURNEY TO DELIVER THAT ORDER, FIRST AND SECOND EMISSARIES OF OUR LORD THE *SHŌGUN*.
LORD HOTTA?!
....
....

THE HOTTA CLAN IS THE *ROCK* OF THE TOKUGAWA *FUDAI*...

AND MASANOBU HIMSELF IS A TRUE SAMURAI, *UPRIGHT* AND *RESOLUTE*. YOU HAVE EVERY REASON TO BE SURPRISED.

HOTTA-SAMA HAS LONG BEEN DISMAYED BY THE GOVERNANCE OF THE *RŌJŪ*. THIS TWENTY-EIGHTH OF SEPTEMBER, IT CAME TO A HEAD. HE SUDDENLY RETURNED TO SAKURA FROM EDO, AND WITHDREW TO HIS CASTLE. HE THEN SENT A *KANSHO* TO THE SHŌGUNATE.

A MOST *STINGING* DOCUMENT...

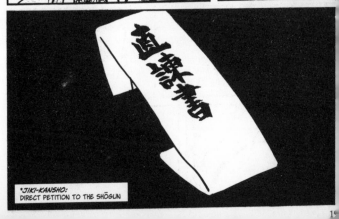

*JIKI-KANSHO: DIRECT PETITION TO THE SHŌGUN

19

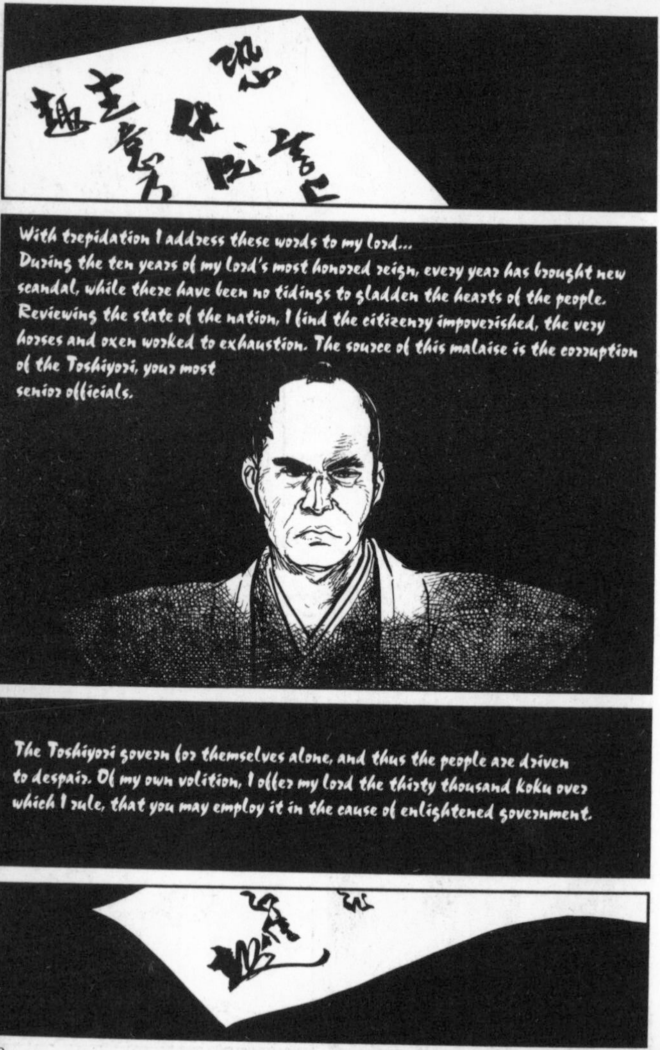
With trepidation I address these words to my lord...
During the ten years of my lord's most honored reign, every year has brought new scandal, while there have been no tidings to gladden the hearts of the people. Reviewing the state of the nation, I find the citizenry impoverished, the very horses and oxen worked to exhaustion. The source of this malaise is the corruption of the Toshiyori, your most senior officials.
The Toshiyori govern for themselves alone, and thus the people are driven to despair. Of my own volition, I offer my lord the thirty thousand koku over which I rule, that you may employ it in the cause of enlightened government.

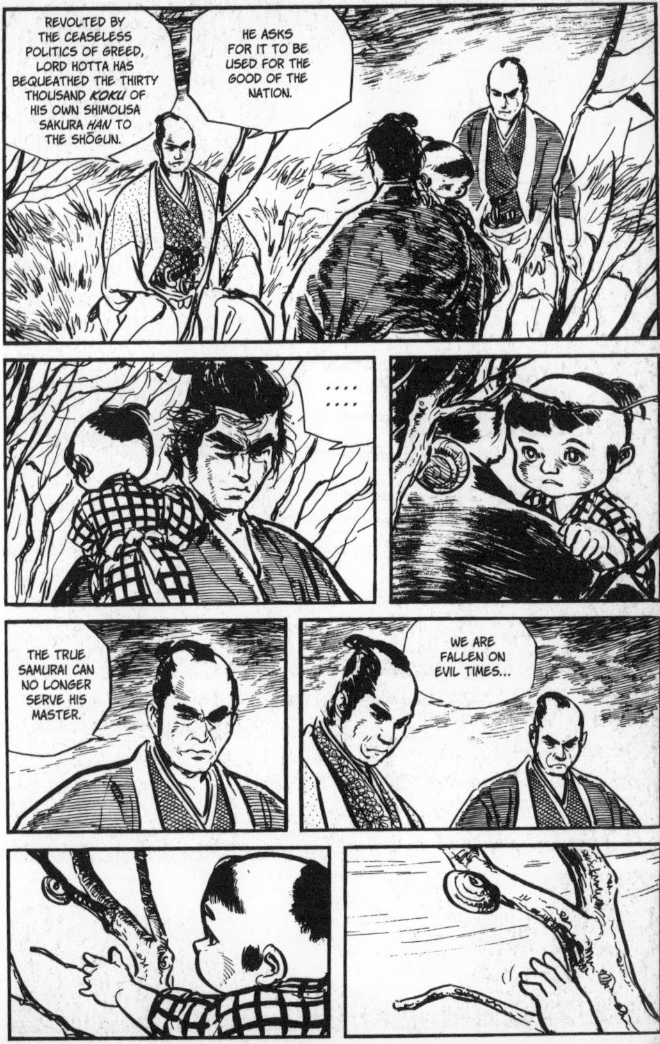
REVOLTED BY THE CEASELESS POLITICS OF GREED, LORD HOTTA HAS BEQUEATHED THE THIRTY THOUSAND *KOKU* OF HIS OWN SHIMOUSA SAKURA *HAN* TO THE SHŌGUN.
HE ASKS FOR IT TO BE USED FOR THE GOOD OF THE NATION.
....
....
THE TRUE SAMURAI CAN NO LONGER SERVE HIS MASTER.
WE ARE FALLEN ON EVIL TIMES...

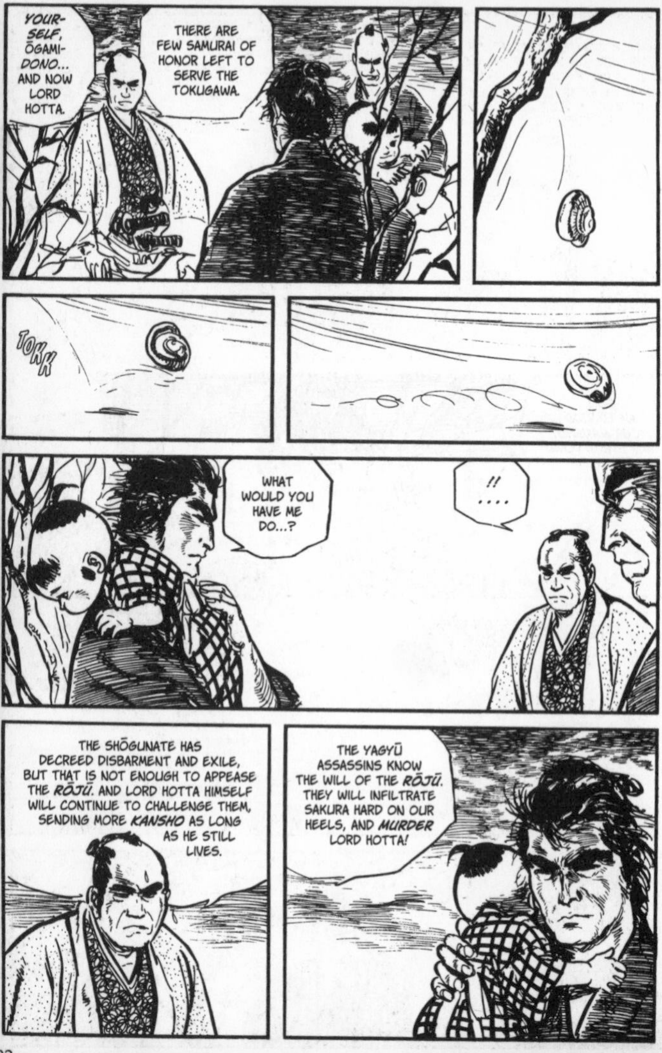
THERE ARE FEW SAMURAI OF HONOR LEFT TO SERVE THE TOKUGAWA.
YOURSELF, ŌGAMI-DONO... AND NOW LORD HOTTA.
TOKK
WHAT WOULD YOU HAVE ME DO...?
!! ....
THE SHŌGUNATE HAS DECREED DISBARMENT AND EXILE, BUT THAT IS NOT ENOUGH TO APPEASE THE *RŌJŪ*. AND LORD HOTTA HIMSELF WILL CONTINUE TO CHALLENGE THEM, SENDING MORE *KANSHO* AS LONG AS HE STILL LIVES.
THE YAGYŪ ASSASSINS KNOW THE WILL OF THE *RŌJŪ*. THEY WILL INFILTRATE SAKURA HARD ON OUR HEELS, AND *MURDER* LORD HOTTA!

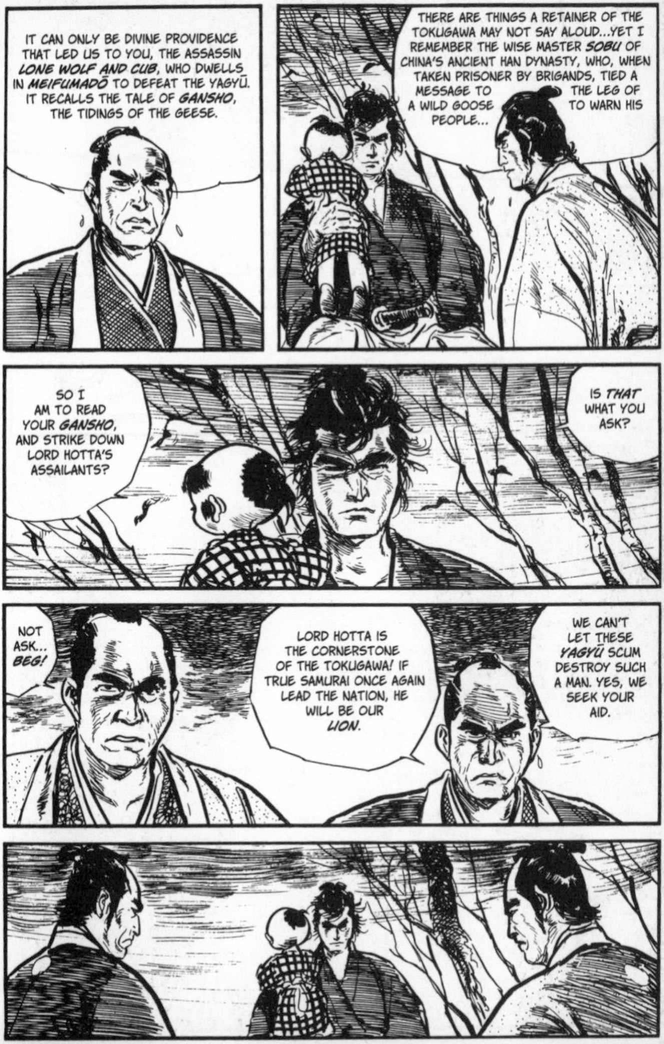
IT CAN ONLY BE DIVINE PROVIDENCE THAT LED US TO YOU, THE ASSASSIN *LONE WOLF AND CUB*, WHO DWELLS IN *MEIFUMADŌ* TO DEFEAT THE YAGYŪ. IT RECALLS THE TALE OF *GANSHO*, THE TIDINGS OF THE GEESE.
THERE ARE THINGS A RETAINER OF THE TOKUGAWA MAY NOT SAY ALOUD...YET I REMEMBER THE WISE MASTER *SOBU* OF CHINA'S ANCIENT HAN DYNASTY, WHO, WHEN TAKEN PRISONER BY BRIGANDS, TIED A MESSAGE TO THE LEG OF A WILD GOOSE TO WARN HIS PEOPLE...
SO I AM TO READ YOUR *GANSHO*, AND STRIKE DOWN LORD HOTTA'S ASSAILANTS?
IS *THAT* WHAT YOU ASK?
NOT ASK... *BEG!*
LORD HOTTA IS THE CORNERSTONE OF THE TOKUGAWA! IF TRUE SAMURAI ONCE AGAIN LEAD THE NATION, HE WILL BE OUR *LION*.
WE CAN'T LET THESE *YAGYŪ* SCUM DESTROY SUCH A MAN. YES, WE SEEK YOUR AID.

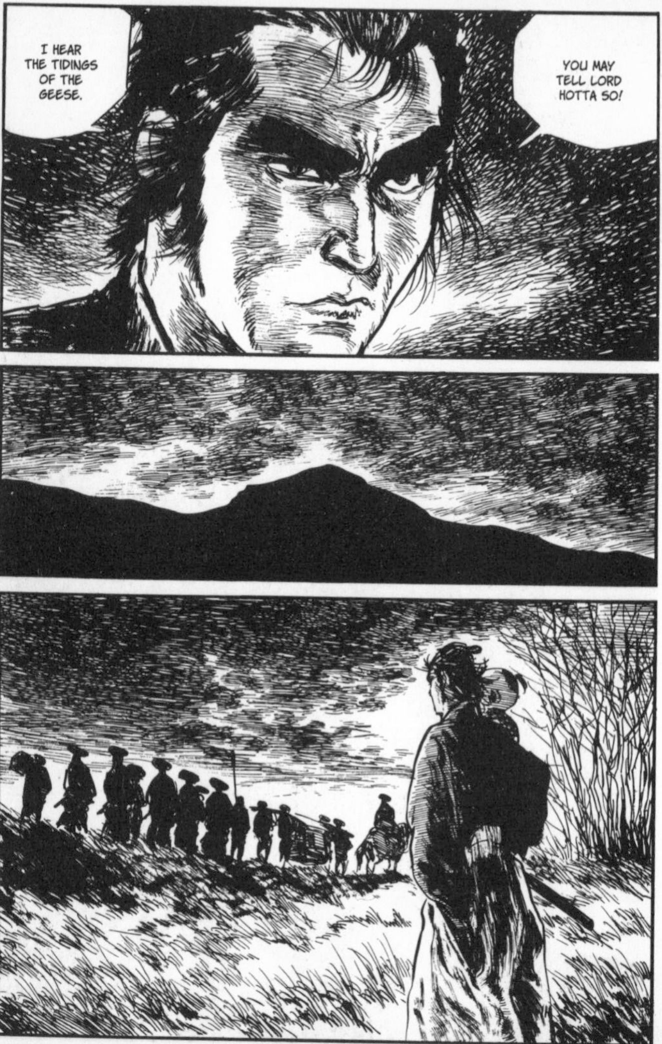
I HEAR THE TIDINGS OF THE GEESE.
YOU MAY TELL LORD HOTTA SO!

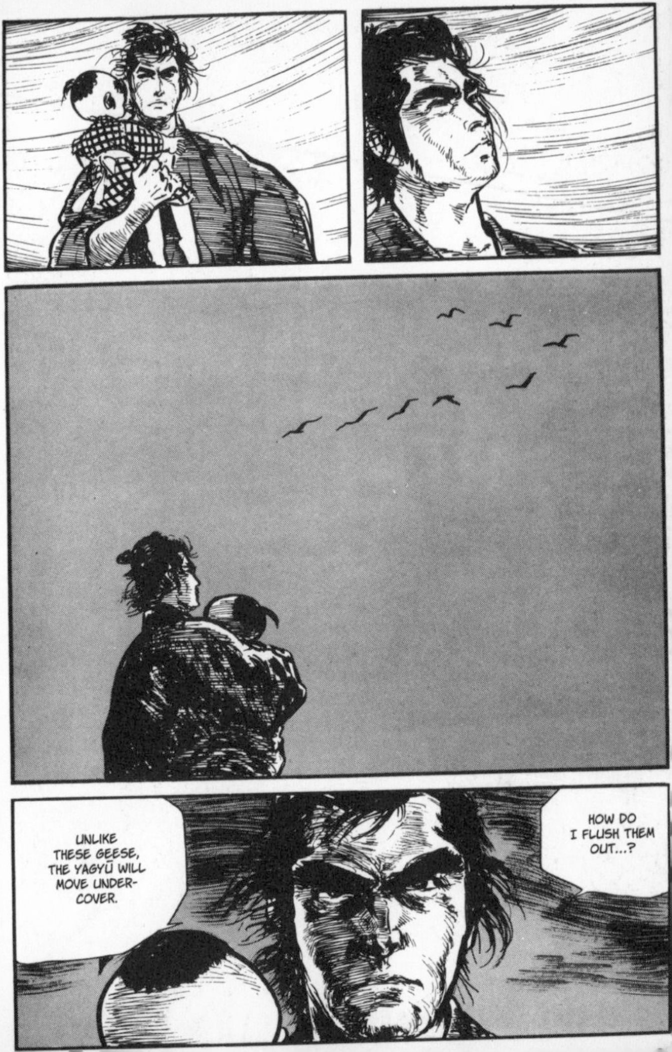
UNLIKE THESE GEESE, THE YAGYŪ WILL MOVE UNDER-COVER.
HOW DO I FLUSH THEM OUT...?

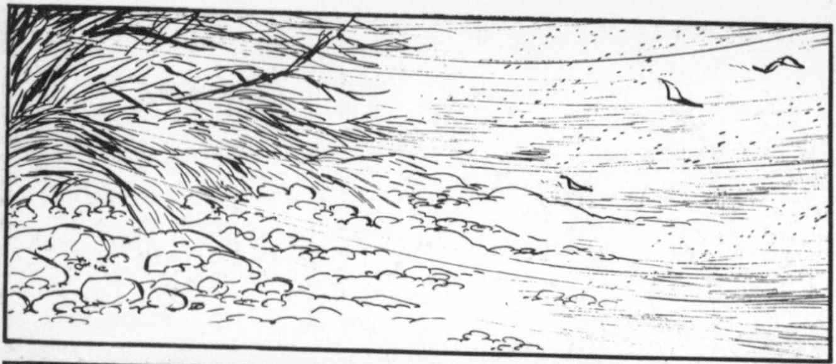
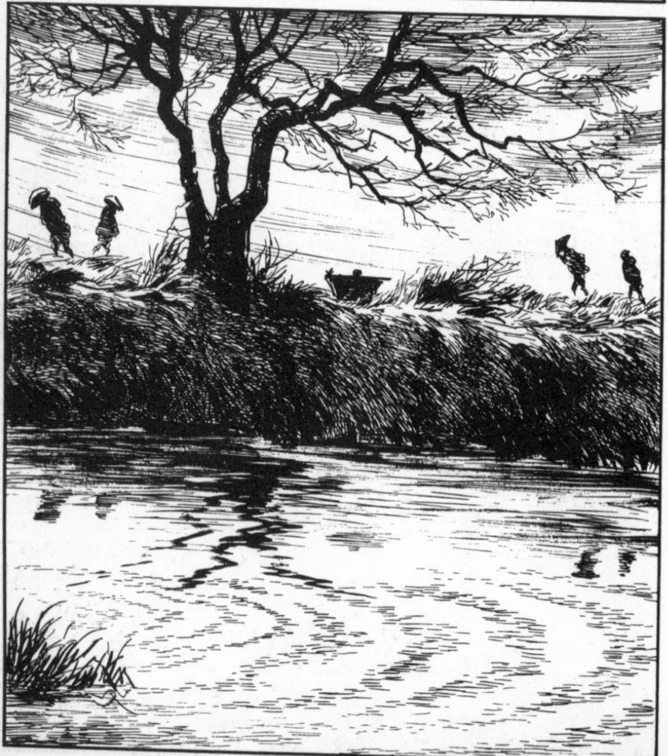

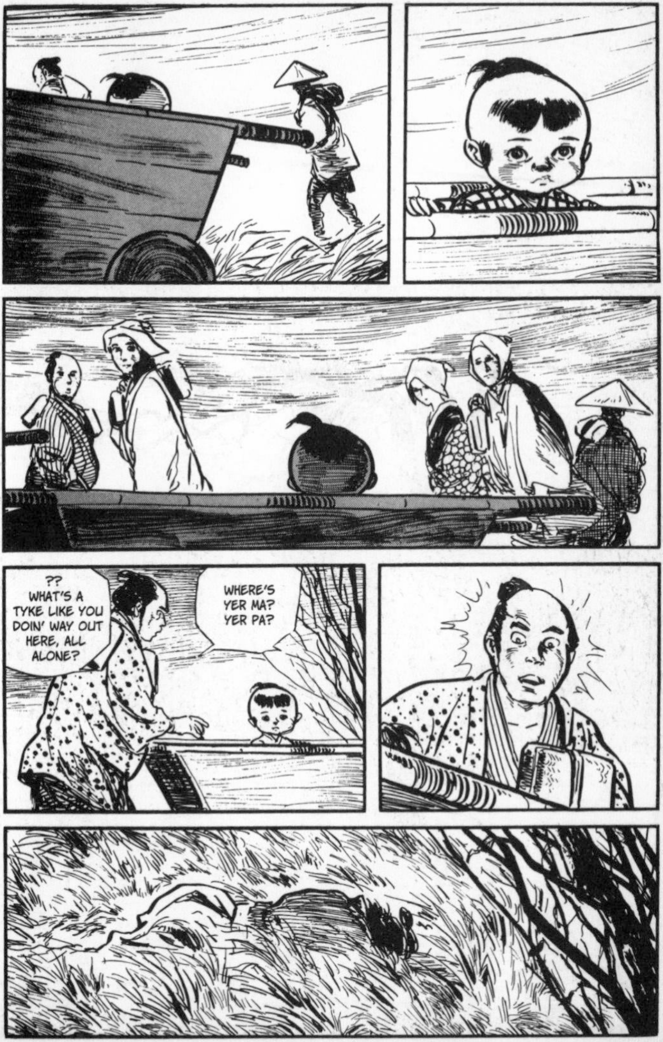
??
WHAT'S A TYKE LIKE YOU DOIN' WAY OUT HERE, ALL ALONE?
WHERE'S YER MA? YER PA?

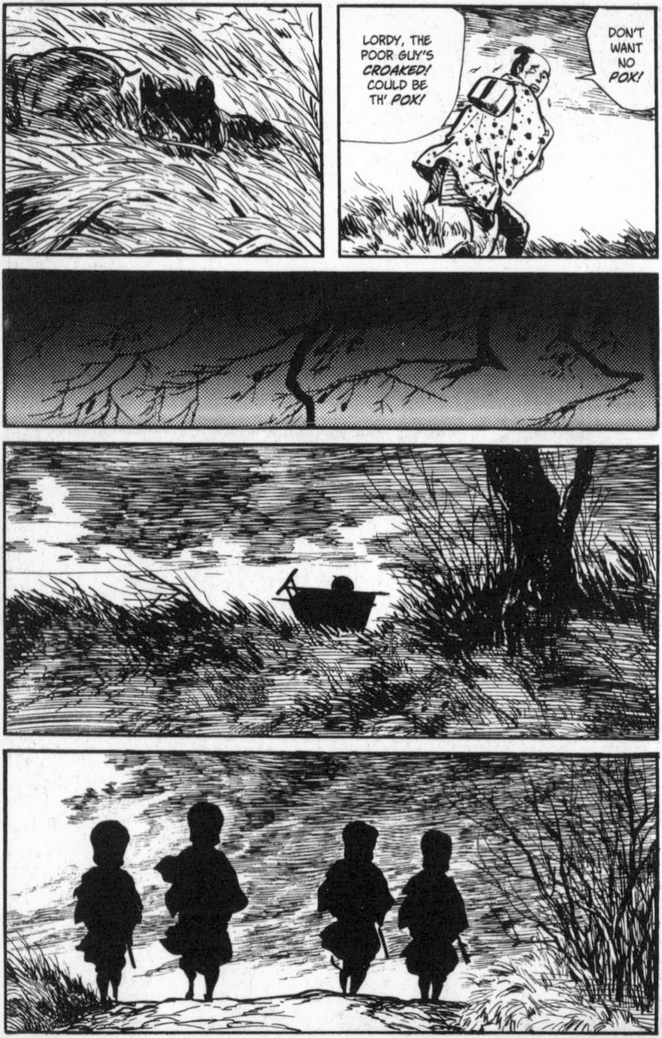
LORDY, THE POOR GUY'S *CROAKED!* COULD BE TH' *POX!*
DON'T WANT NO *POX!*

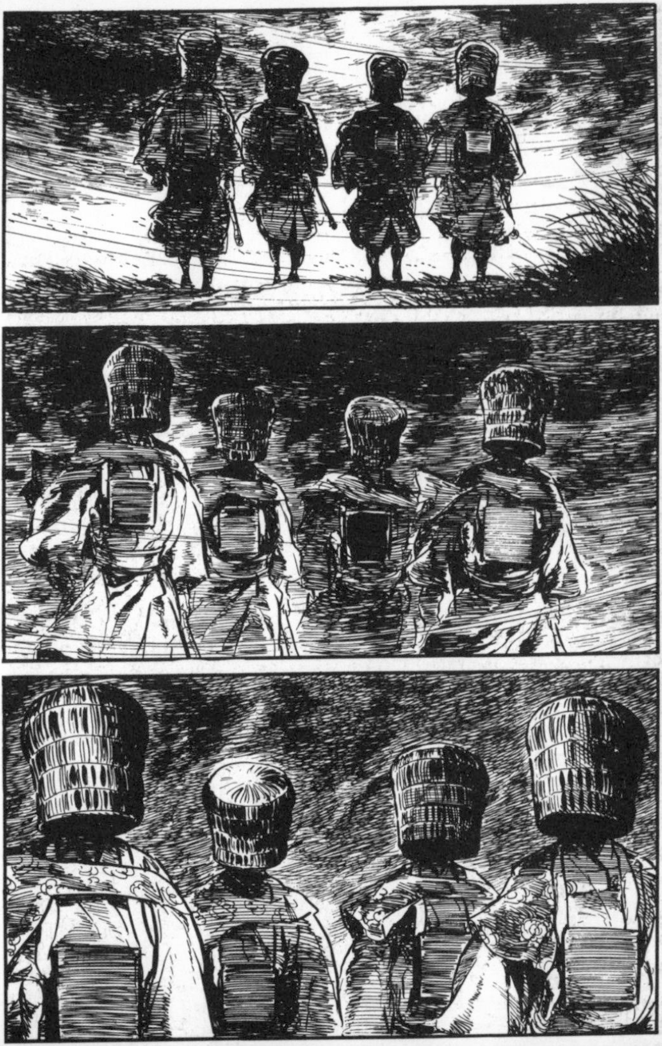

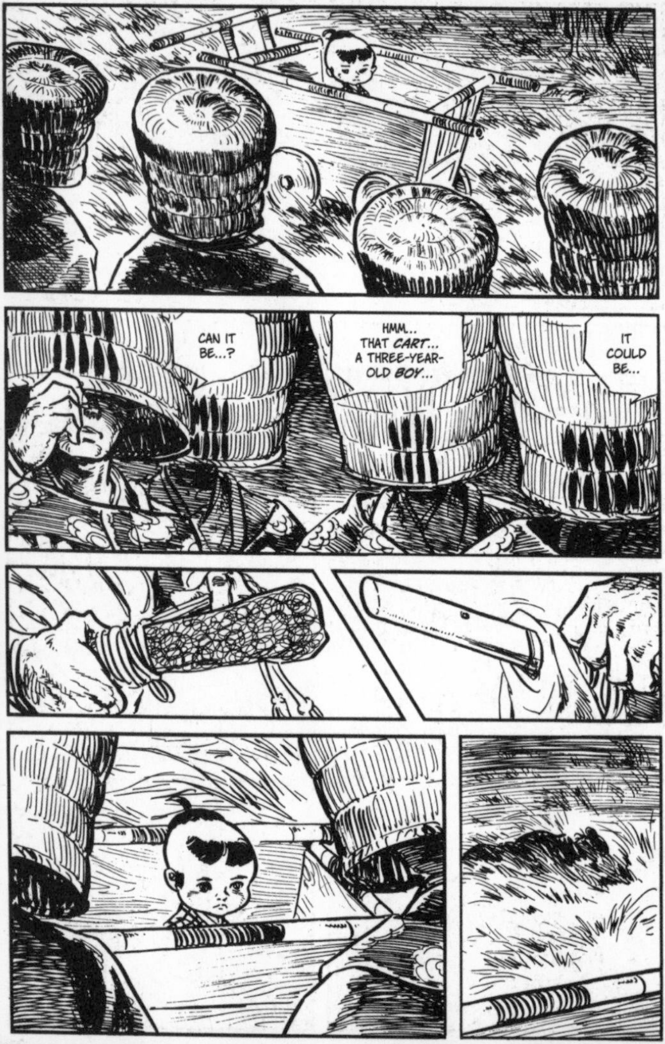
IT COULD BE...
HMM... THAT *CART*... A THREE-YEAR-OLD *BOY*...
CAN IT BE...?

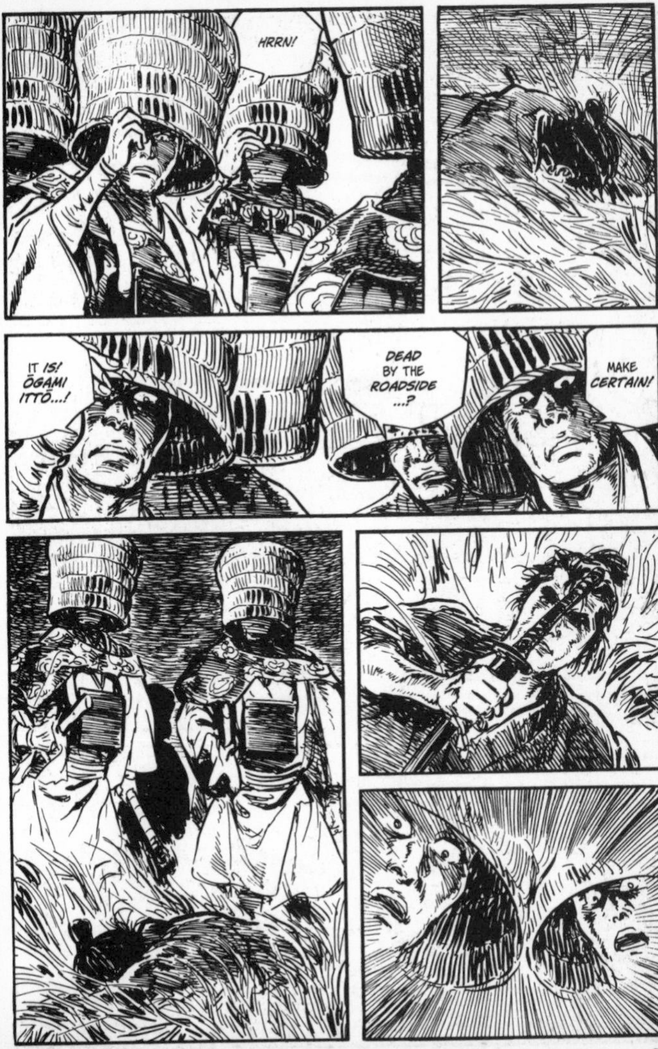
HRRN!
MAKE CERTAIN!
DEAD BY THE ROADSIDE ...?
IT IS! ŌGAMI ITTŌ...!

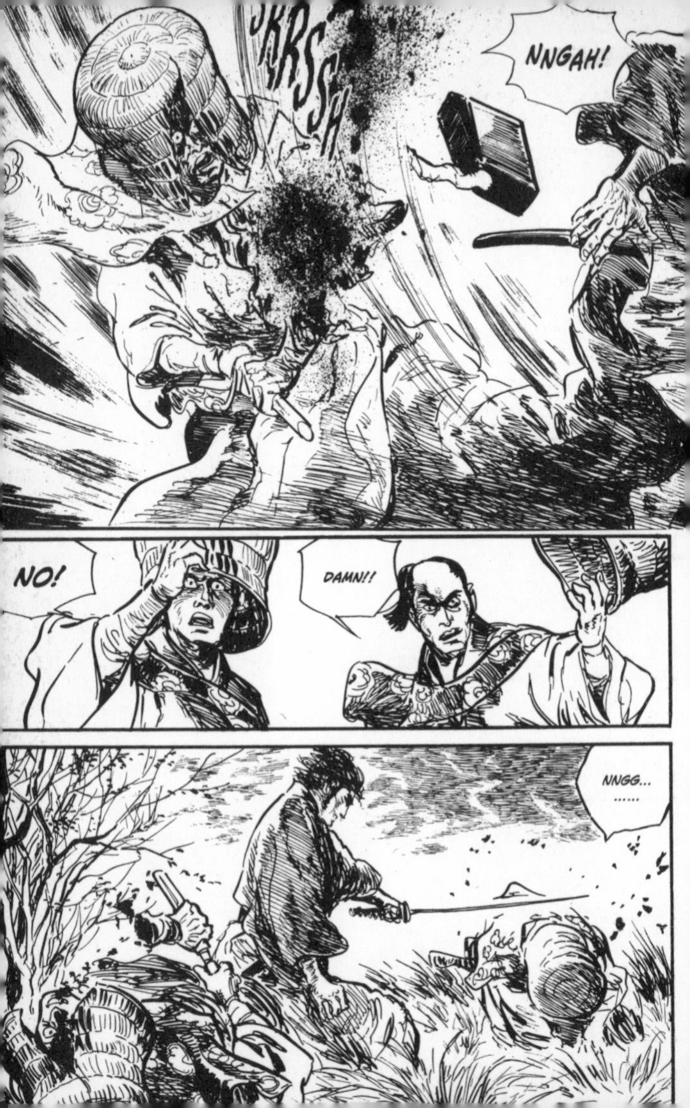
NNGAH!
KRSSH
DAMN!!
NO!
NNGG...
......

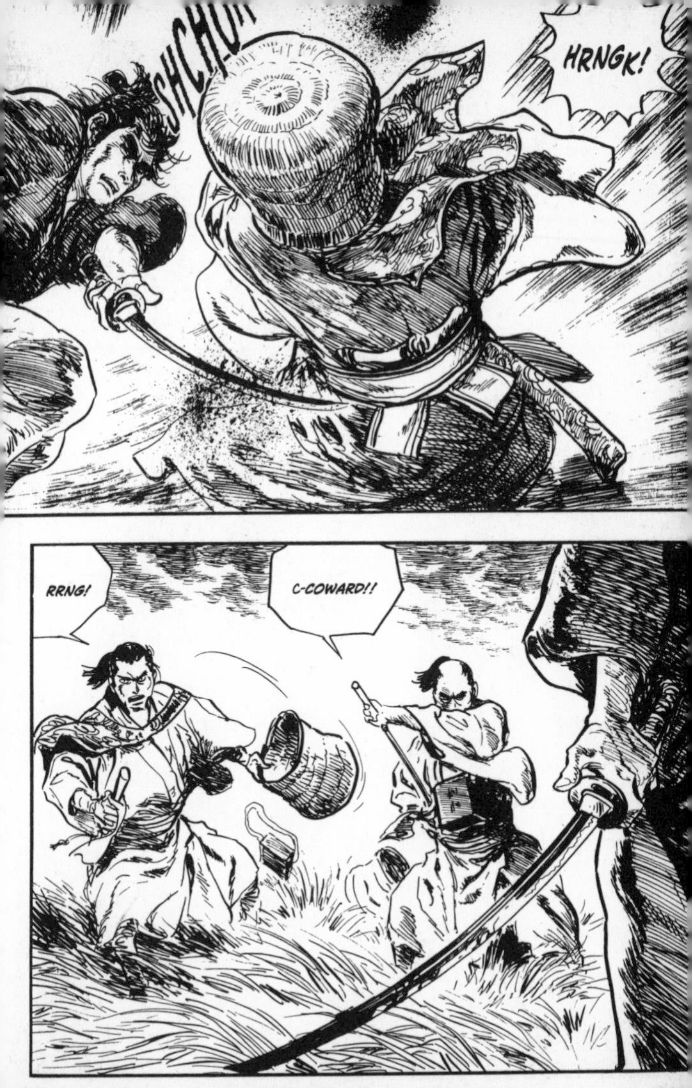
SHCHU
HRNGK!
RRNG!
C-COWARD!!

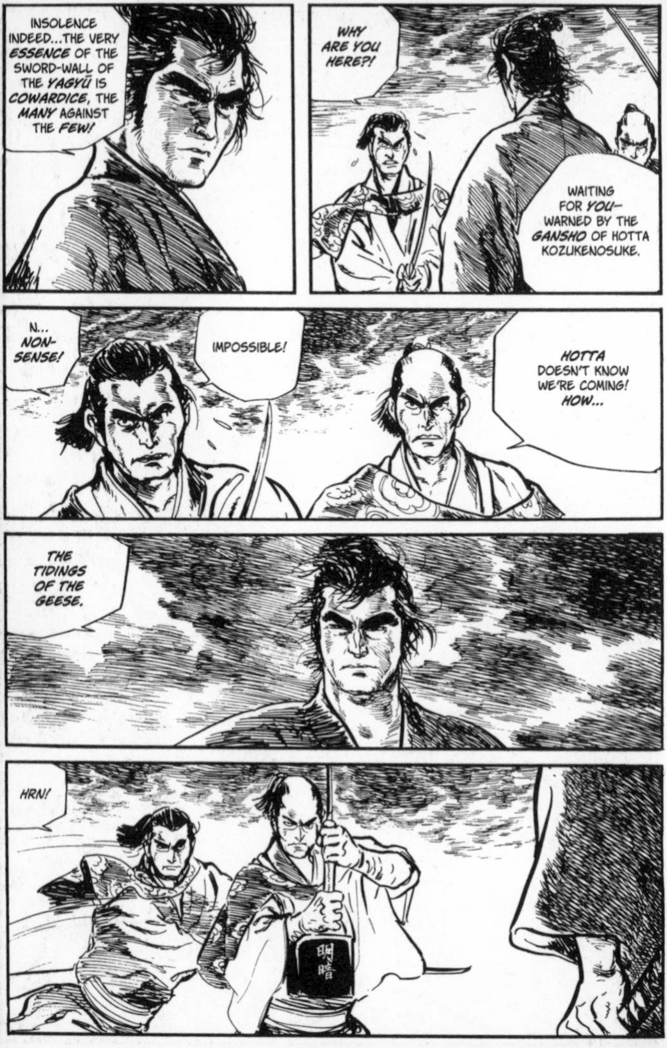
INSOLENCE INDEED...THE VERY ESSENCE OF THE SWORD-WALL OF THE YAGYŪ IS COWARDICE, THE MANY AGAINST THE FEW!
WHY ARE YOU HERE?!
WAITING FOR YOU— WARNED BY THE GANSHO OF HOTTA KOZUKENOSUKE.
N... NON-SENSE!
IMPOSSIBLE!
HOTTA DOESN'T KNOW WE'RE COMING! HOW...
THE TIDINGS OF THE GEESE.
HRN!
明暗

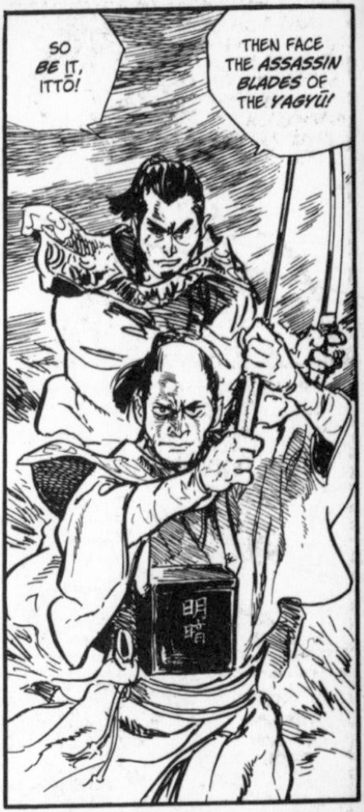
SO BE IT, ITTŌ!
THEN FACE THE ASSASSIN BLADES OF THE YAGYŪ!
明暗
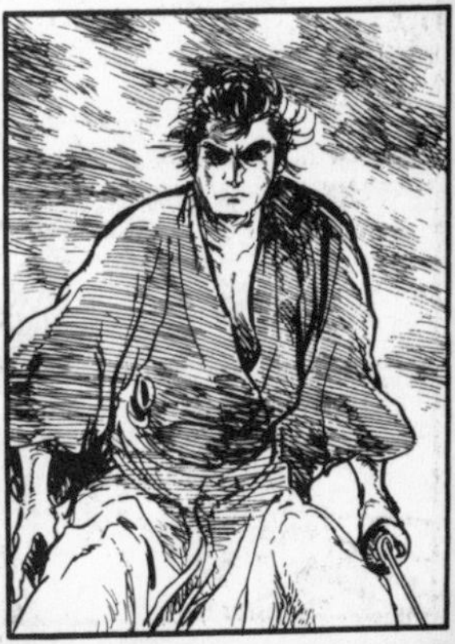
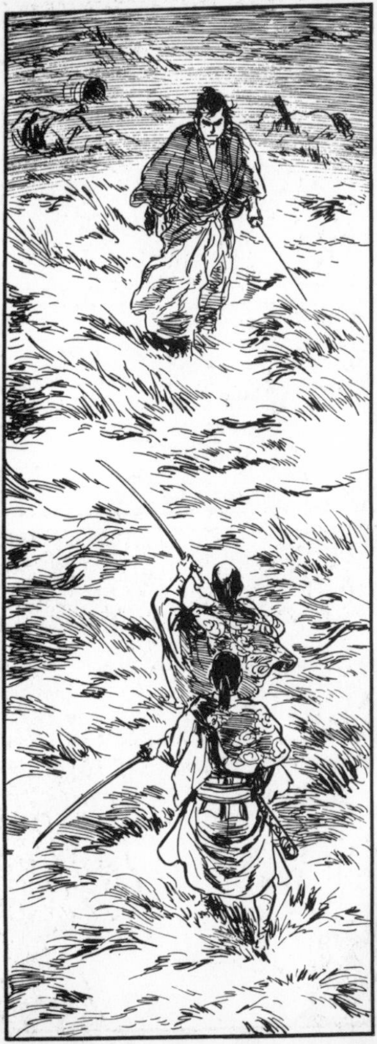

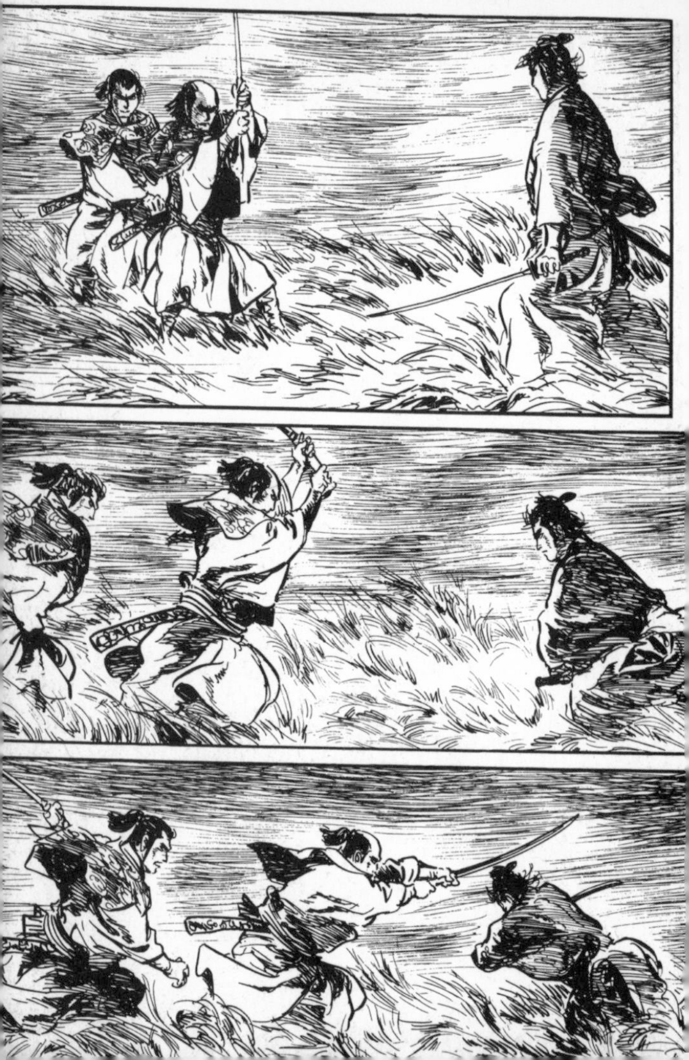

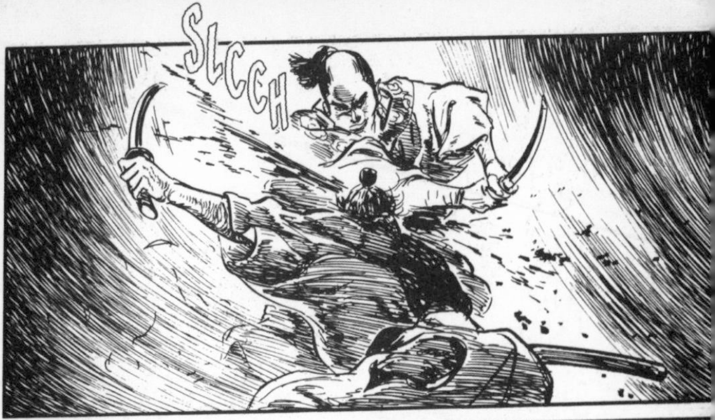
SLCCH

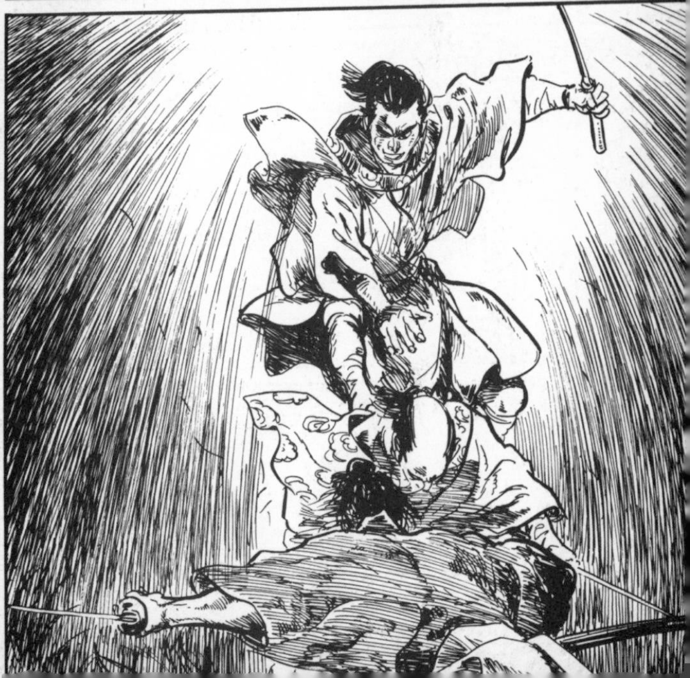

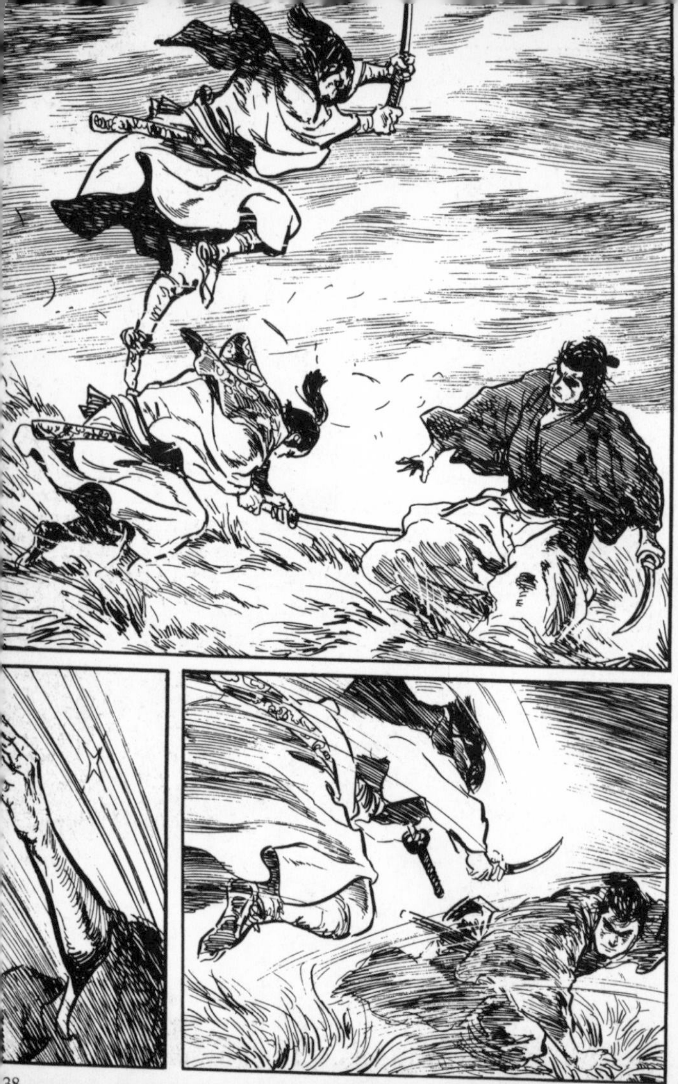

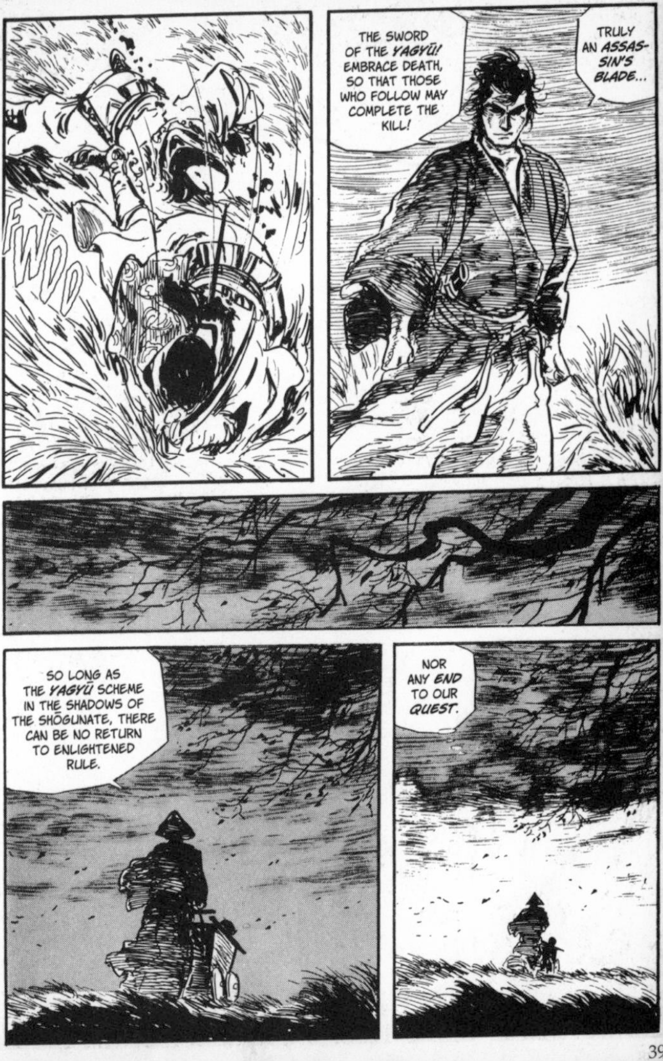
FWOO
THE SWORD OF THE YAGYŪ! EMBRACE DEATH, SO THAT THOSE WHO FOLLOW MAY COMPLETE THE KILL!
TRULY AN ASSAS-SIN'S BLADE...
SO LONG AS THE YAGYŪ SCHEME IN THE SHADOWS OF THE SHŌGUNATE, THERE CAN BE NO RETURN TO ENLIGHTENED RULE.
NOR ANY END TO OUR QUEST.

the fortieth

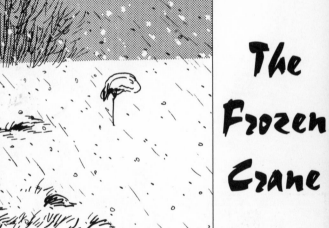

The Frozen Crane

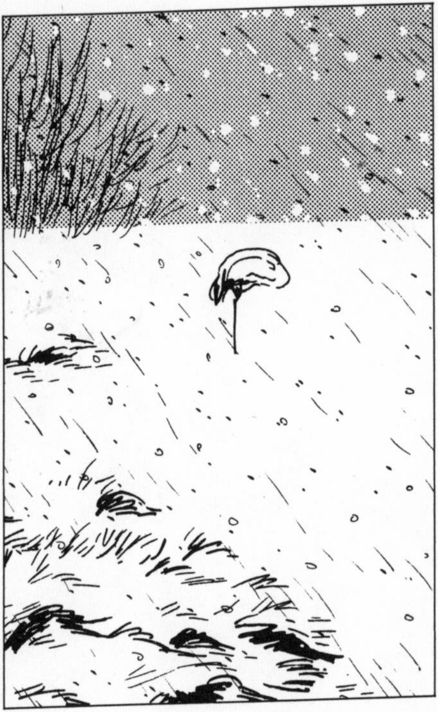

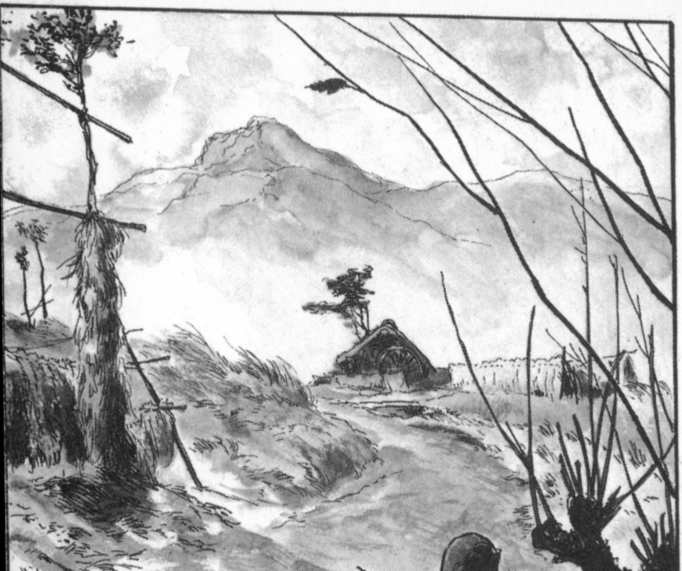
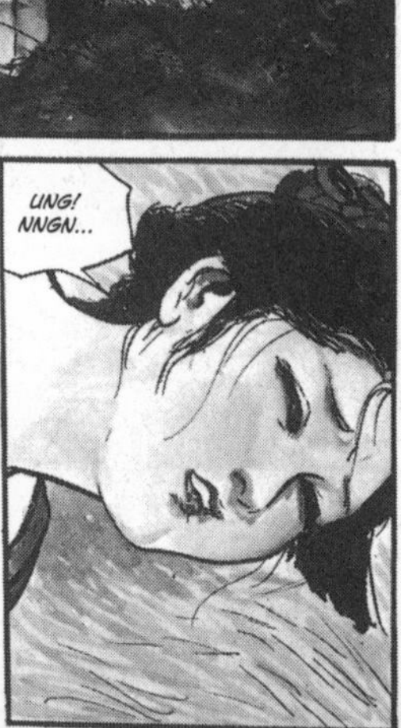
UNG!
NNGN...
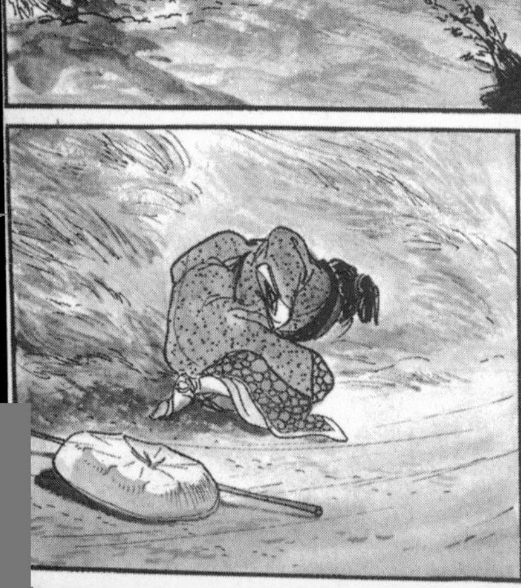

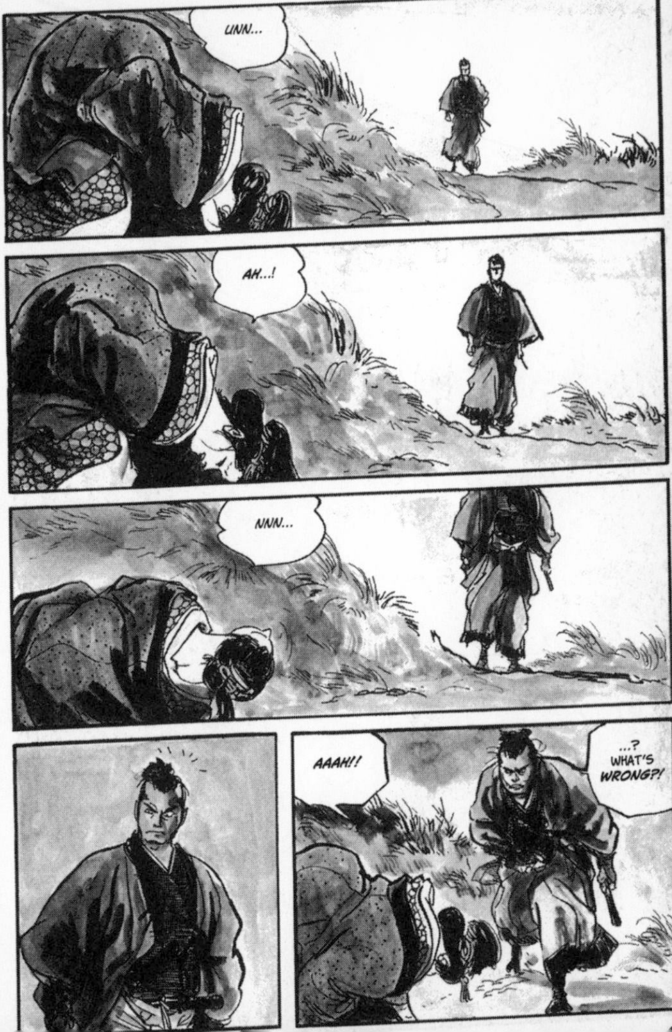
UNN...
AH...!
NNN...
AAAH!!
...? WHAT'S WRONG?!

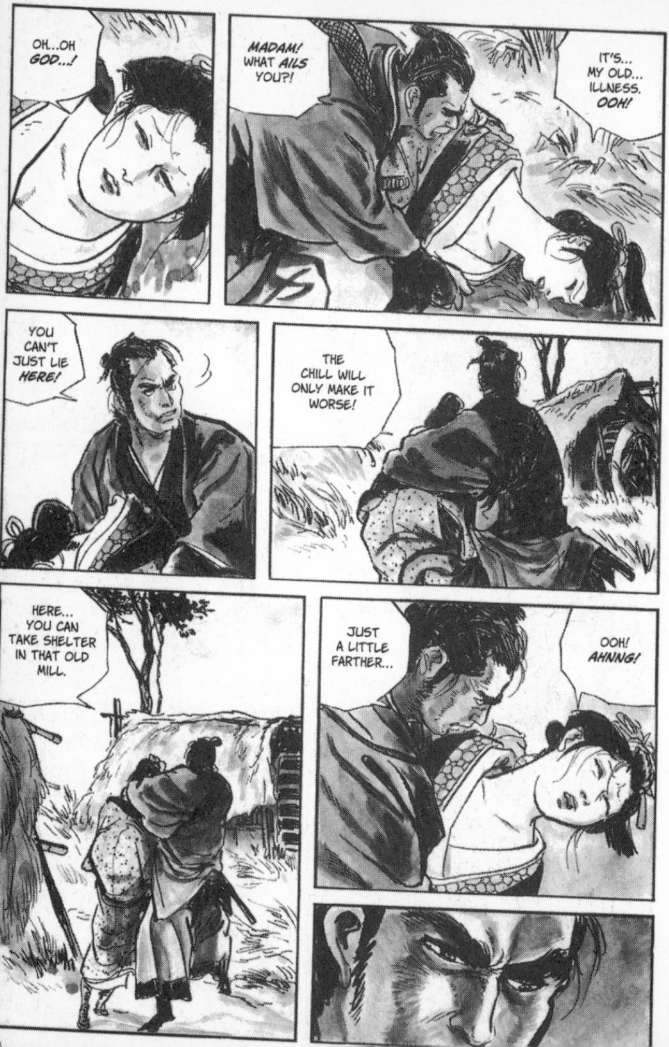
OH...OH GOD...!
MADAM! WHAT AILS YOU?!
IT'S... MY OLD... ILLNESS. OOH!
YOU CAN'T JUST LIE HERE!
THE CHILL WILL ONLY MAKE IT WORSE!
HERE... YOU CAN TAKE SHELTER IN THAT OLD MILL.
JUST A LITTLE FARTHER...
OOH! AHNNG!

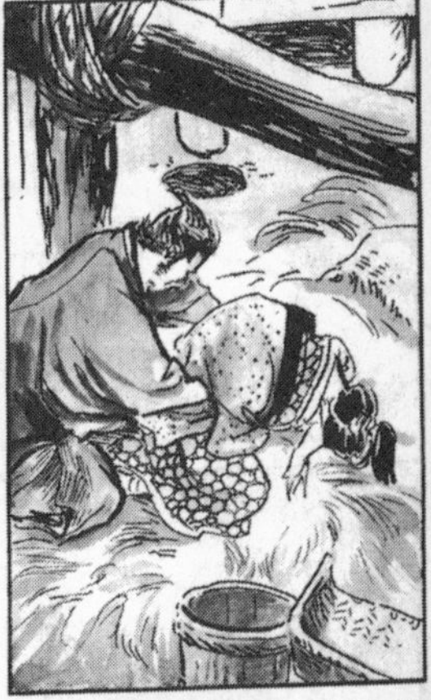

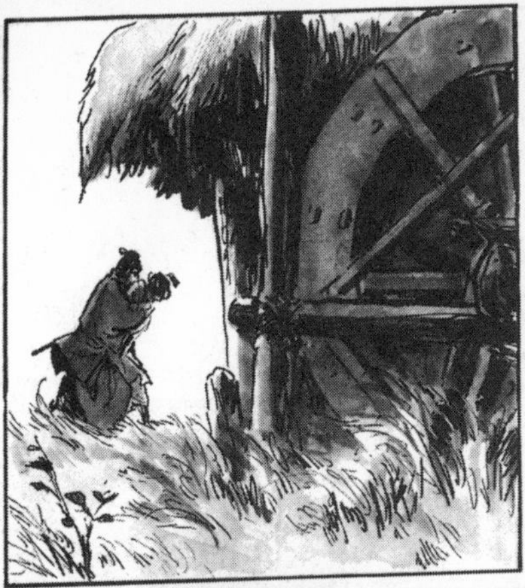

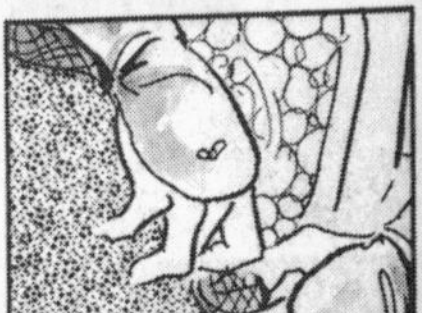

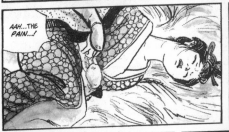

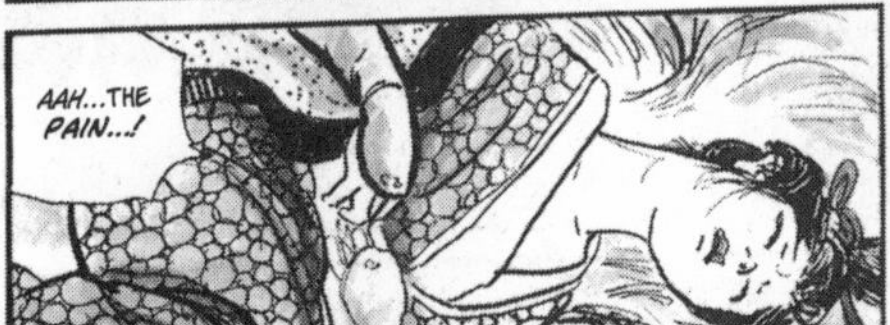
AAH...THE PAIN...!

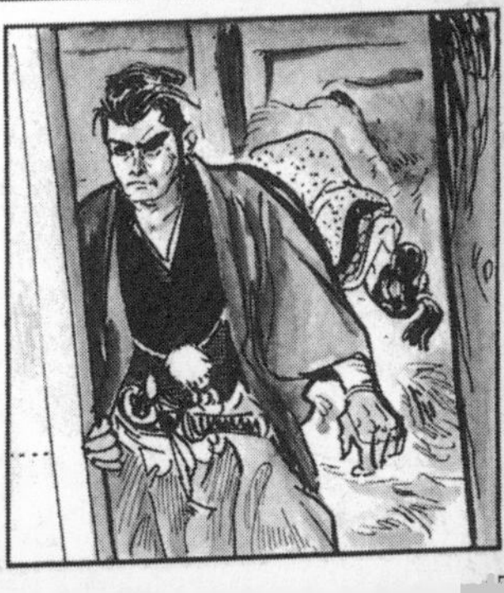

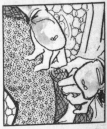

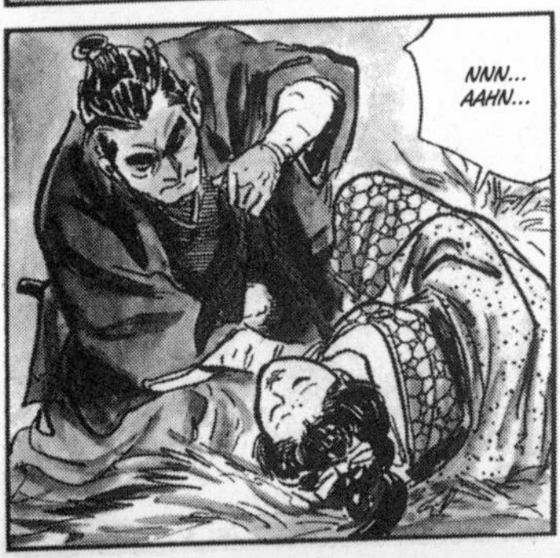
NNN... AAHN...

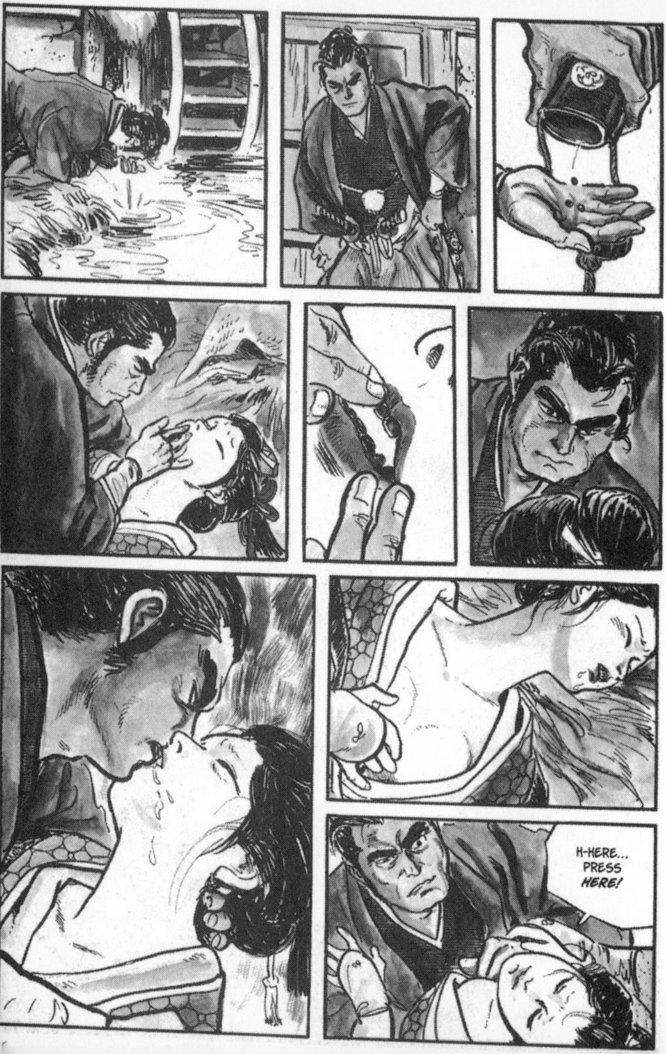
H-HERE... PRESS HERE!

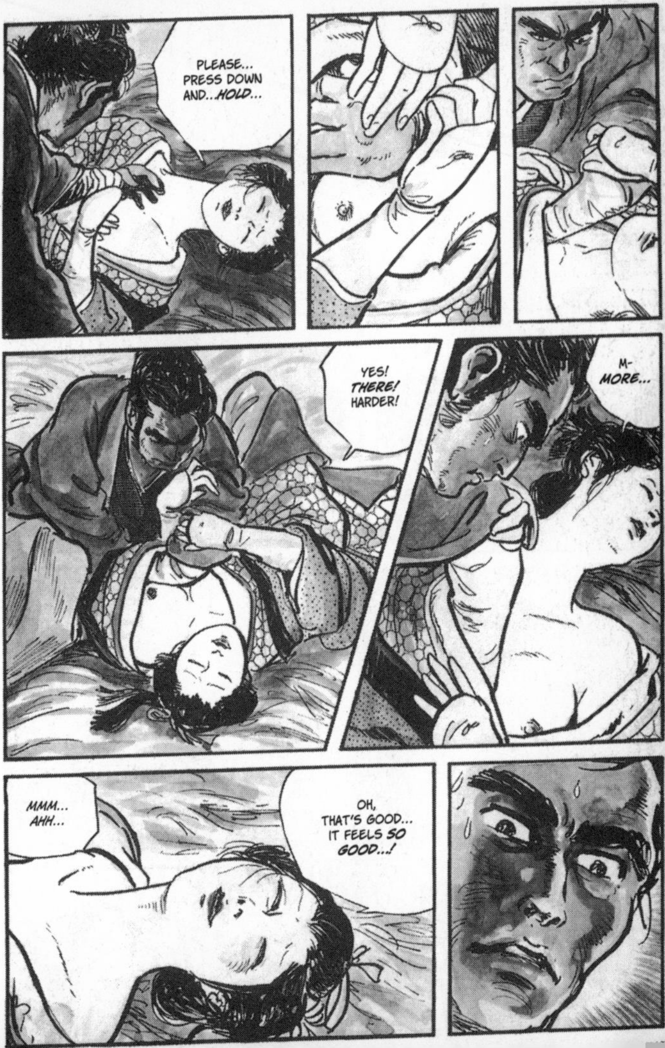
PLEASE... PRESS DOWN AND...*HOLD*...
M- *MORE*...
YES! *THERE!* HARDER!
OH, THAT'S GOOD... IT FEELS *SO GOOD*...!
MMM... AHH...

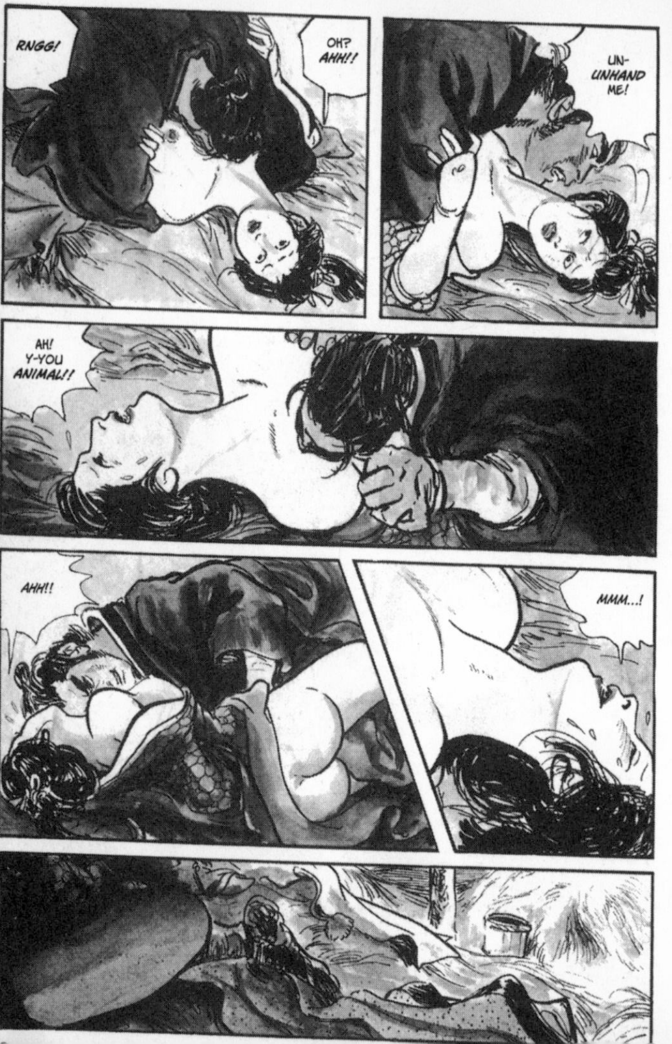
UN-
UNHAND
ME!
OH?
AHH!!
RNGG!
AH!
Y-YOU
ANIMAL!!
MMM...!
AHH!!

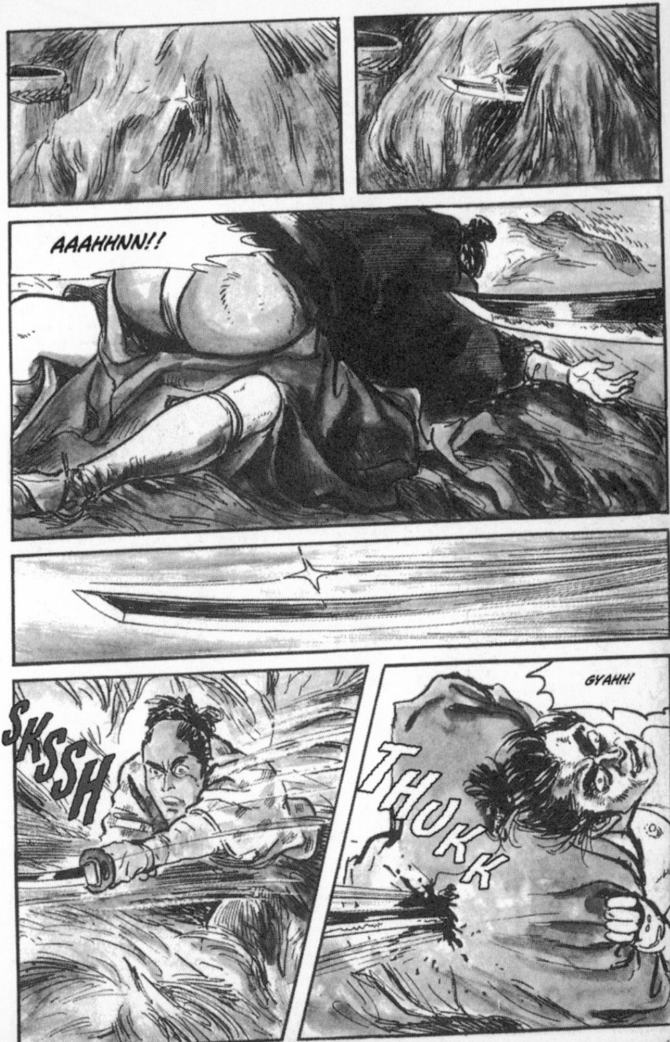
AAAHHNN!!
SKSSH
GYAHH!
THUKK

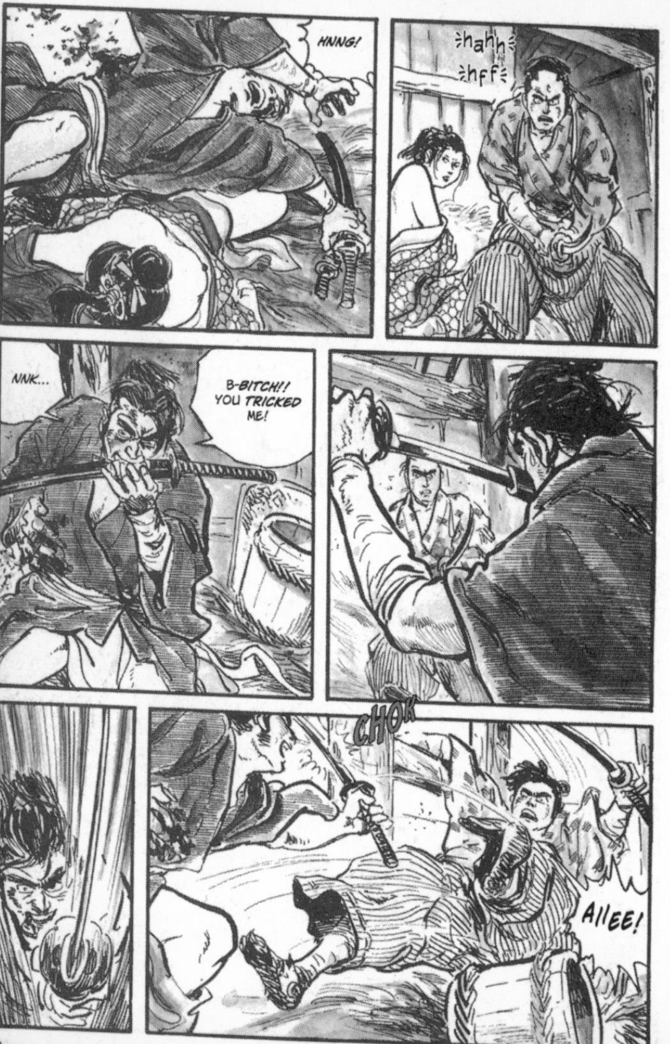
hahh
hff
HNNG!
NNK...
B-BITCH!! YOU TRICKED ME!
CHOK
AIIEE!

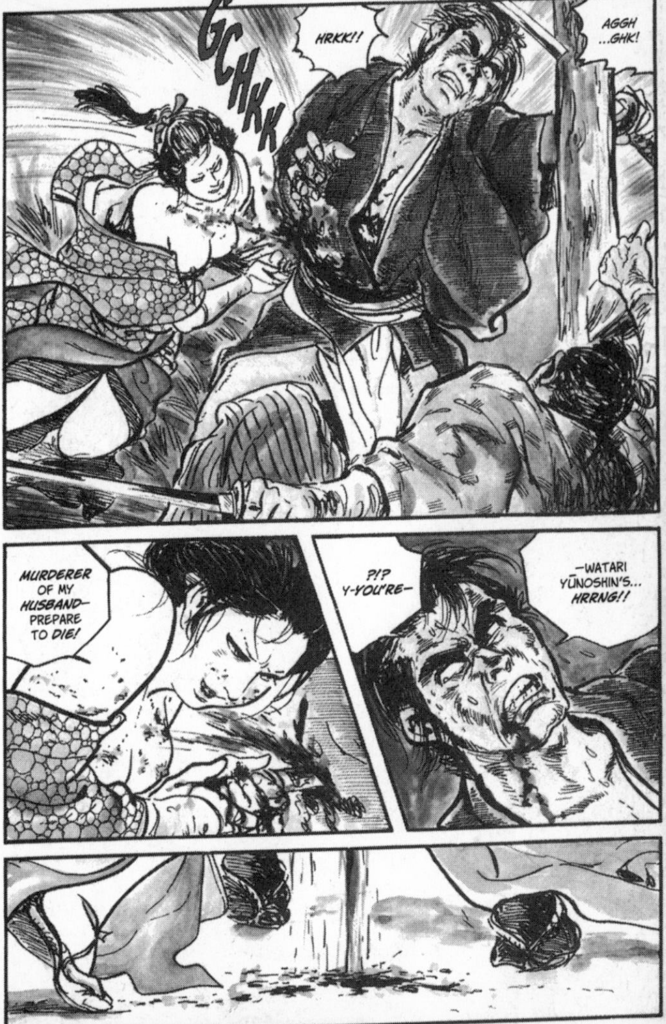
AGGH ...GHK!
HRKK!!
GCHKK
?!? Y-YOU'RE—
—WATARI YŪNOSHIN'S... HRRNG!!
MURDERER OF MY HUSBAND— PREPARE TO DIE!

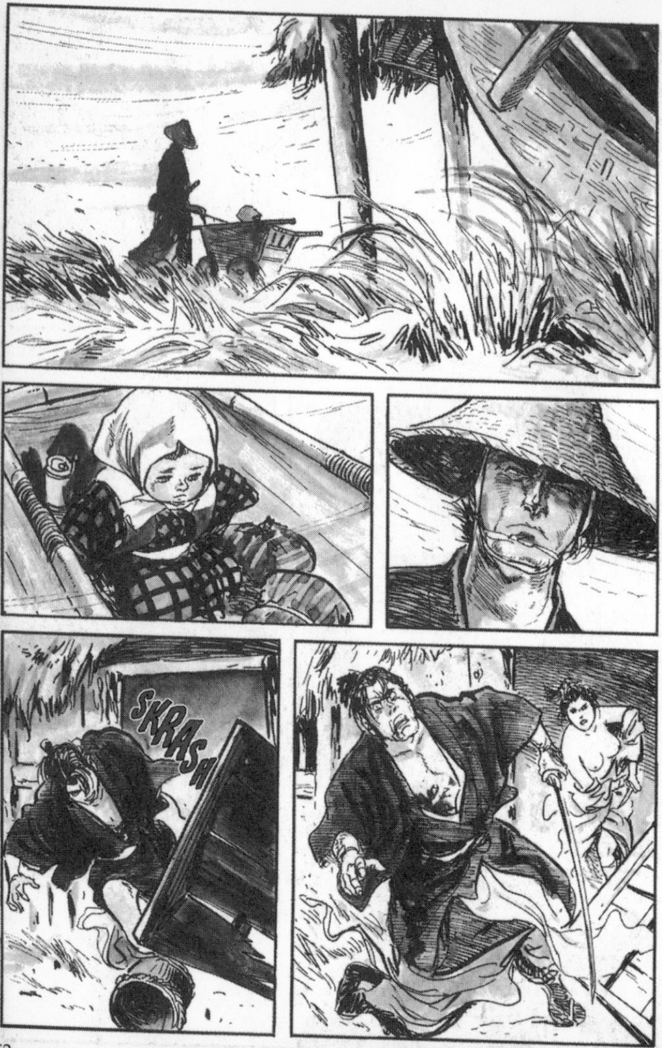
SKRASH

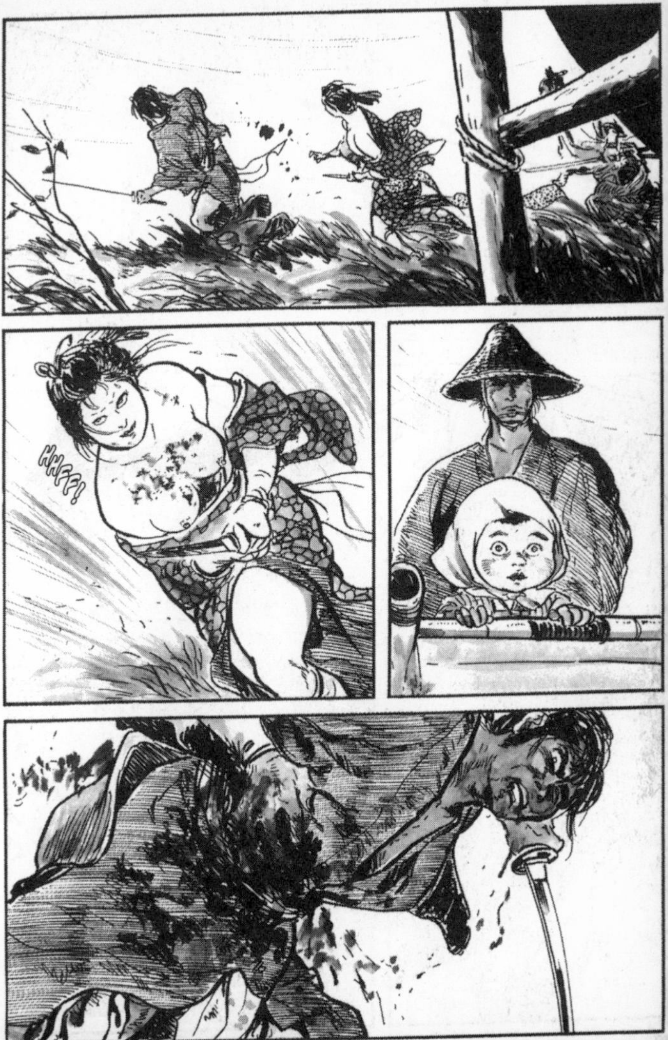
HHFFF!

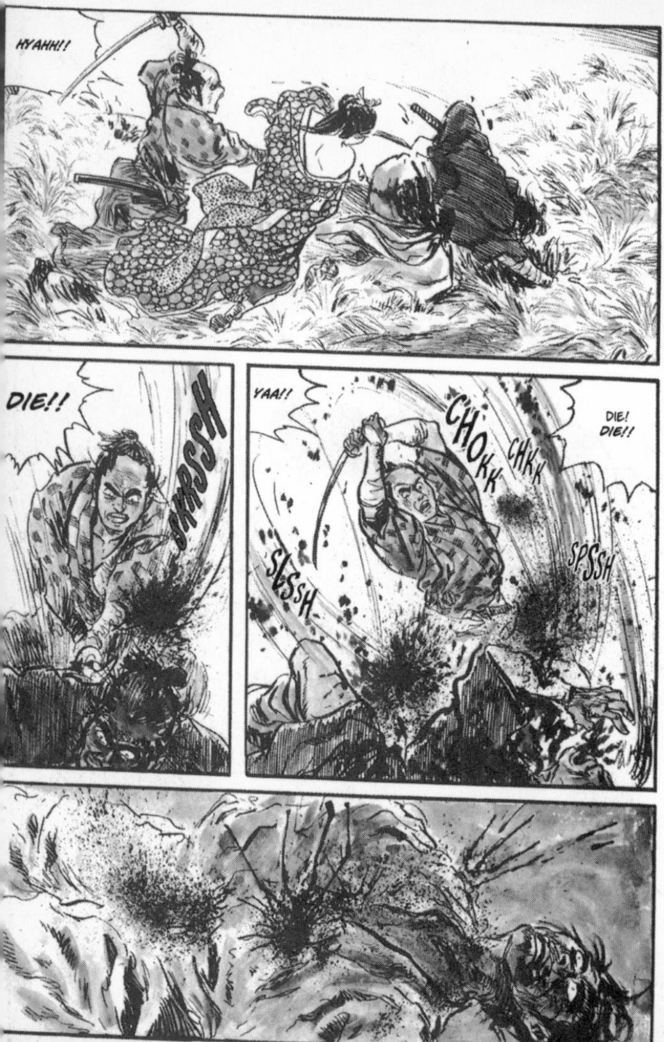
HYAHH!!
DIE!
DIE!!
CHKK
CHOKK
YAA!!
SPSSH
SLSSH
DIE!!
SKRSSH

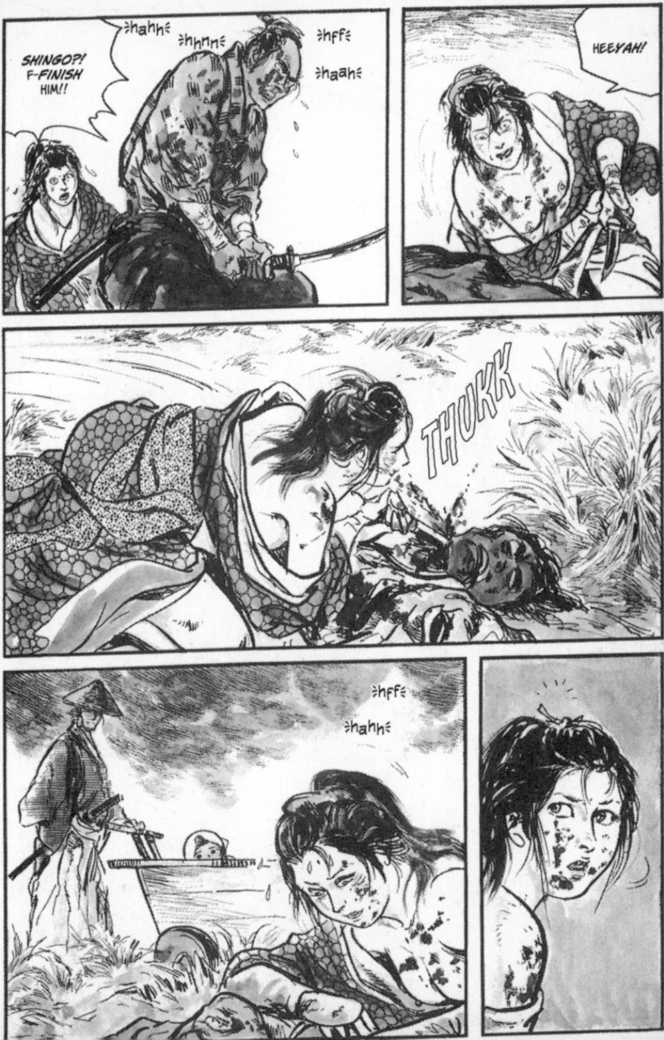
SHINGO?! F-FINISH HIM!!
hahn
hhnn
hff
haah
HEEYAH!
THUKK
hff
hahn

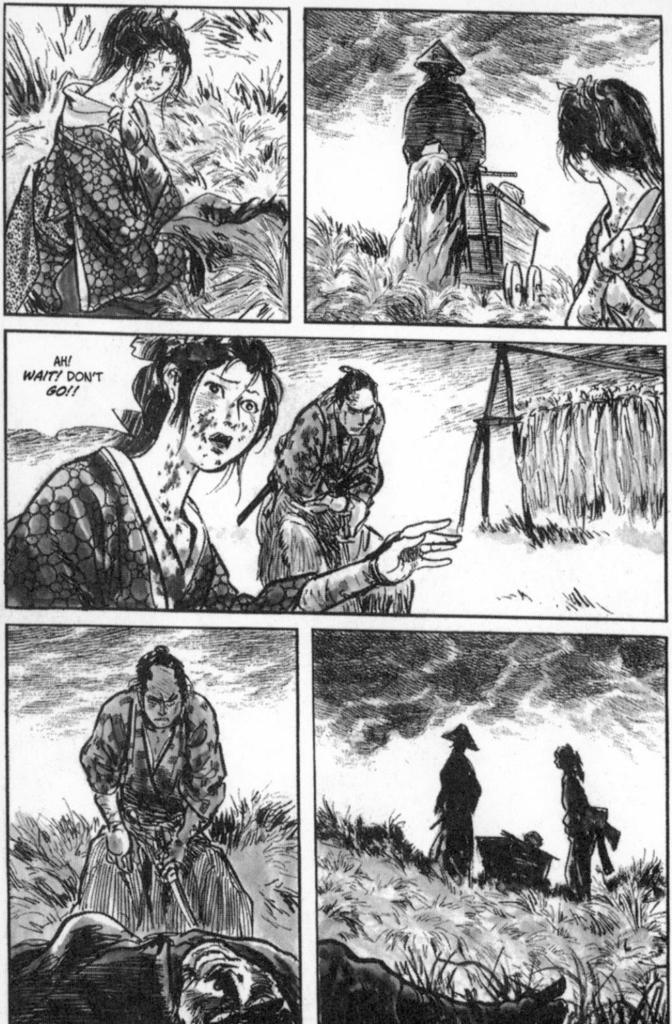
AH!
WAIT! DON'T GO!!

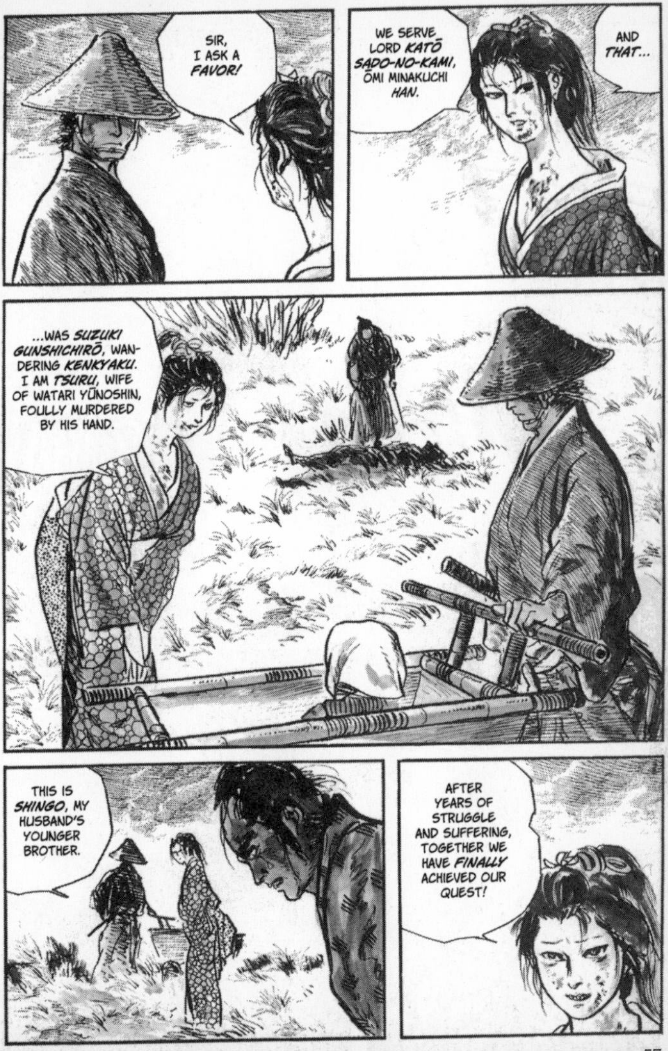
SIR, I ASK A *FAVOR!*
WE SERVE LORD *KATŌ SADO-NO-KAMI*, ŌMI MINAKUCHI *HAN.*
AND *THAT...*
...WAS *SUZUKI GUNSHICHIRŌ*, WANDERING *KENKYAKU*. I AM *TSURU*, WIFE OF WATARI YŪNOSHIN, FOULLY MURDERED BY HIS HAND.
THIS IS *SHINGO*, MY HUSBAND'S YOUNGER BROTHER.
AFTER YEARS OF STRUGGLE AND SUFFERING, TOGETHER WE HAVE *FINALLY* ACHIEVED OUR QUEST!

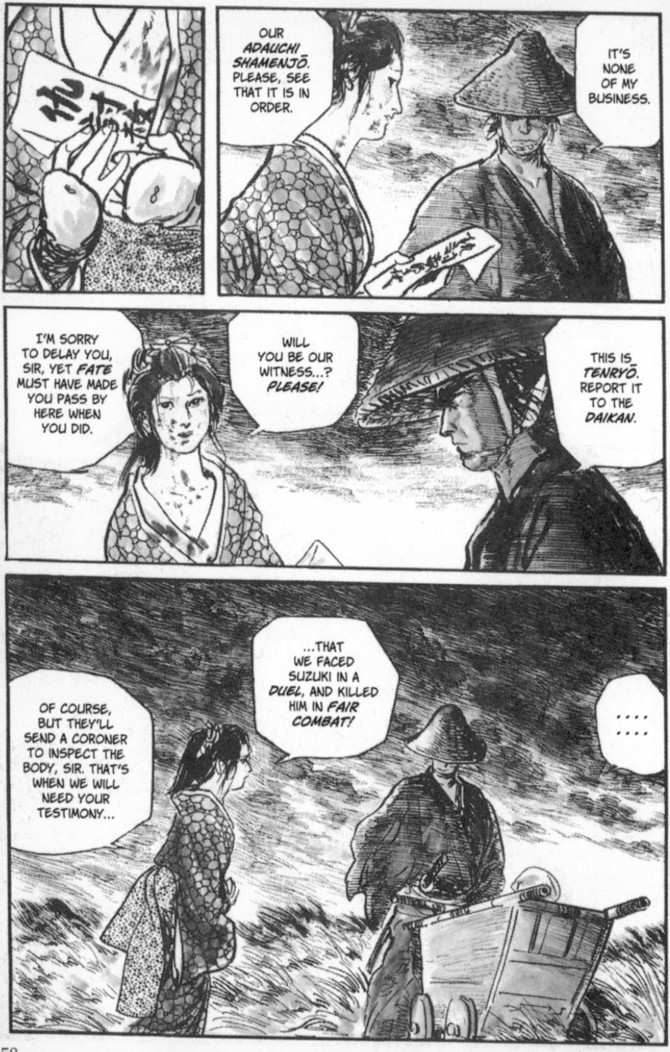
OUR ADAUCHI SHAMENJŌ. PLEASE, SEE THAT IT IS IN ORDER.
IT'S NONE OF MY BUSINESS.
I'M SORRY TO DELAY YOU, SIR, YET FATE MUST HAVE MADE YOU PASS BY HERE WHEN YOU DID.
WILL YOU BE OUR WITNESS...? PLEASE!
THIS IS TENRYŌ. REPORT IT TO THE DAIKAN.
OF COURSE, BUT THEY'LL SEND A CORONER TO INSPECT THE BODY, SIR. THAT'S WHEN WE WILL NEED YOUR TESTIMONY...
...THAT WE FACED SUZUKI IN A DUEL, AND KILLED HIM IN FAIR COMBAT!
....
....

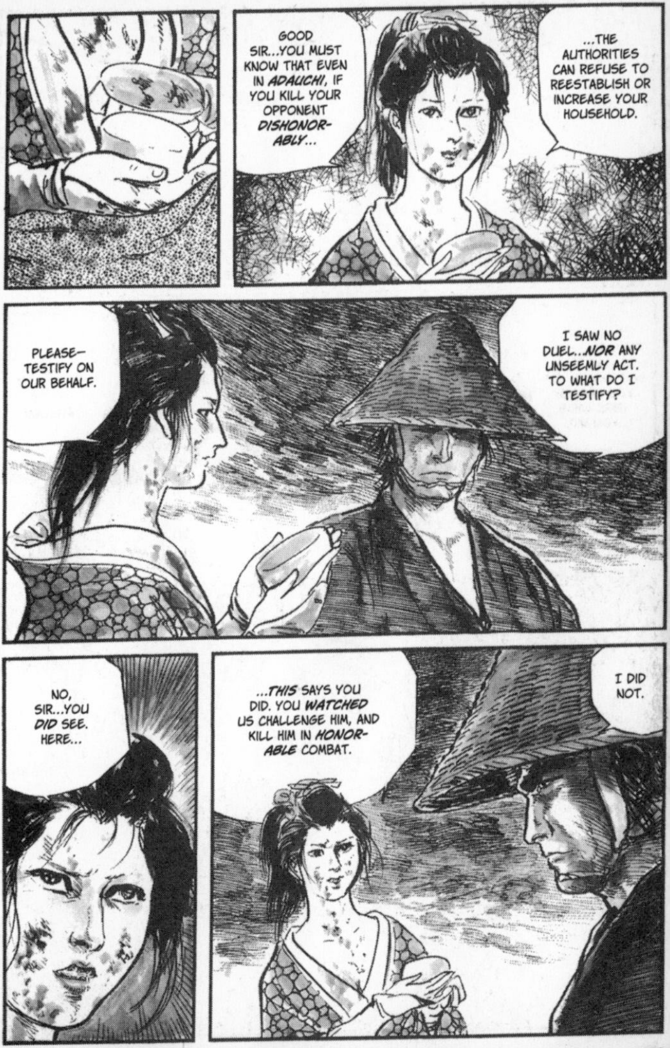
GOOD SIR...YOU MUST KNOW THAT EVEN IN *ADAUCHI*, IF YOU KILL YOUR OPPONENT *DISHONOR-ABLY*...
...THE AUTHORITIES CAN REFUSE TO REESTABLISH OR INCREASE YOUR HOUSEHOLD.
PLEASE—TESTIFY ON OUR BEHALF.
I SAW NO DUEL...*NOR* ANY UNSEEMLY ACT. TO WHAT DO I TESTIFY?
NO, SIR...YOU *DID* SEE. HERE...
...*THIS* SAYS YOU DID. YOU *WATCHED* US CHALLENGE HIM, AND KILL HIM IN *HONOR-ABLE* COMBAT.
I DID NOT.

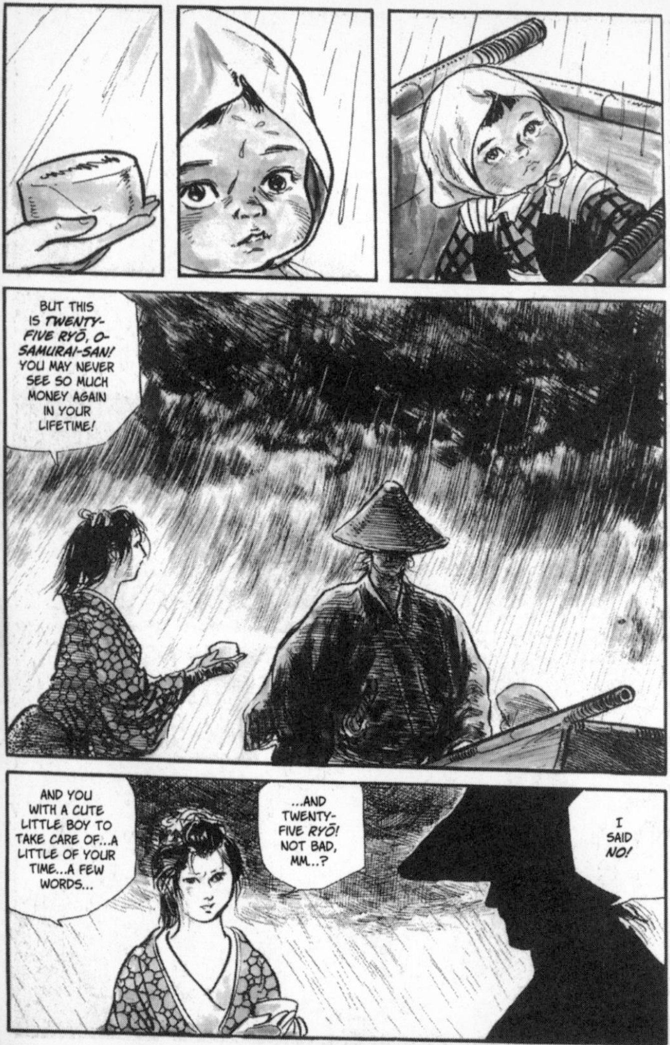
BUT THIS IS *TWENTY-FIVE RYŌ*, O-*SAMURAI-SAN!* YOU MAY NEVER SEE SO MUCH MONEY AGAIN IN YOUR LIFETIME!
AND YOU WITH A CUTE LITTLE BOY TO TAKE CARE OF...A LITTLE OF YOUR TIME...A FEW WORDS...
...AND TWENTY-FIVE *RYŌ!* NOT BAD, MM..?
I SAID *NO!*

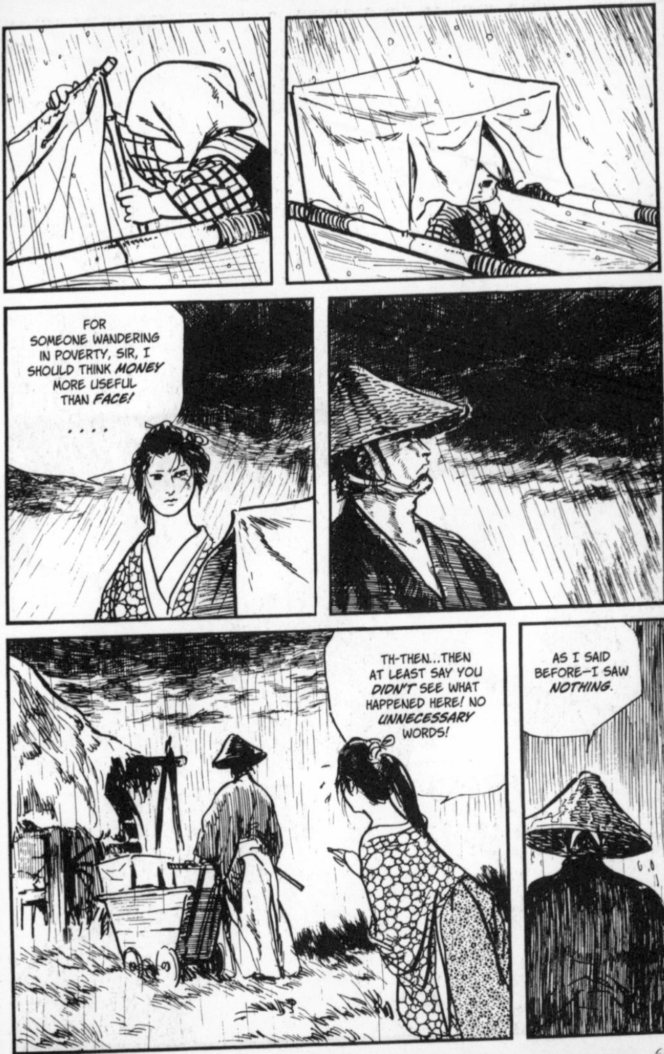
FOR SOMEONE WANDERING IN POVERTY, SIR, I SHOULD THINK MONEY MORE USEFUL THAN FACE!
. . . .
TH-THEN...THEN AT LEAST SAY YOU DIDN'T SEE WHAT HAPPENED HERE! NO UNNECESSARY WORDS!
AS I SAID BEFORE—I SAW NOTHING.

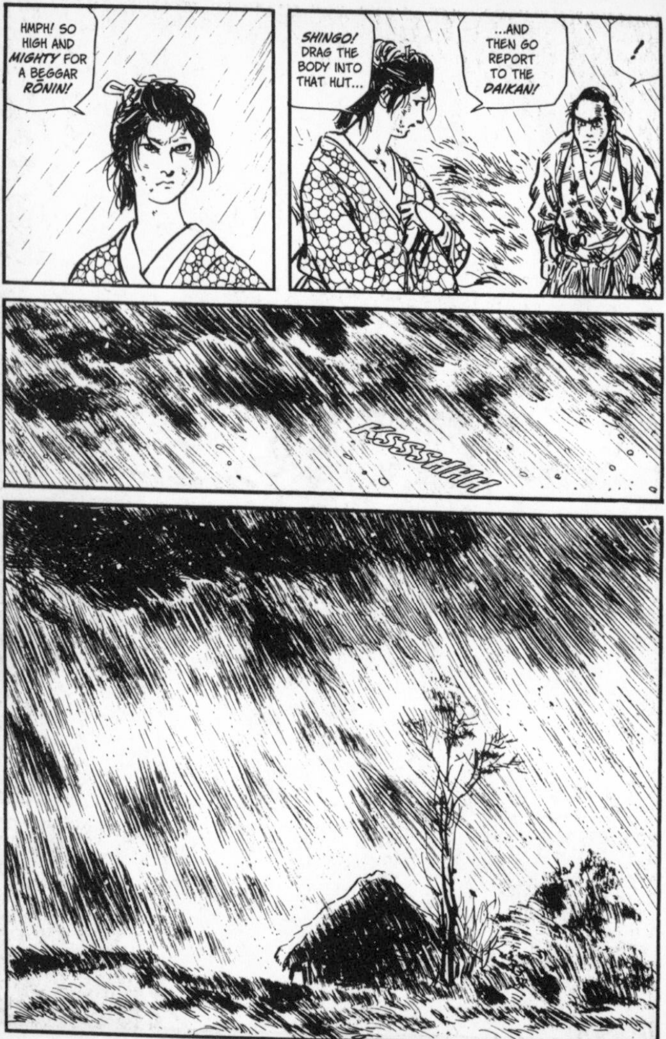
HMPH! SO HIGH AND MIGHTY FOR A BEGGAR RŌNIN!
SHINGO! DRAG THE BODY INTO THAT HUT...
...AND THEN GO REPORT TO THE DAIKAN!
!
KSSSSHHH

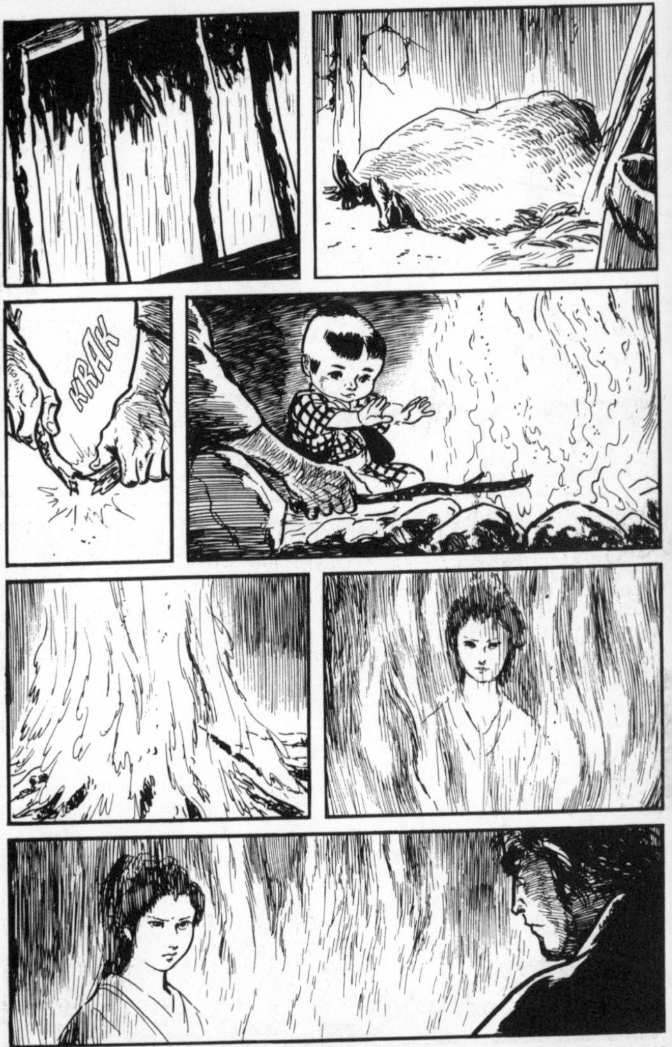
KRAK

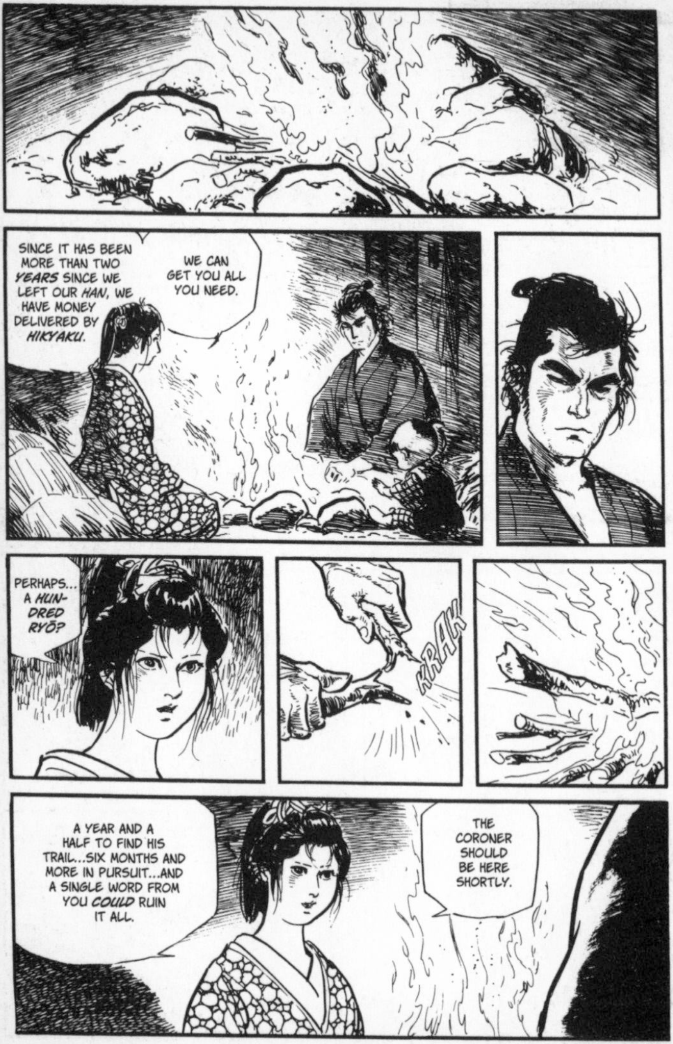
SINCE IT HAS BEEN MORE THAN TWO *YEARS* SINCE WE LEFT OUR *HAN*, WE HAVE MONEY DELIVERED BY ***HIKYAKU***.
WE CAN GET YOU ALL YOU NEED.
PERHAPS... A *HUN-DRED RYŌ*?
KRAK
A YEAR AND A HALF TO FIND HIS TRAIL...SIX MONTHS AND MORE IN PURSUIT...AND A SINGLE WORD FROM YOU *COULD* RUIN IT ALL.
THE CORONER SHOULD BE HERE SHORTLY.

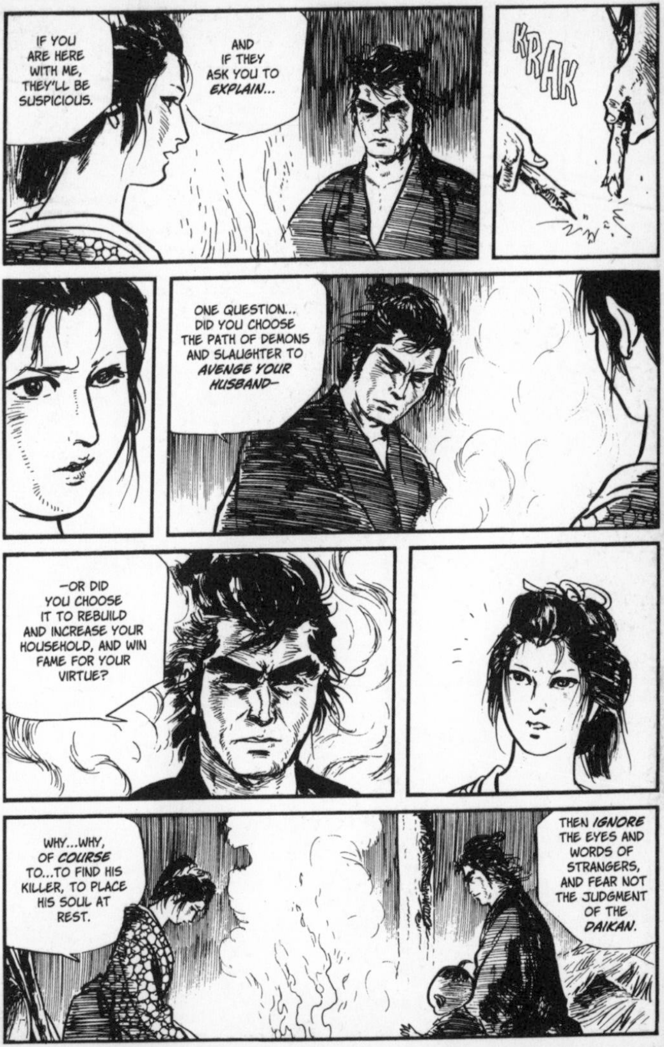
IF YOU ARE HERE WITH ME, THEY'LL BE SUSPICIOUS.
AND IF THEY ASK YOU TO *EXPLAIN*...
KRAK
ONE QUESTION... DID YOU CHOOSE THE PATH OF DEMONS AND SLAUGHTER TO *AVENGE YOUR HUSBAND*—
—OR DID YOU CHOOSE IT TO REBUILD AND INCREASE YOUR HOUSEHOLD, AND WIN FAME FOR YOUR VIRTUE?
WHY...WHY, OF *COURSE* TO...TO FIND HIS KILLER, TO PLACE HIS SOUL AT REST.
THEN *IGNORE* THE EYES AND WORDS OF STRANGERS, AND FEAR NOT THE JUDGMENT OF THE *DAIKAN*.

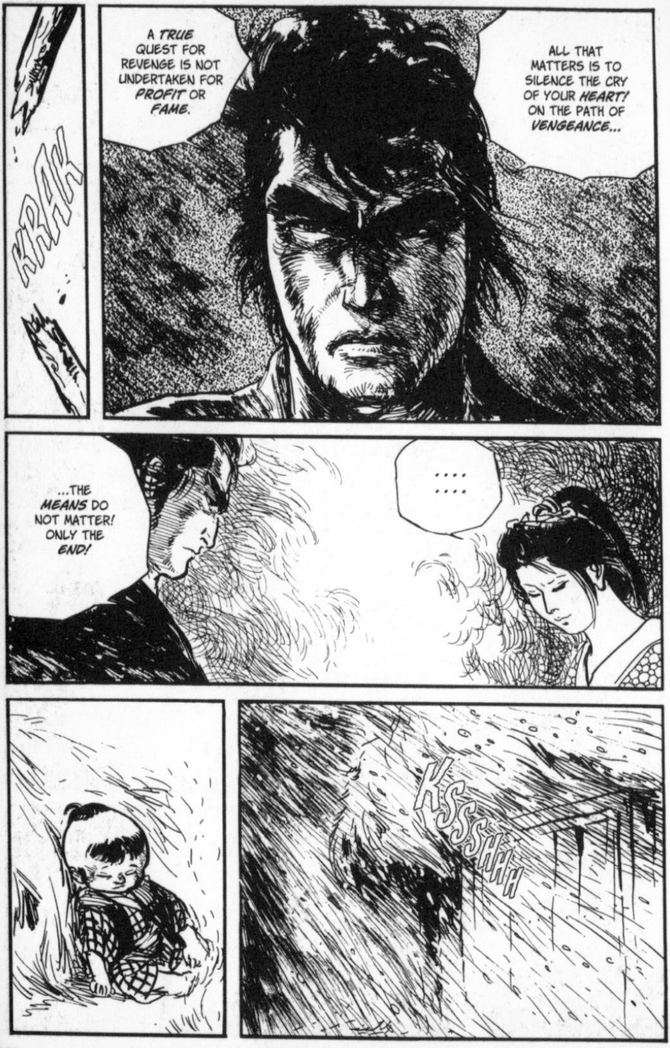
KRAK
A TRUE QUEST FOR REVENGE IS NOT UNDERTAKEN FOR PROFIT OR FAME.
ALL THAT MATTERS IS TO SILENCE THE CRY OF YOUR HEART! ON THE PATH OF VENGEANCE...
...THE MEANS DO NOT MATTER! ONLY THE END!
....
....
KSSSHHH

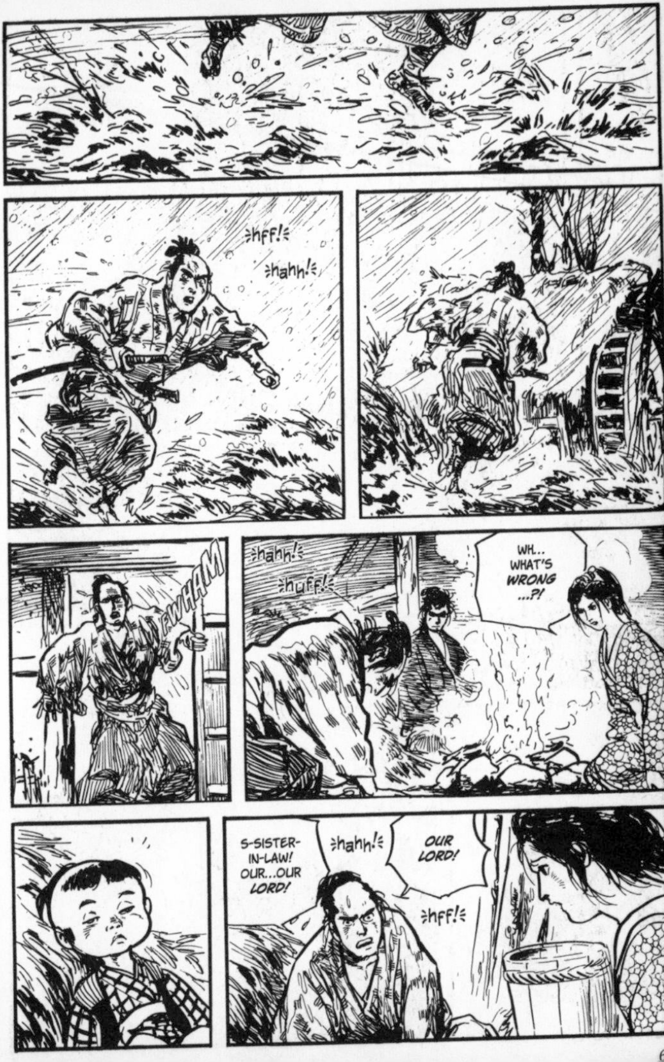
hff!
hahh!
FWHAM
hahh!
huff!
WH... WHAT'S WRONG ...?!
S-SISTER-IN-LAW! OUR...OUR LORD!
hahh!
OUR LORD!
hff!

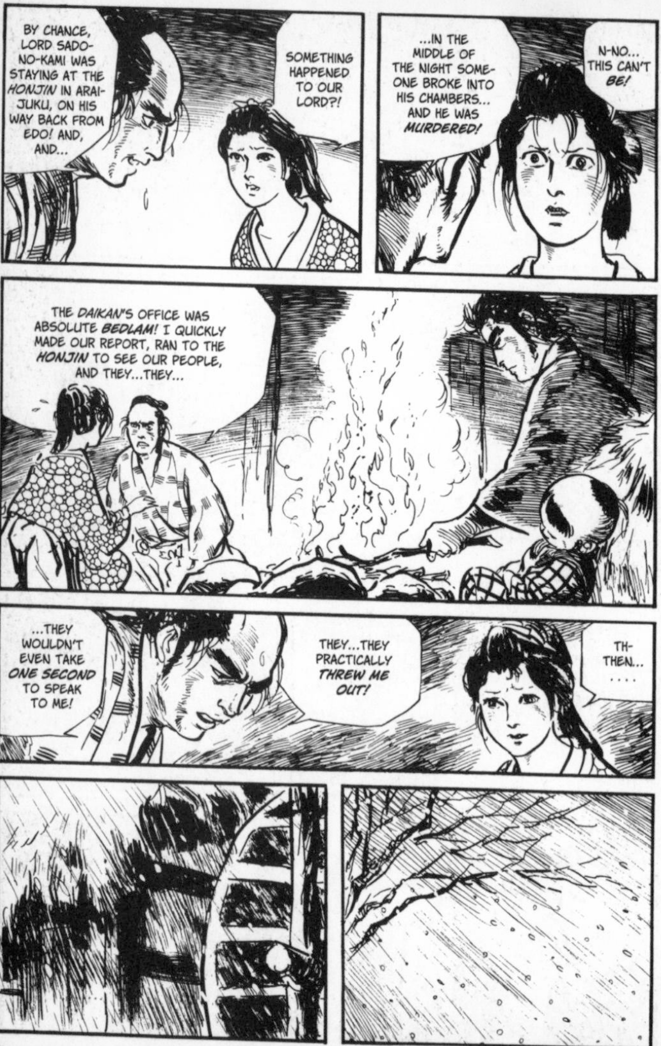
BY CHANCE, LORD SADO-NO-KAMI WAS STAYING AT THE HONJIN IN ARAI-JUKU, ON HIS WAY BACK FROM EDO! AND, AND...
SOMETHING HAPPENED TO OUR LORD?!
...IN THE MIDDLE OF THE NIGHT SOME-ONE BROKE INTO HIS CHAMBERS... AND HE WAS MURDERED!
N-NO... THIS CAN'T BE!
THE DAIKAN'S OFFICE WAS ABSOLUTE BEDLAM! I QUICKLY MADE OUR REPORT, RAN TO THE HONJIN TO SEE OUR PEOPLE, AND THEY...THEY...
...THEY WOULDN'T EVEN TAKE ONE SECOND TO SPEAK TO ME!
THEY...THEY PRACTICALLY THREW ME OUT!
TH-THEN... ....

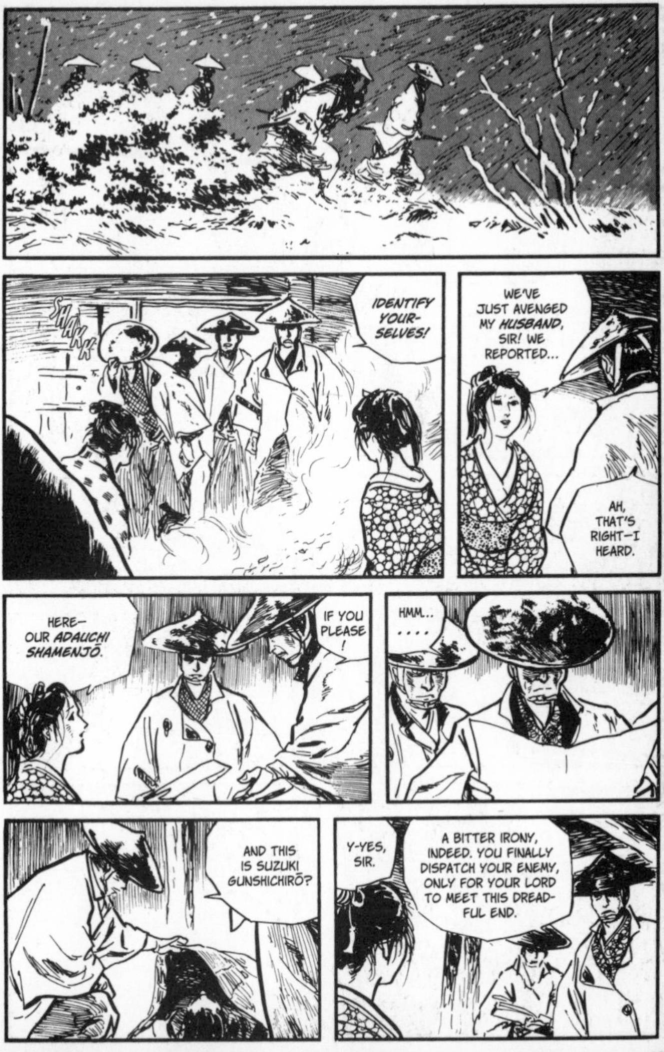

SHAKK
IDENTIFY YOURSELVES!
WE'VE JUST AVENGED MY *HUSBAND*, SIR! WE REPORTED...
AH, THAT'S RIGHT—I HEARD.
HERE— OUR *ADAUCHI SHAMENJŌ*.
IF YOU PLEASE!
HMM... ....
AND THIS IS SUZUKI GUNSHICHIRŌ?
Y-YES, SIR.
A BITTER IRONY, INDEED. YOU FINALLY DISPATCH YOUR ENEMY, ONLY FOR YOUR LORD TO MEET THIS DREADFUL END.

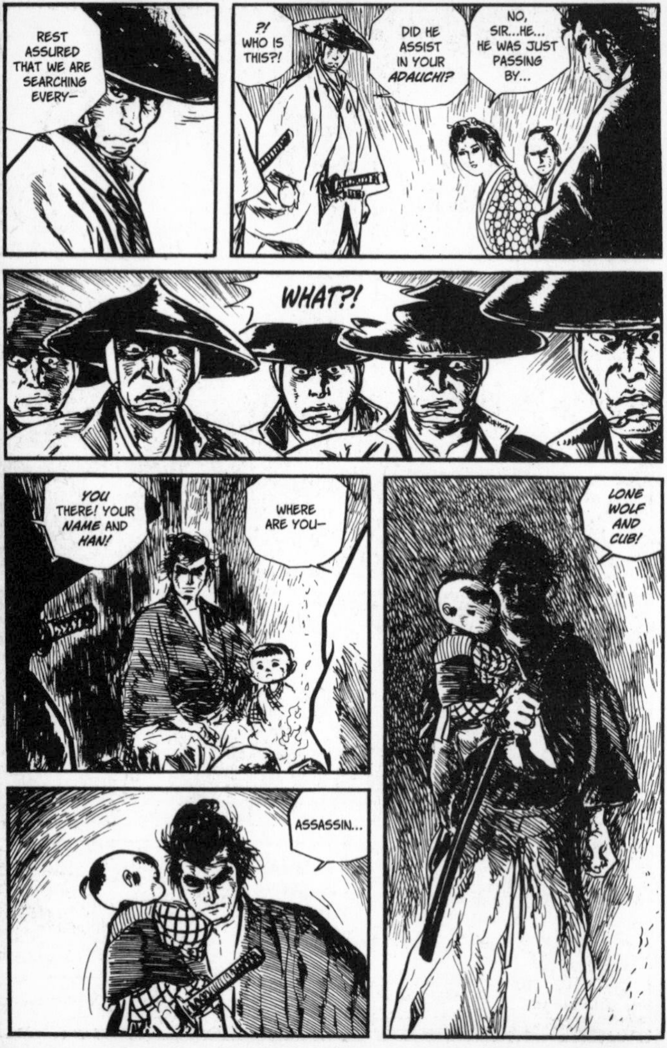
REST ASSURED THAT WE ARE SEARCHING EVERY—
?! WHO IS THIS?!
DID HE ASSIST IN YOUR ADAUCHI?
NO, SIR...HE... HE WAS JUST PASSING BY...
WHAT?!
YOU THERE! YOUR NAME AND HAN!
WHERE ARE YOU—
ASSASSIN...
LONE WOLF AND CUB!

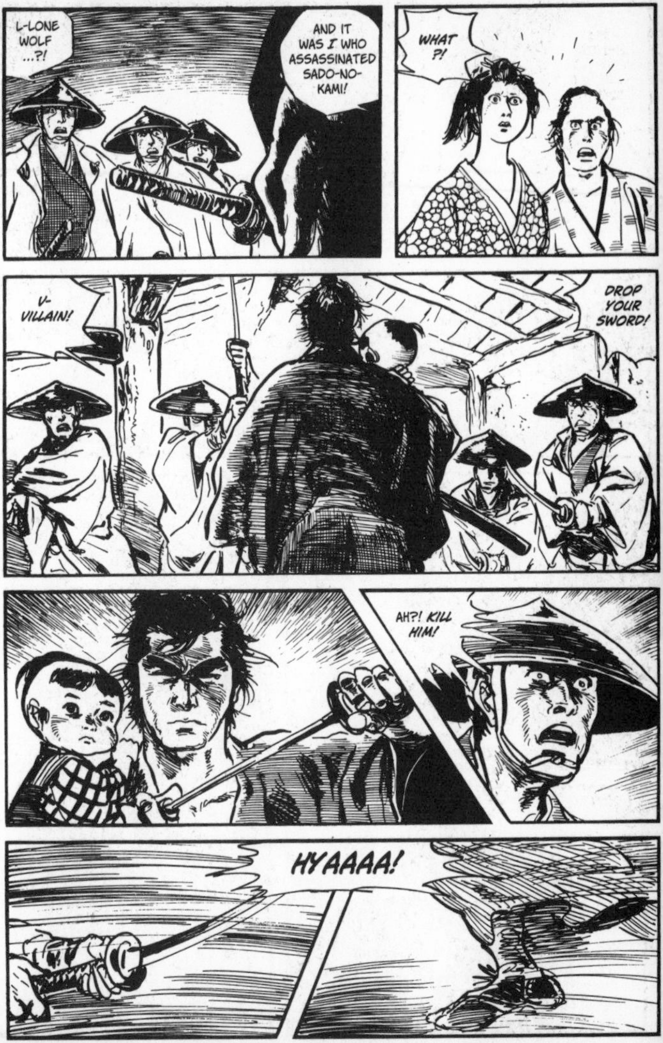
L-LONE WOLF ...?!
AND IT WAS I WHO ASSASSINATED SADO-NO-KAMI!
WHAT ?!
V-VILLAIN!
DROP YOUR SWORD!
AH?! KILL HIM!
HYAAAA!

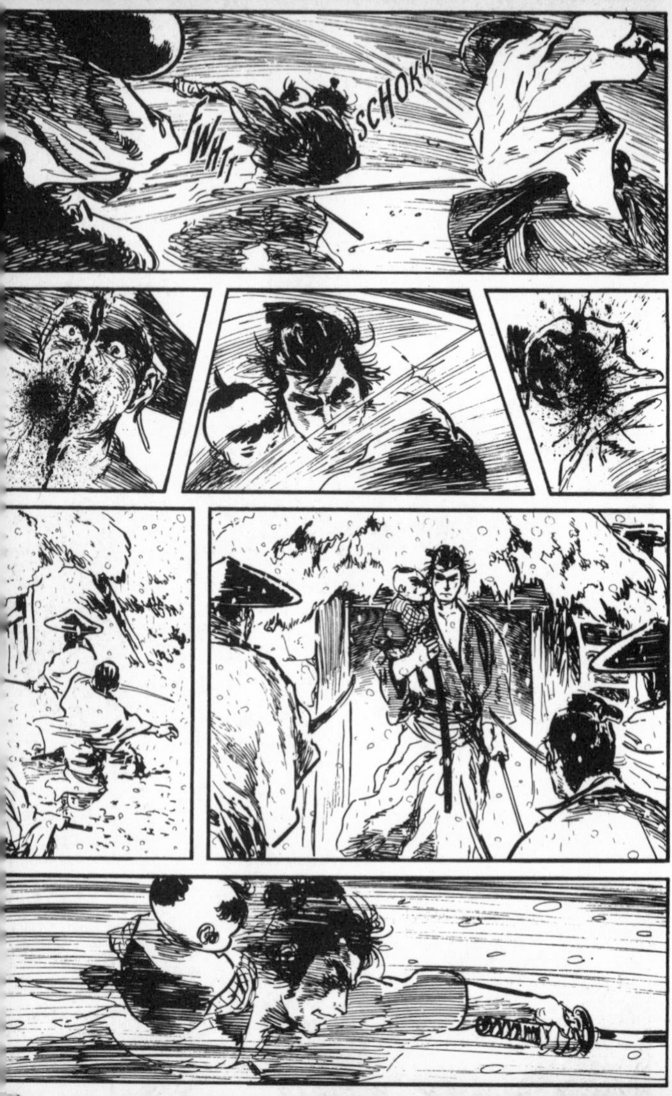
SCHOKK
WHT

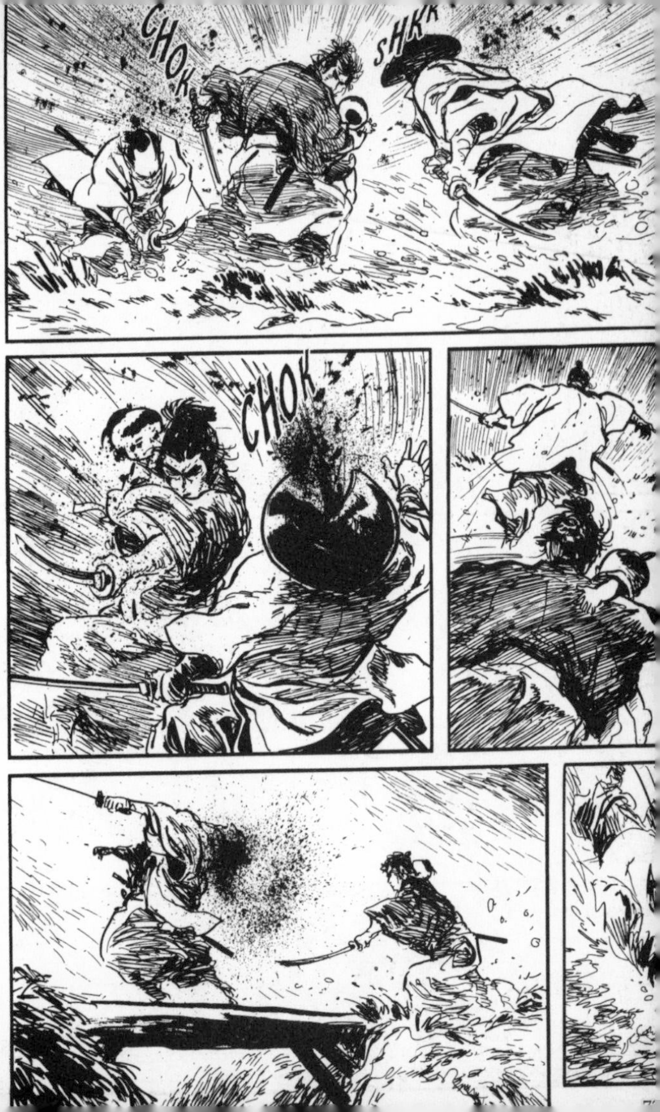
SHKK
CHOK
CHOK

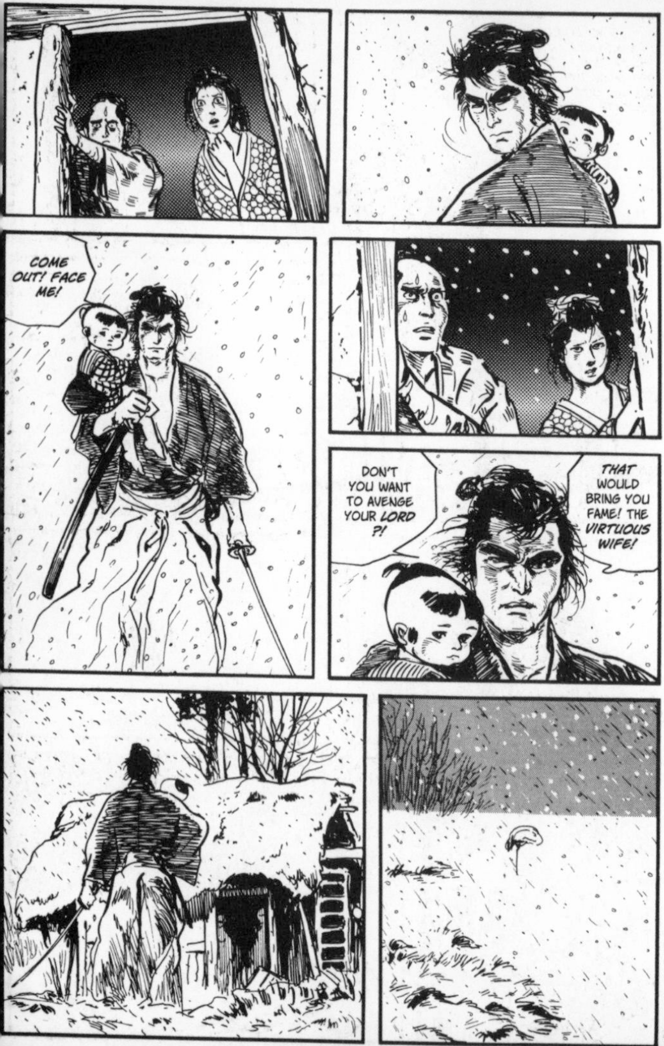
COME OUT! FACE ME!
DON'T YOU WANT TO AVENGE YOUR LORD ?!
THAT WOULD BRING YOU FAME! THE VIRTUOUS WIFE!

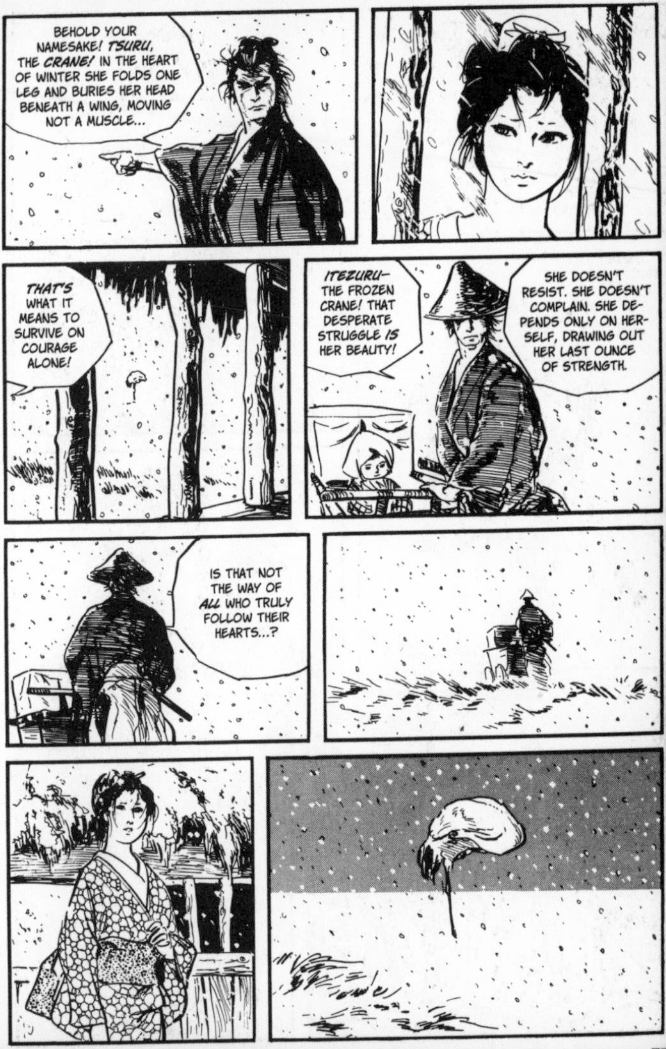
BEHOLD YOUR NAMESAKE! *TSURU,* THE *CRANE!* IN THE HEART OF WINTER SHE FOLDS ONE LEG AND BURIES HER HEAD BENEATH A WING, MOVING NOT A MUSCLE...
SHE DOESN'T RESIST. SHE DOESN'T COMPLAIN. SHE DEPENDS ONLY ON HERSELF, DRAWING OUT HER LAST OUNCE OF STRENGTH.
ITEZURU— THE FROZEN CRANE! THAT DESPERATE STRUGGLE *IS* HER BEAUTY!
THAT'S WHAT IT MEANS TO SURVIVE ON COURAGE ALONE!
IS THAT NOT THE WAY OF *ALL* WHO TRULY FOLLOW THEIR HEARTS...?

the forty-first

Chains

of

Death

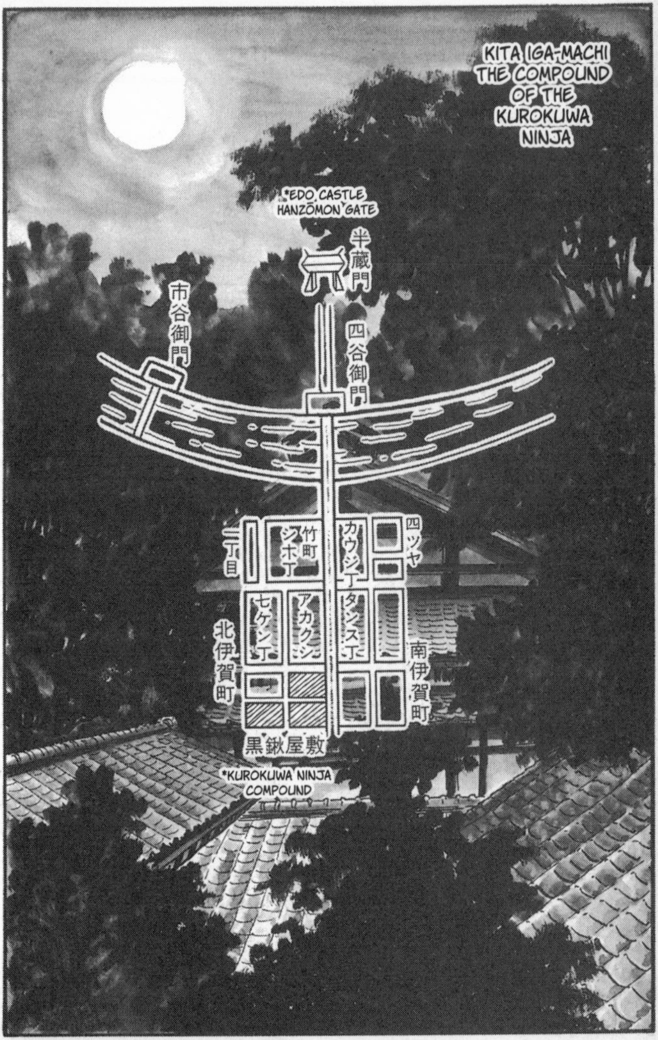
KITA IGA-MACHI
THE COMPOUND OF THE KUROKUWA NINJA
*EDO CASTLE HANZOMON GATE
半蔵門
四谷御門
市谷御門
四ツヤ
カウジ丁
竹町
シホ丁
二丁目
タンス丁
アカクシ
セケン丁
南伊賀町
北伊賀町
黒鍬屋敷
*KUROKUWA NINJA COMPOUND

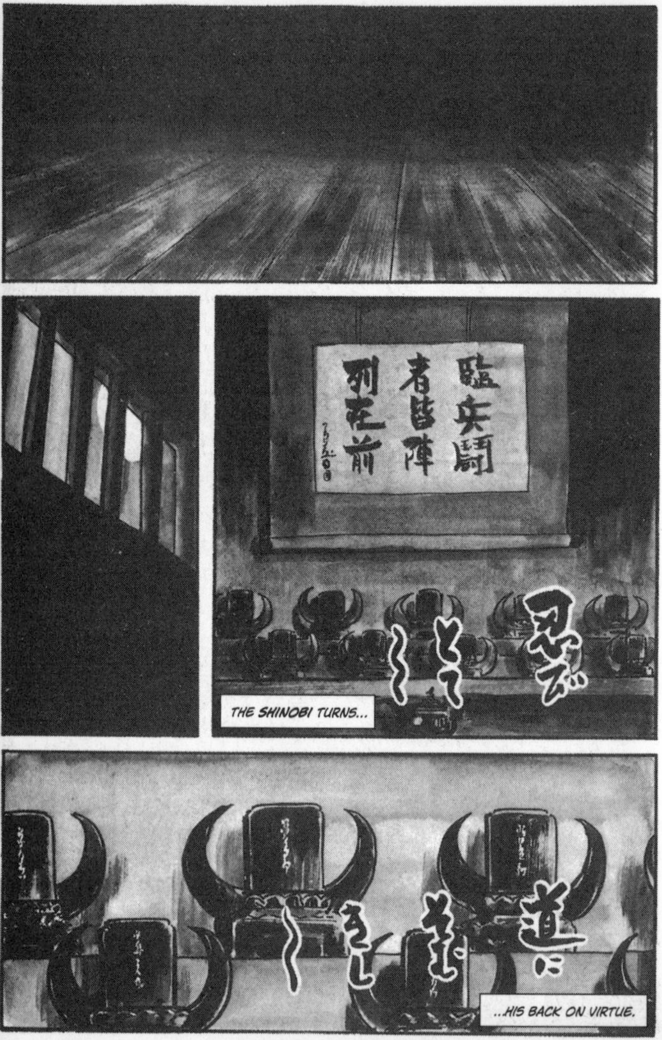
臨兵闘者皆陣列在前
忍ぶとて〜
THE SHINOBI TURNS...
道にそむきし〜
...HIS BACK ON VIRTUE.

SHOW HIM THE WAY!

高井清五郎　平山小三神　椎名喜之神　飯田平武

偸み

亀井嘉十郎　村山兵衛　内田弥作　伊野原喜次郎　松山惣八郎　磯田序助　後藤円進　尾瀬久禾之進

神や仏の

しかで守らん

THE GODS AND BUDDHA CANNOT MAKE HIM OBEY...

THE WARRIOR MUST ALWAYS BELIEVE IN VIRTUE.

ものふは常に信心いたすべじ

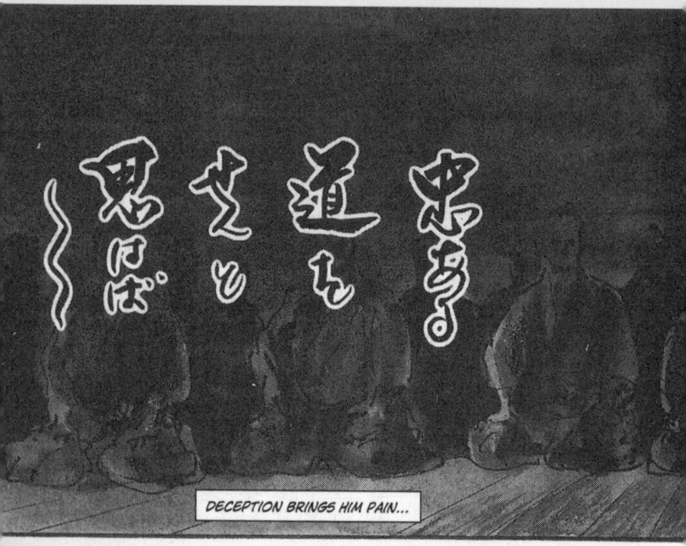
DECEPTION BRINGS HIM PAIN...

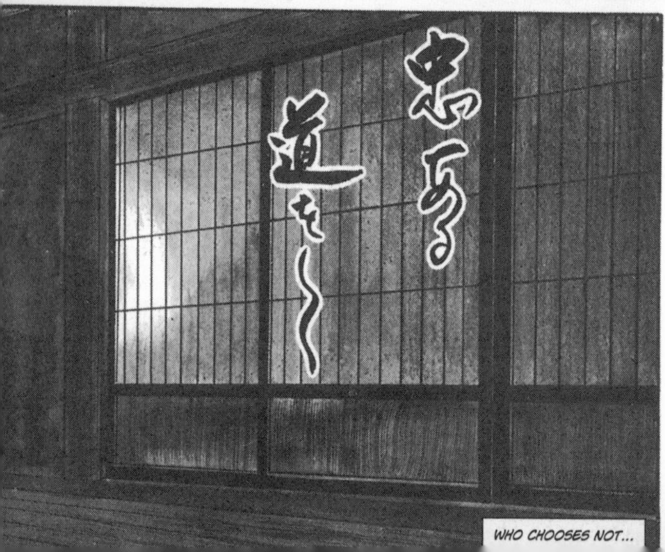
忠ある
道を～
WHO CHOOSES NOT...

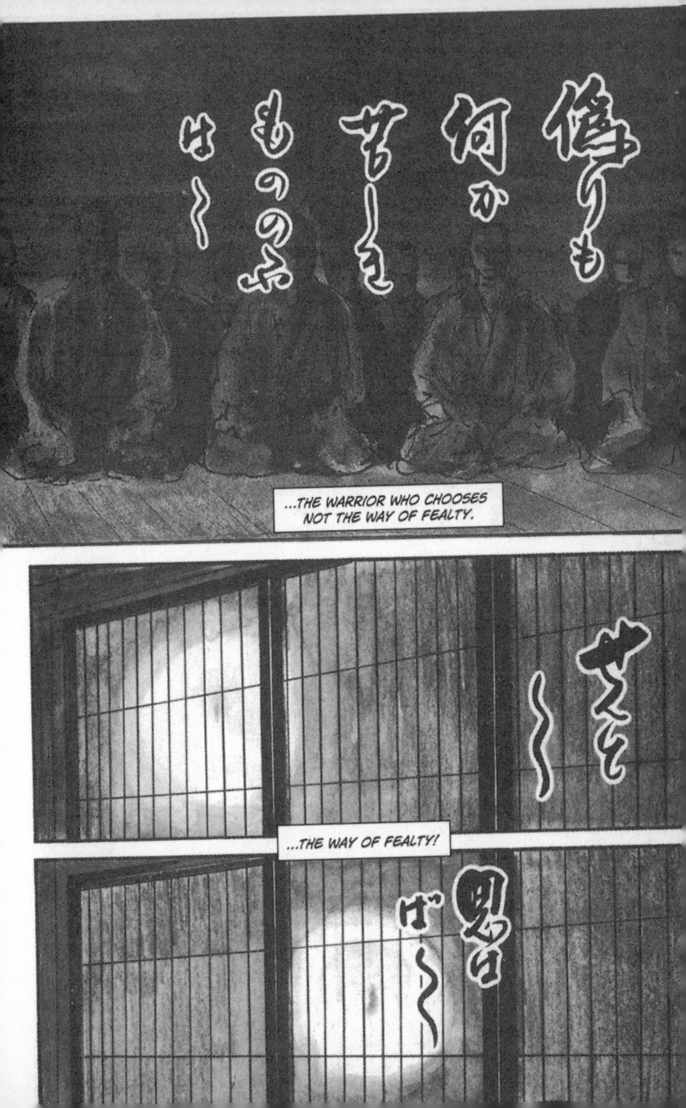
侮りも何か苦しきもののふは〜
...THE WARRIOR WHO CHOOSES NOT THE WAY OF FEALTY.
せくと〜
...THE WAY OF FEALTY!
男はばく〜

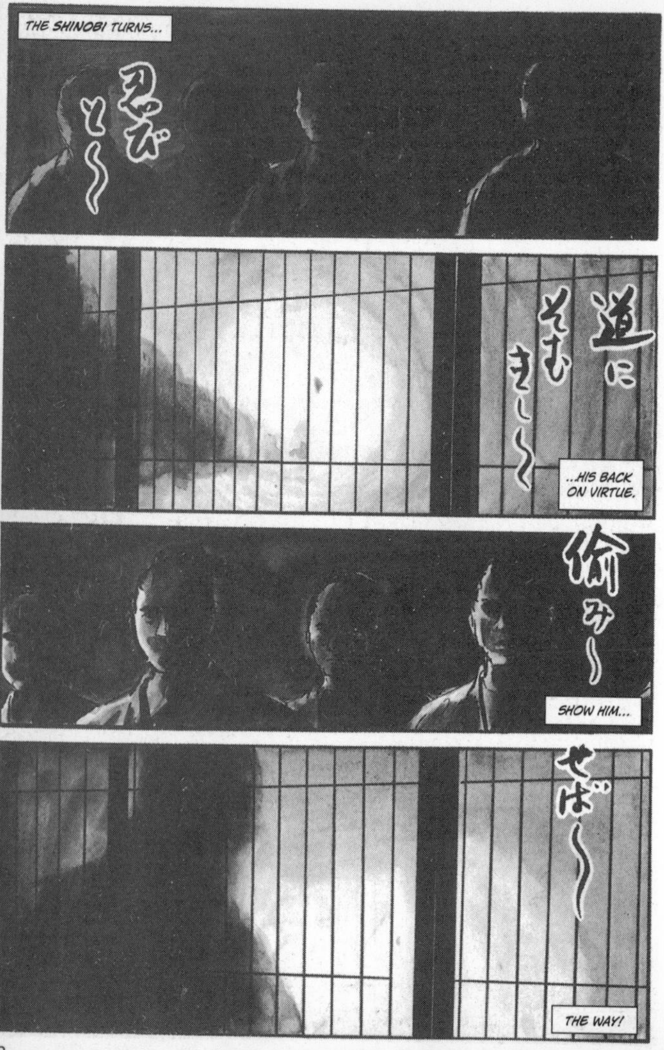
THE SHINOBI TURNS...
忍びと〜
道にそむきし〜
...HIS BACK ON VIRTUE.
偸み〜
SHOW HIM...
せば〜
THE WAY!

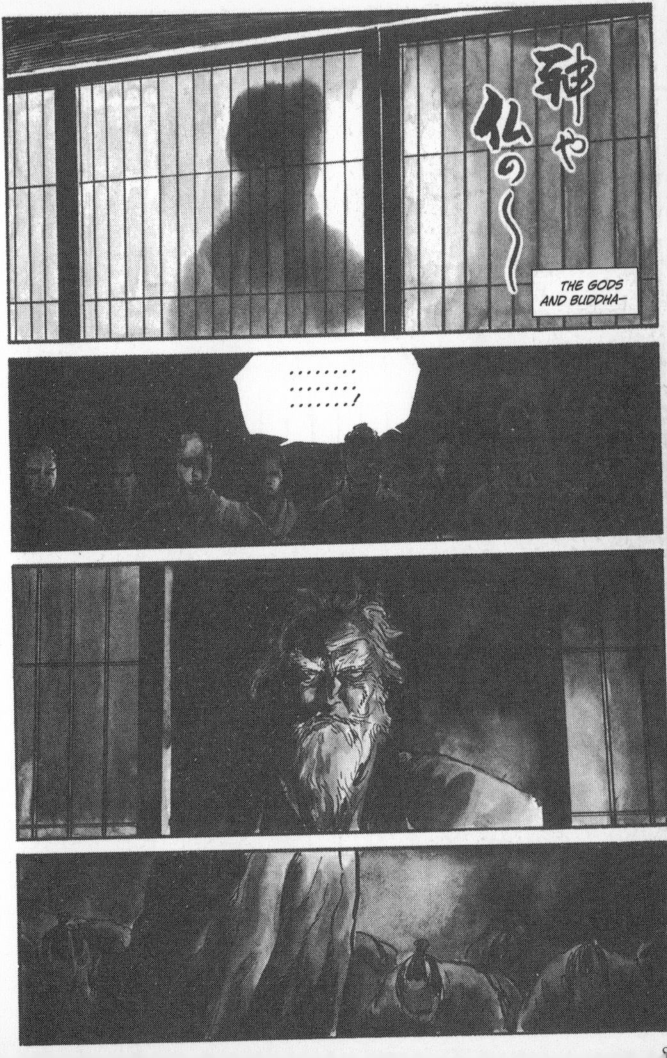
神や仏の〜〜
THE GODS AND BUDDHA—
....!

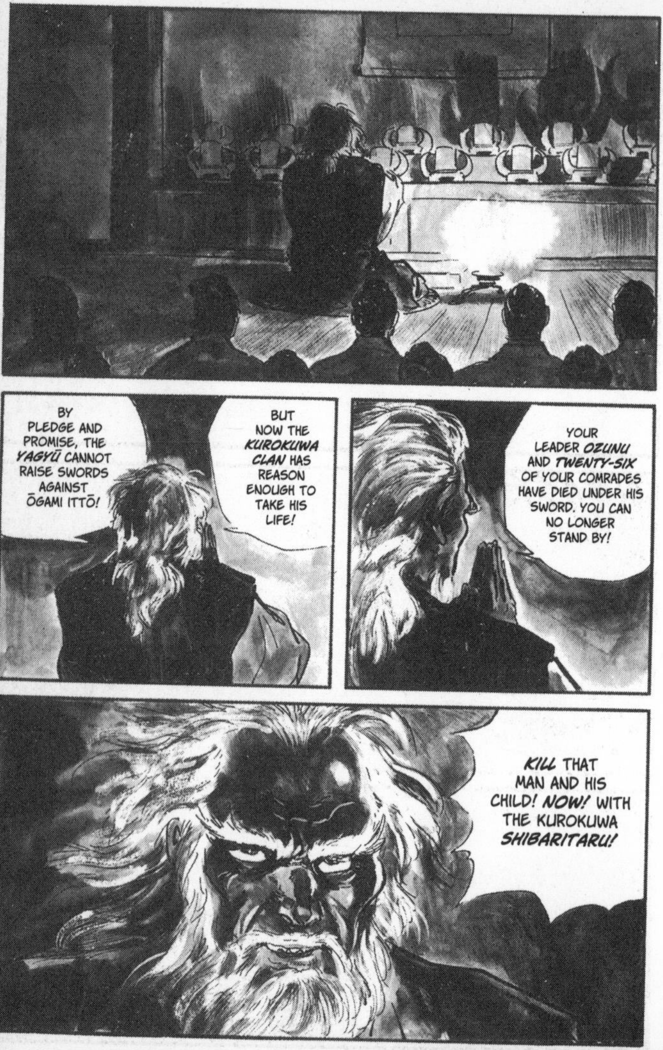
BY PLEDGE AND PROMISE, THE YAGYŪ CANNOT RAISE SWORDS AGAINST ŌGAMI ITTŌ!
BUT NOW THE KUROKUWA CLAN HAS REASON ENOUGH TO TAKE HIS LIFE!
YOUR LEADER OZUNU AND TWENTY-SIX OF YOUR COMRADES HAVE DIED UNDER HIS SWORD. YOU CAN NO LONGER STAND BY!
KILL THAT MAN AND HIS CHILD! NOW! WITH THE KUROKUWA SHIBARITARU!

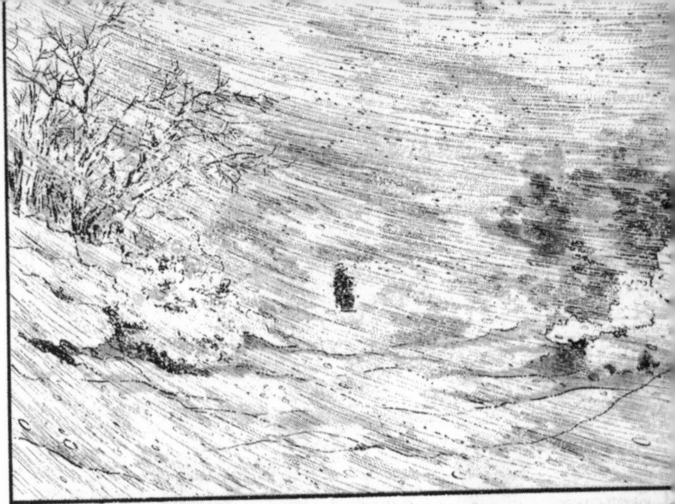
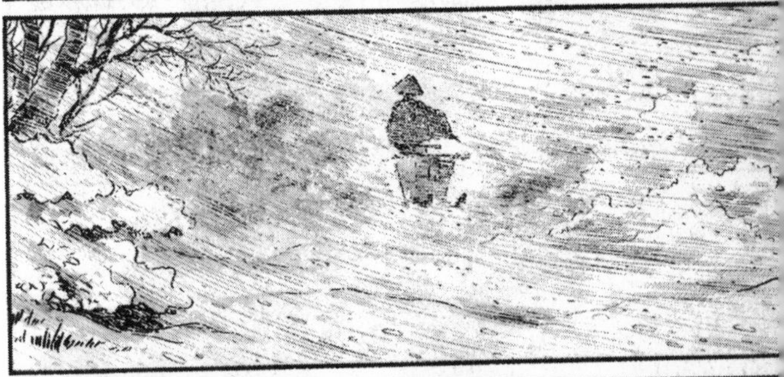
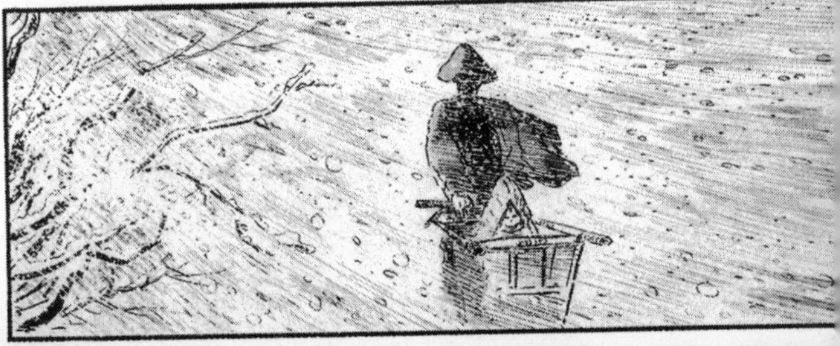

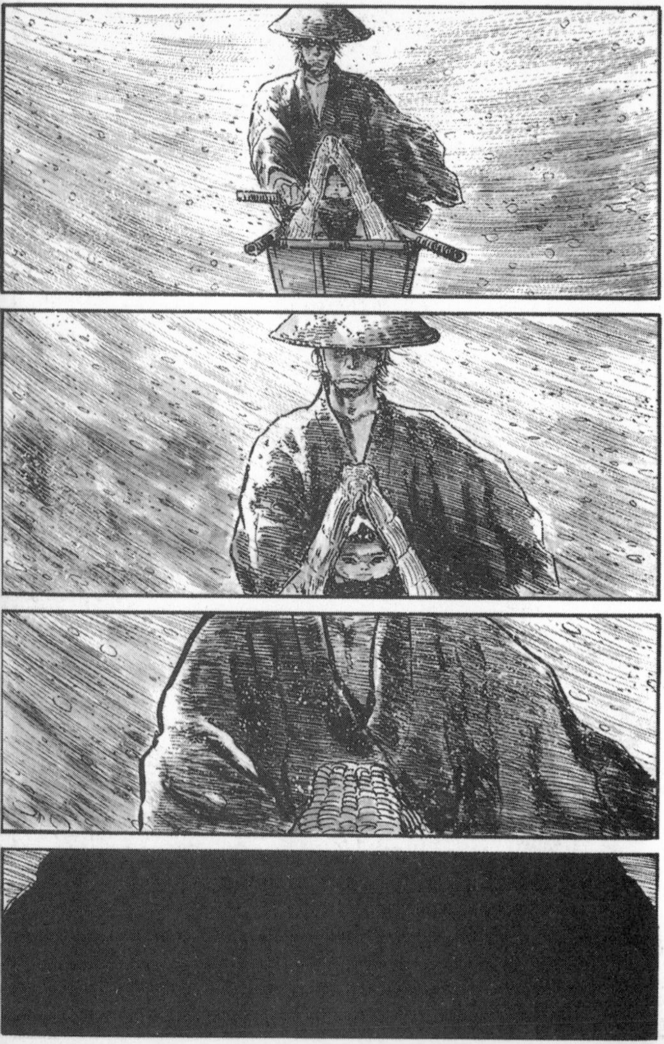

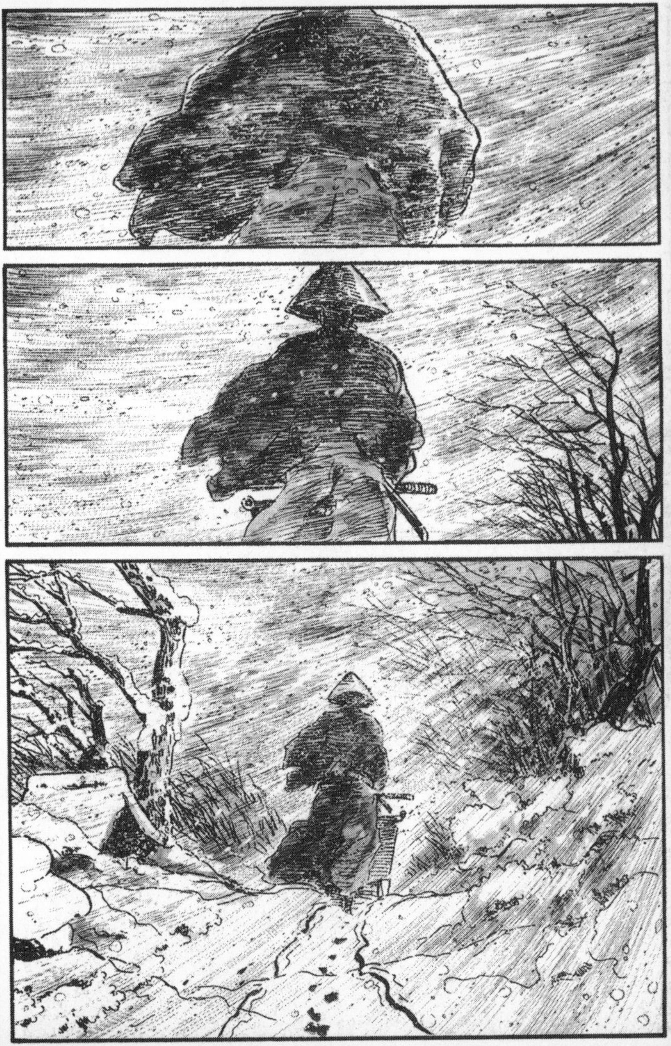

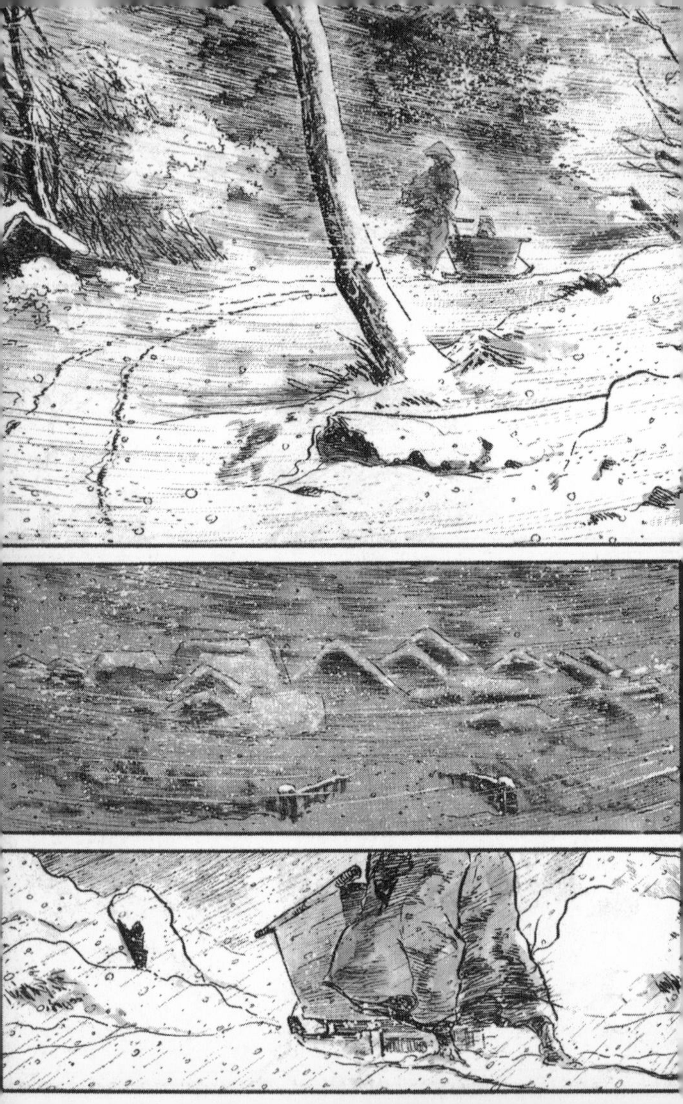

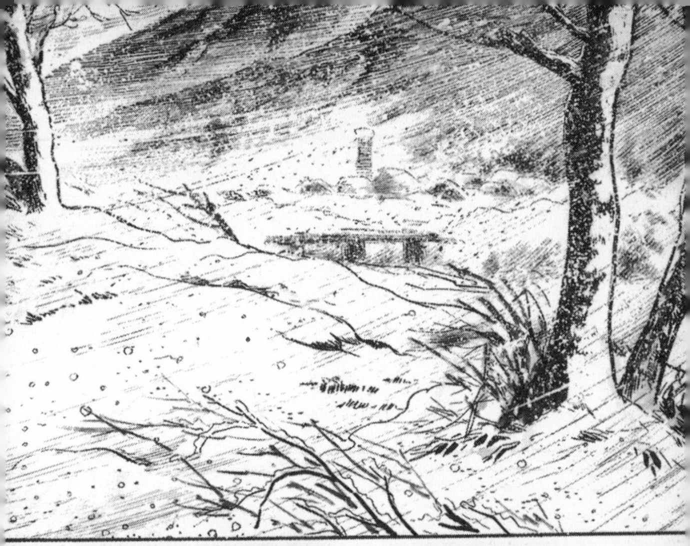

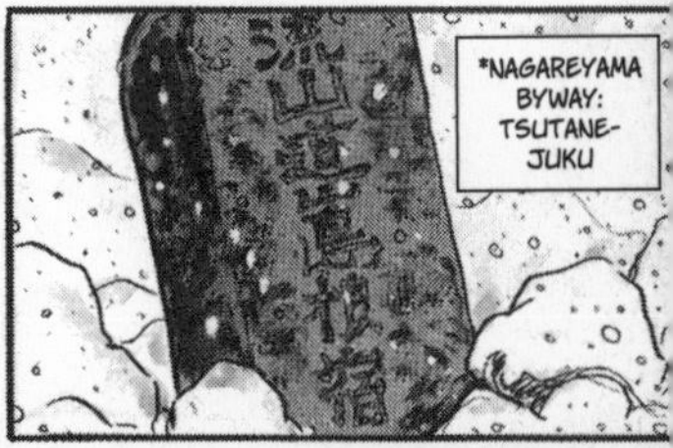
*NAGAREYAMA BYWAY: TSUTANE-JUKU

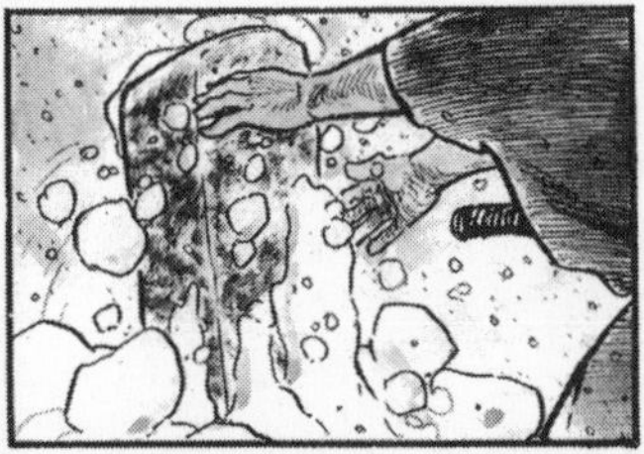

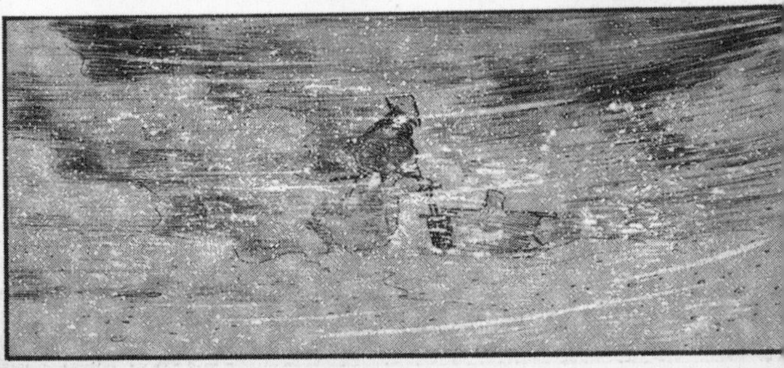

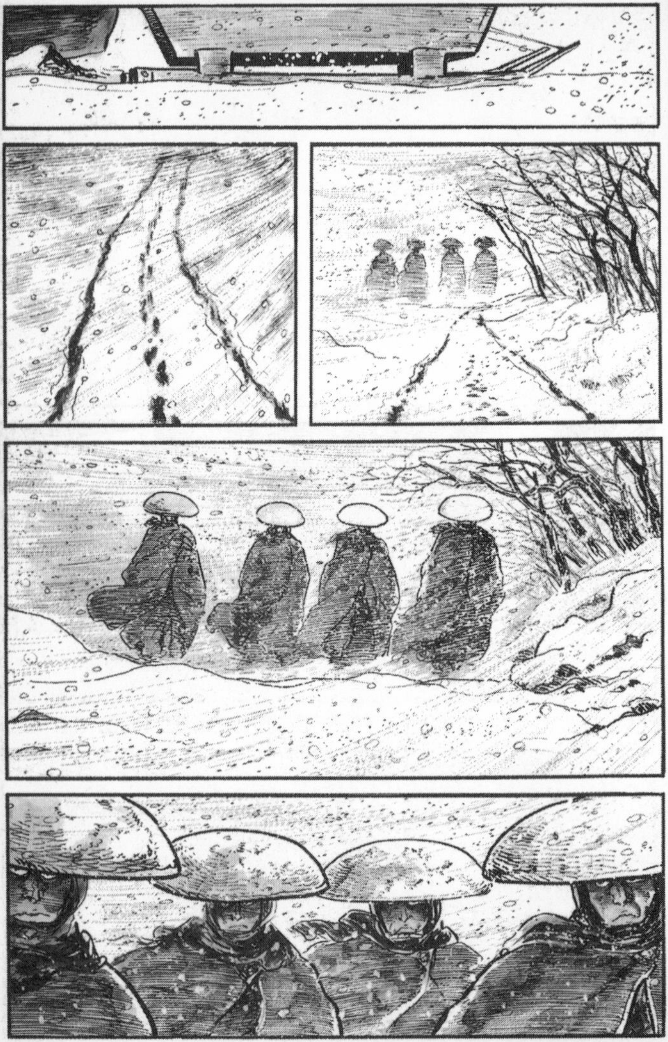

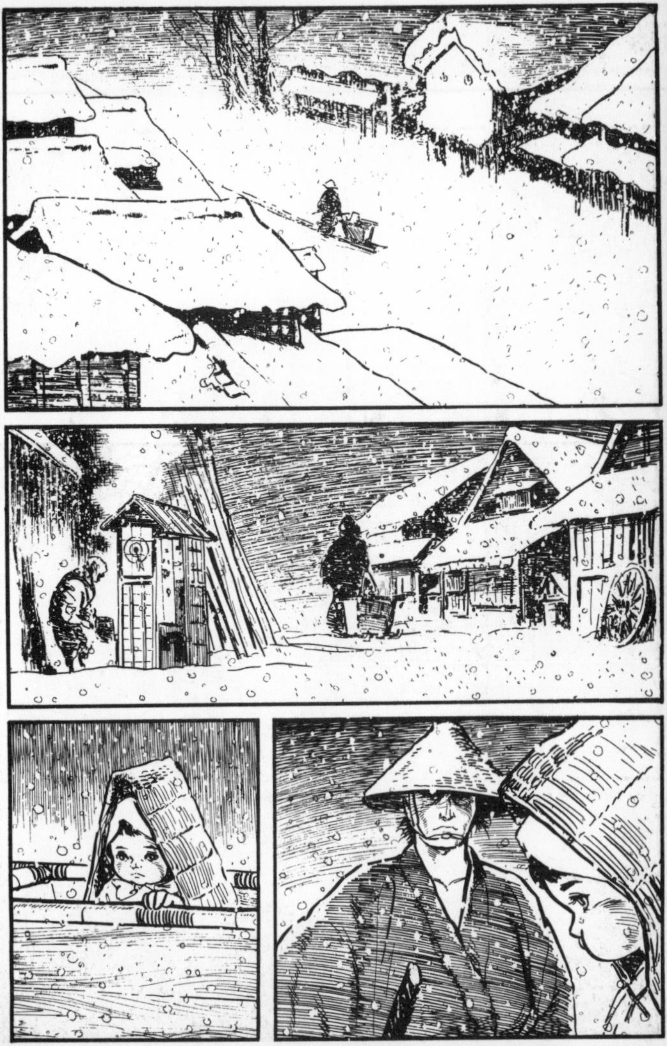

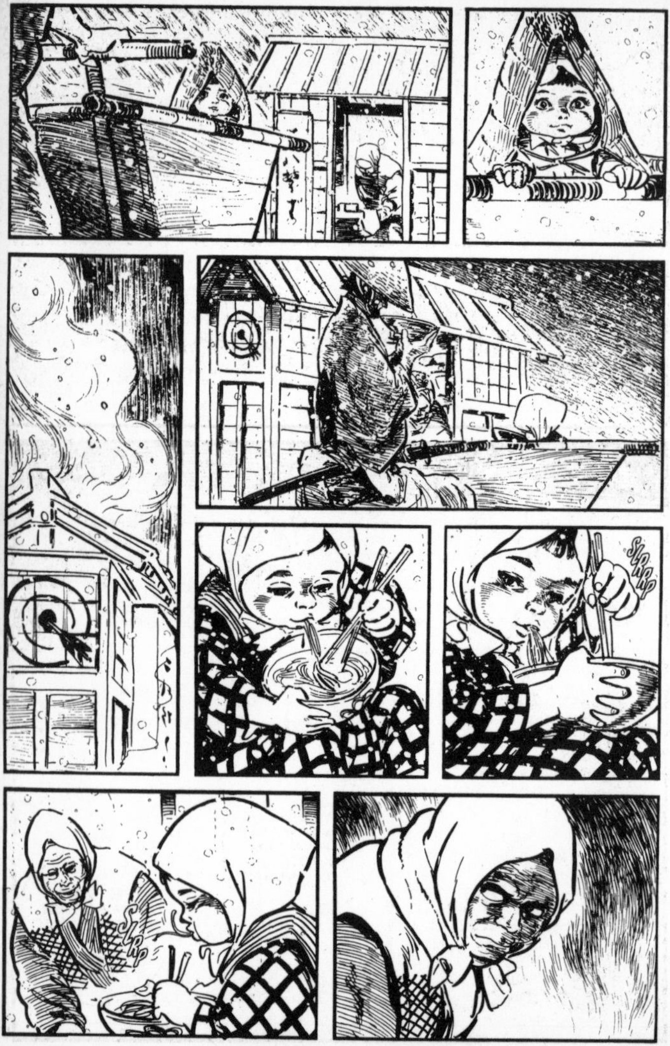
SLRRP
SLRP

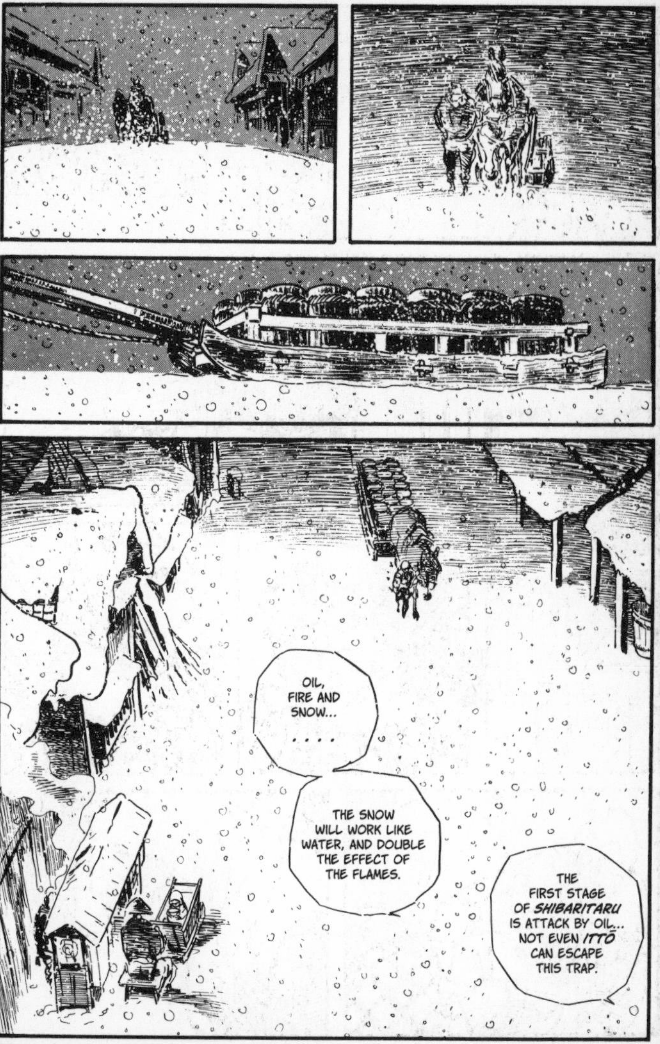
OIL, FIRE AND SNOW... ....
THE SNOW WILL WORK LIKE WATER, AND DOUBLE THE EFFECT OF THE FLAMES.
THE FIRST STAGE OF *SHIBARITARU* IS ATTACK BY OIL... NOT EVEN *ITTŌ* CAN ESCAPE THIS TRAP.

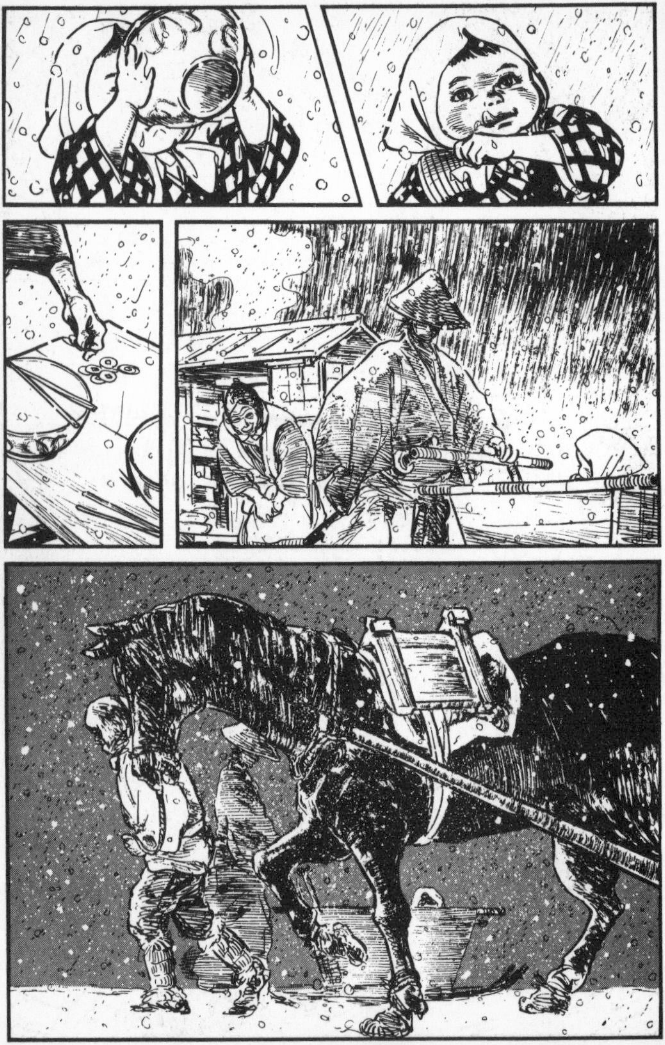

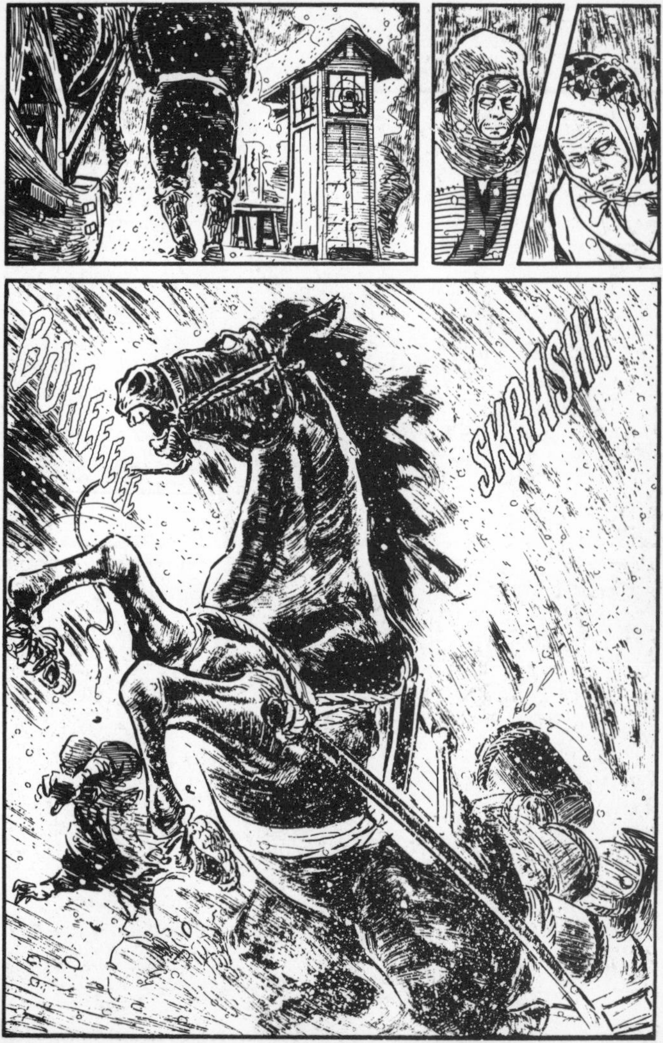
SKRASHH
BUHEEEEE

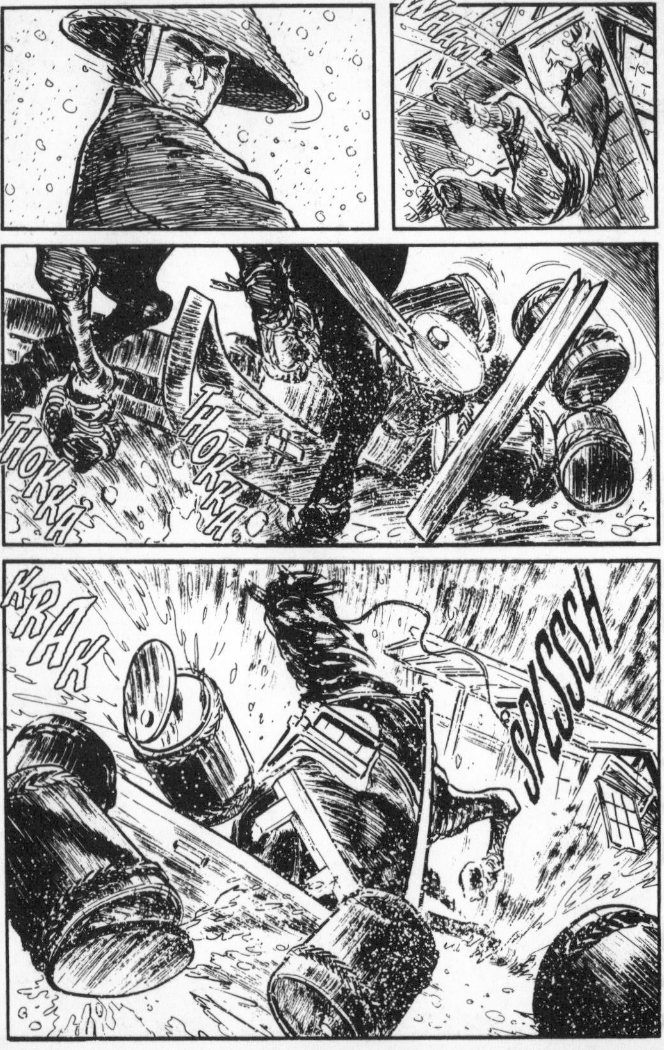
WHAM!
THOKKA
THOKKA
SPLSSH
KRAK

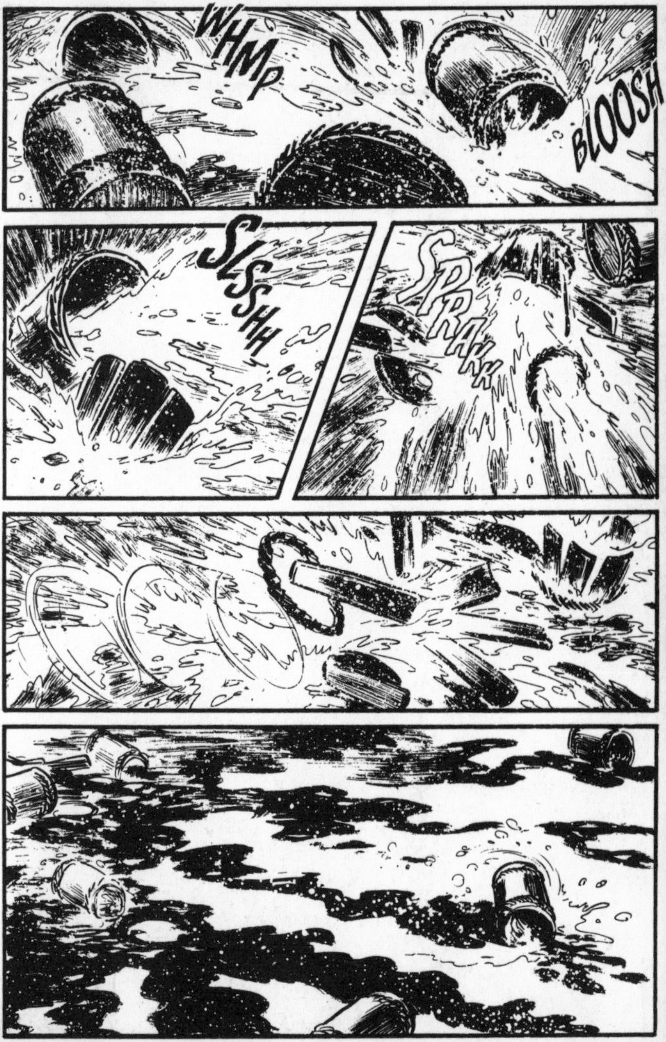
WHMP
BLOOSH
SPRAKK
SLSSHH

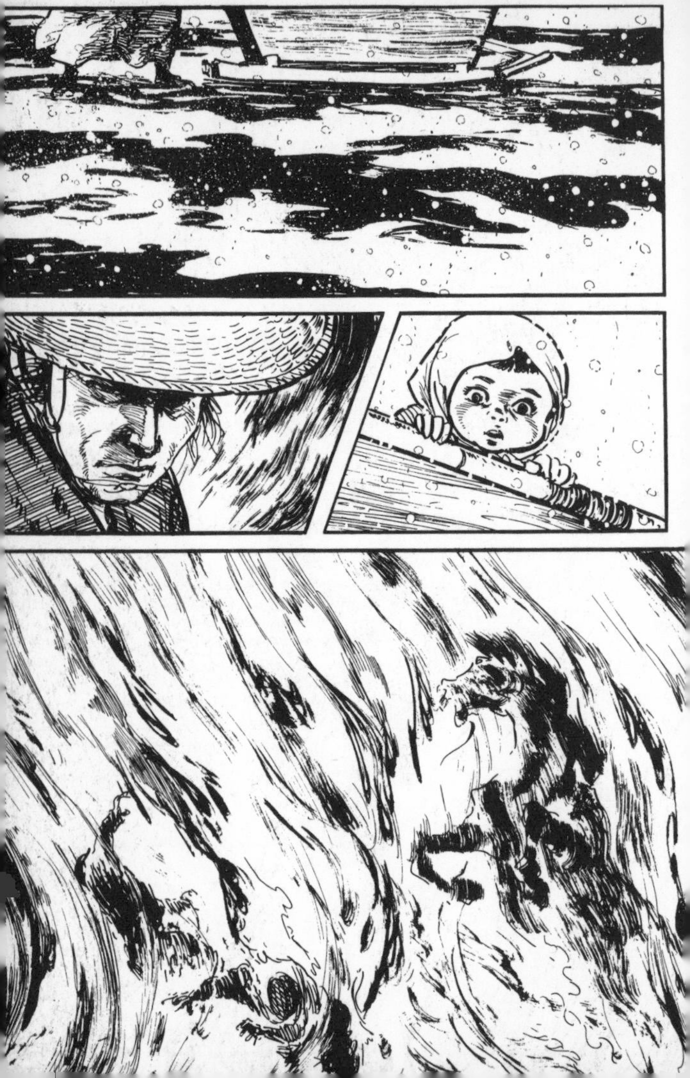

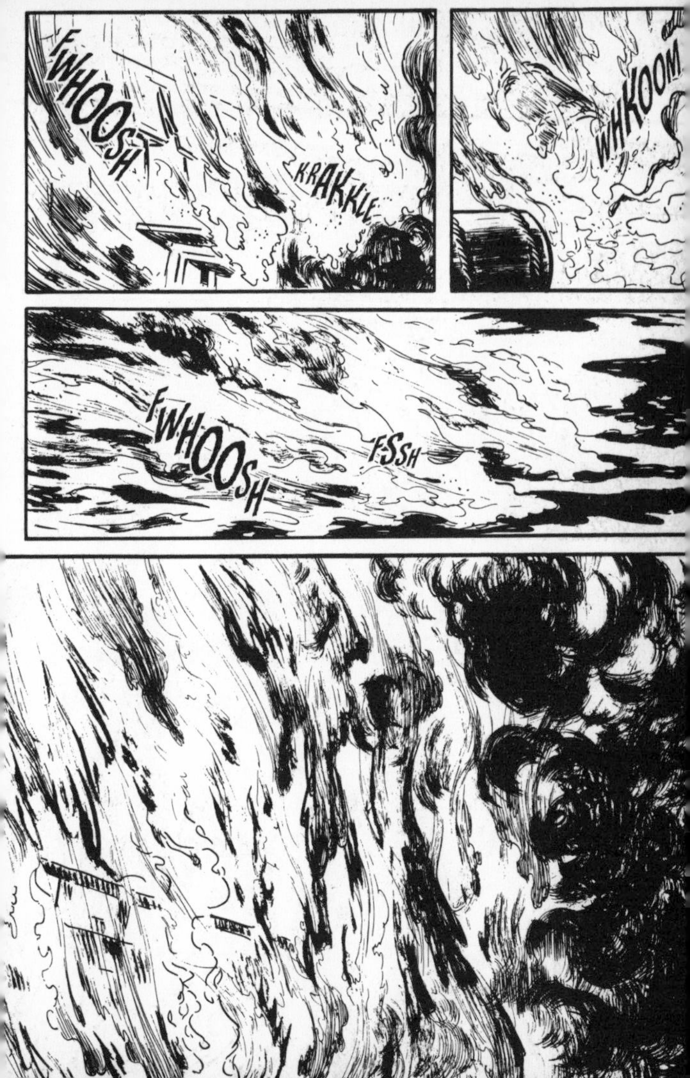
WHKOOM
FWHOOSH
KRAKKLE
FWHOOSH
FSSH

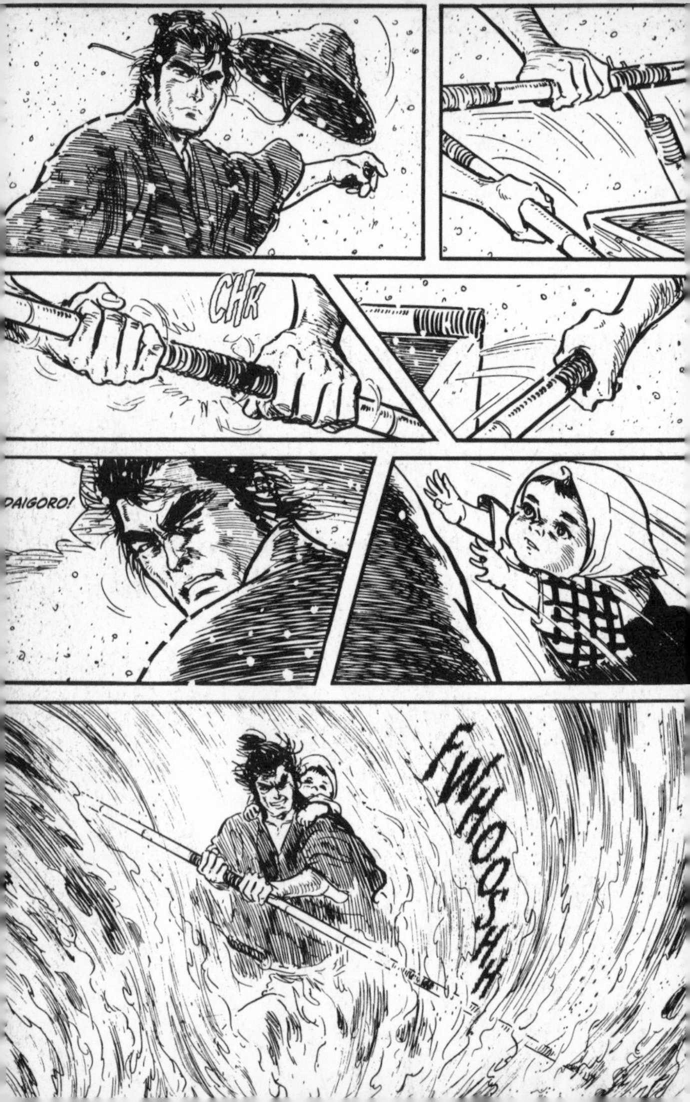
CHK
DAIGORO!
FWHOOSHH

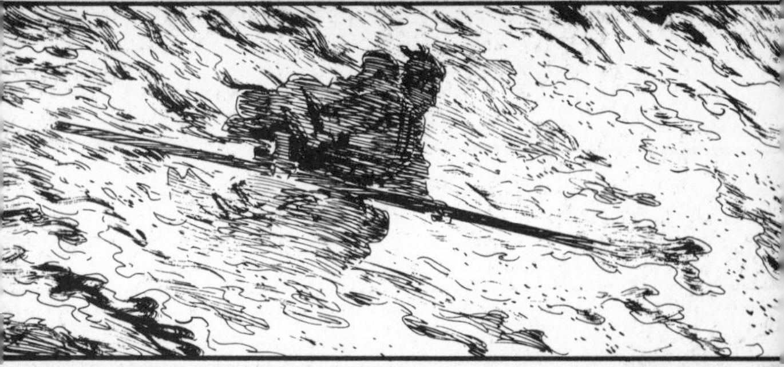
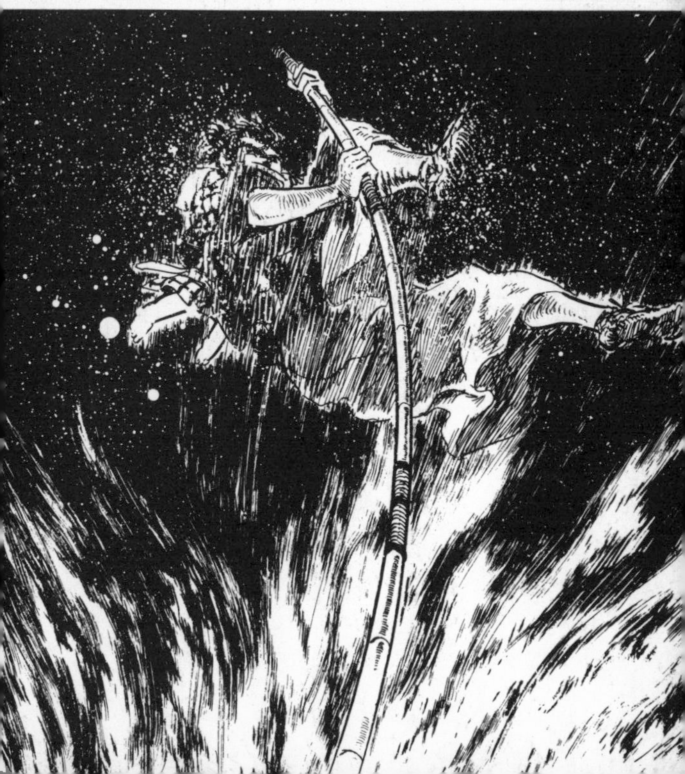

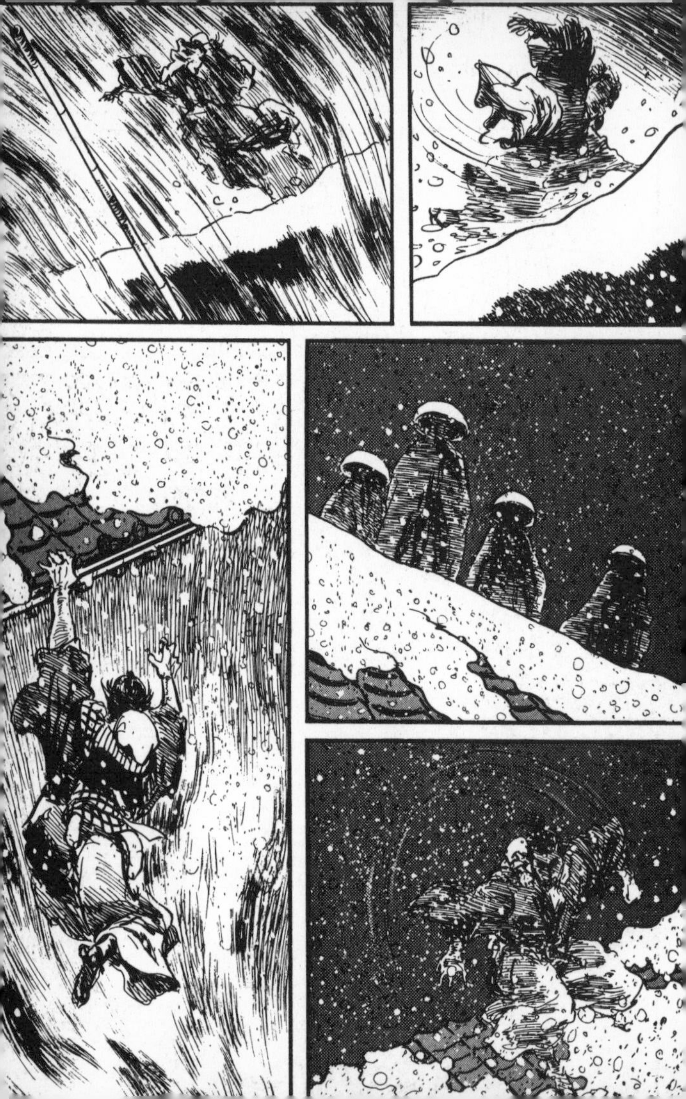

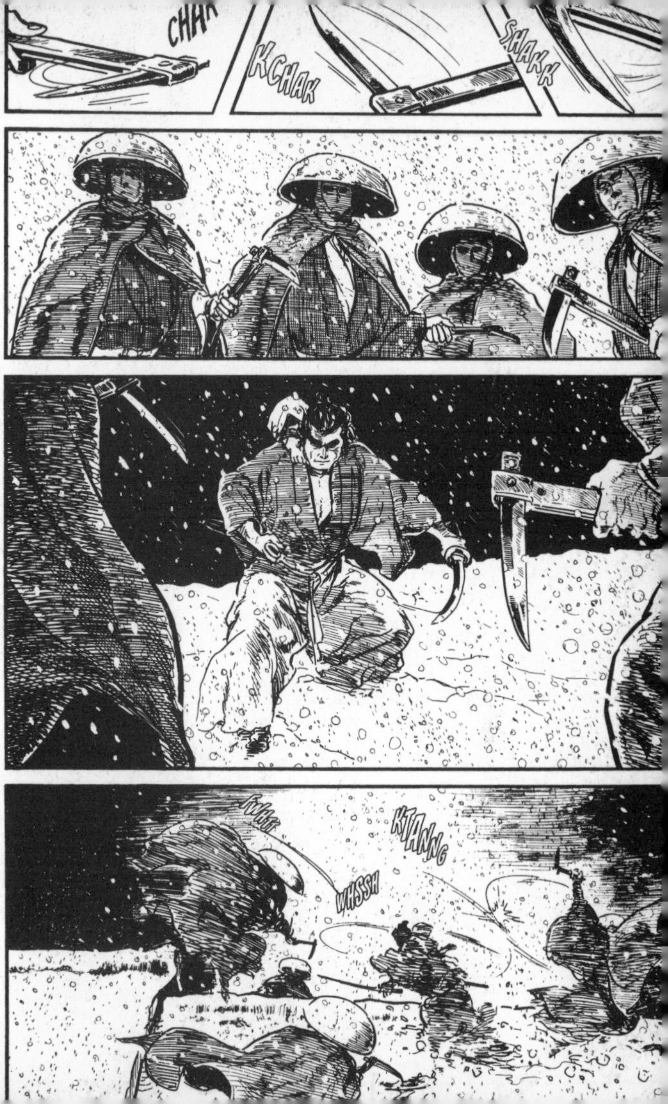
SHAKK
KCHAK
CHAK
KTANNG
FWHTT
WHSSH

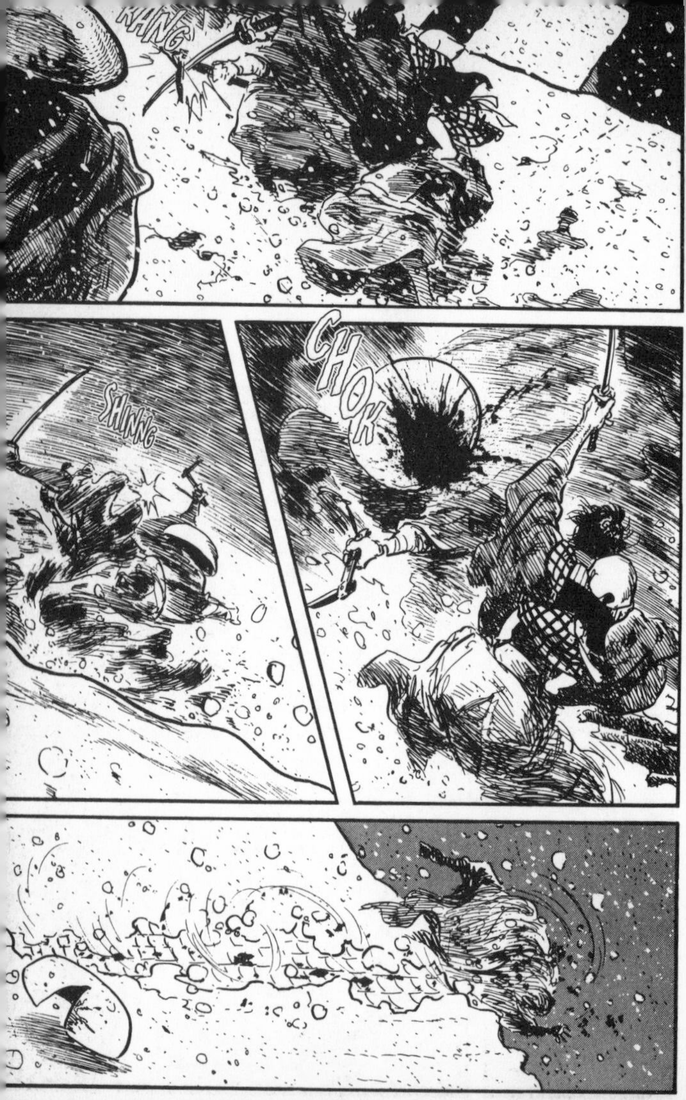
KHANG
CHOK
SHINNG

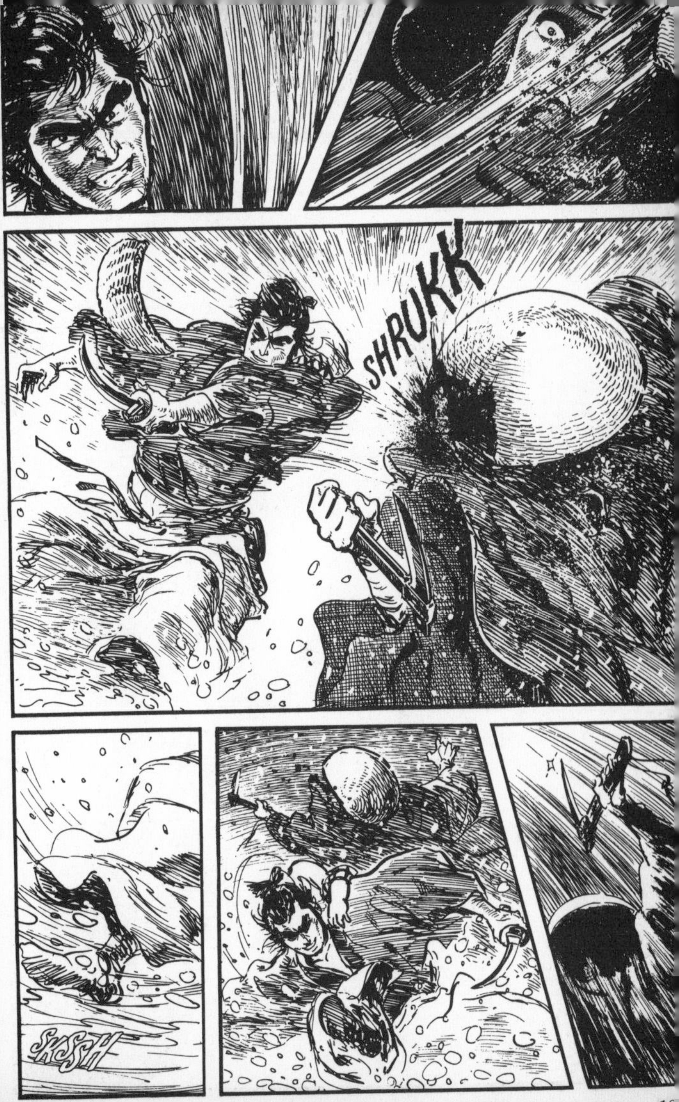
SHRUKK
SKSSH

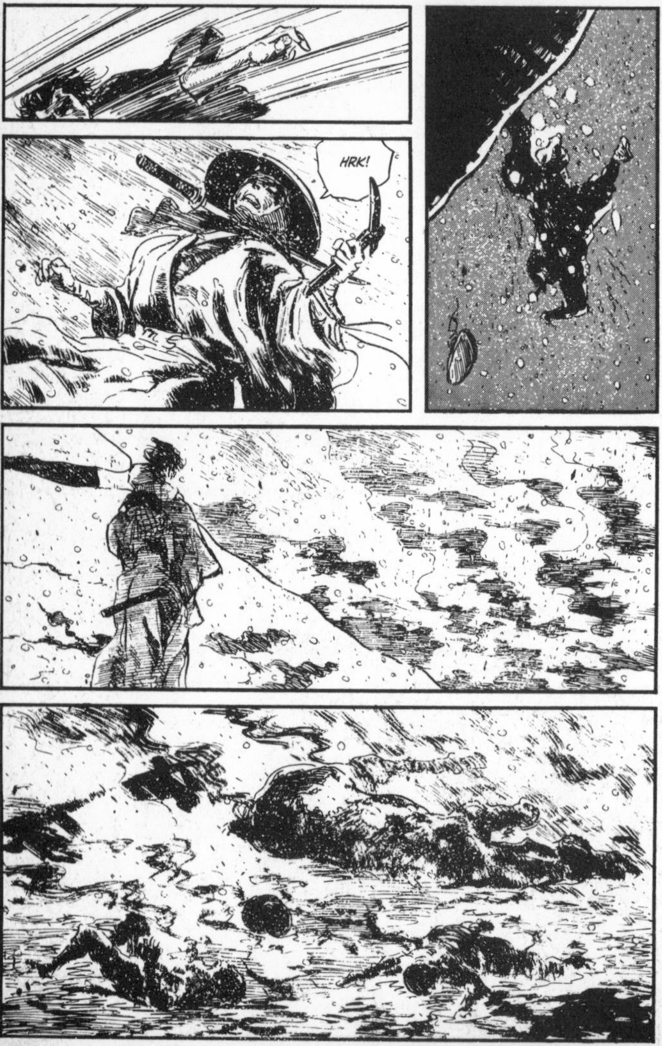
HRK!

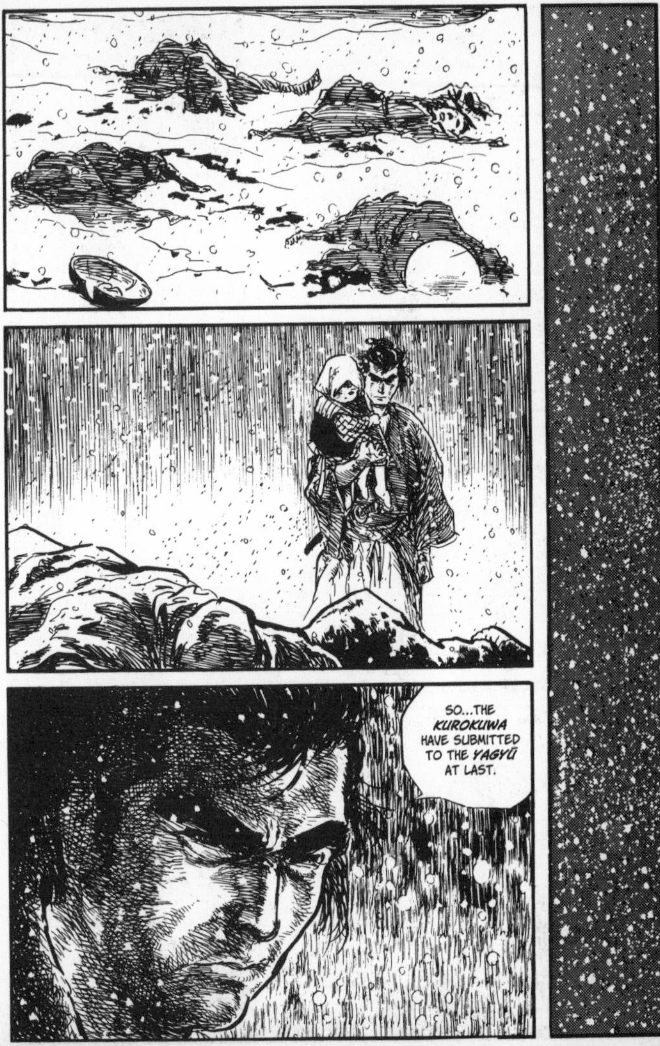
SO...THE *KUROKUWA* HAVE SUBMITTED TO THE *YAGYŪ* AT LAST.

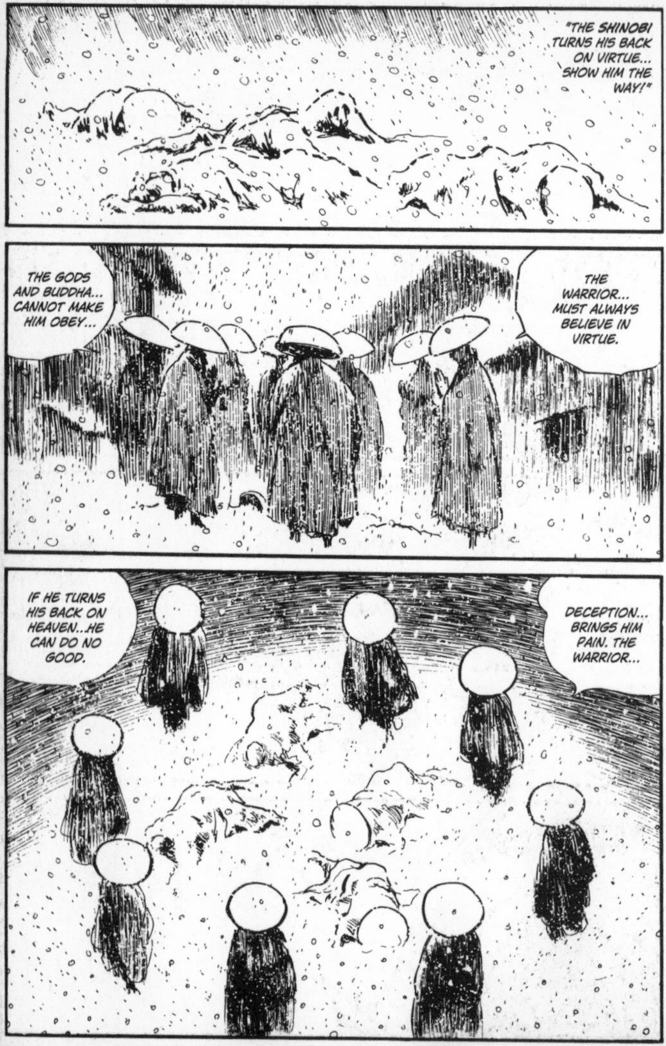
"THE SHINOBI TURNS HIS BACK ON VIRTUE... SHOW HIM THE WAY!"
THE WARRIOR... MUST ALWAYS BELIEVE IN VIRTUE.
THE GODS AND BUDDHA... CANNOT MAKE HIM OBEY...
DECEPTION... BRINGS HIM PAIN. THE WARRIOR...
IF HE TURNS HIS BACK ON HEAVEN...HE CAN DO NO GOOD.

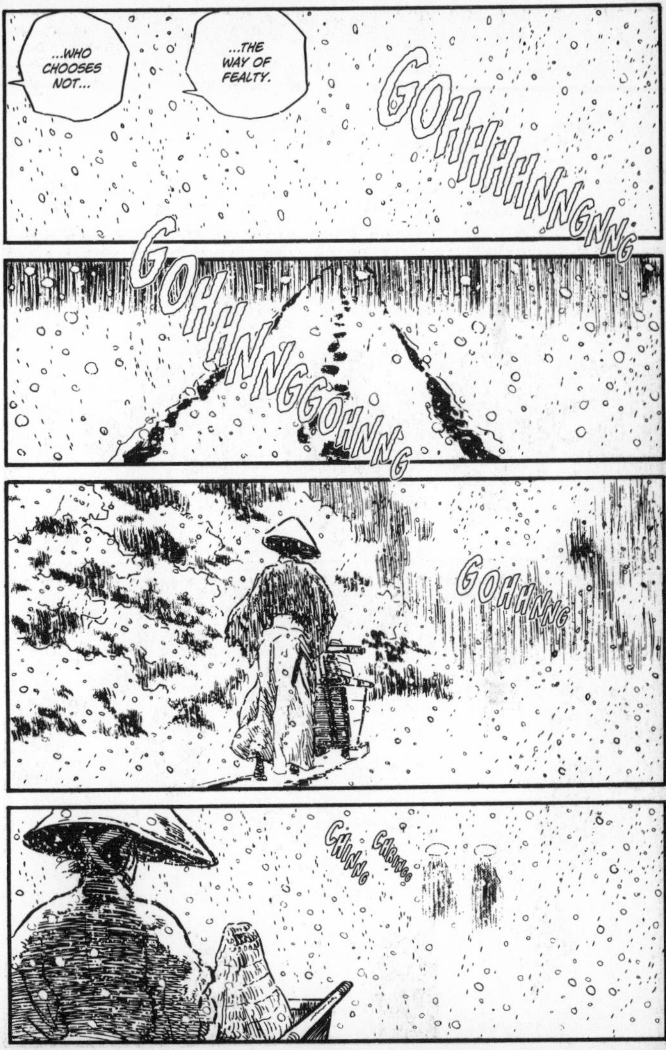
...THE WAY OF FEALTY.
...WHO CHOOSES NOT...
GOHHHHHNNGNNG
GOHHNNGGOHNNG
GOHHNNG
CHRINGG
CHINNG

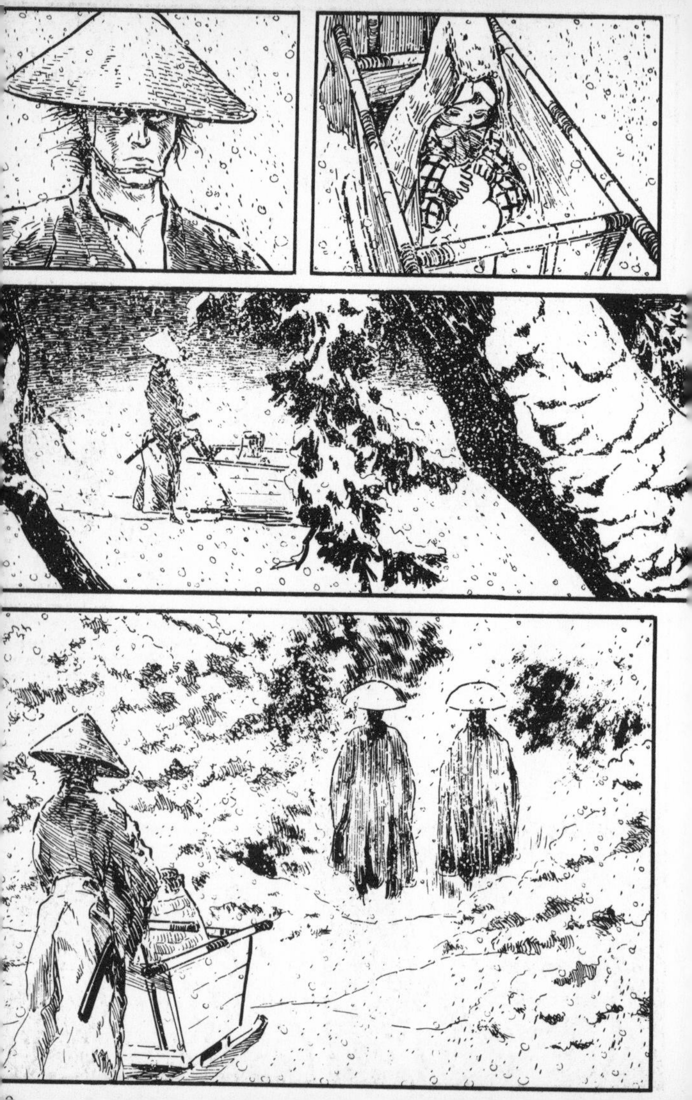

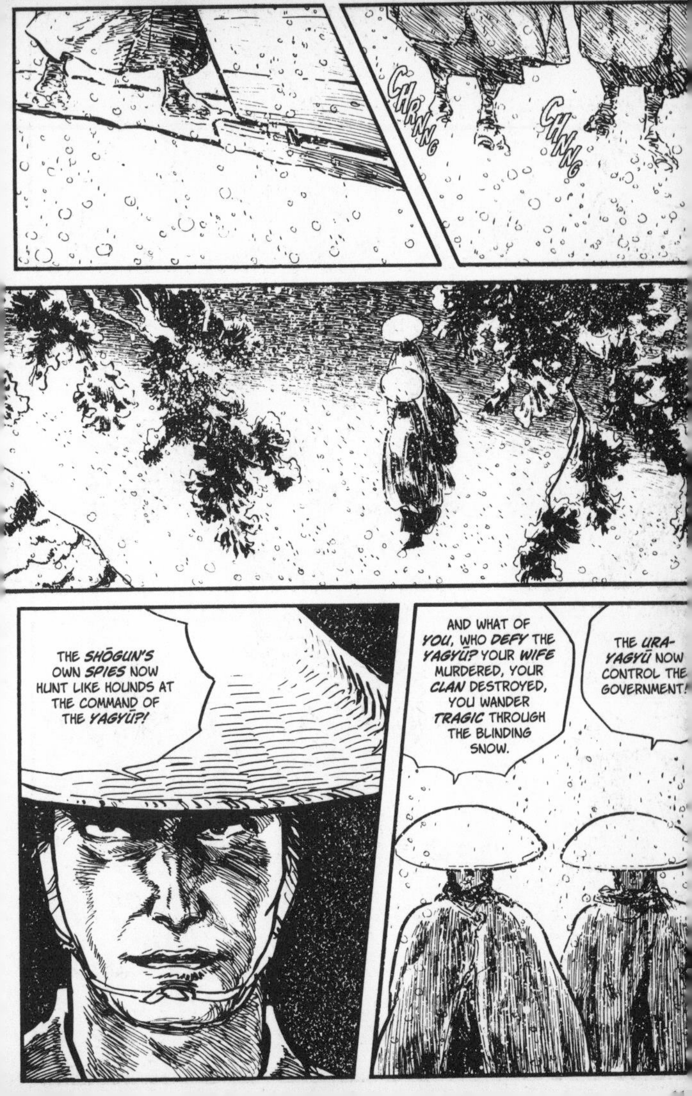
CHRNNG
CHNNG
THE SHŌGUN'S OWN SPIES NOW HUNT LIKE HOUNDS AT THE COMMAND OF THE YAGYŪ?!
AND WHAT OF YOU, WHO DEFY THE YAGYŪ? YOUR WIFE MURDERED, YOUR CLAN DESTROYED, YOU WANDER TRAGIC THROUGH THE BLINDING SNOW.
THE URA-YAGYŪ NOW CONTROL THE GOVERNMENT!

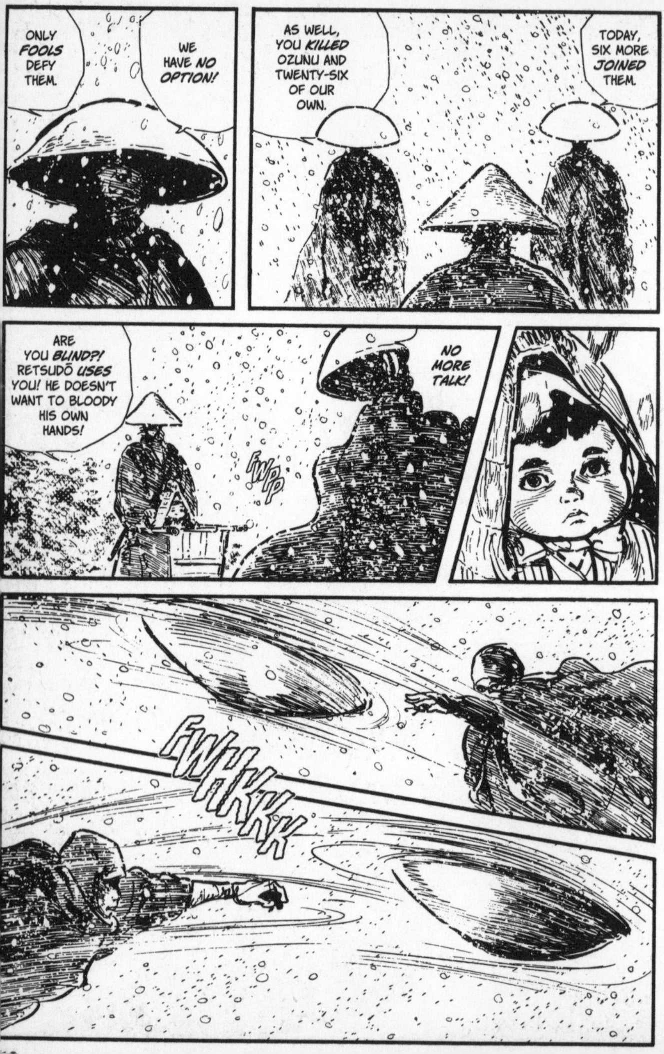
ONLY *FOOLS* DEFY THEM.
WE HAVE *NO OPTION!*
AS WELL, YOU *KILLED* OZUNU AND TWENTY-SIX OF OUR OWN.
TODAY, SIX MORE *JOINED* THEM.
ARE YOU *BLIND?!* RETSUDŌ *USES* YOU! HE DOESN'T WANT TO BLOODY HIS OWN HANDS!
NO MORE TALK!
FWPP
FWHKKK

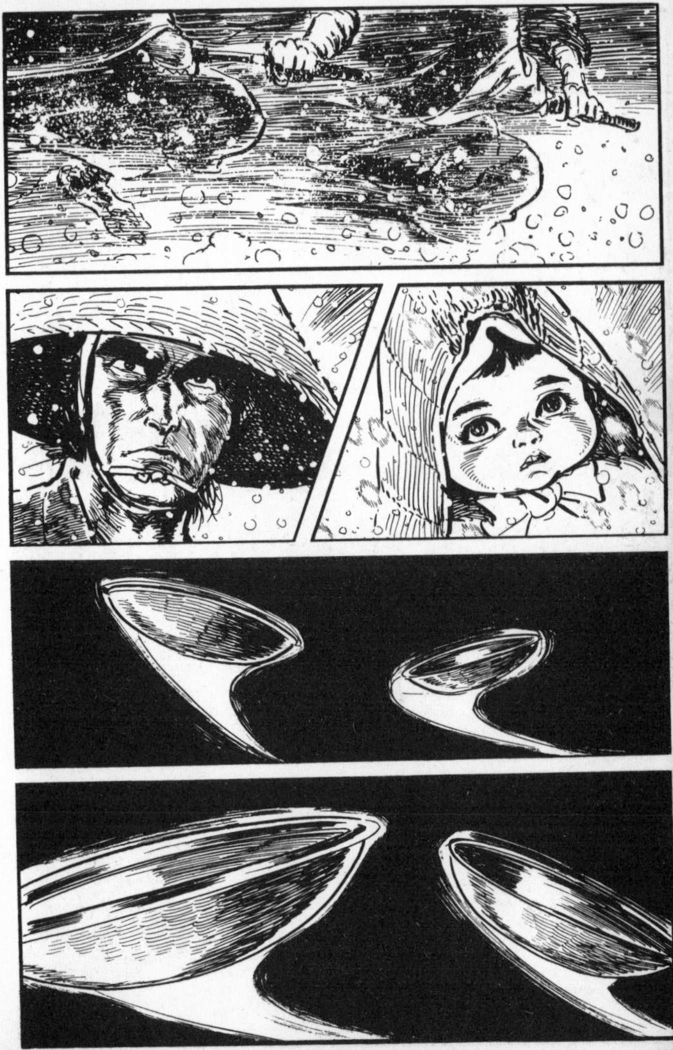

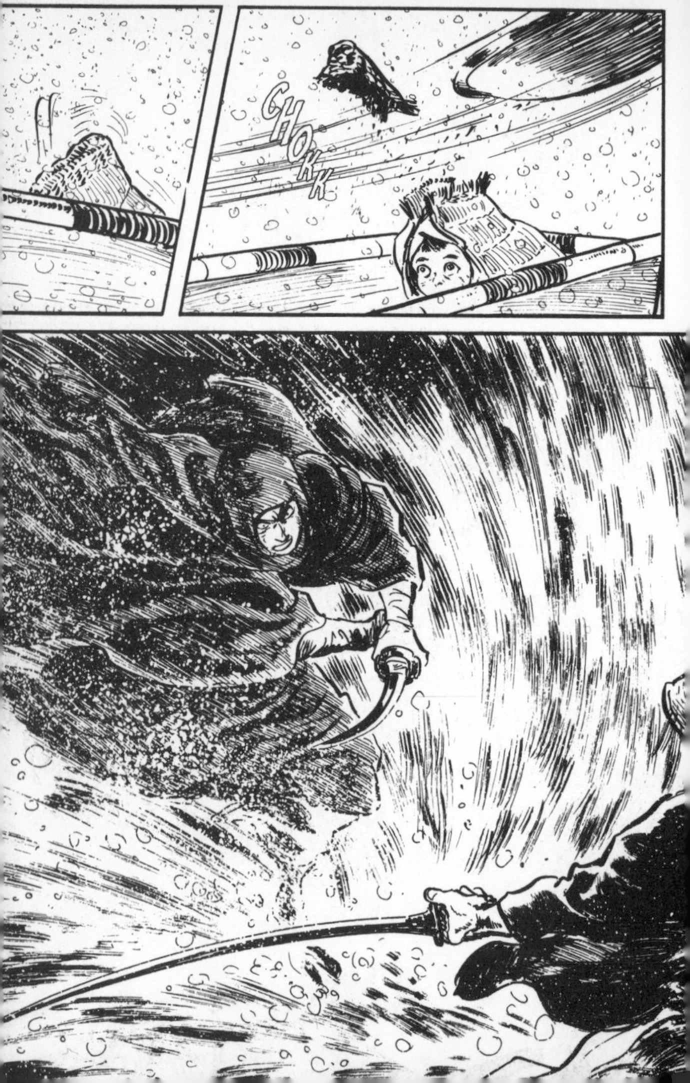
CHOKK

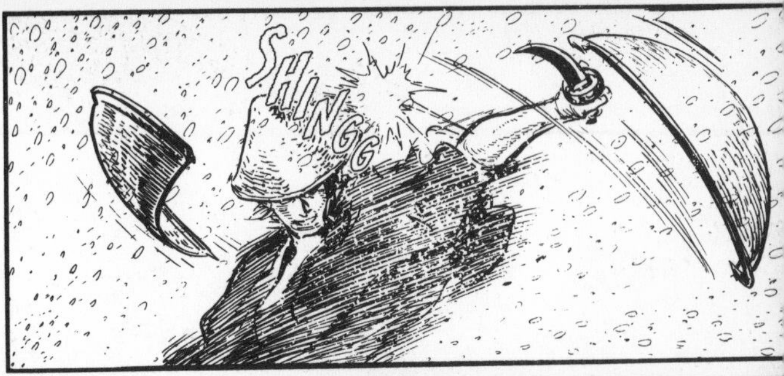
SHINGG
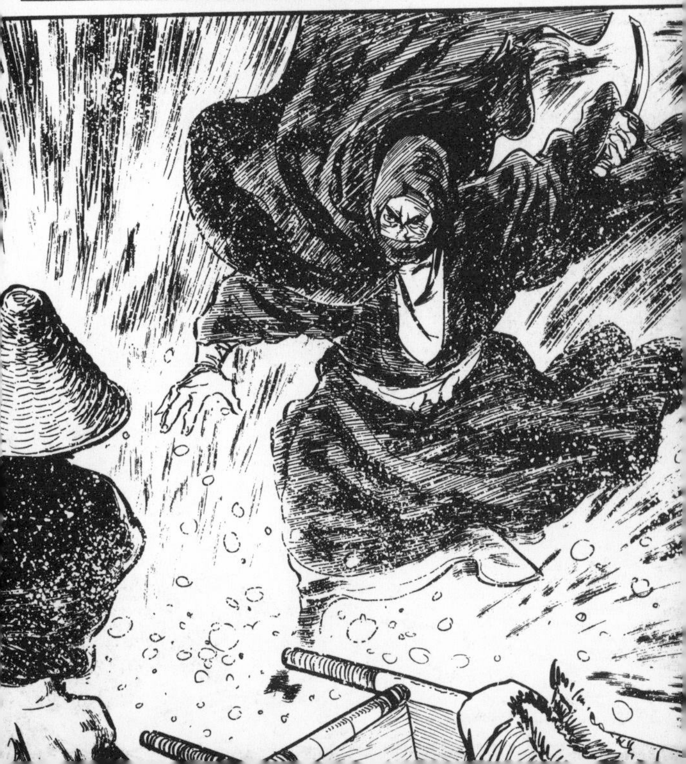

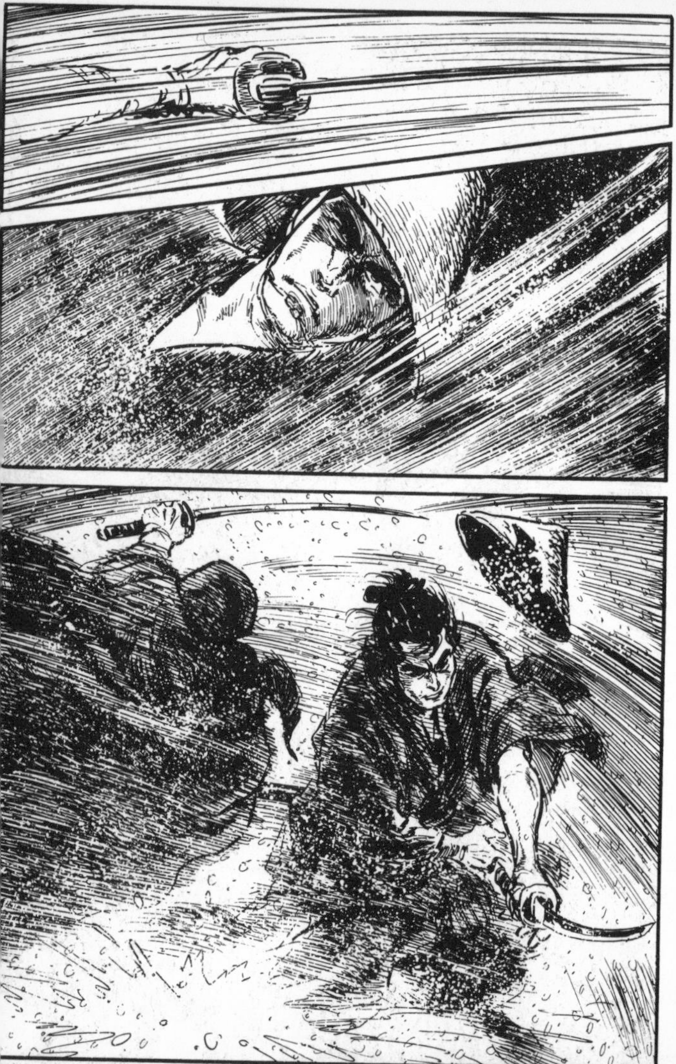

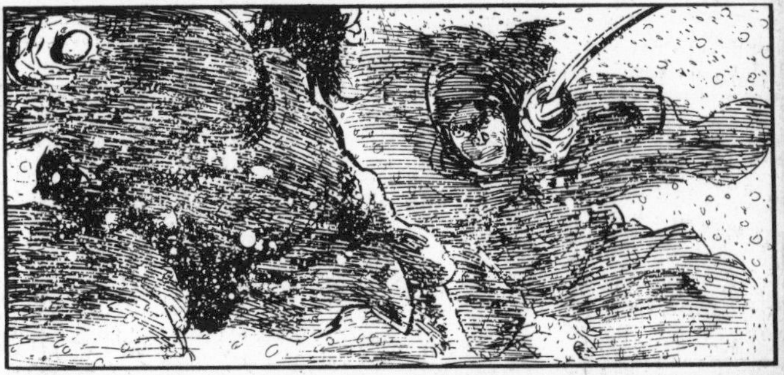

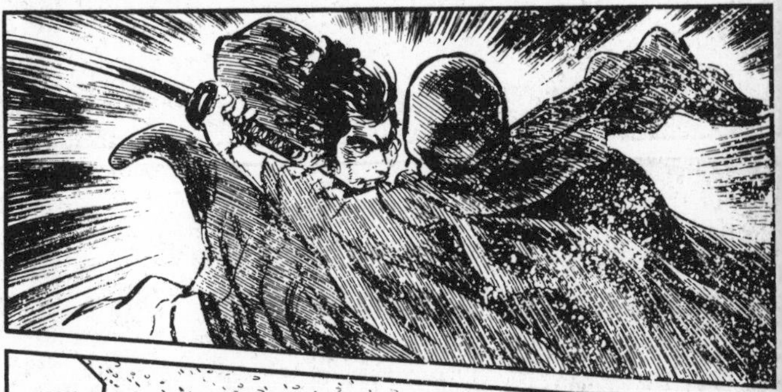

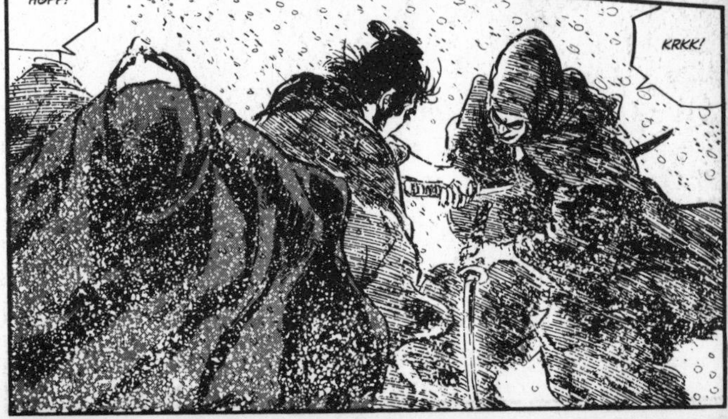
KRKK!
HGFF!

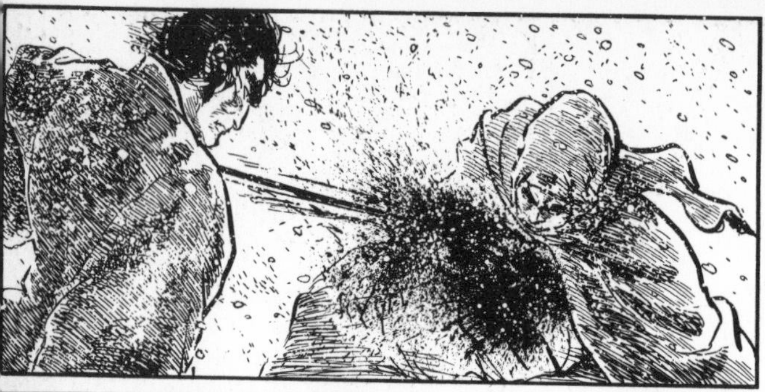
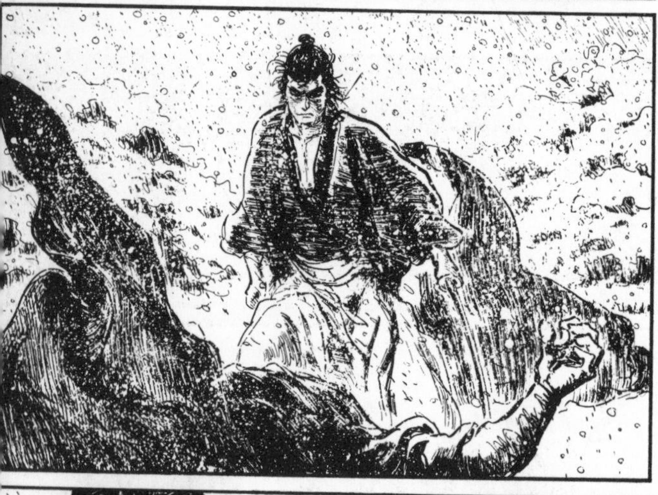
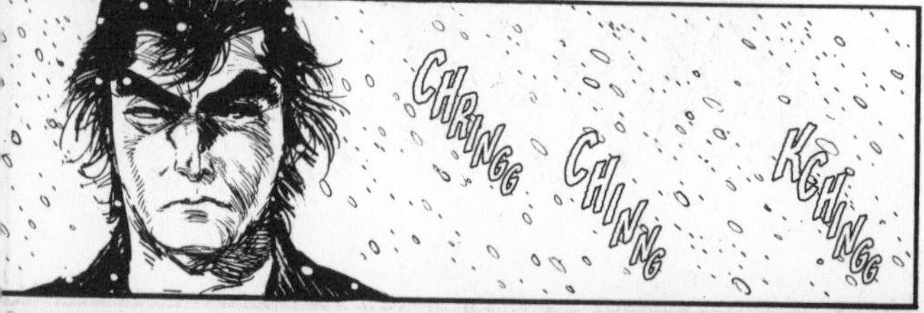
KCHINGG
CHINNG
CHRINGG

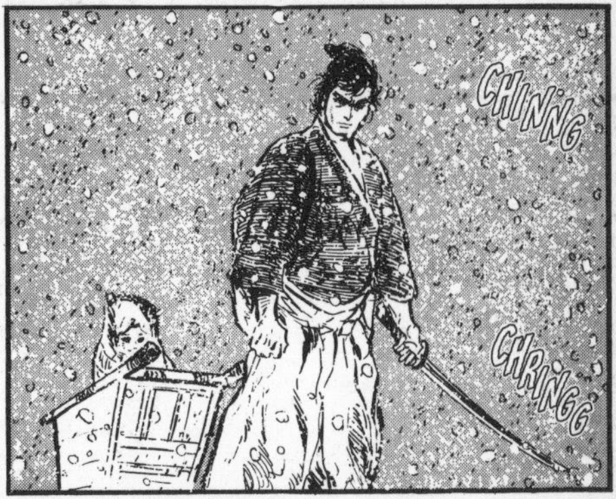
CHINNG
CHRINGG
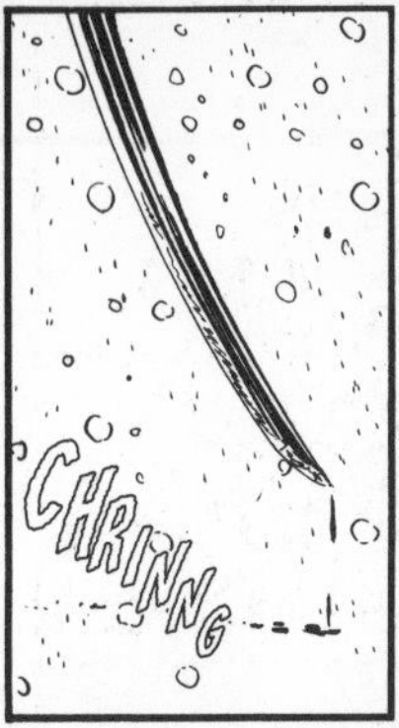
CHRINNG
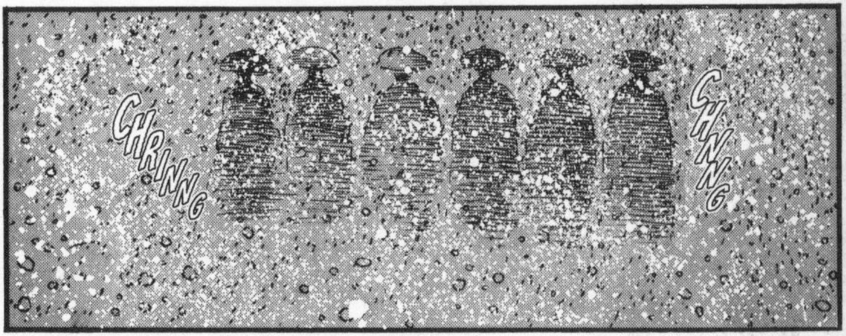
CHNNG
CHRINNG
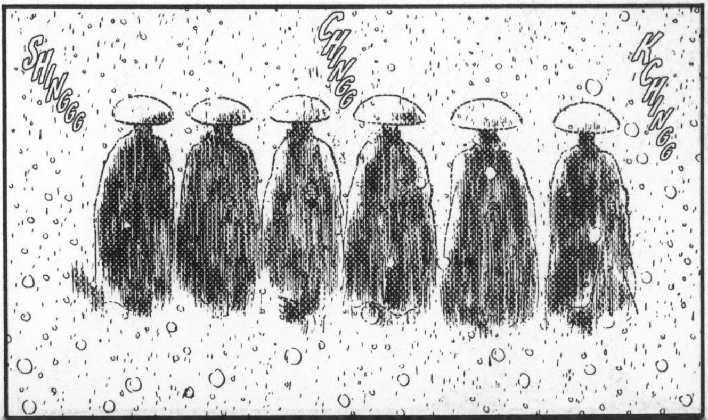
KCHINGG
CHINGG
SHINGGG

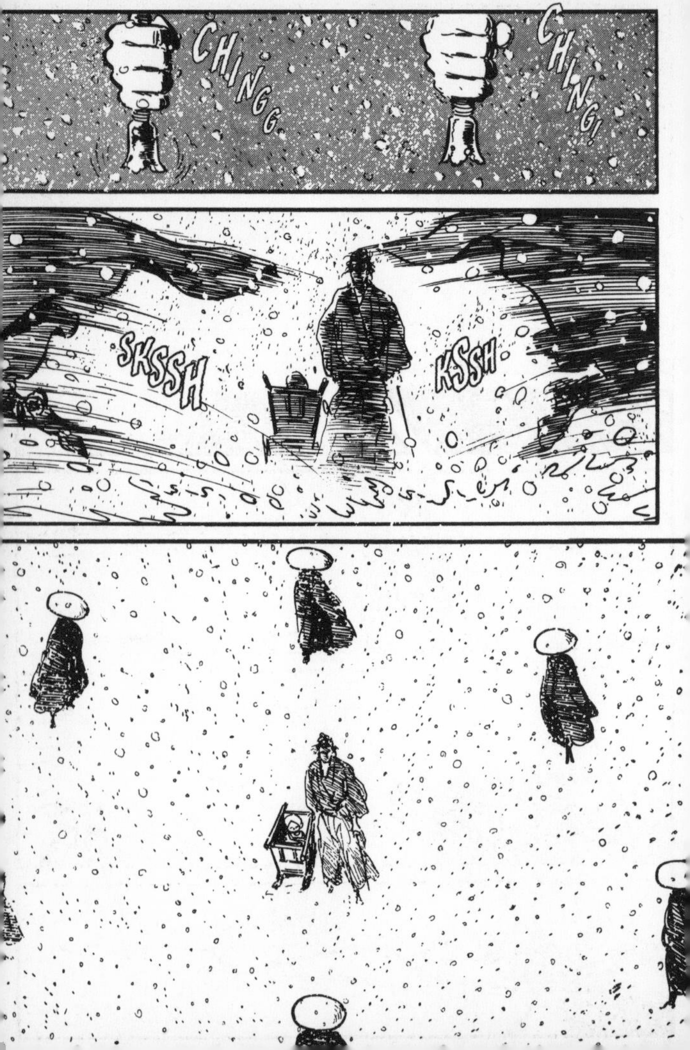
CHING!
CHINGG
KSSH
SKSSH

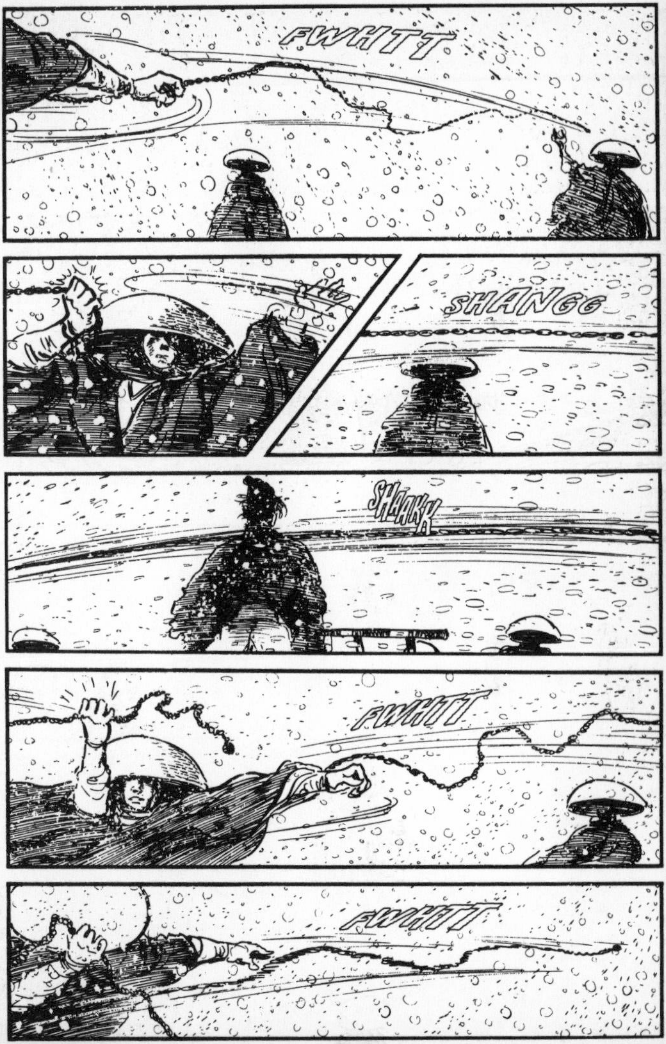
FWHTT
SHANGG
SHAAKK
FWHTT
FWHTT

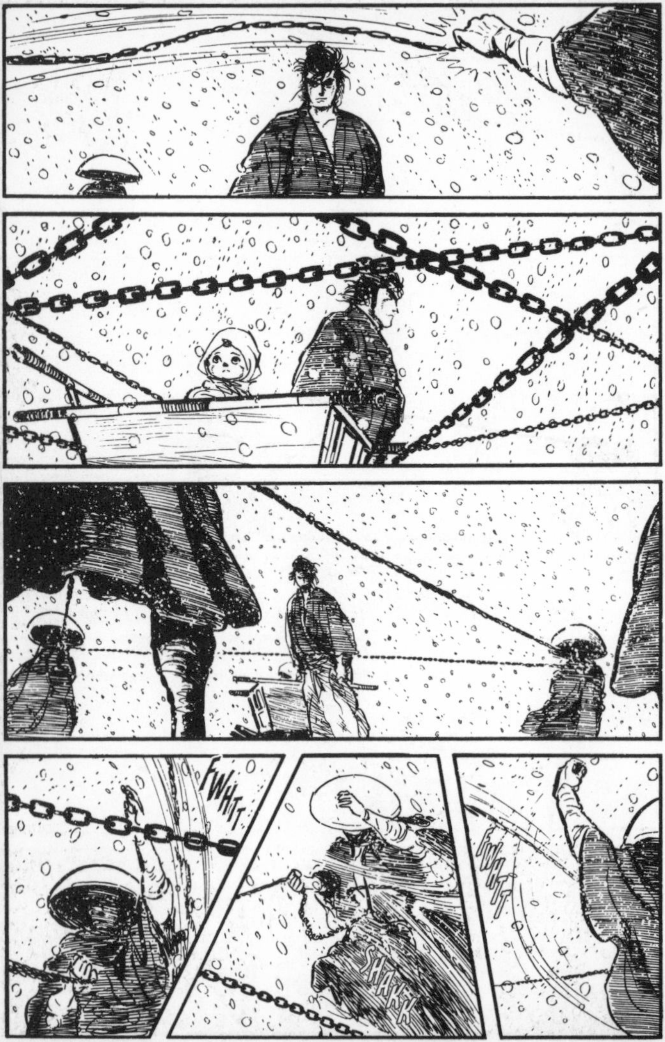
FWHTT
SHAKK
FWHTT

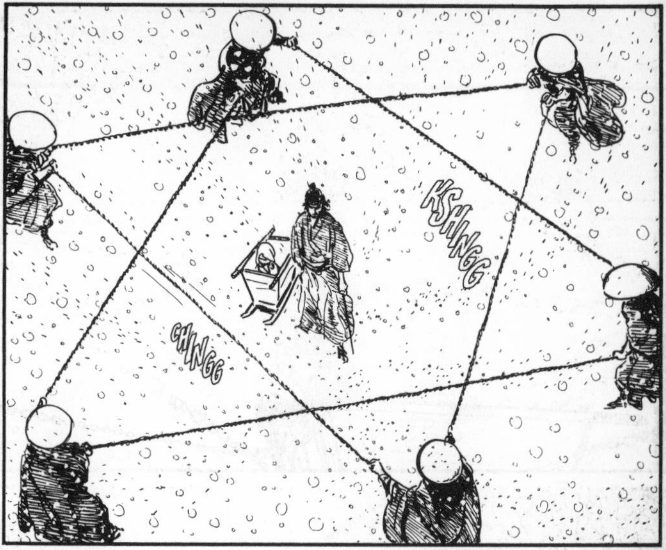
KSHINGG
CHINGG
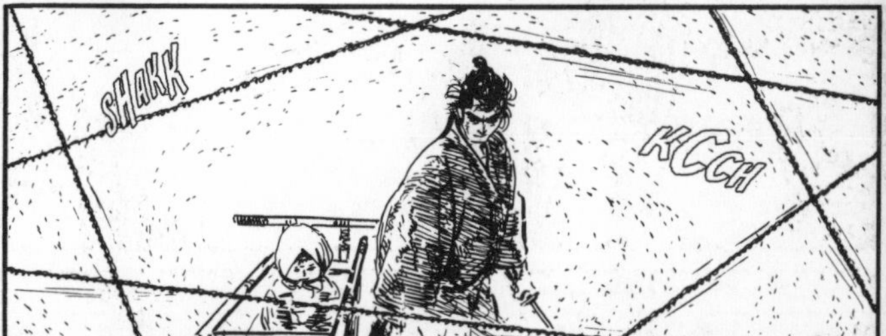
KCCH
SHAKK
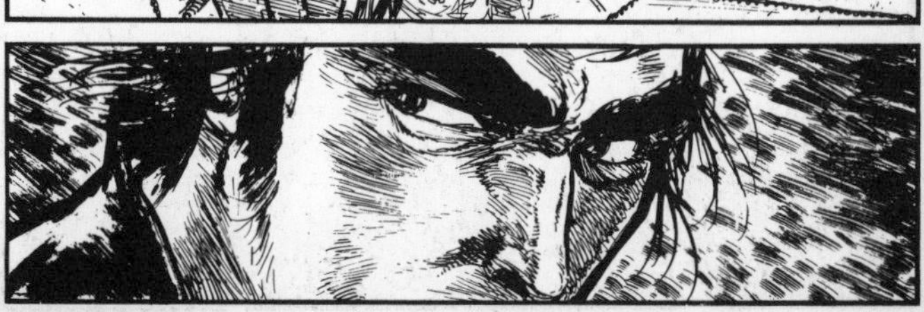

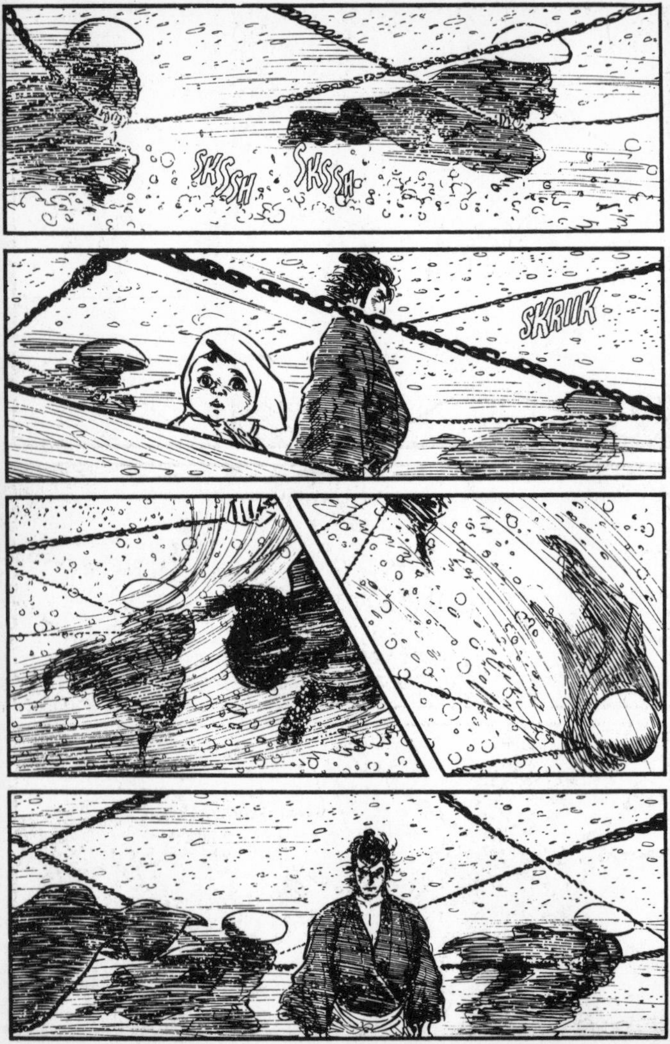
SKSSH
SKSSH
SKRIIK

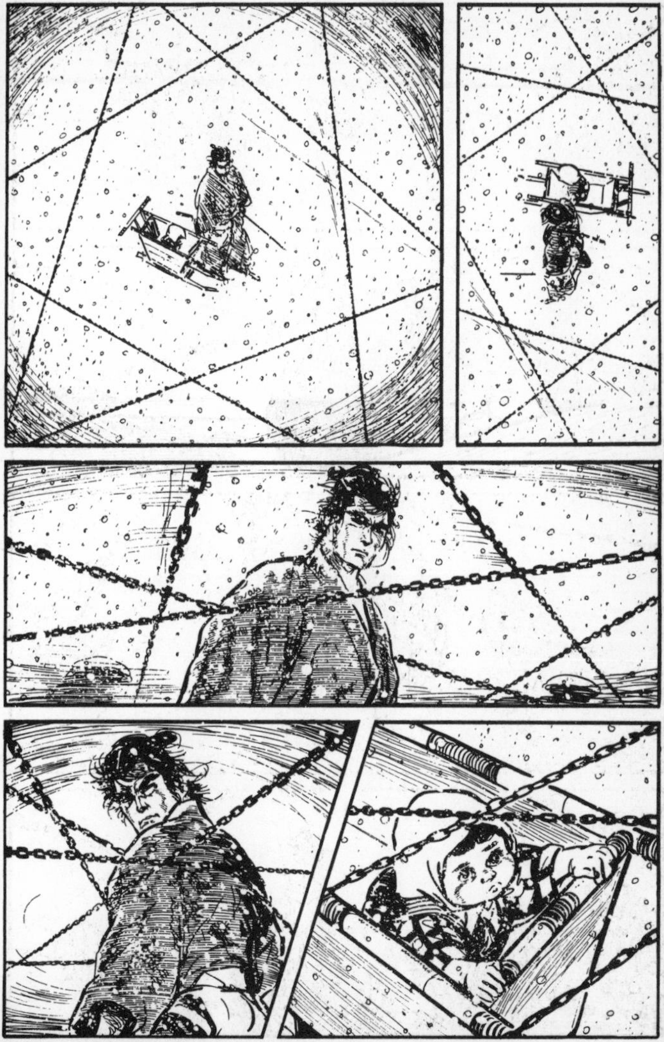

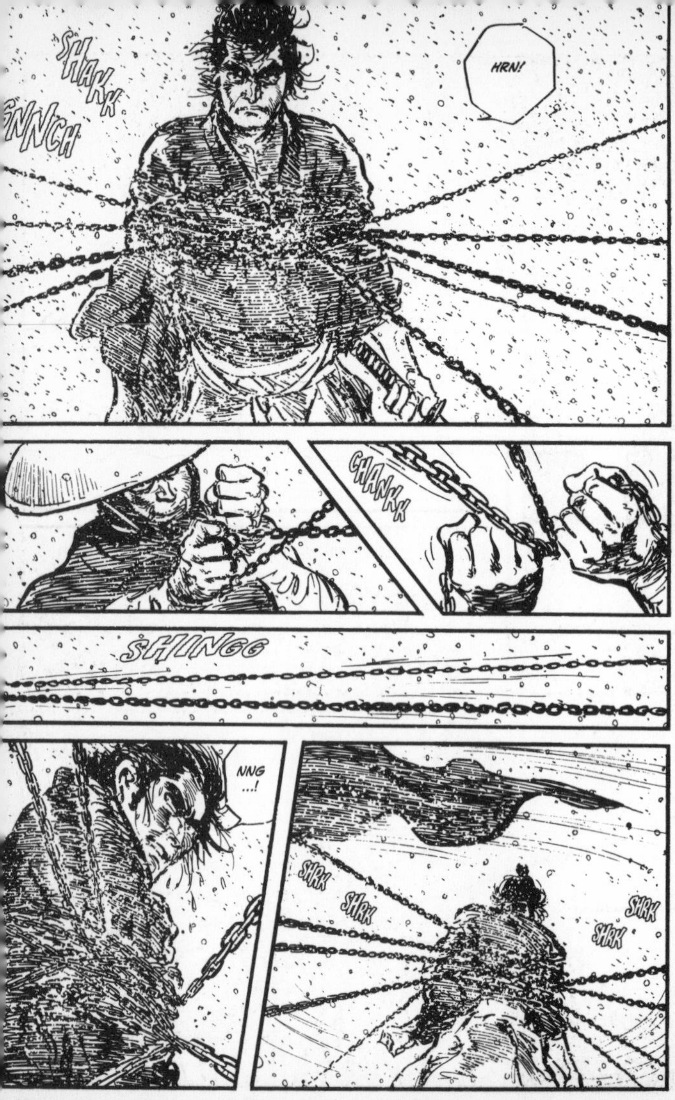
HRN!
SHAKK
GNNCH
CHANKK
SHINGG
SHRK
SHRK
SHRK
SHRK
NNG ...!

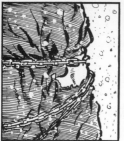

....!
....!

THE KUROKUWA *SHIBARI-TARU!*

WELL, ITTŌ?!

ACCEPT YOUR FATE!

SHKK

SHNGG

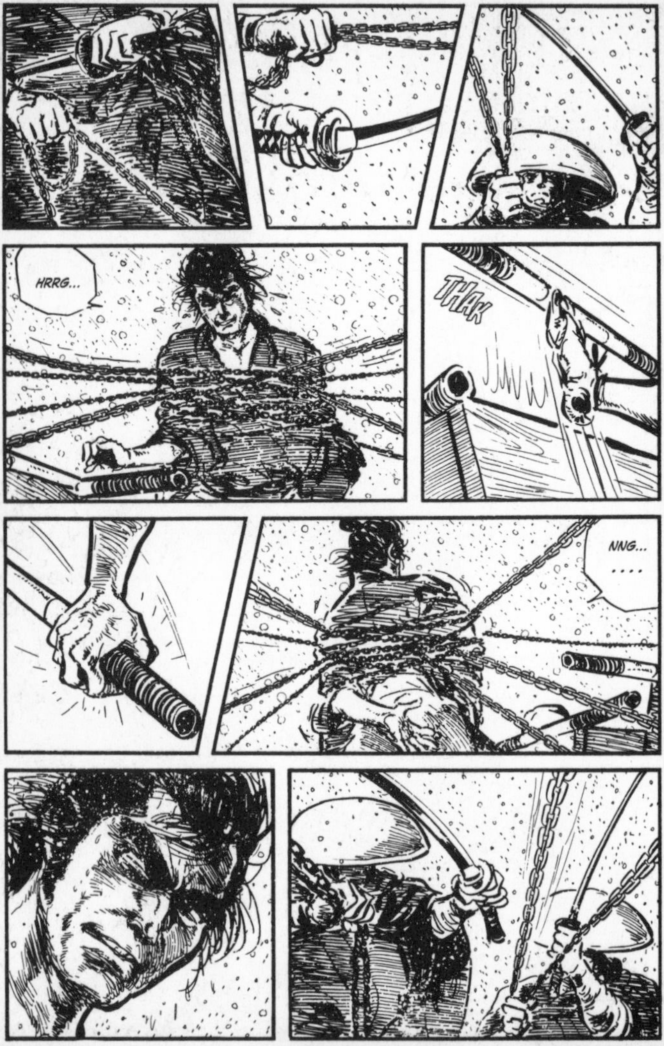
HRRG...
THAK
NNG...
....

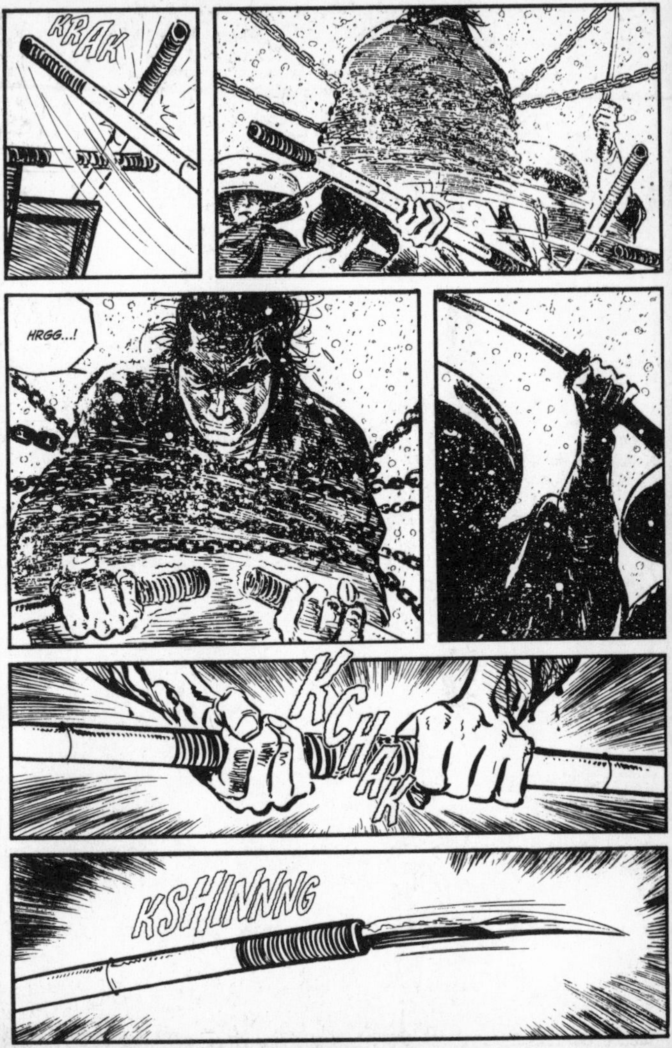
KRAK
HRGG...!
KCHAK
KSHINNNG

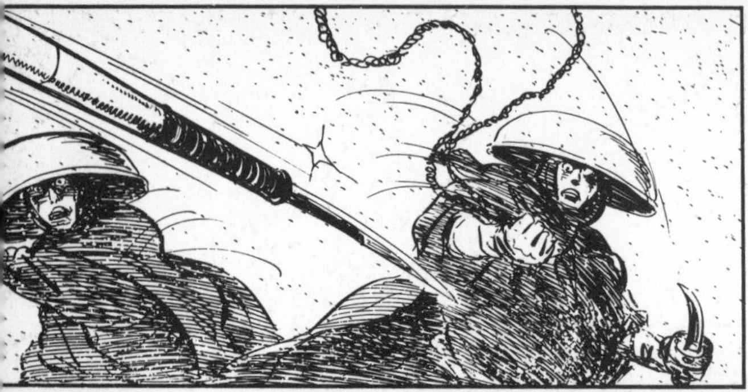
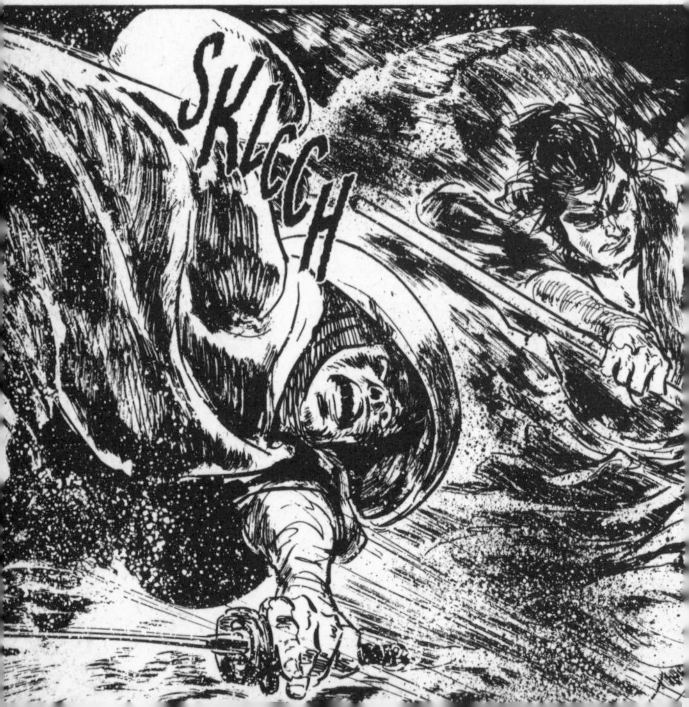
SKLCCH

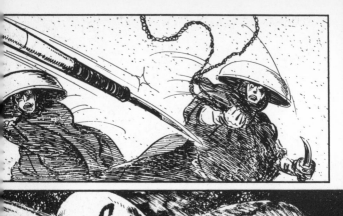

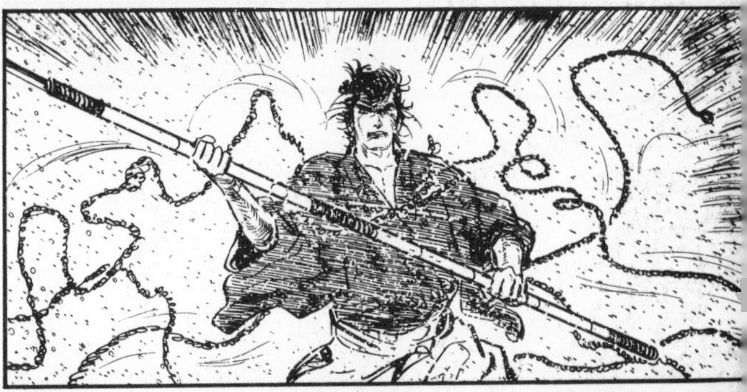
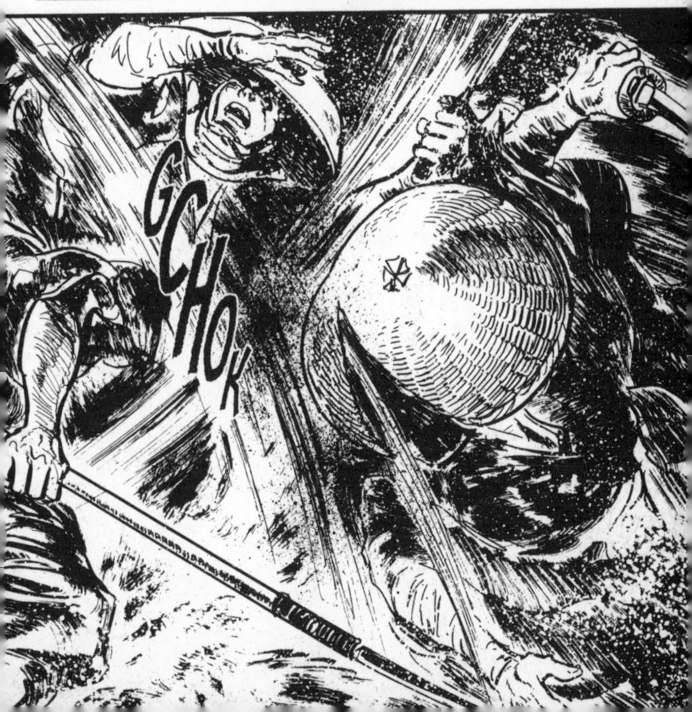
GCHOK

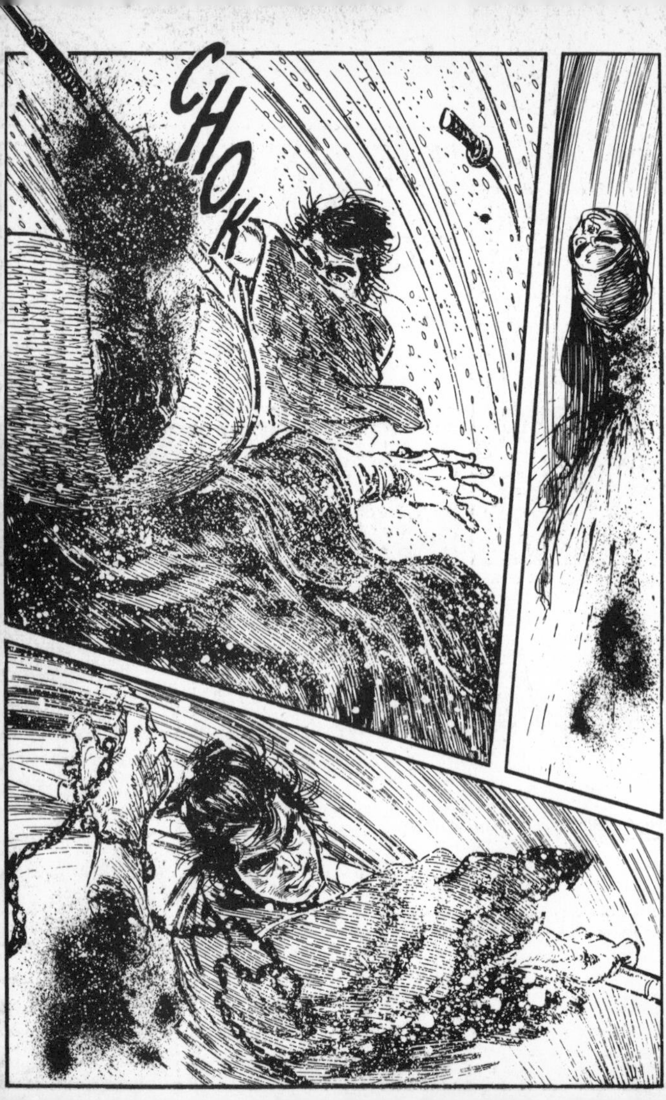
CHOK

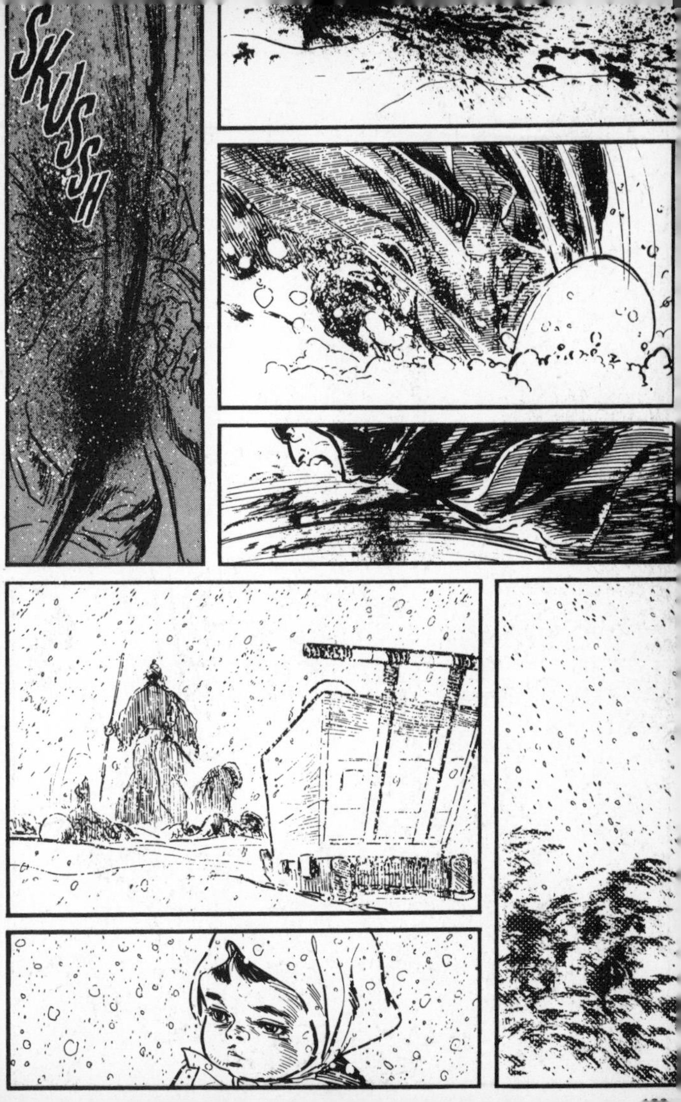
SKUSSH

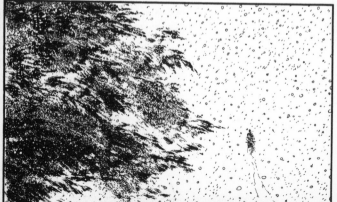

the forty-second

The Infinite Path

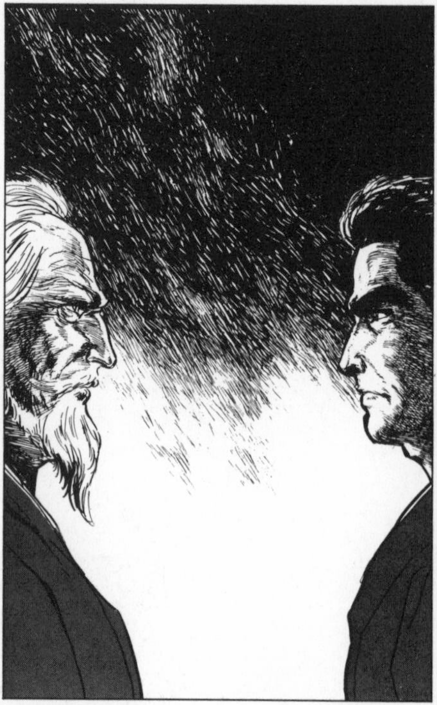

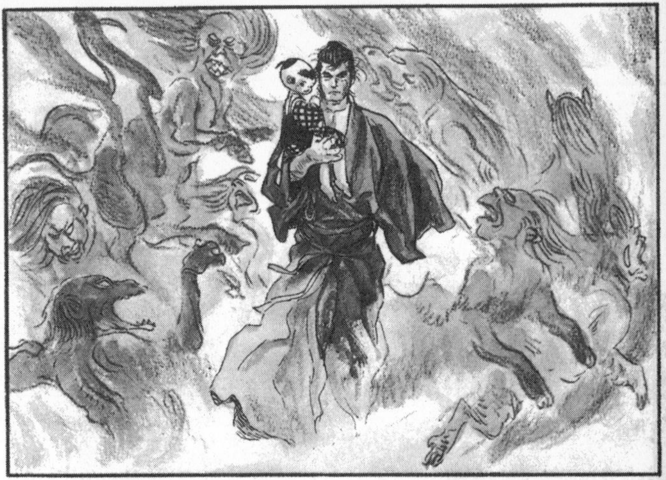
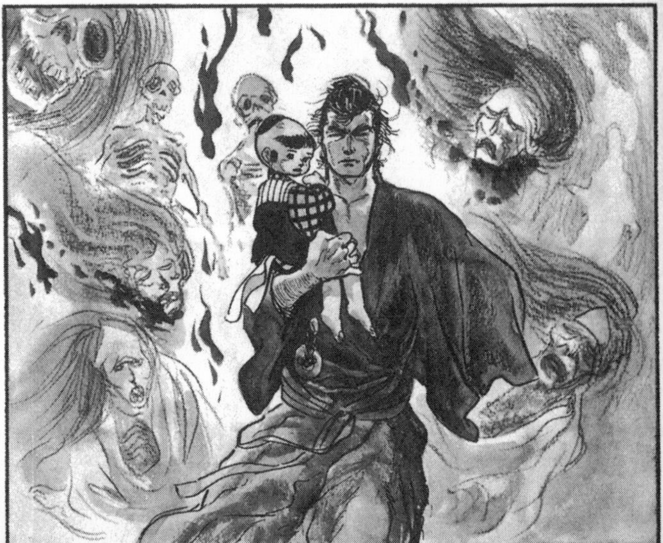

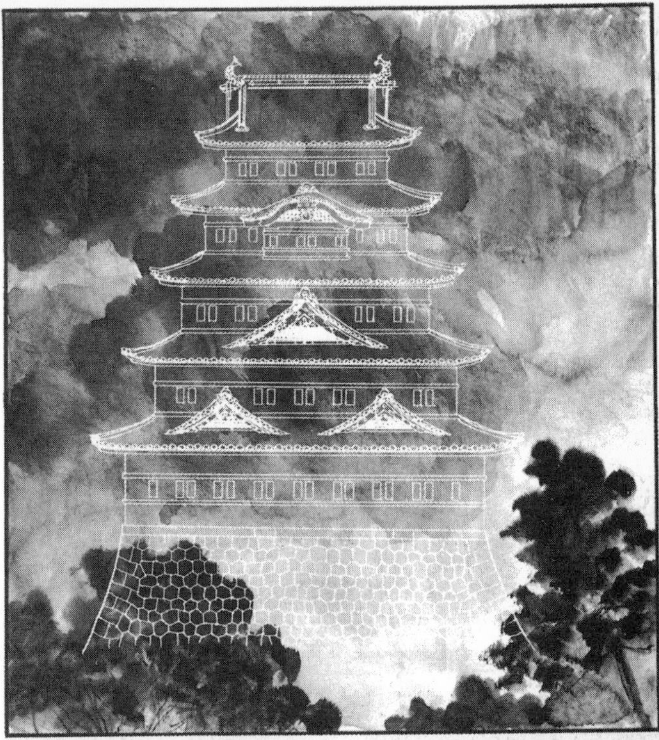
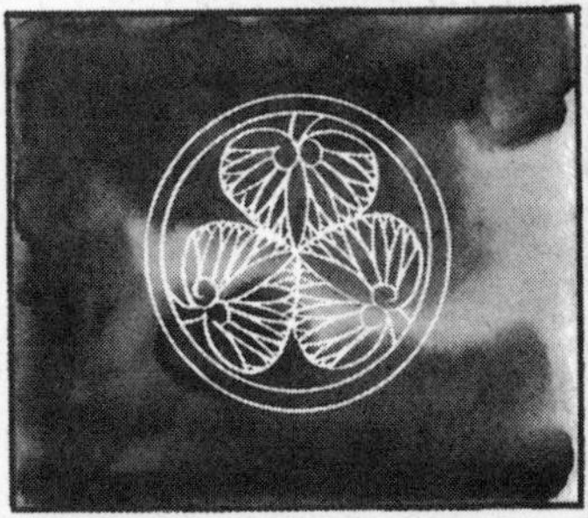
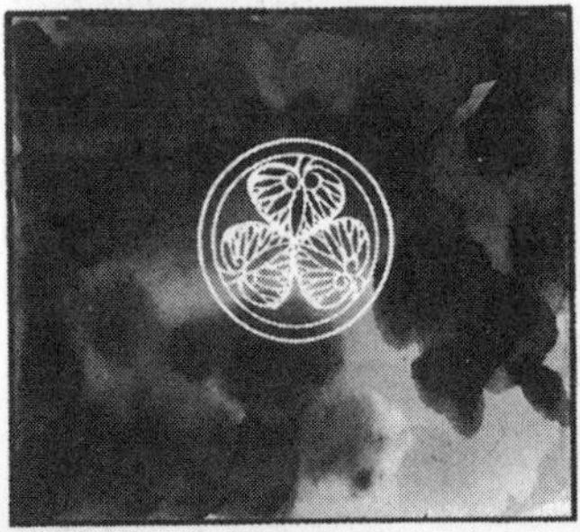

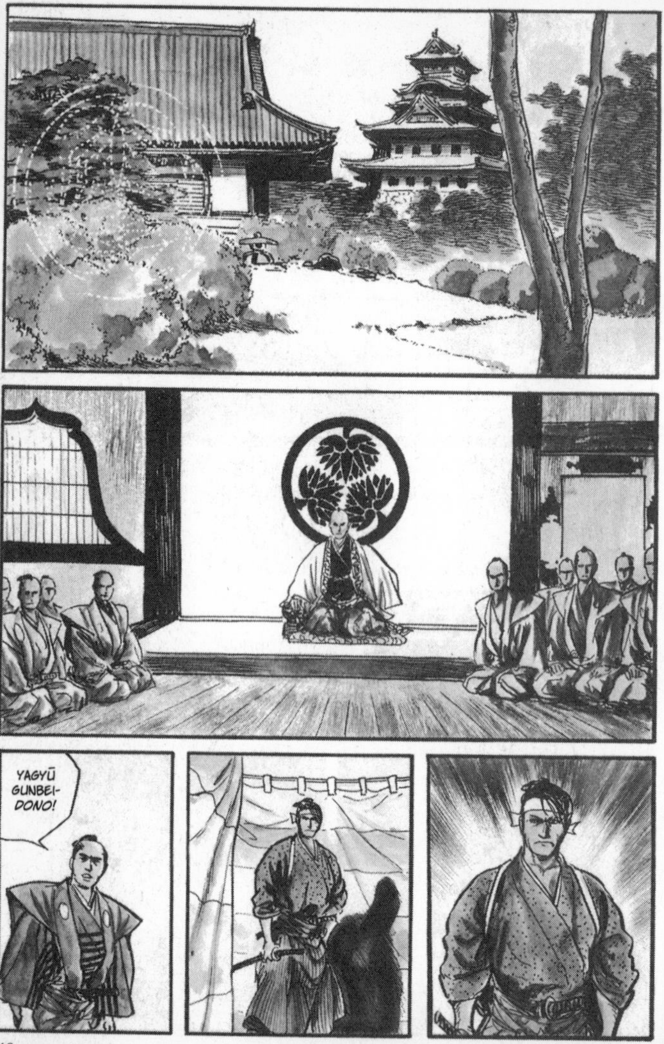
YAGYŪ GUNBEI-DONO!

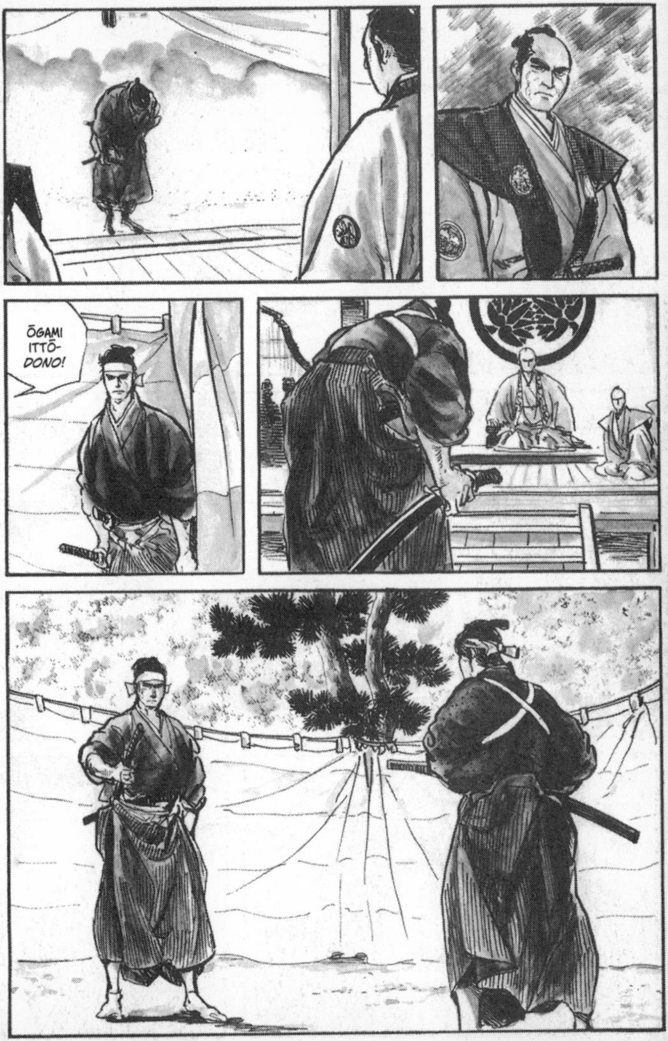
ŌGAMI ITTŌ-DONO!

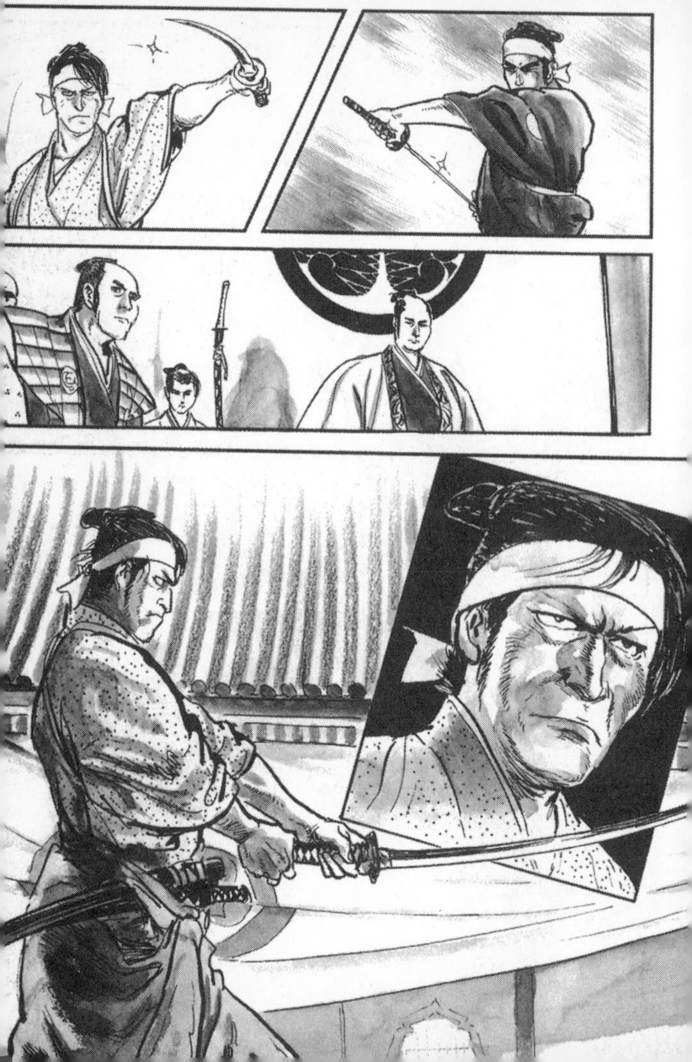

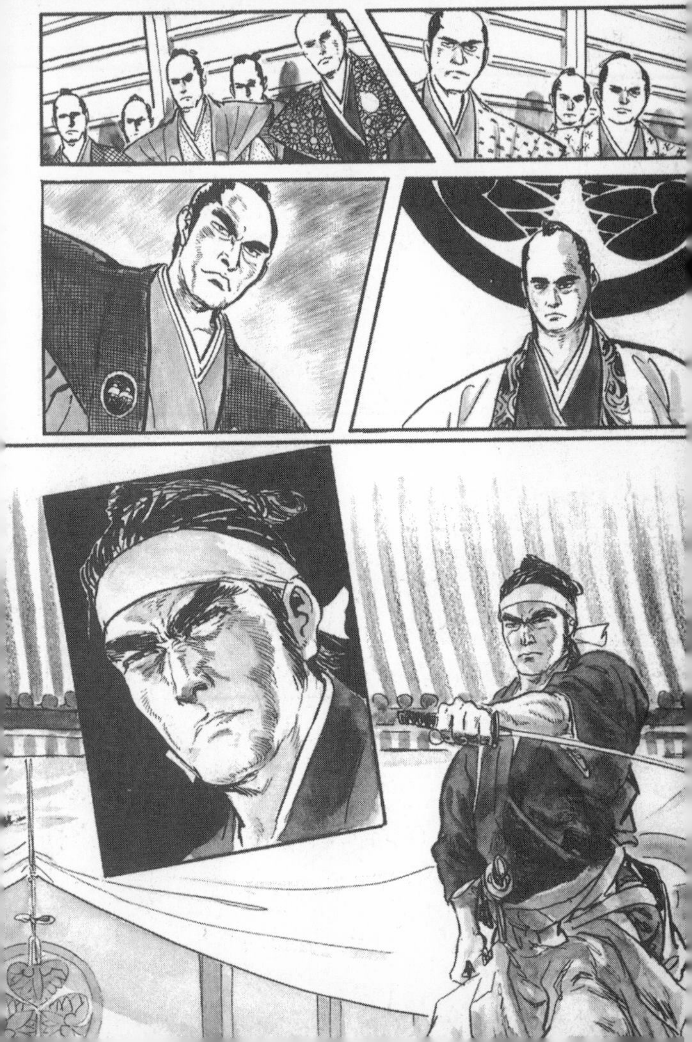

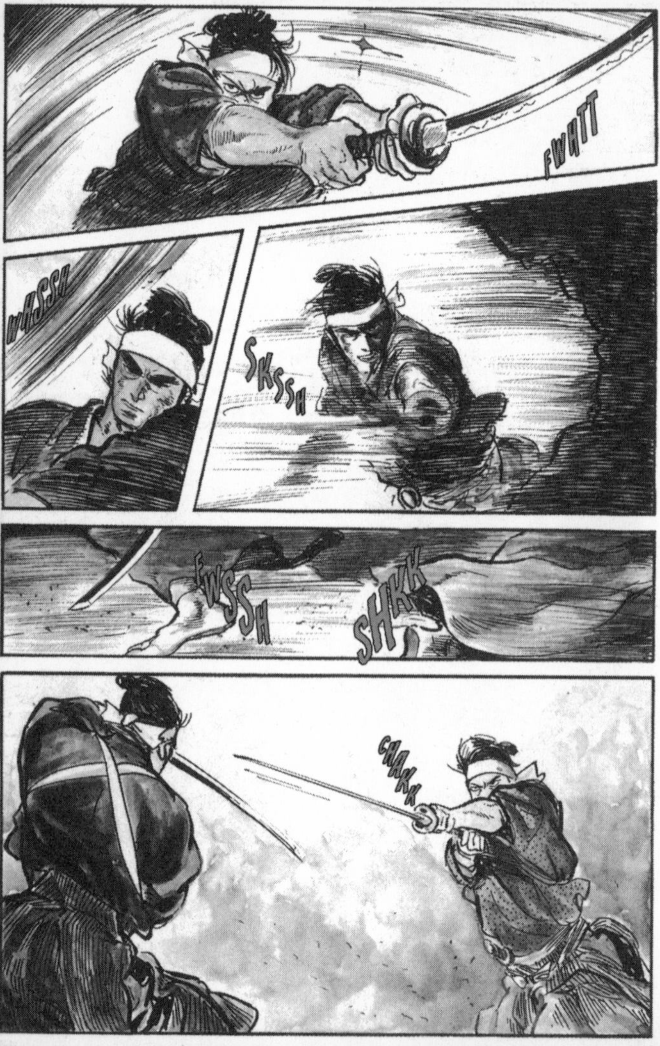
FWHTT
SKSSH
WHSSH
SHKK
FWSSH
CHAKK

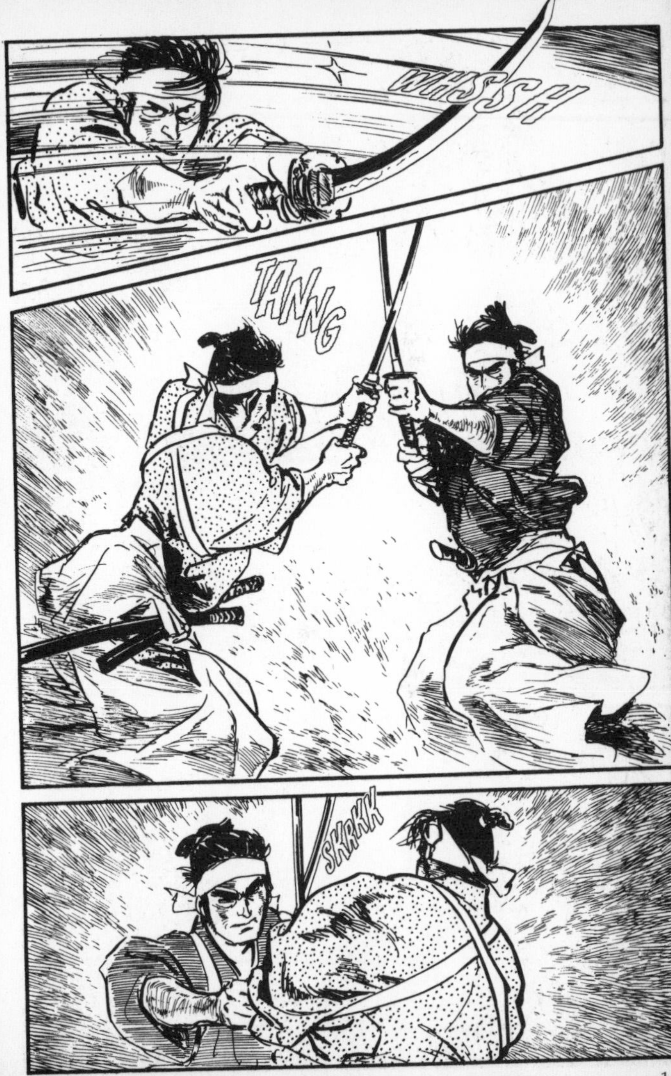
WHSSH
TANNG
SKRKK

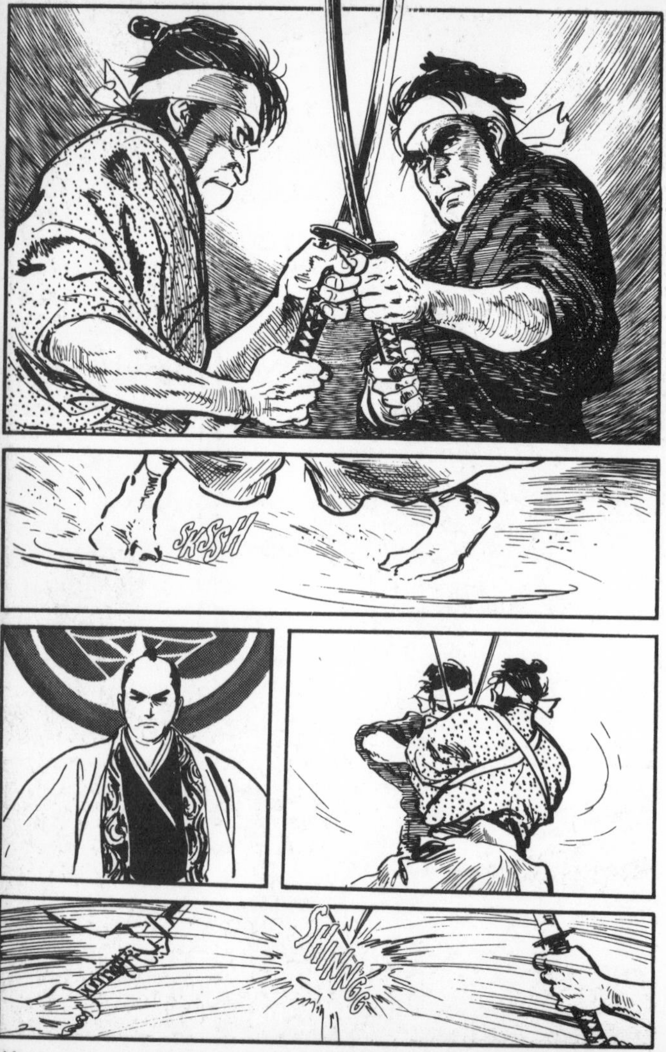
SKSSH
SHINNGG

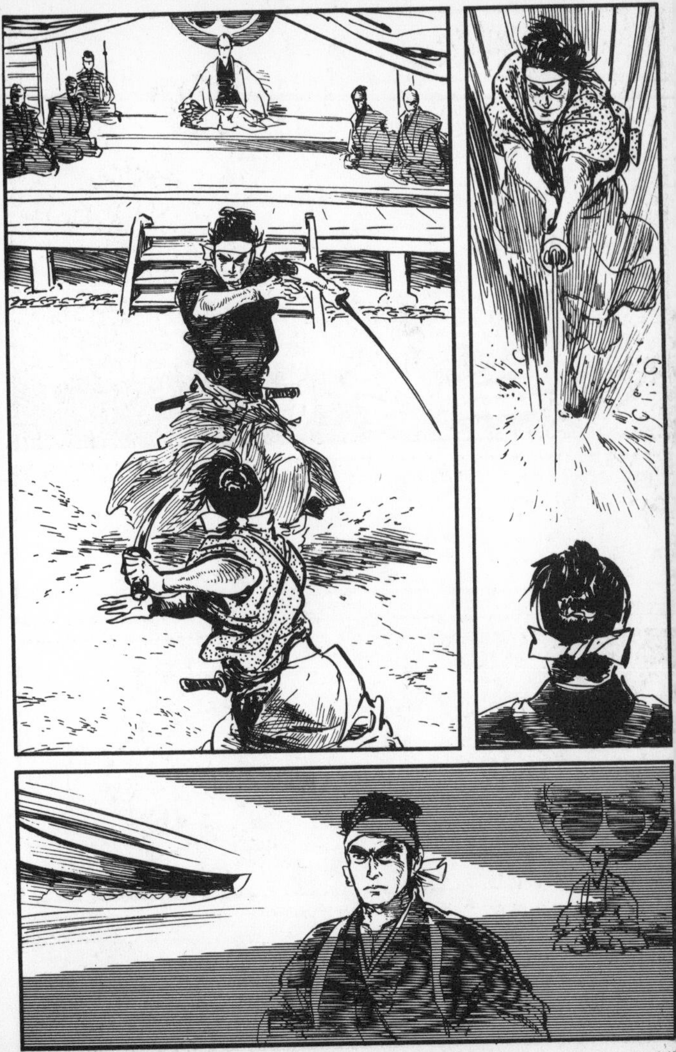

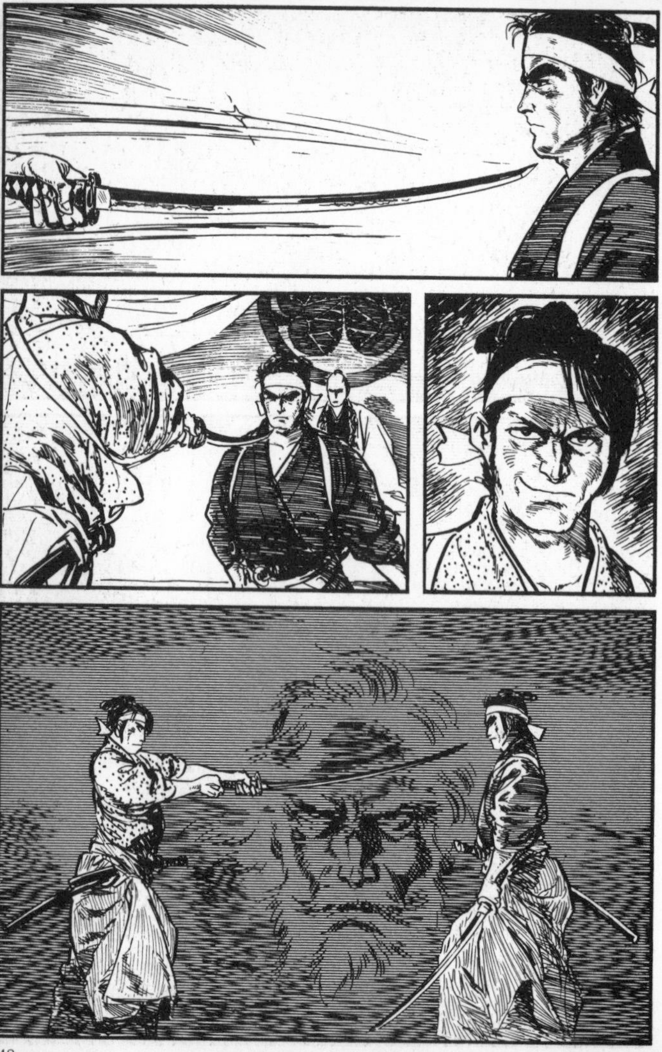

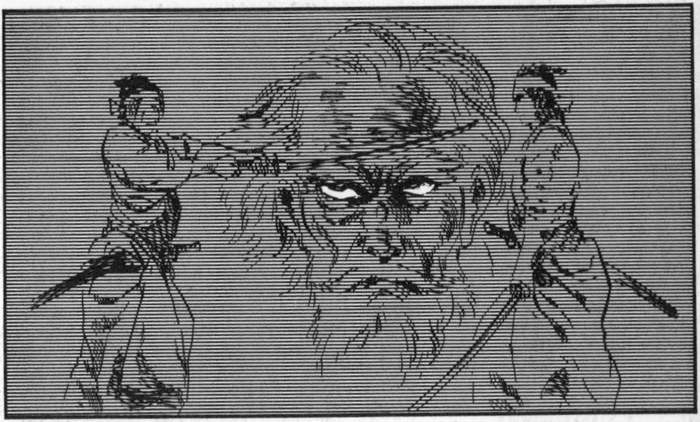

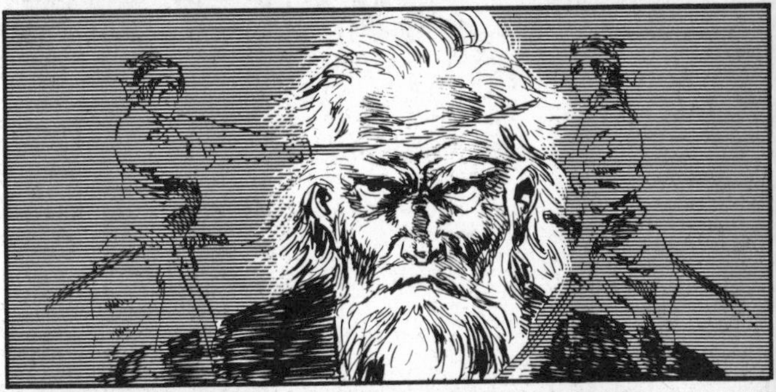

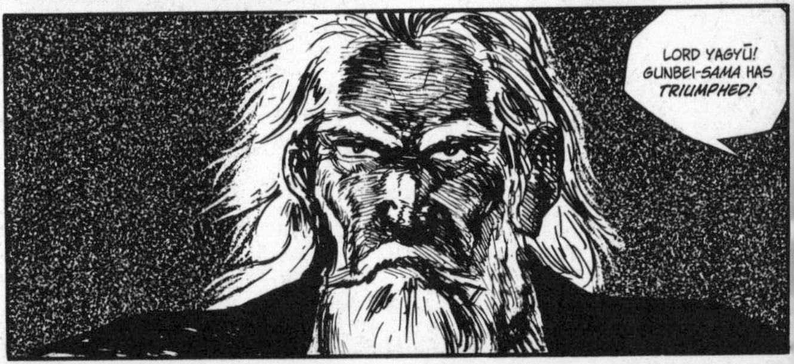
LORD YAGYŪ! GUNBEI-SAMA HAS *TRIUMPHED!*

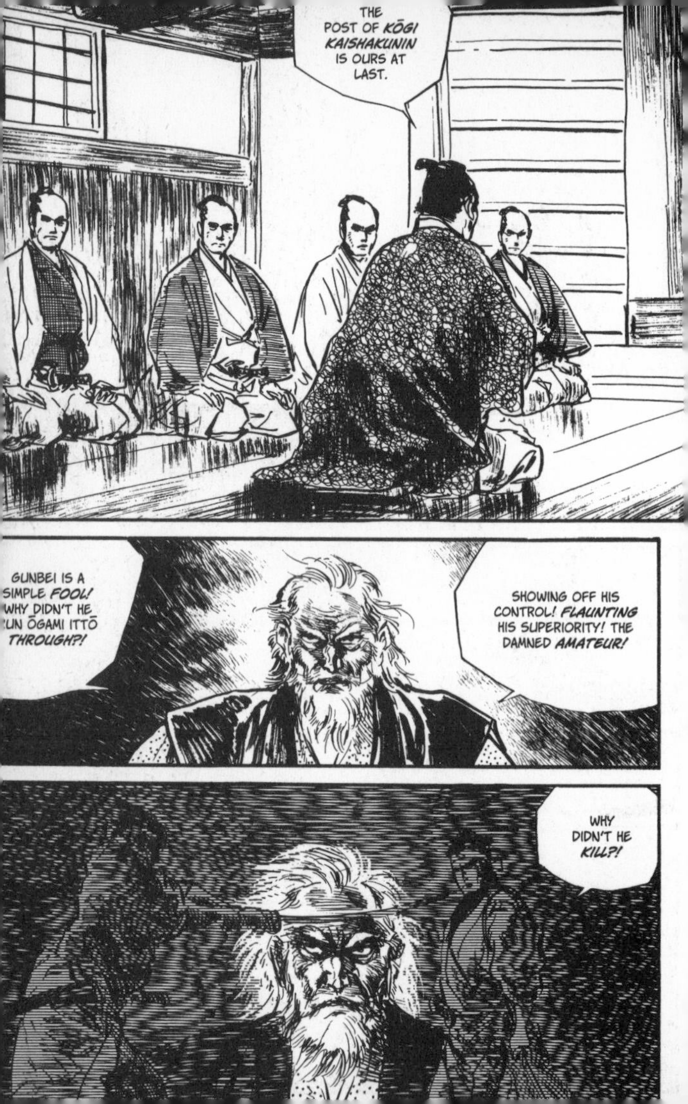
THE POST OF *KŌGI KAISHAKUNIN* IS OURS AT LAST.
GUNBEI IS A SIMPLE *FOOL!* WHY DIDN'T HE RUN ŌGAMI ITTŌ *THROUGH?!*
SHOWING OFF HIS CONTROL! *FLAUNTING* HIS SUPERIORITY! THE DAMNED *AMATEUR!*
WHY DIDN'T HE *KILL?!*

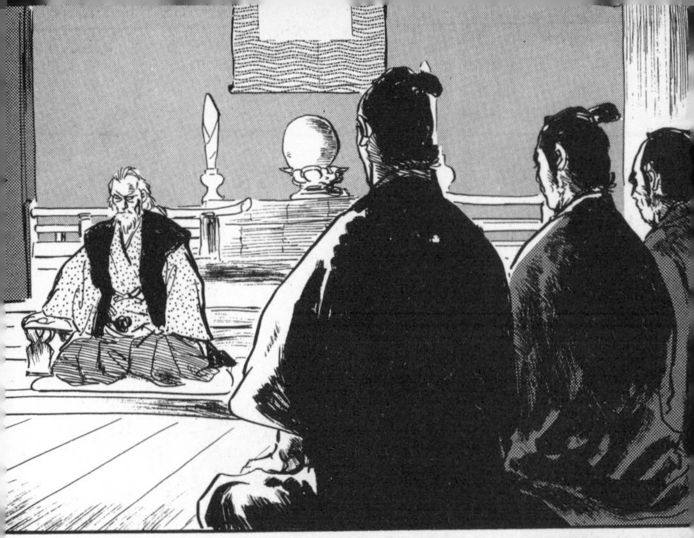

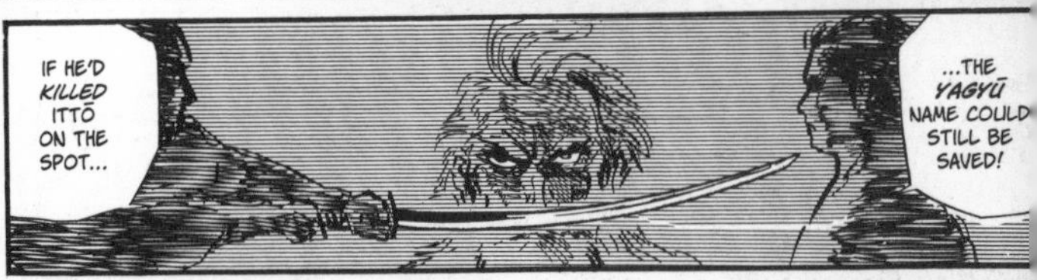
IF HE'D KILLED ITTŌ ON THE SPOT...
...THE YAGYŪ NAME COULD STILL BE SAVED!

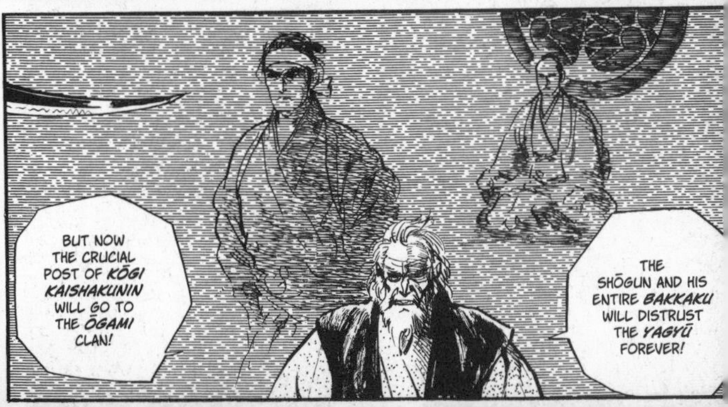
BUT NOW THE CRUCIAL POST OF KŌGI KAISHAKUNIN WILL GO TO THE ŌGAMI CLAN!
THE SHŌGUN AND HIS ENTIRE BAKKAKU WILL DISTRUST THE YAGYŪ FOREVER!

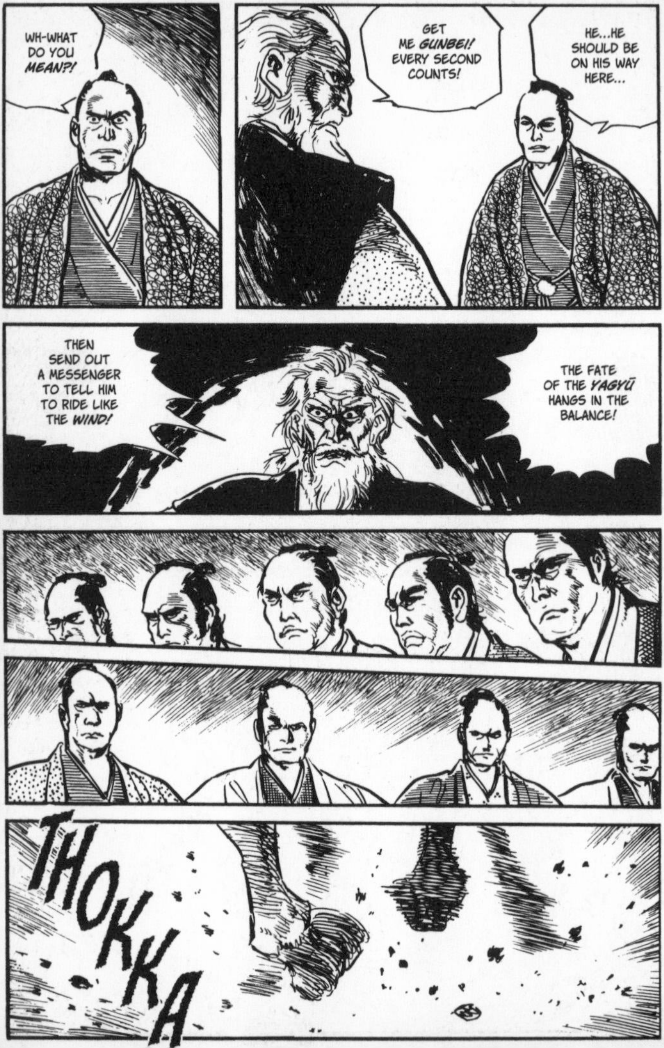
WH-WHAT DO YOU *MEAN?!*
GET ME *GUNBEI!* EVERY SECOND COUNTS!
HE...HE SHOULD BE ON HIS WAY HERE...
THEN SEND OUT A MESSENGER TO TELL HIM TO RIDE LIKE THE *WIND!*
THE FATE OF THE *YAGYŪ* HANGS IN THE BALANCE!
THOKKA

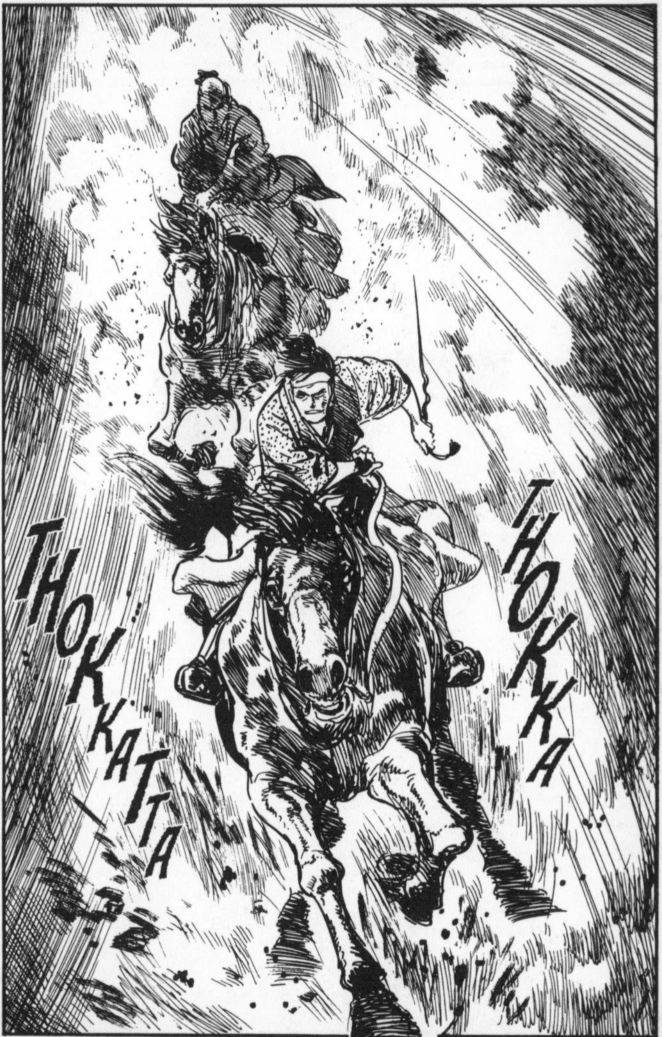
THOKKA
THOKATTA

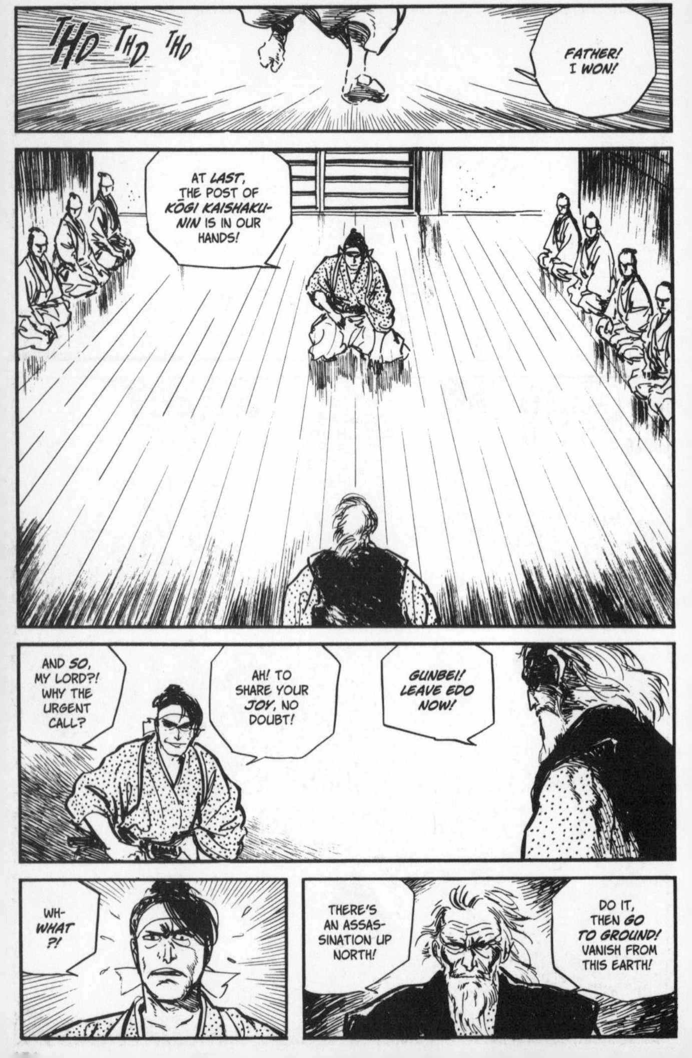
THD THD THD
FATHER! I WON!
AT LAST, THE POST OF KŌGI KAISHAKU-NIN IS IN OUR HANDS!
AND SO, MY LORD?! WHY THE URGENT CALL?
AH! TO SHARE YOUR JOY, NO DOUBT!
GUNBEI! LEAVE EDO NOW!
WH- WHAT ?!
THERE'S AN ASSAS-SINATION UP NORTH!
DO IT, THEN GO TO GROUND! VANISH FROM THIS EARTH!

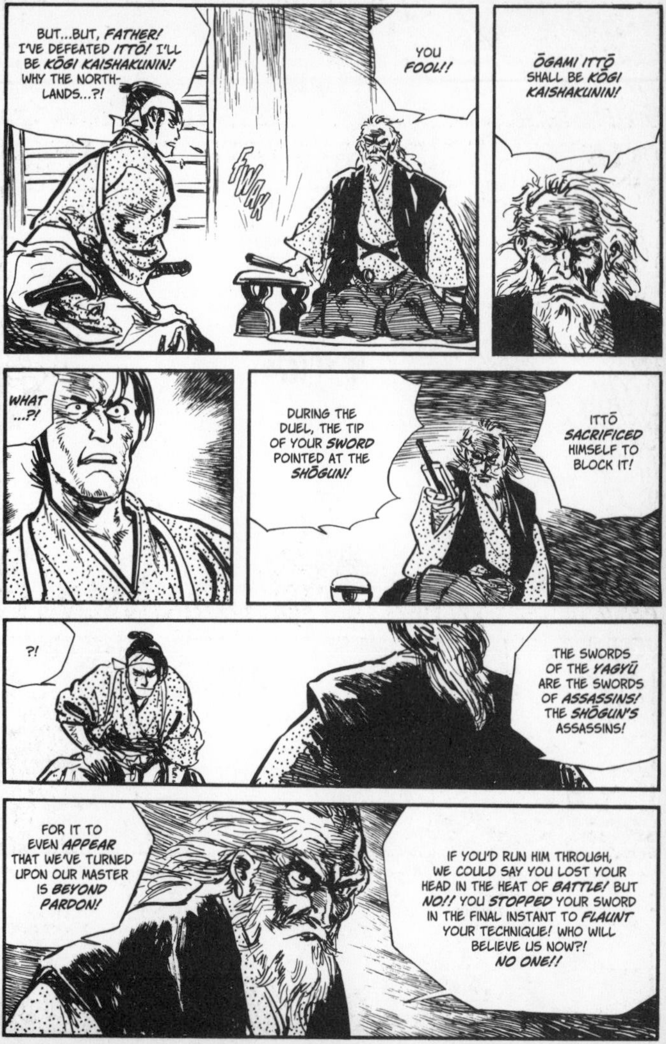
BUT...BUT, FATHER! I'VE DEFEATED ITTŌ! I'LL BE KŌGI KAISHAKUNIN! WHY THE NORTH-LANDS...?!
FWAK
YOU FOOL!!
ŌGAMI ITTŌ SHALL BE KŌGI KAISHAKUNIN!
WHAT ...?!
DURING THE DUEL, THE TIP OF YOUR SWORD POINTED AT THE SHŌGUN!
ITTŌ SACRIFICED HIMSELF TO BLOCK IT!
?!
THE SWORDS OF THE YAGYŪ ARE THE SWORDS OF ASSASSINS! THE SHŌGUN'S ASSASSINS!
FOR IT TO EVEN APPEAR THAT WE'VE TURNED UPON OUR MASTER IS BEYOND PARDON!
IF YOU'D RUN HIM THROUGH, WE COULD SAY YOU LOST YOUR HEAD IN THE HEAT OF BATTLE! BUT NO!! YOU STOPPED YOUR SWORD IN THE FINAL INSTANT TO FLAUNT YOUR TECHNIQUE! WHO WILL BELIEVE US NOW?! NO ONE!!

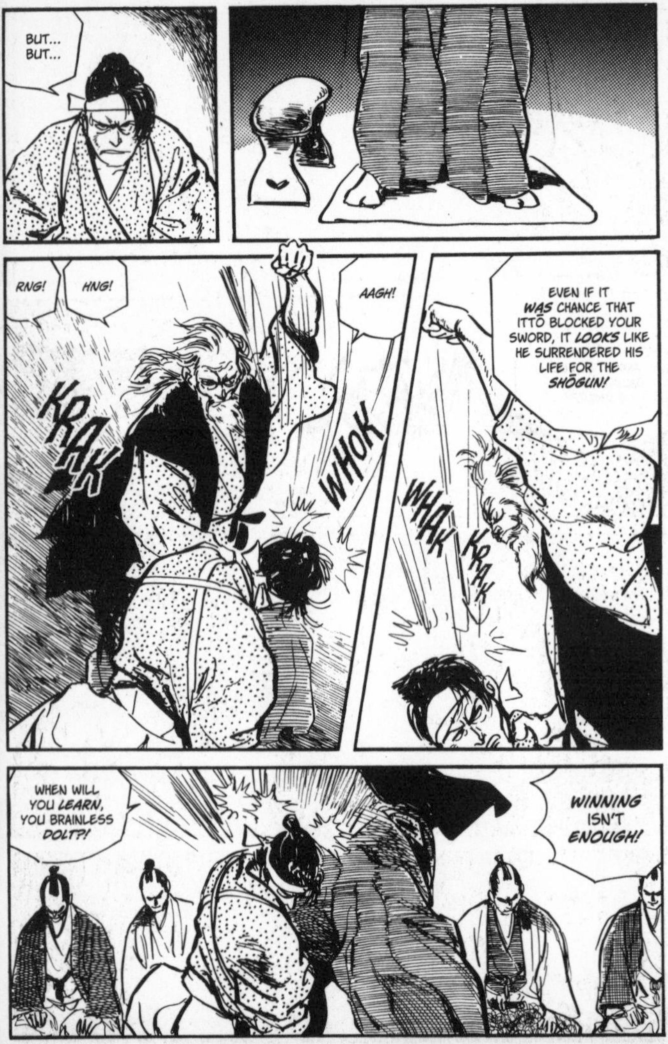
BUT...
BUT...
RNG!
HNG!
KRAK
AAGH!
WHOK
EVEN IF IT *WAS* CHANCE THAT ITTŌ BLOCKED YOUR SWORD, IT *LOOKS* LIKE HE SURRENDERED HIS LIFE FOR THE *SHŌGUN!*
WHAK
KRAK
WHEN WILL YOU *LEARN*, YOU BRAINLESS *DOLT?!*
WINNING ISN'T *ENOUGH!*

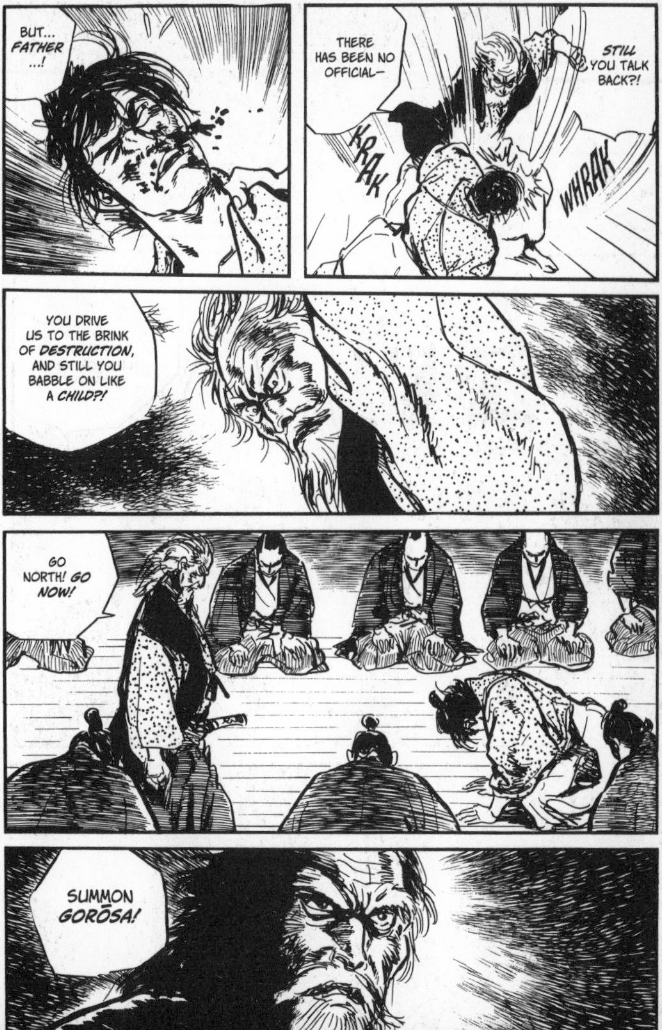
BUT... FATHER ...!
THERE HAS BEEN NO OFFICIAL—
STILL YOU TALK BACK?!
KRAK
WHRAK
YOU DRIVE US TO THE BRINK OF DESTRUCTION, AND STILL YOU BABBLE ON LIKE A CHILD?!
GO NORTH! GO NOW!
SUMMON GORŌSA!

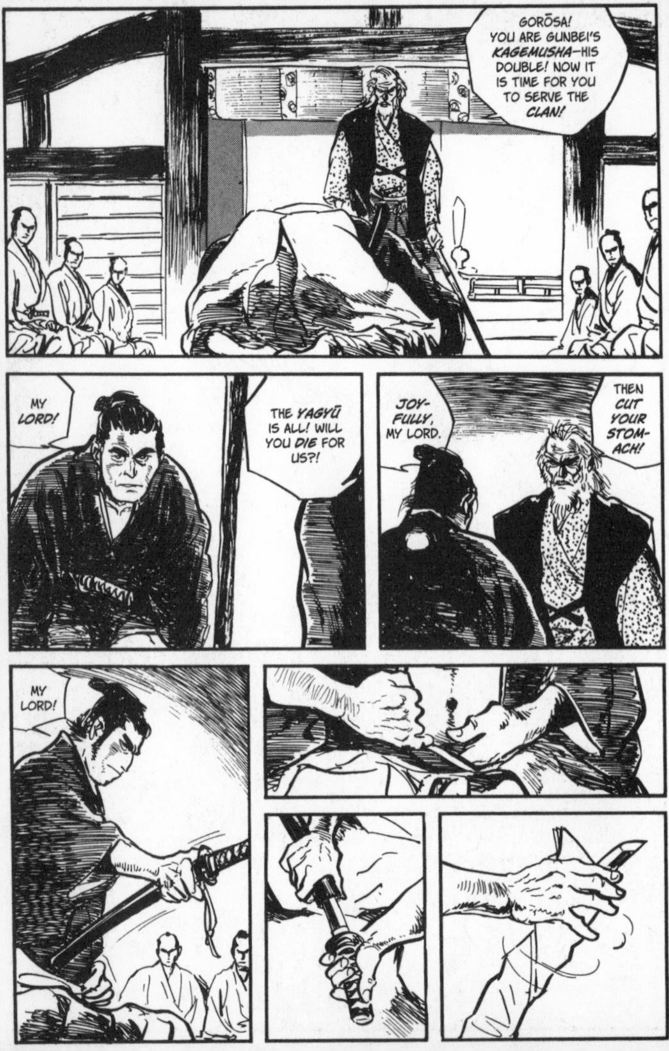
GORŌSA! YOU ARE GUNBEI'S *KAGEMUSHA*—HIS DOUBLE! NOW IT IS TIME FOR YOU TO SERVE THE *CLAN!*
MY *LORD!*
THE *YAGYŪ* IS ALL! WILL YOU *DIE* FOR US?!
JOY-FULLY, MY LORD.
THEN *CUT YOUR STOM-ACH!*
MY LORD!

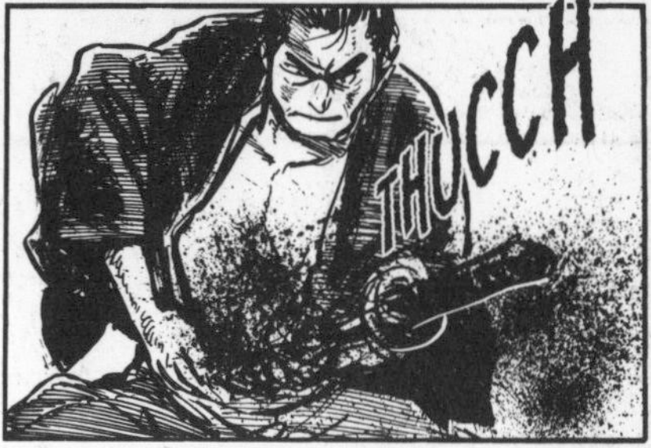
THUCCH
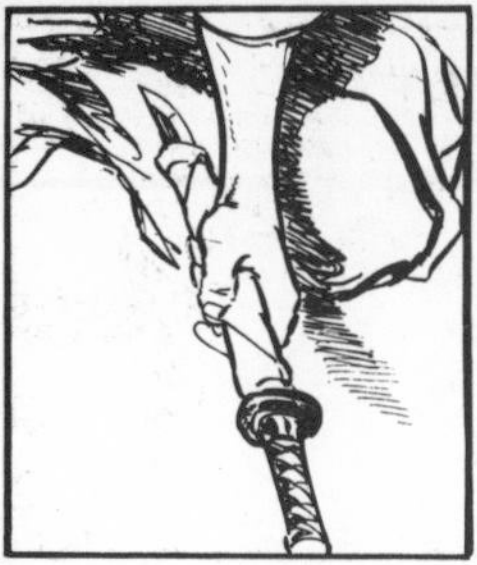
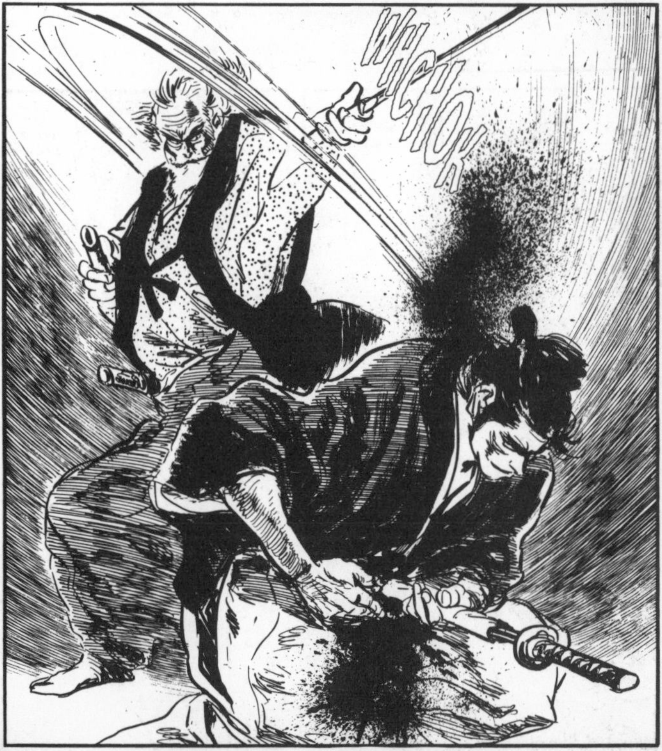
WHCHOK

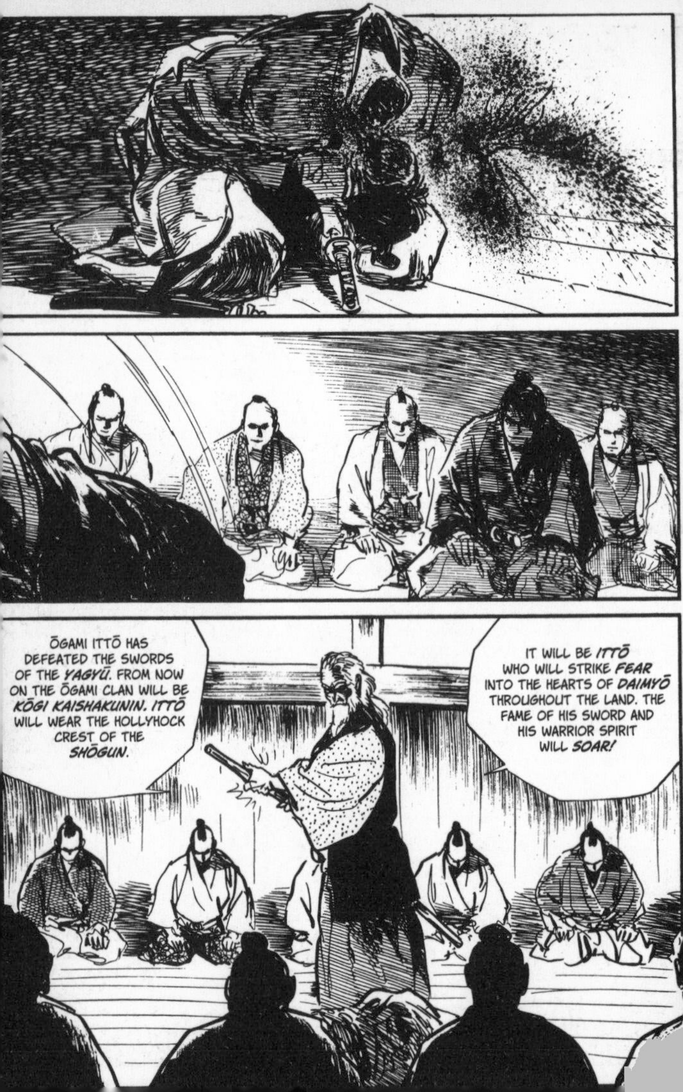
ŌGAMI ITTŌ HAS DEFEATED THE SWORDS OF THE *YAGYŪ*. FROM NOW ON THE ŌGAMI CLAN WILL BE *KŌGI KAISHAKUNIN*. *ITTŌ* WILL WEAR THE HOLLYHOCK CREST OF THE *SHŌGUN*.
IT WILL BE *ITTŌ* WHO WILL STRIKE *FEAR* INTO THE HEARTS OF *DAIMYŌ* THROUGHOUT THE LAND. THE FAME OF HIS SWORD AND HIS WARRIOR SPIRIT WILL *SOAR!*

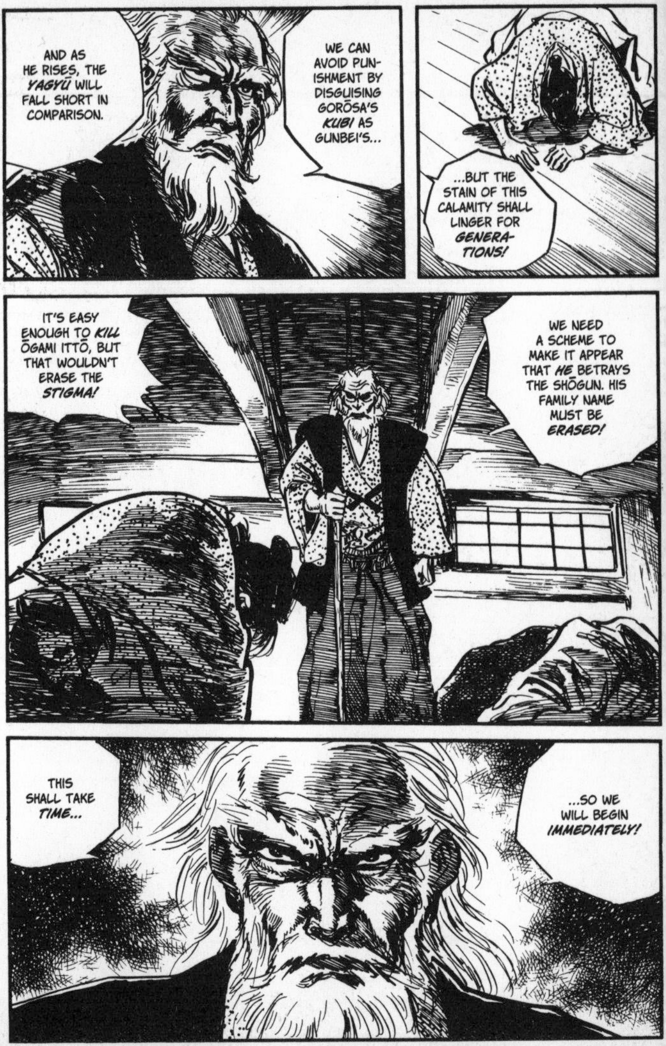
AND AS HE RISES, THE *YAGYŪ* WILL FALL SHORT IN COMPARISON.
WE CAN AVOID PUN-ISHMENT BY DISGUISING GORŌSA'S *KUBI* AS GUNBEI'S...
...BUT THE STAIN OF THIS CALAMITY SHALL LINGER FOR *GENERA-TIONS!*
IT'S EASY ENOUGH TO *KILL* ŌGAMI ITTŌ, BUT THAT WOULDN'T ERASE THE *STIGMA!*
WE NEED A SCHEME TO MAKE IT APPEAR THAT *HE* BETRAYS THE SHŌGUN. HIS FAMILY NAME MUST BE *ERASED!*
THIS SHALL TAKE *TIME...*
...SO WE WILL BEGIN *IMMEDIATELY!*

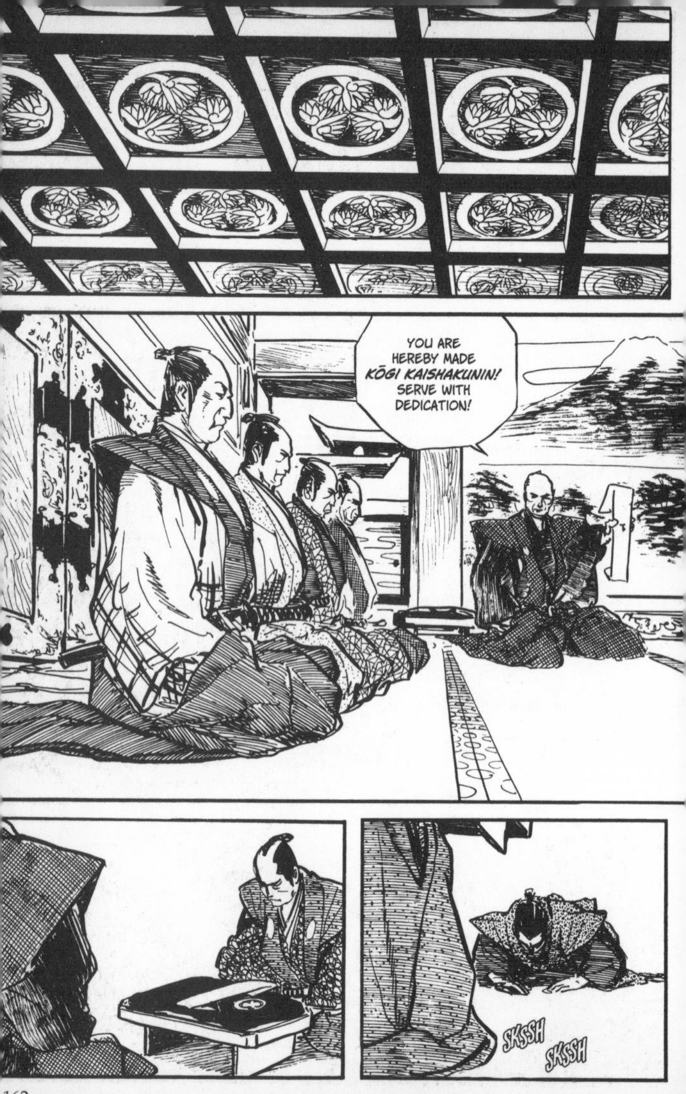
YOU ARE HEREBY MADE *KŌGI KAISHAKUNIN!* SERVE WITH DEDICATION!
SKSSH
SKSSH

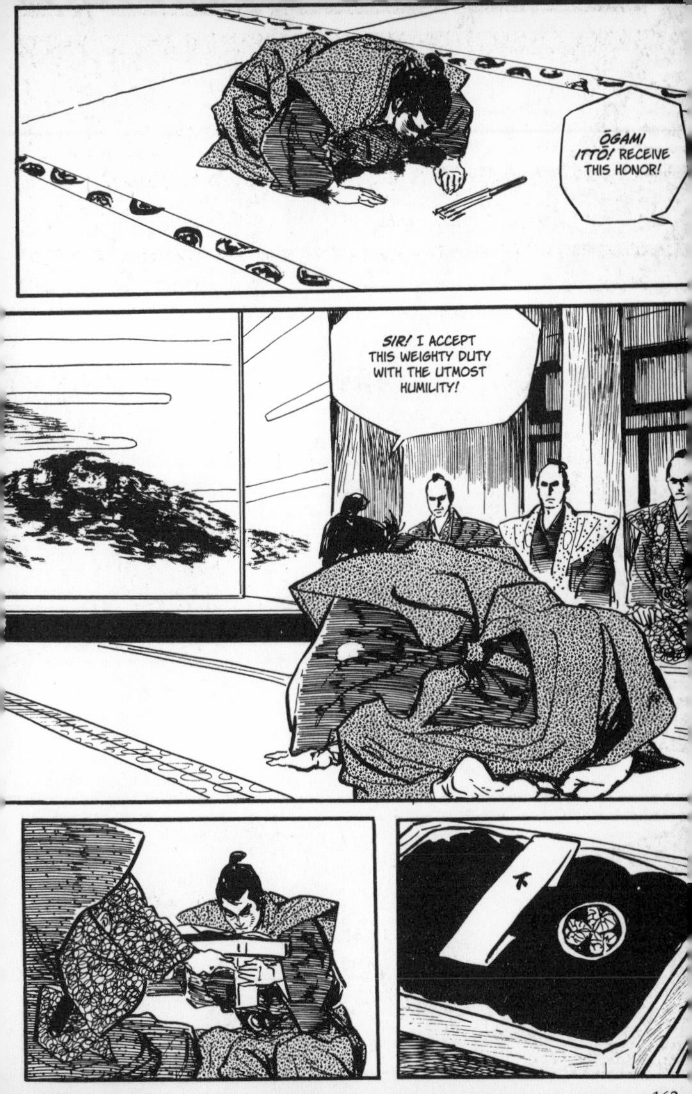
ŌGAMI ITTŌ! RECEIVE THIS HONOR!
SIR! I ACCEPT THIS WEIGHTY DUTY WITH THE UTMOST HUMILITY!

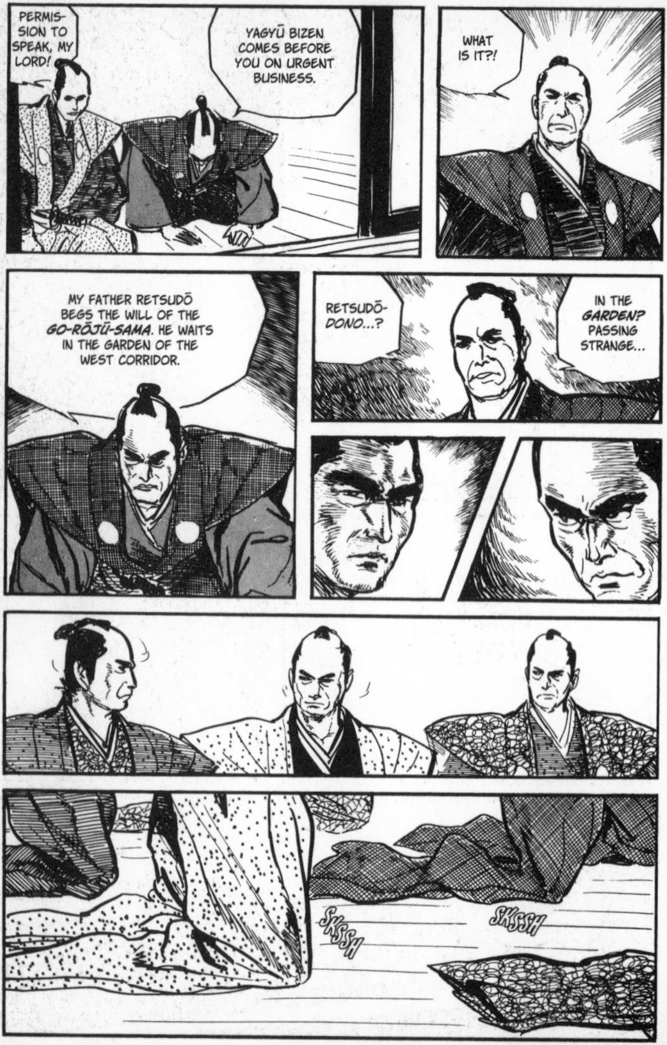
PERMISSION TO SPEAK, MY LORD!
YAGYŪ BIZEN COMES BEFORE YOU ON URGENT BUSINESS.
WHAT IS IT?!
MY FATHER RETSUDŌ BEGS THE WILL OF THE *GO-RŌJŪ-SAMA*. HE WAITS IN THE GARDEN OF THE WEST CORRIDOR.
RETSUDŌ-DONO...?
IN THE *GARDEN?* PASSING STRANGE...
SKSSH
SKSSH

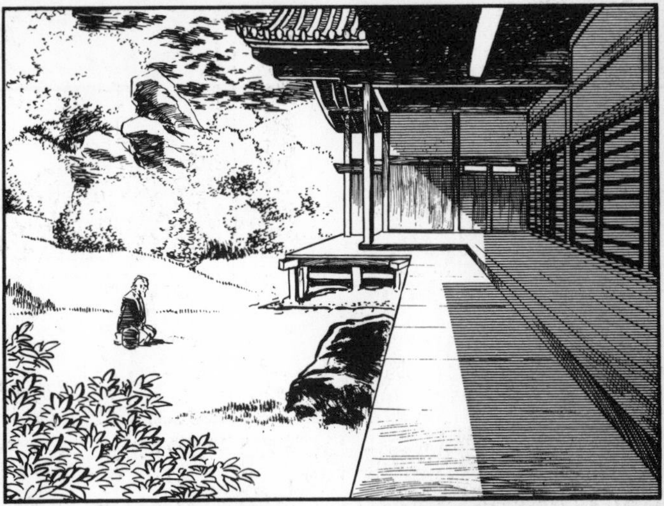

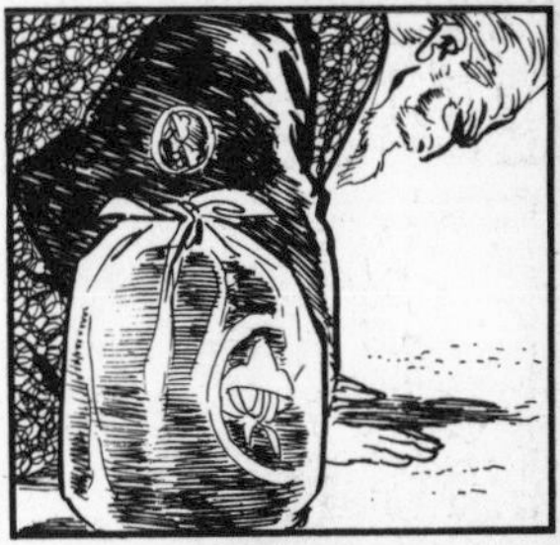

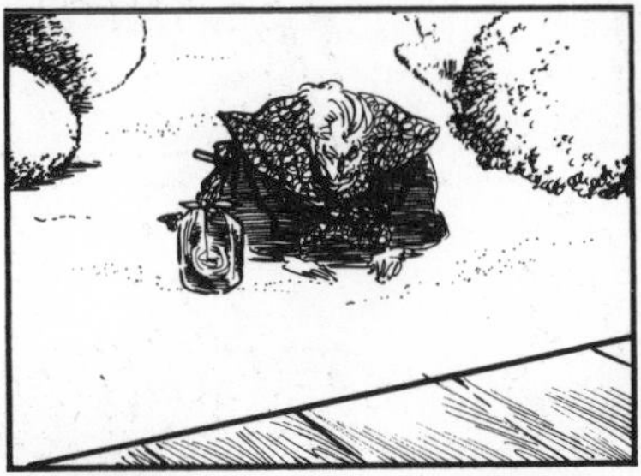

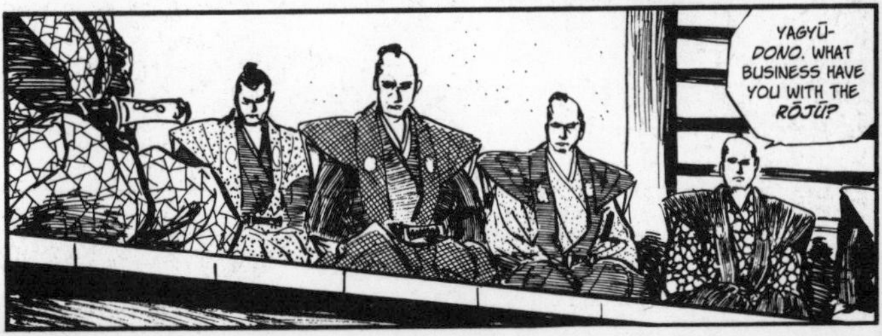
YAGYŪ-DONO. WHAT BUSINESS HAVE YOU WITH THE RŌJŪ?

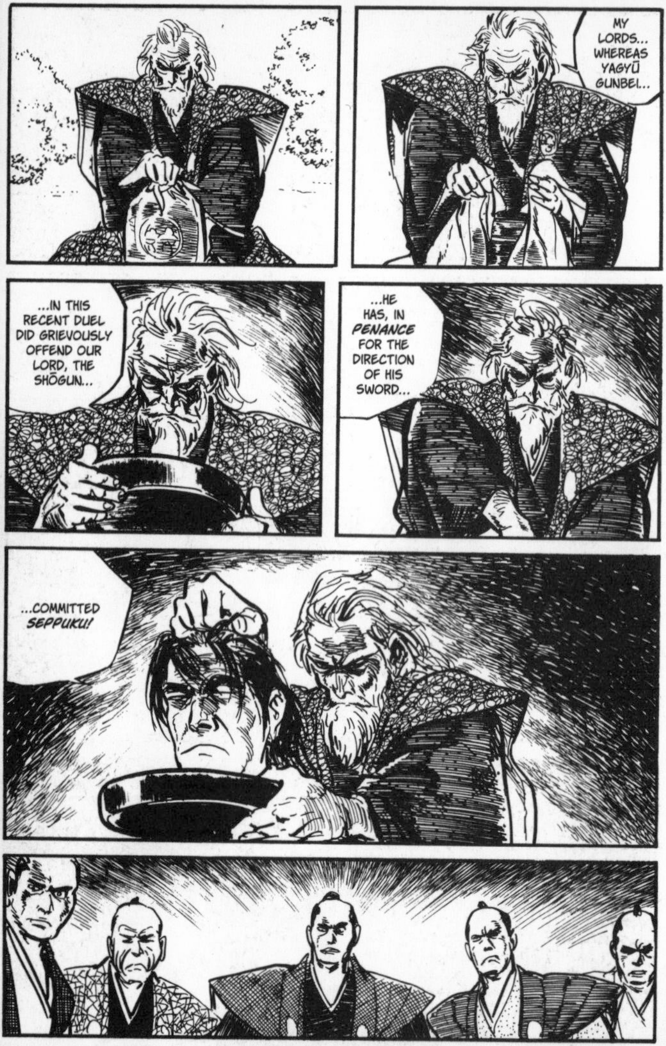
MY LORDS... WHEREAS YAGYŪ GUNBEI...
...IN THIS RECENT DUEL DID GRIEVOUSLY OFFEND OUR LORD, THE SHŌGUN...
...HE HAS, IN *PENANCE* FOR THE DIRECTION OF HIS SWORD...
...COMMITTED *SEPPUKU!*

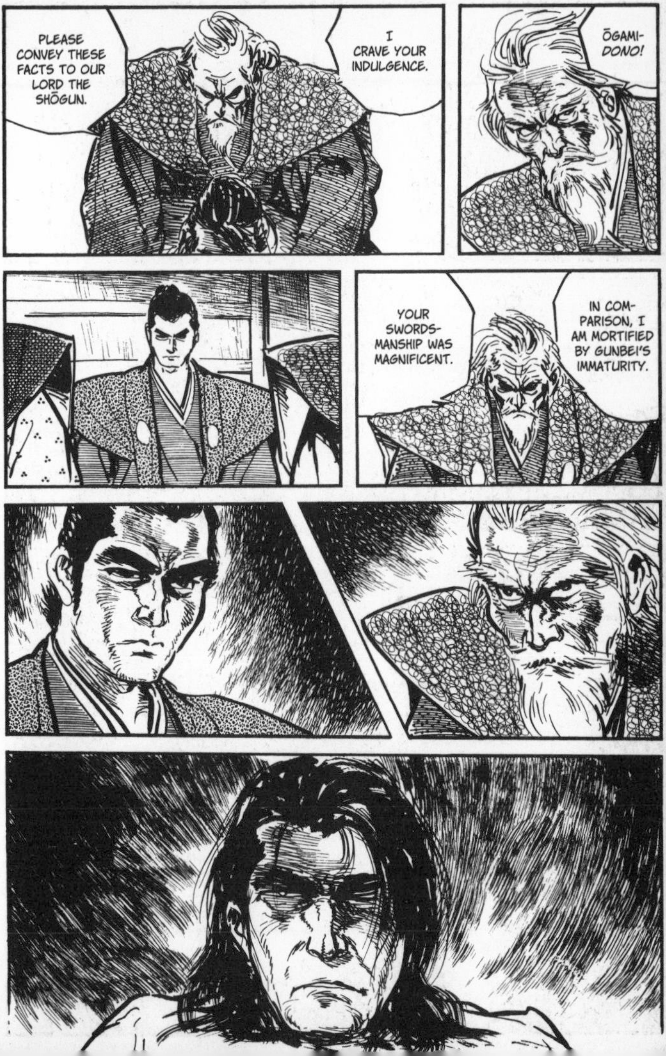
PLEASE CONVEY THESE FACTS TO OUR LORD THE SHŌGUN.
I CRAVE YOUR INDULGENCE.
ŌGAMI-DONO!
YOUR SWORDS-MANSHIP WAS MAGNIFICENT.
IN COM-PARISON, I AM MORTIFIED BY GUNBEI'S IMMATURITY.

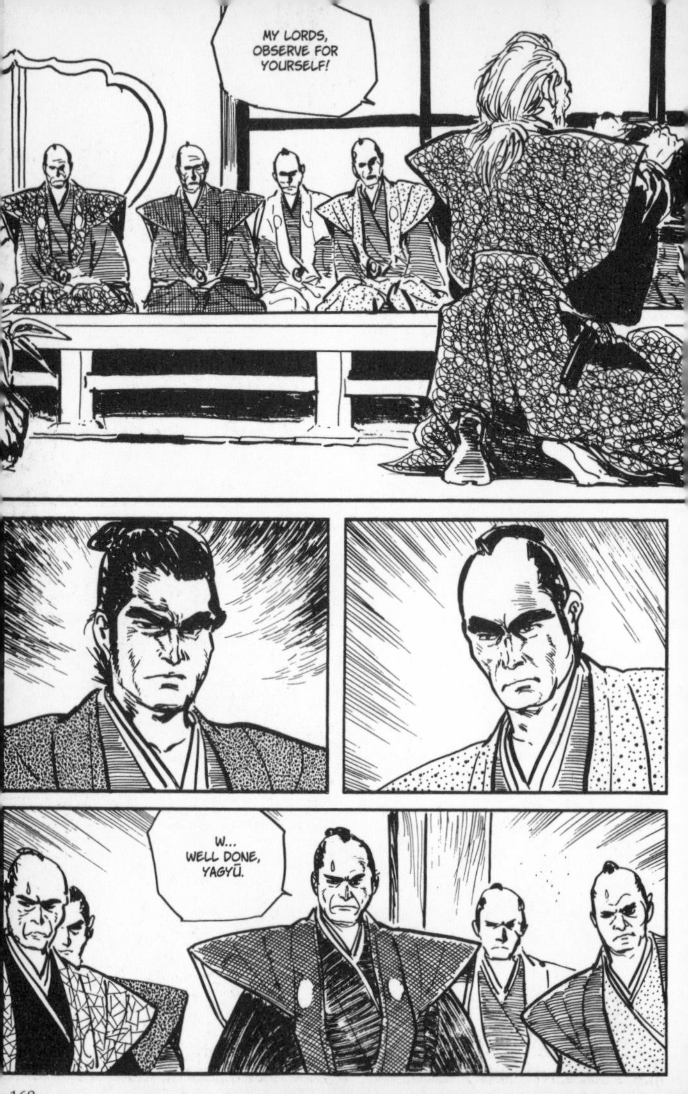
MY LORDS, OBSERVE FOR YOURSELF!
W... WELL DONE, YAGYŪ.

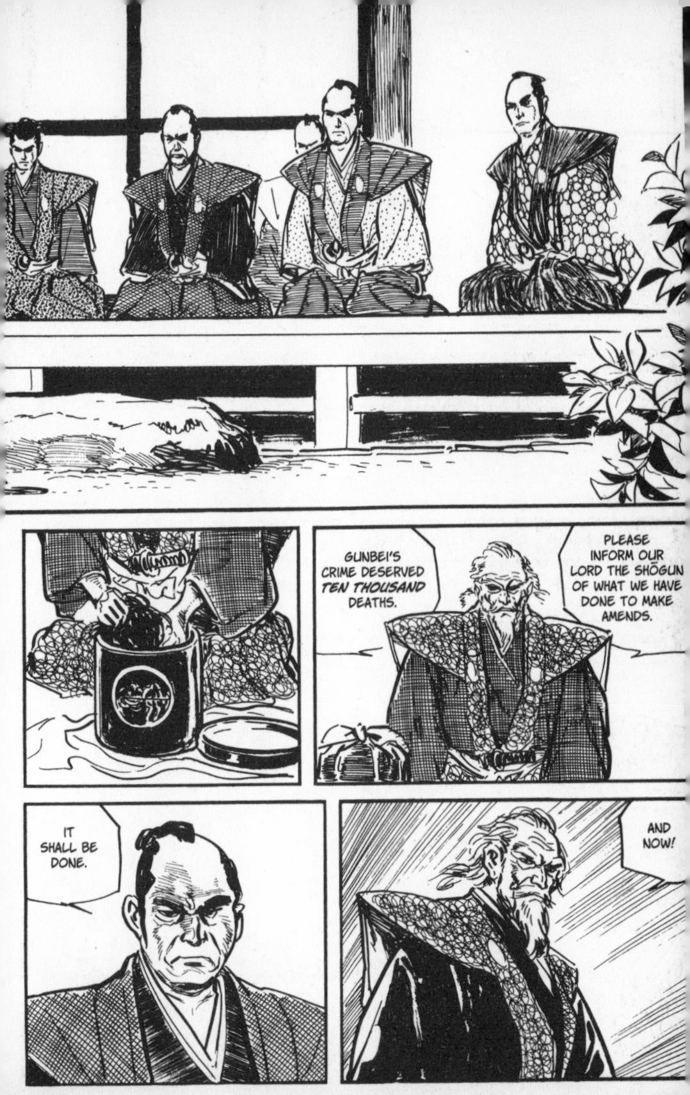
GUNBEI'S CRIME DESERVED *TEN THOUSAND* DEATHS.
PLEASE INFORM OUR LORD THE SHŌGUN OF WHAT WE HAVE DONE TO MAKE AMENDS.
IT SHALL BE DONE.
AND NOW!

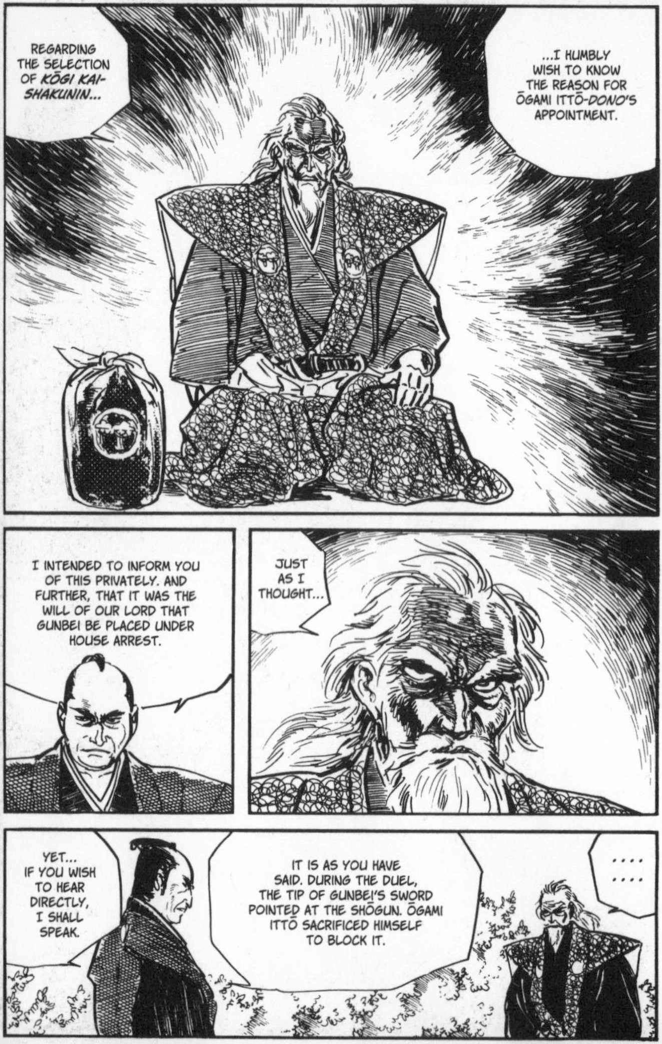

REGARDING THE SELECTION OF *KŌGI KAI-SHAKUNIN*...
...I HUMBLY WISH TO KNOW THE REASON FOR ŌGAMI ITTŌ-*DONO*'S APPOINTMENT.
I INTENDED TO INFORM YOU OF THIS PRIVATELY. AND FURTHER, THAT IT WAS THE WILL OF OUR LORD THAT GUNBEI BE PLACED UNDER HOUSE ARREST.
JUST AS I THOUGHT...
YET... IF YOU WISH TO HEAR DIRECTLY, I SHALL SPEAK.
IT IS AS YOU HAVE SAID. DURING THE DUEL, THE TIP OF GUNBEI'S SWORD POINTED AT THE SHŌGUN. ŌGAMI ITTŌ SACRIFICED HIMSELF TO BLOCK IT.
....

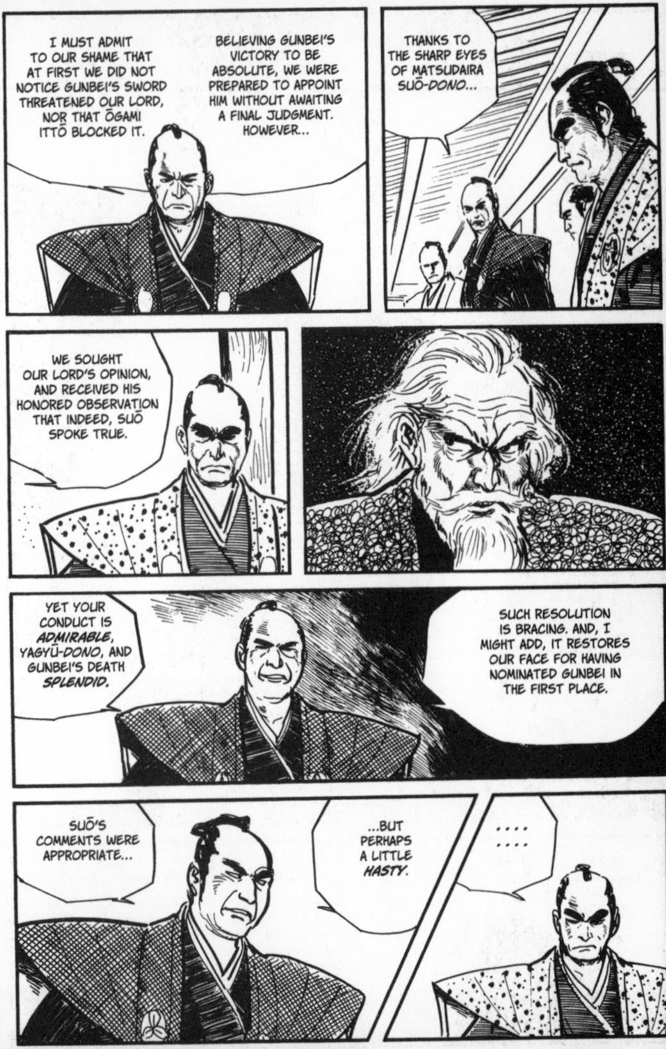
I MUST ADMIT TO OUR SHAME THAT AT FIRST WE DID NOT NOTICE GUNBEI'S SWORD THREATENED OUR LORD, NOR THAT ŌGAMI ITTŌ BLOCKED IT.
BELIEVING GUNBEI'S VICTORY TO BE ABSOLUTE, WE WERE PREPARED TO APPOINT HIM WITHOUT AWAITING A FINAL JUDGMENT. HOWEVER...
THANKS TO THE SHARP EYES OF MATSUDAIRA SUŌ-DONO...
WE SOUGHT OUR LORD'S OPINION, AND RECEIVED HIS HONORED OBSERVATION THAT INDEED, SUŌ SPOKE TRUE.
YET YOUR CONDUCT IS ADMIRABLE, YAGYŪ-DONO, AND GUNBEI'S DEATH SPLENDID.
SUCH RESOLUTION IS BRACING. AND, I MIGHT ADD, IT RESTORES OUR FACE FOR HAVING NOMINATED GUNBEI IN THE FIRST PLACE.
SUŌ'S COMMENTS WERE APPROPRIATE...
...BUT PERHAPS A LITTLE HASTY.
....
....

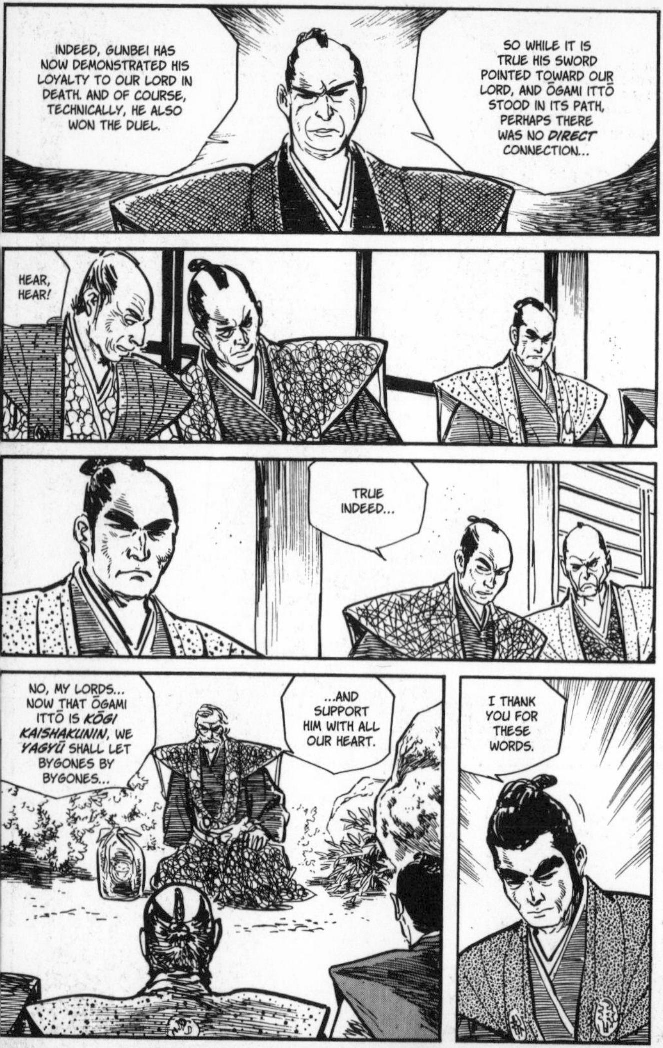
INDEED, GUNBEI HAS NOW DEMONSTRATED HIS LOYALTY TO OUR LORD IN DEATH. AND OF COURSE, TECHNICALLY, HE ALSO WON THE DUEL.
SO WHILE IT IS TRUE HIS SWORD POINTED TOWARD OUR LORD, AND ŌGAMI ITTŌ STOOD IN ITS PATH, PERHAPS THERE WAS NO *DIRECT* CONNECTION...
HEAR, HEAR!
TRUE INDEED...
NO, MY LORDS... NOW THAT ŌGAMI ITTŌ IS *KŌGI KAISHAKUNIN*, WE *YAGYŪ* SHALL LET BYGONES BY BYGONES...
...AND SUPPORT HIM WITH ALL OUR HEART.
I THANK YOU FOR THESE WORDS.

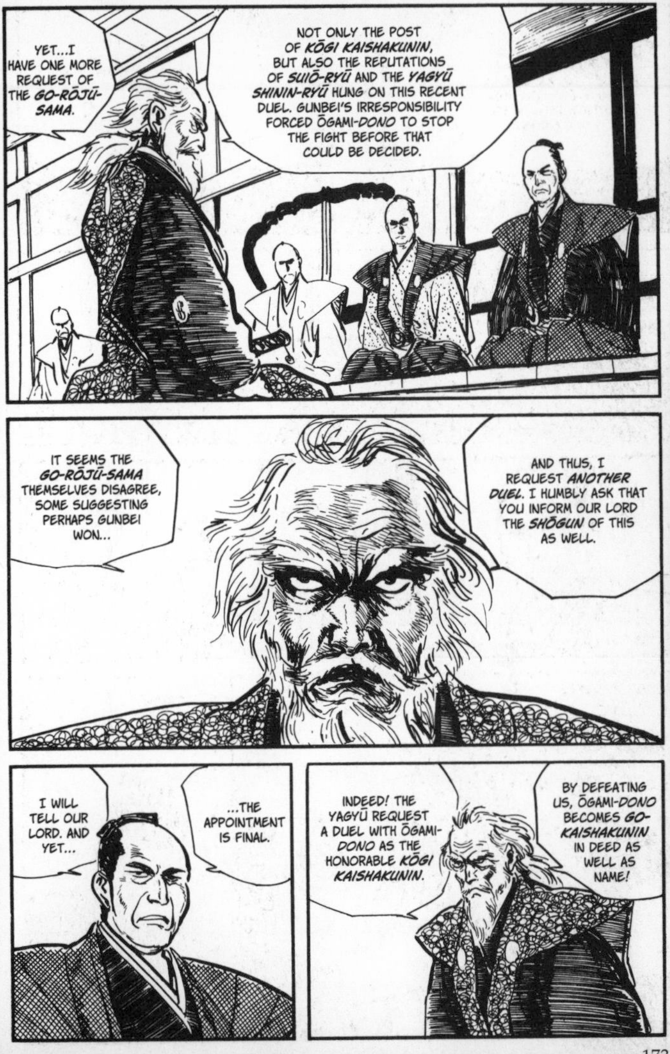
YET...I HAVE ONE MORE REQUEST OF THE GO-RŌJŪ-SAMA.
NOT ONLY THE POST OF KŌGI KAISHAKUNIN, BUT ALSO THE REPUTATIONS OF SUIŌ-RYŪ AND THE YAGYŪ SHININ-RYŪ HUNG ON THIS RECENT DUEL. GUNBEI'S IRRESPONSIBILITY FORCED ŌGAMI-DONO TO STOP THE FIGHT BEFORE THAT COULD BE DECIDED.
IT SEEMS THE GO-RŌJŪ-SAMA THEMSELVES DISAGREE, SOME SUGGESTING PERHAPS GUNBEI WON...
AND THUS, I REQUEST ANOTHER DUEL. I HUMBLY ASK THAT YOU INFORM OUR LORD THE SHŌGUN OF THIS AS WELL.
I WILL TELL OUR LORD. AND YET...
...THE APPOINTMENT IS FINAL.
INDEED! THE YAGYŪ REQUEST A DUEL WITH ŌGAMI-DONO AS THE HONORABLE KŌGI KAISHAKUNIN.
BY DEFEATING US, ŌGAMI-DONO BECOMES GO-KAISHAKUNIN IN DEED AS WELL AS NAME!

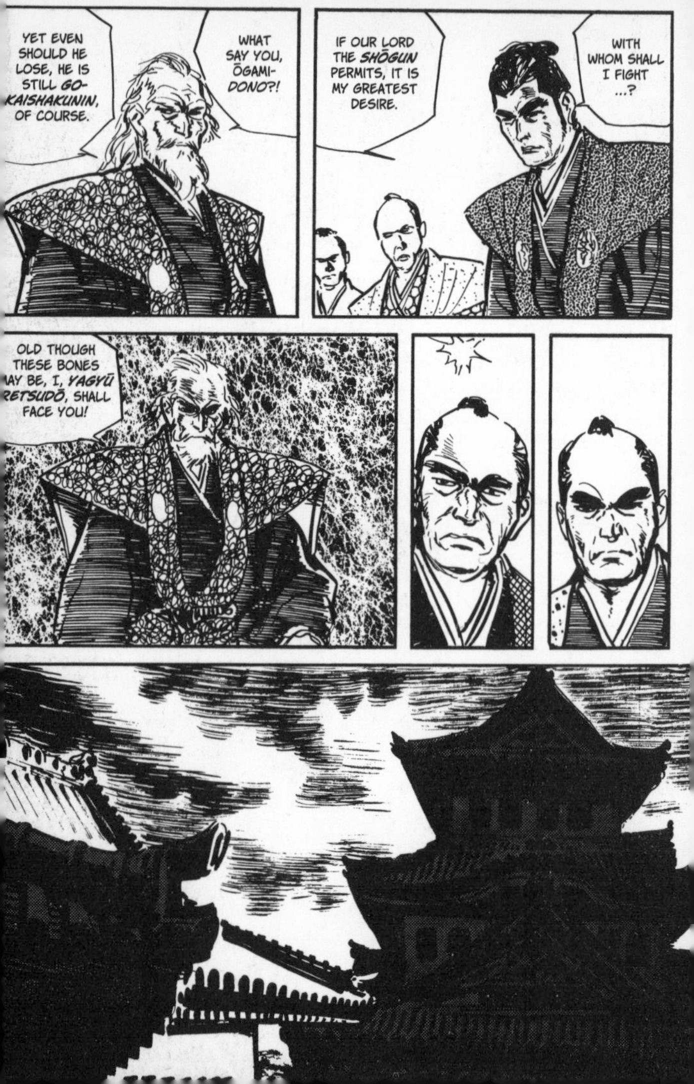
YET EVEN SHOULD HE LOSE, HE IS STILL *GO-KAISHAKUNIN*, OF COURSE.
WHAT SAY YOU, ŌGAMI-*DONO*?!
IF OUR LORD THE *SHŌGUN* PERMITS, IT IS MY GREATEST DESIRE.
WITH WHOM SHALL I FIGHT ...?
OLD THOUGH THESE BONES AY BE, I, *YAGYŪ RETSUDŌ*, SHALL FACE YOU!

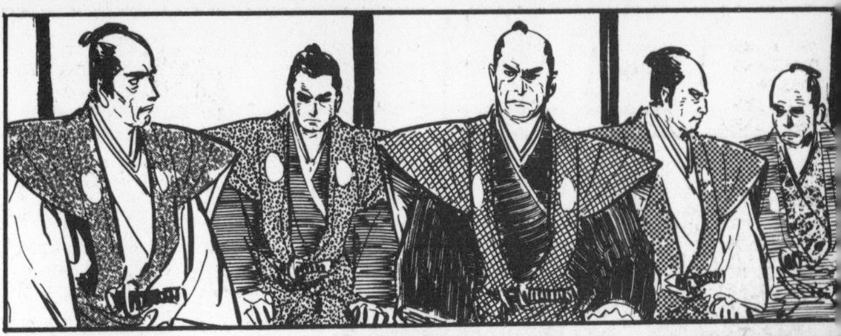
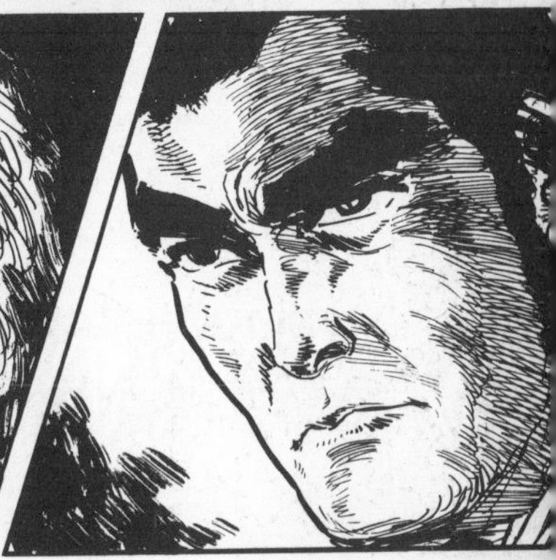
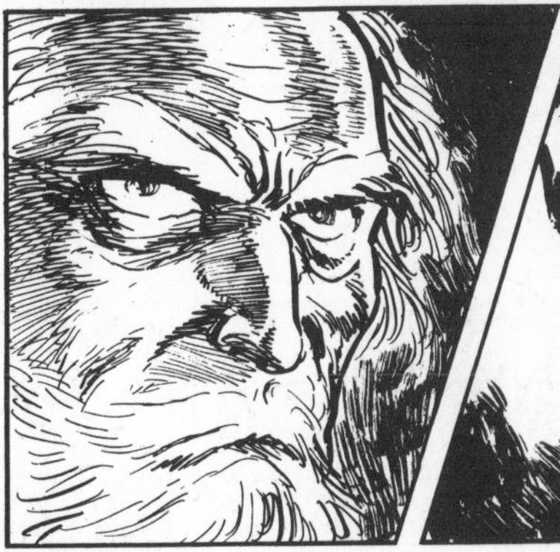
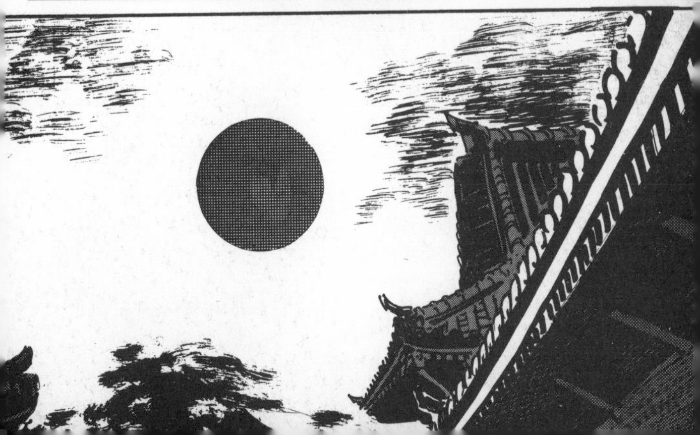

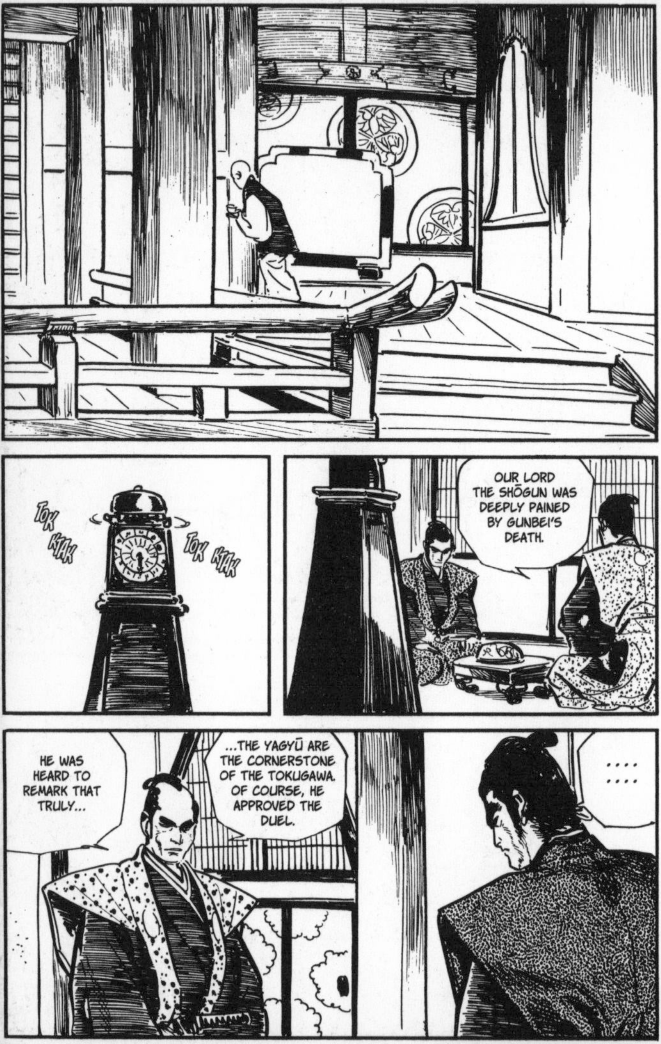
TOK KTAK
TOK KTAK
OUR LORD THE SHŌGUN WAS DEEPLY PAINED BY GUNBEI'S DEATH.
HE WAS HEARD TO REMARK THAT TRULY...
...THE YAGYŪ ARE THE CORNERSTONE OF THE TOKUGAWA. OF COURSE, HE APPROVED THE DUEL.
....
....

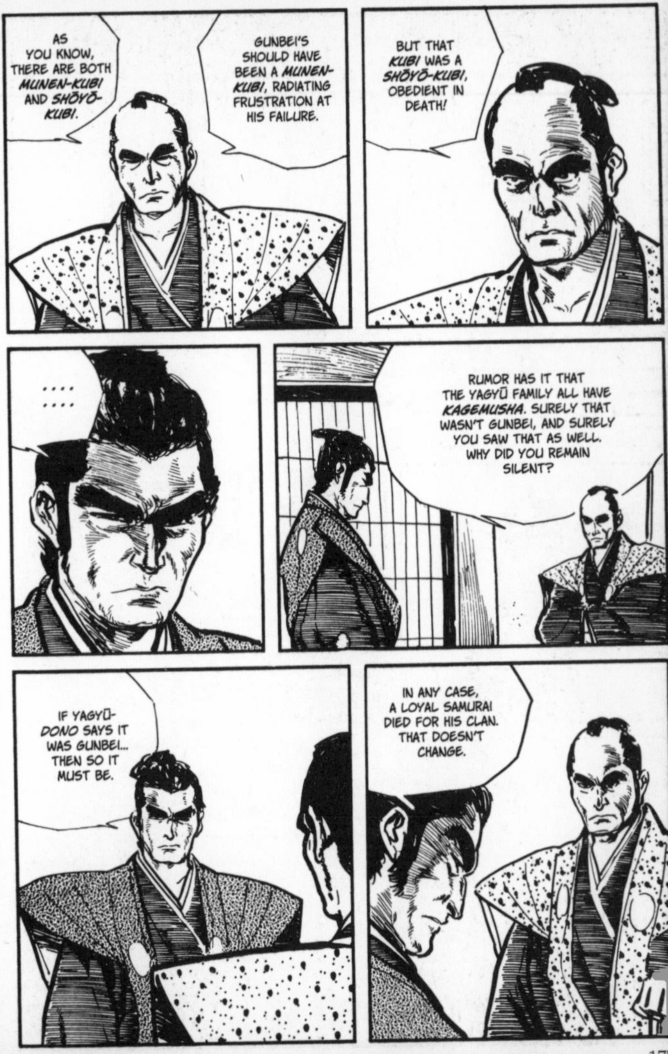
AS YOU KNOW, THERE ARE BOTH *MUNEN-KUBI* AND *SHŌYŌ-KUBI*.
GUNBEI'S SHOULD HAVE BEEN A *MUNEN-KUBI*, RADIATING FRUSTRATION AT HIS FAILURE.
BUT THAT *KUBI* WAS A *SHŌYŌ-KUBI*, OBEDIENT IN DEATH!
....
....
RUMOR HAS IT THAT THE YAGYŪ FAMILY ALL HAVE *KAGEMUSHA*. SURELY THAT WASN'T GUNBEI, AND SURELY YOU SAW THAT AS WELL. WHY DID YOU REMAIN SILENT?
IF YAGYŪ-*DONO* SAYS IT WAS GUNBEI... THEN SO IT MUST BE.
IN ANY CASE, A LOYAL SAMURAI DIED FOR HIS CLAN. THAT DOESN'T CHANGE.

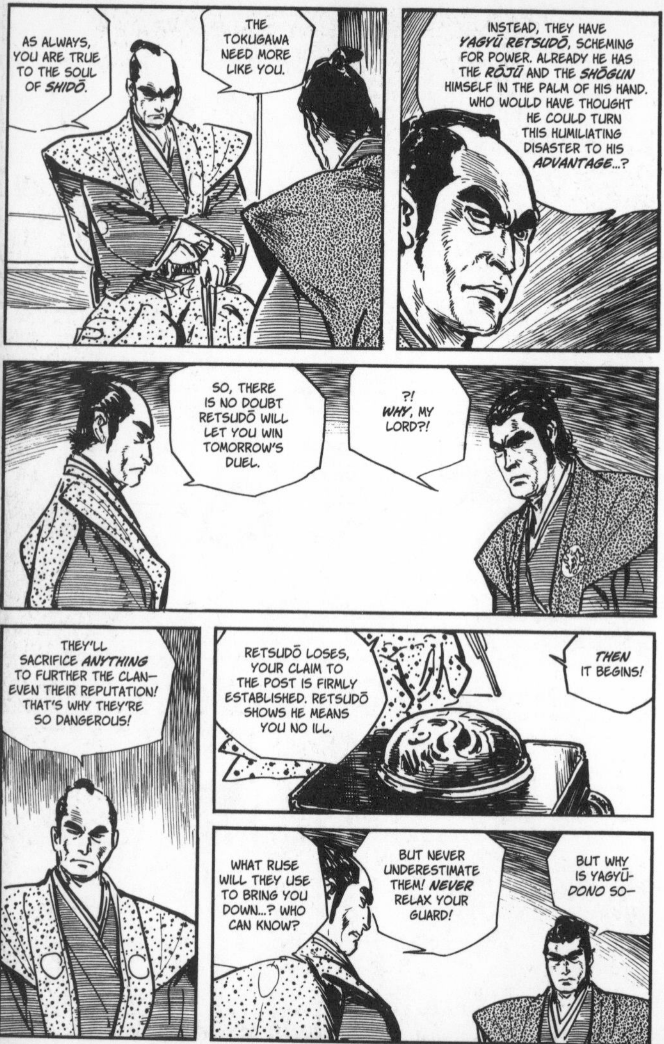
AS ALWAYS, YOU ARE TRUE TO THE SOUL OF *SHIDŌ*.
THE TOKUGAWA NEED MORE LIKE YOU.
INSTEAD, THEY HAVE *YAGYŪ RETSUDŌ*, SCHEMING FOR POWER. ALREADY HE HAS THE *RŌJŪ* AND THE *SHŌGUN* HIMSELF IN THE PALM OF HIS HAND. WHO WOULD HAVE THOUGHT HE COULD TURN THIS HUMILIATING DISASTER TO HIS *ADVANTAGE*...?
SO, THERE IS NO DOUBT RETSUDŌ WILL LET YOU WIN TOMORROW'S DUEL.
?! *WHY*, MY LORD?!
THEY'LL SACRIFICE *ANYTHING* TO FURTHER THE CLAN— EVEN THEIR REPUTATION! THAT'S WHY THEY'RE SO DANGEROUS!
RETSUDŌ LOSES, YOUR CLAIM TO THE POST IS FIRMLY ESTABLISHED. RETSUDŌ SHOWS HE MEANS YOU NO ILL.
THEN IT BEGINS!
WHAT RUSE WILL THEY USE TO BRING YOU DOWN...? WHO CAN KNOW?
BUT NEVER UNDERESTIMATE THEM! *NEVER* RELAX YOUR GUARD!
BUT WHY IS YAGYŪ-*DONO* SO—

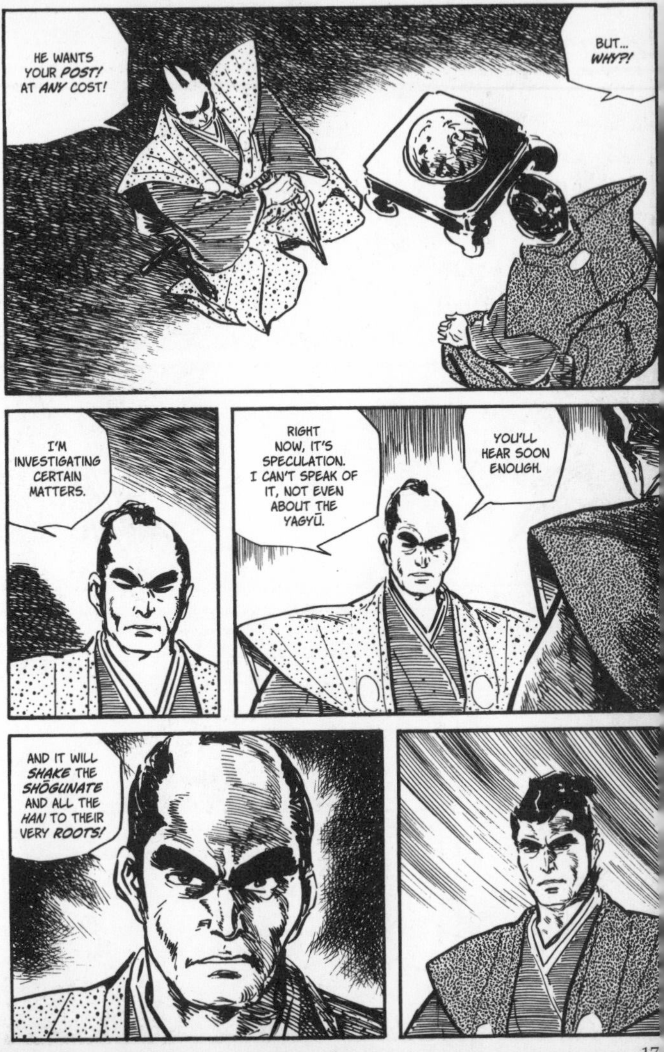
HE WANTS YOUR *POST!* AT *ANY* COST!
BUT... *WHY?!*
I'M INVESTIGATING CERTAIN MATTERS.
RIGHT NOW, IT'S SPECULATION. I CAN'T SPEAK OF IT, NOT EVEN ABOUT THE YAGYŪ.
YOU'LL HEAR SOON ENOUGH.
AND IT WILL *SHAKE* THE *SHŌGUNATE* AND ALL THE *HAN* TO THEIR VERY *ROOTS!*

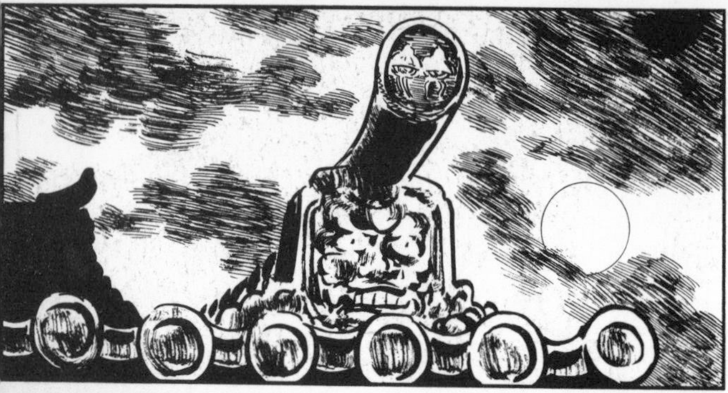

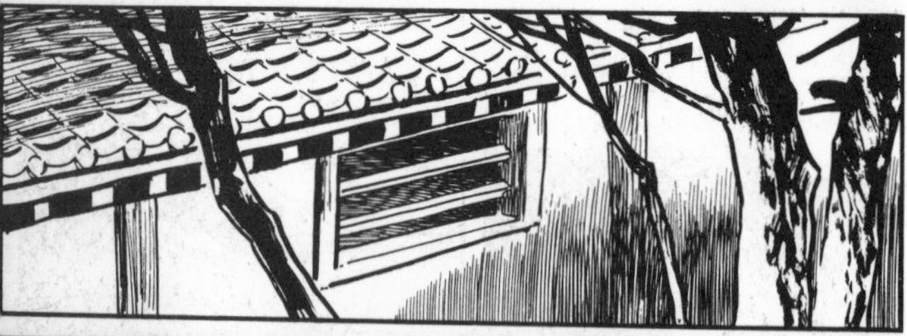

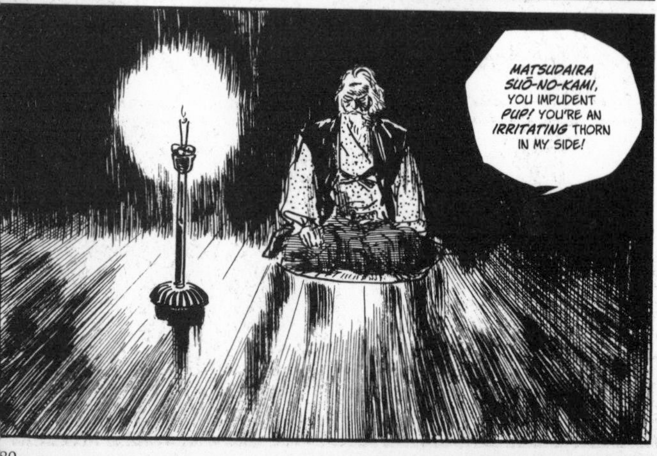
MATSUDAIRA SUŌ-NO-KAMI, YOU IMPUDENT PUP! YOU'RE AN IRRITATING THORN IN MY SIDE!

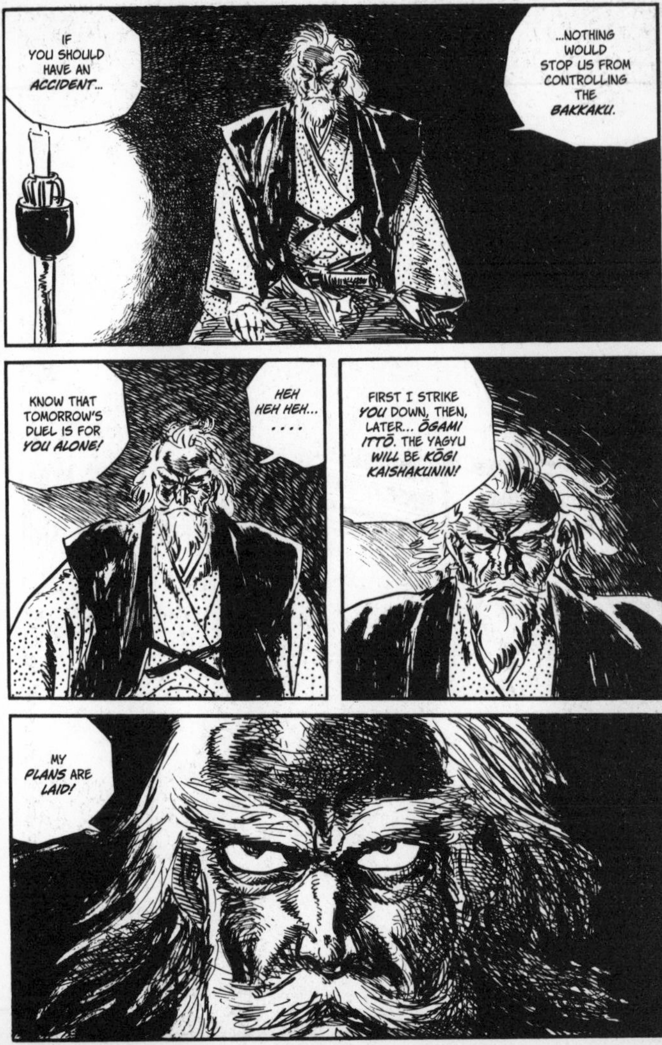
IF YOU SHOULD HAVE AN ACCIDENT...
...NOTHING WOULD STOP US FROM CONTROLLING THE BAKKAKU.
KNOW THAT TOMORROW'S DUEL IS FOR YOU ALONE!
HEH HEH HEH... . . . .
FIRST I STRIKE YOU DOWN, THEN, LATER... ŌGAMI ITTŌ. THE YAGYU WILL BE KŌGI KAISHAKUNIN!
MY PLANS ARE LAID!

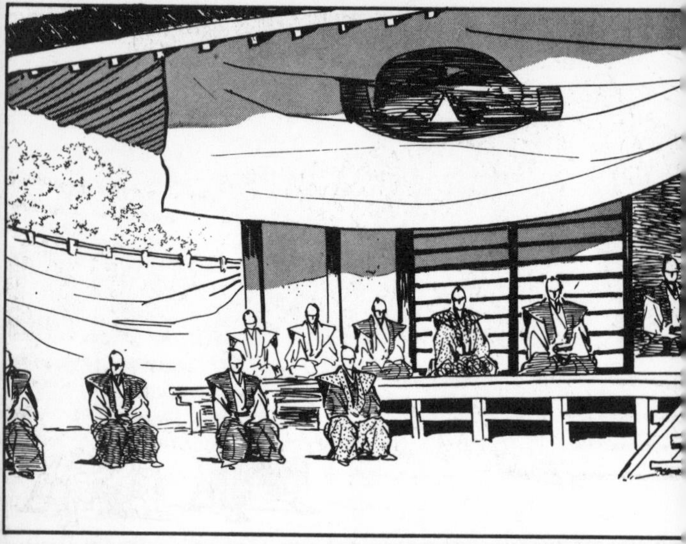
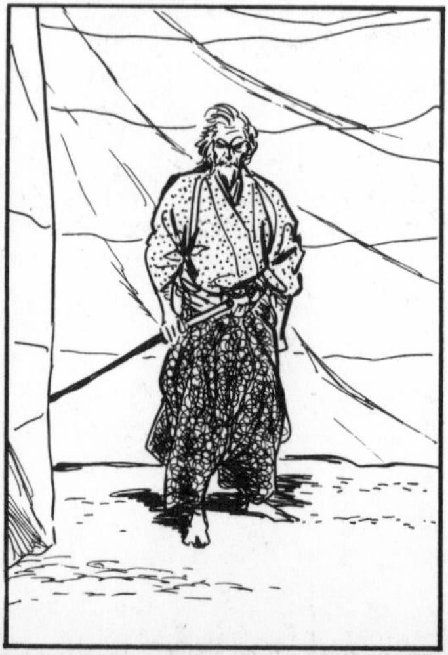
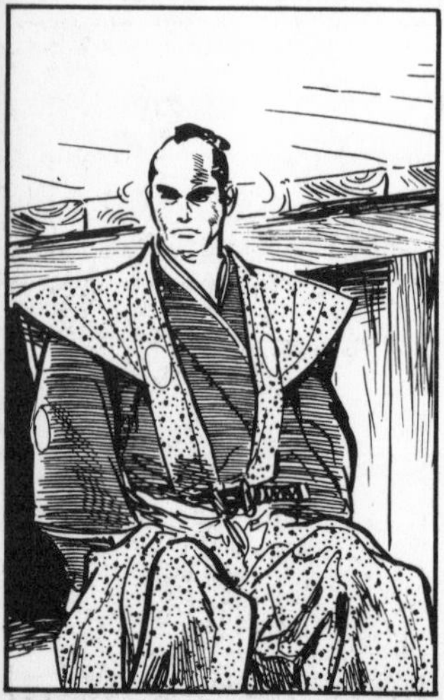

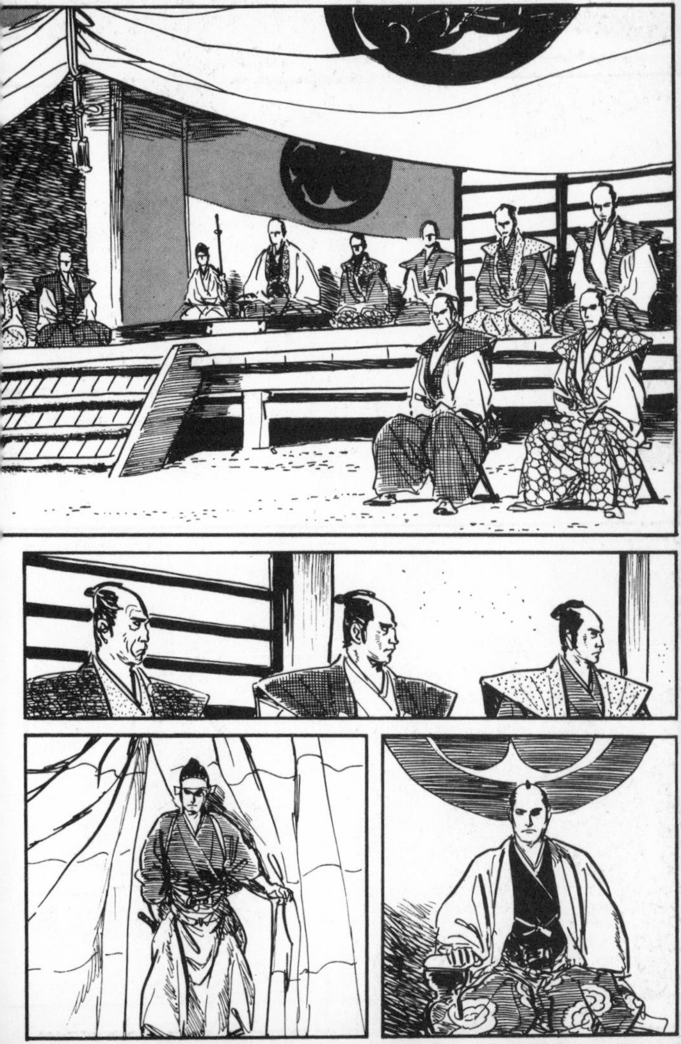

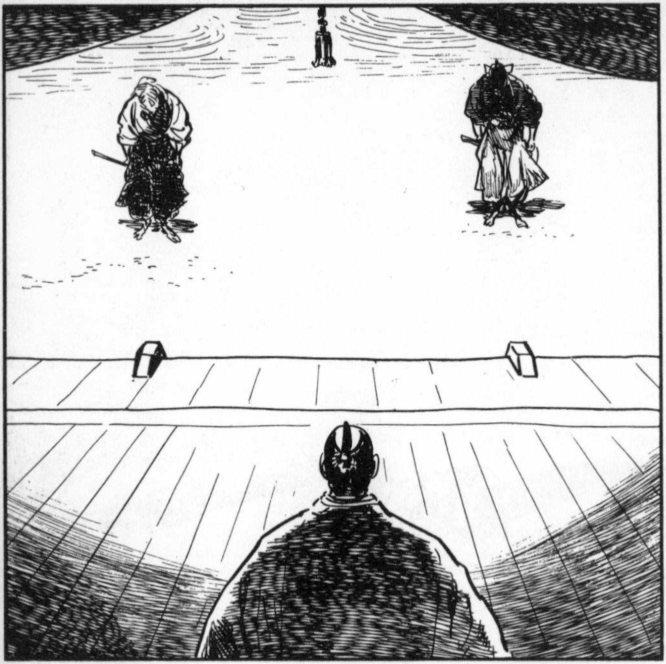
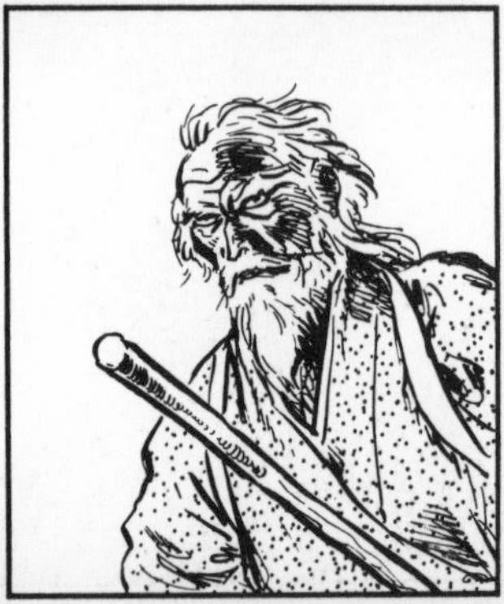
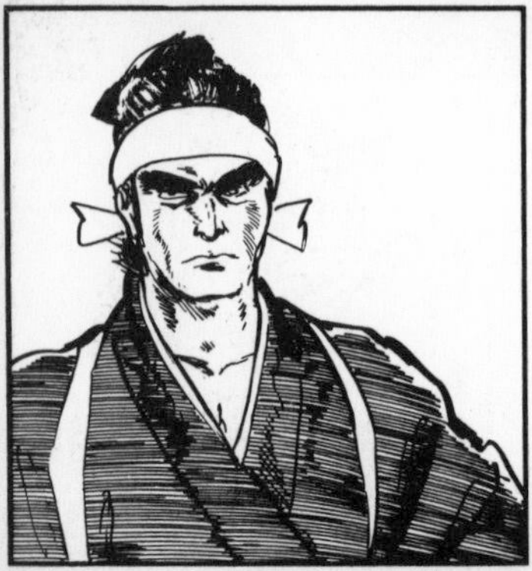

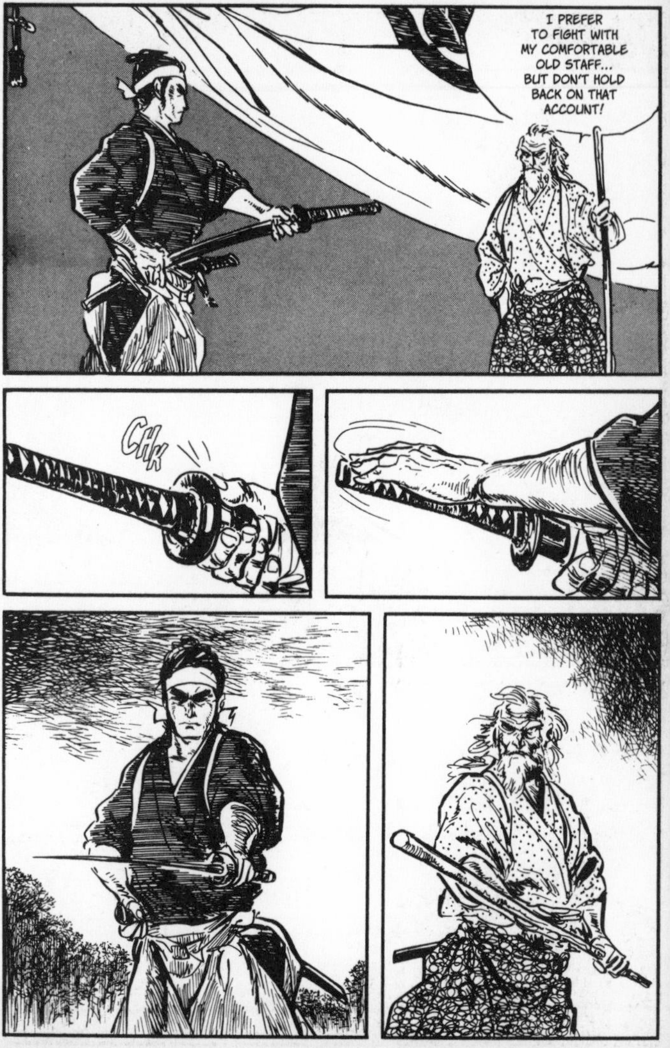
I PREFER TO FIGHT WITH MY COMFORTABLE OLD STAFF... BUT DON'T HOLD BACK ON THAT ACCOUNT!
CHK

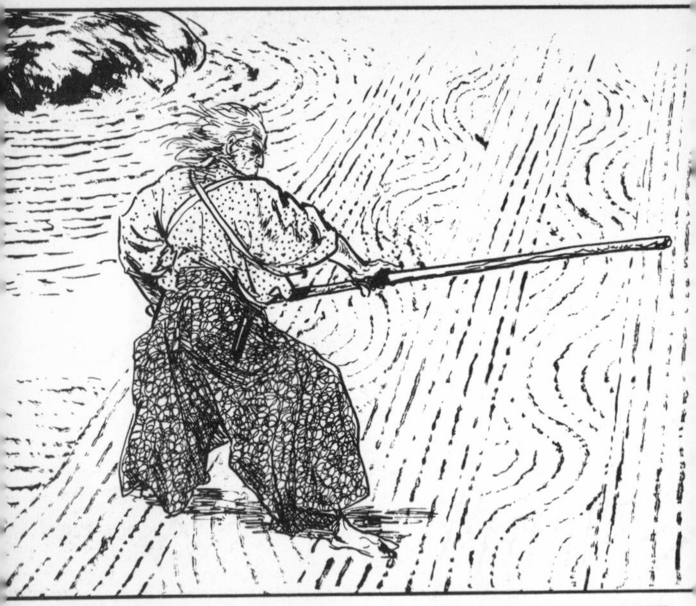
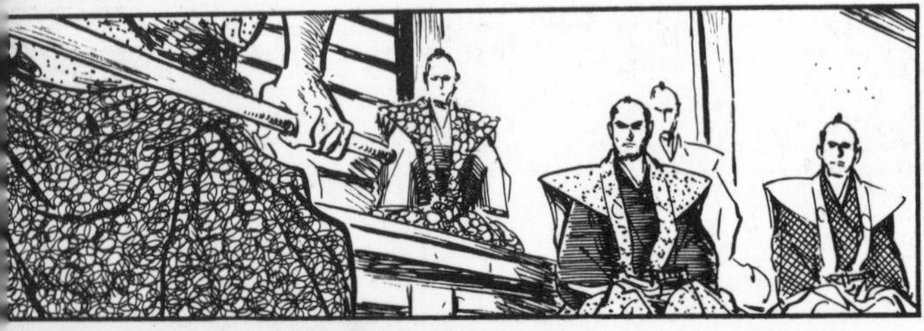
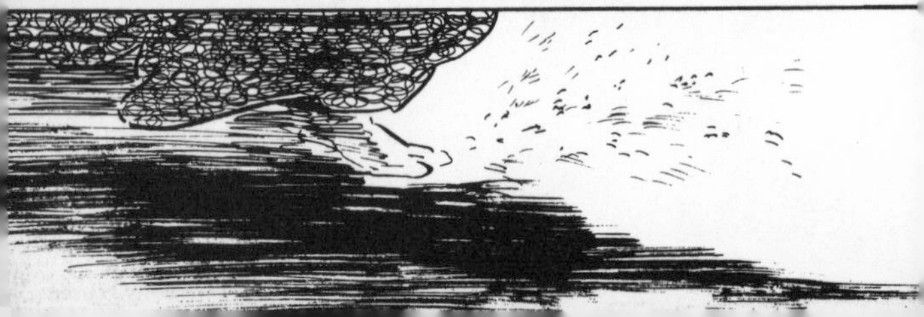

SKSSSH

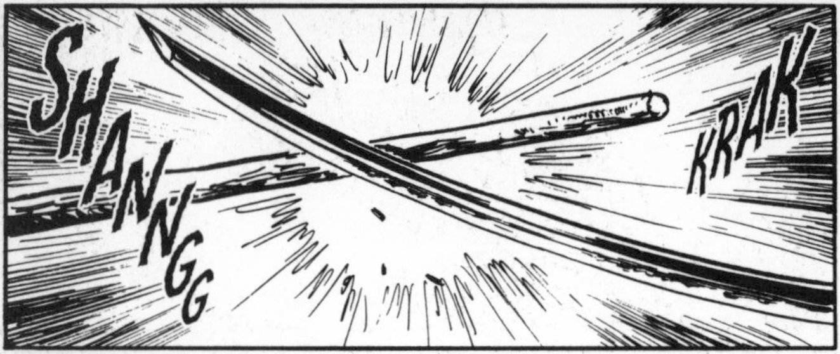
KRAK
SHANNGG
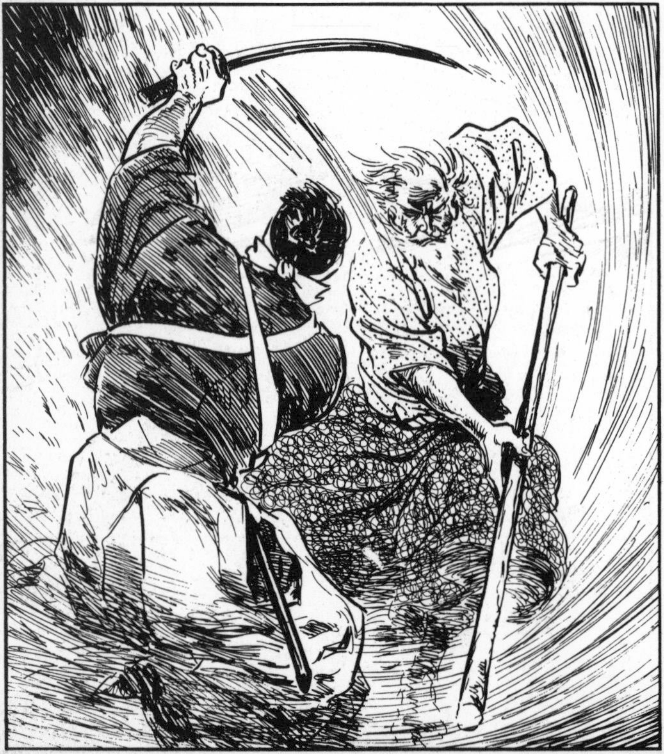

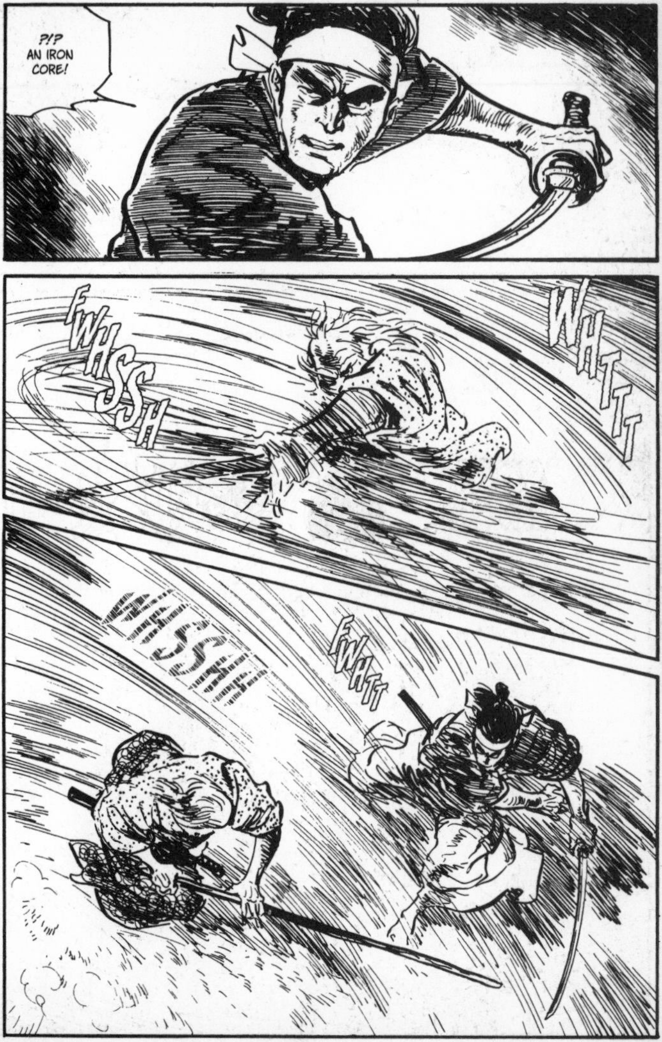
?!? AN IRON CORE!
WHTTTT
FWHSSH
FWHTT
WHSSH

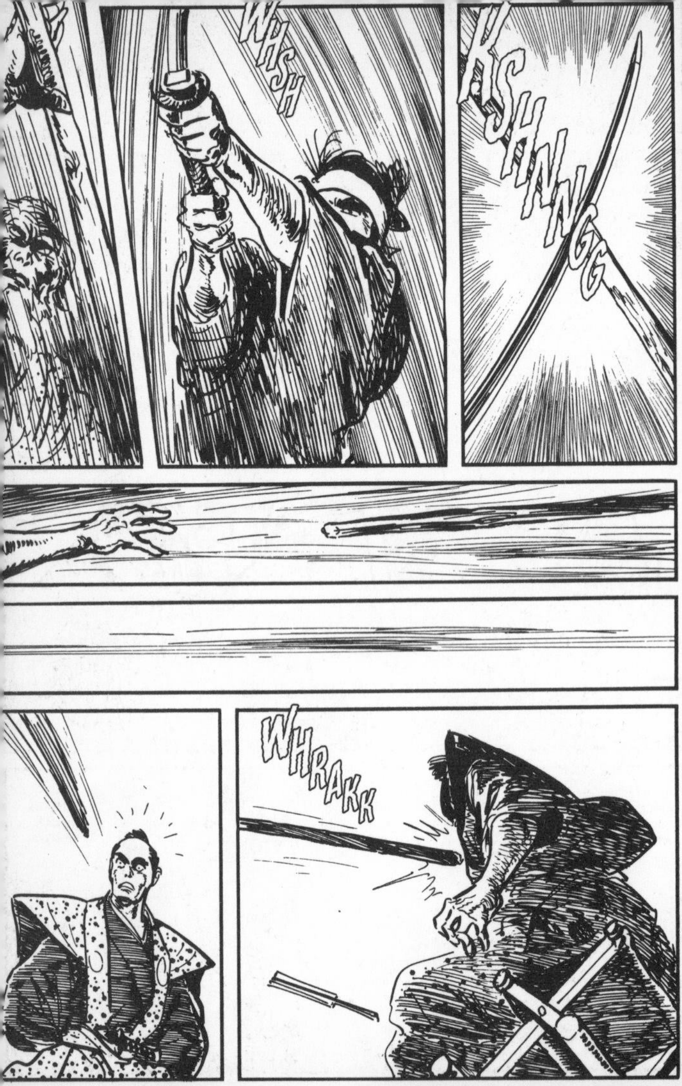
KSHINNGG
WHSH
WHRAKK

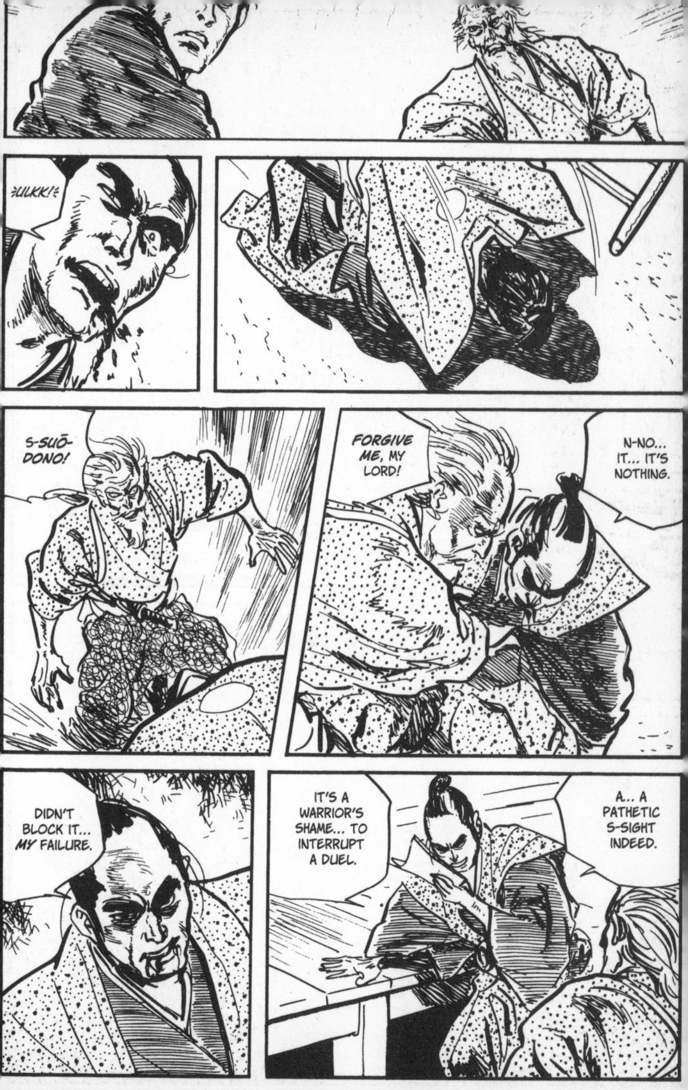

ULKK!
N-NO... IT... IT'S NOTHING.
FORGIVE ME, MY LORD!
S-SUŌ-DONO!
A... A PATHETIC S-SIGHT INDEED.
IT'S A WARRIOR'S SHAME... TO INTERRUPT A DUEL.
DIDN'T BLOCK IT... MY FAILURE.

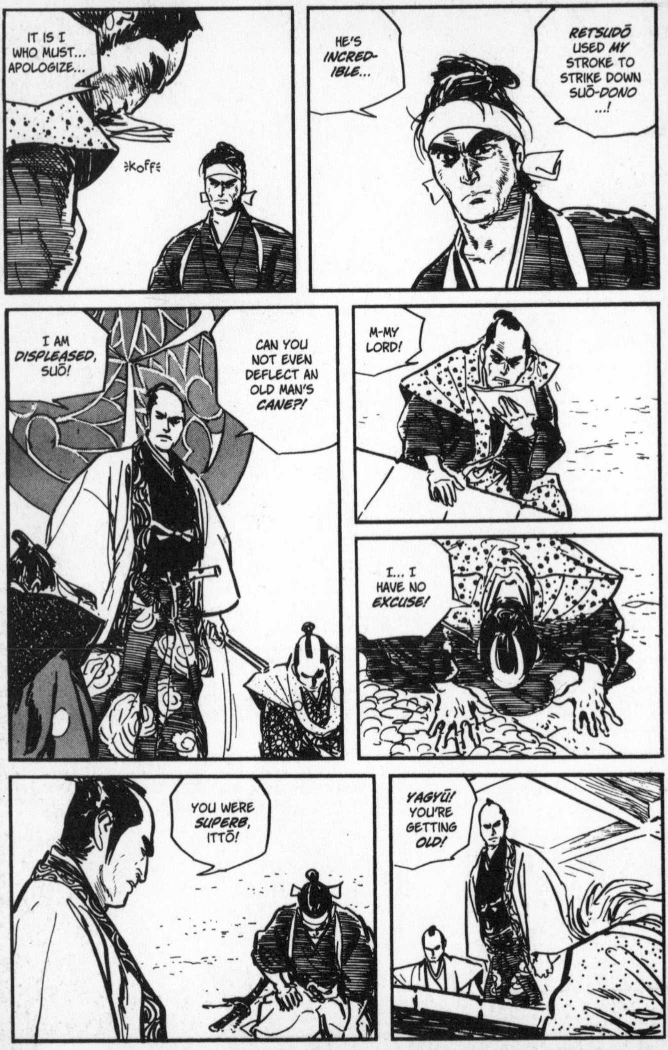
IT IS I WHO MUST... APOLOGIZE...
KOFF
HE'S INCREDIBLE...
RETSUDŌ USED MY STROKE TO STRIKE DOWN SUŌ-DONO ...!
I AM DISPLEASED, SUŌ!
CAN YOU NOT EVEN DEFLECT AN OLD MAN'S CANE?!
M-MY LORD!
I... I HAVE NO EXCUSE!
YOU WERE SUPERB, ITTŌ!
YAGYŪ! YOU'RE GETTING OLD!

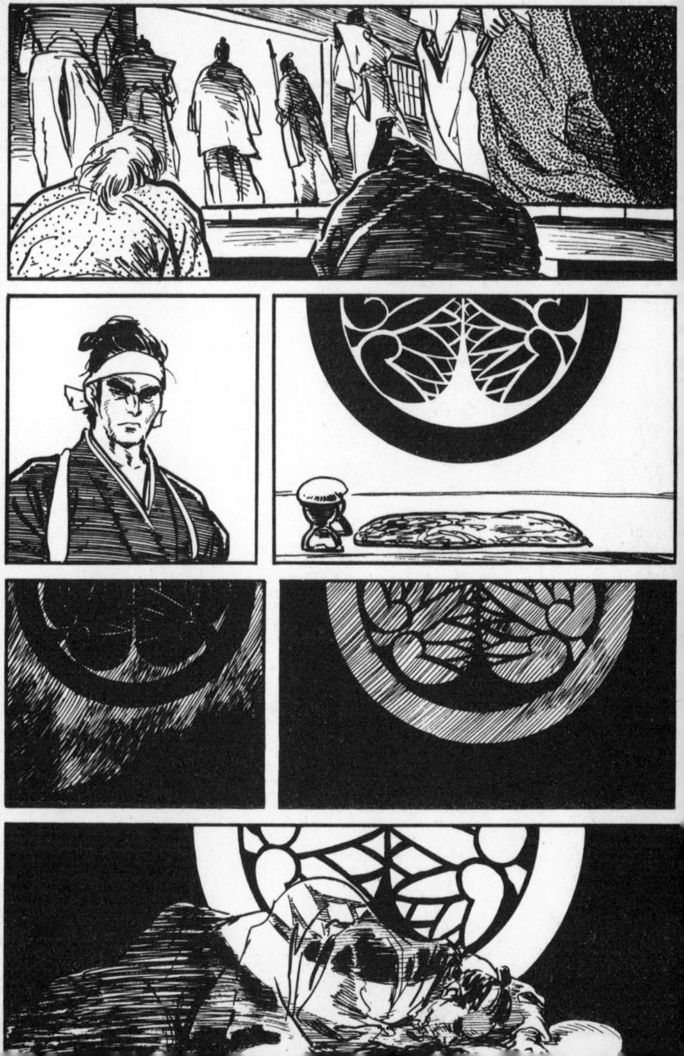

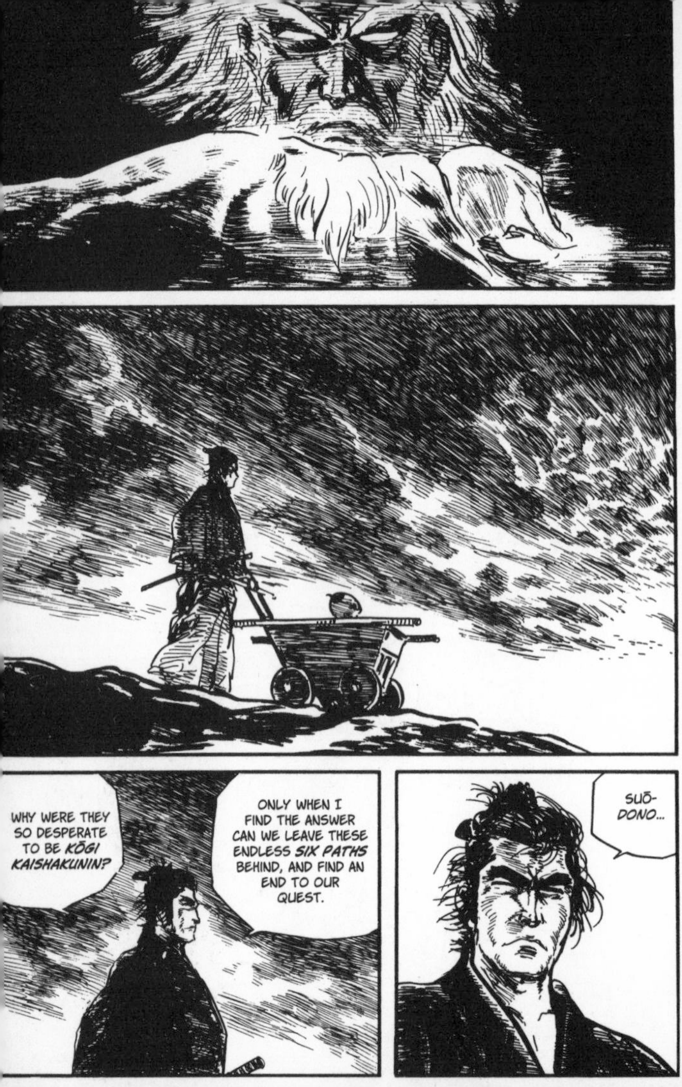
WHY WERE THEY SO DESPERATE TO BE *KŌGI KAISHAKUNIN?*
ONLY WHEN I FIND THE ANSWER CAN WE LEAVE THESE ENDLESS *SIX PATHS* BEHIND, AND FIND AN END TO OUR QUEST.
SUŌ-DONO...

the forty-third

Thread of Tears

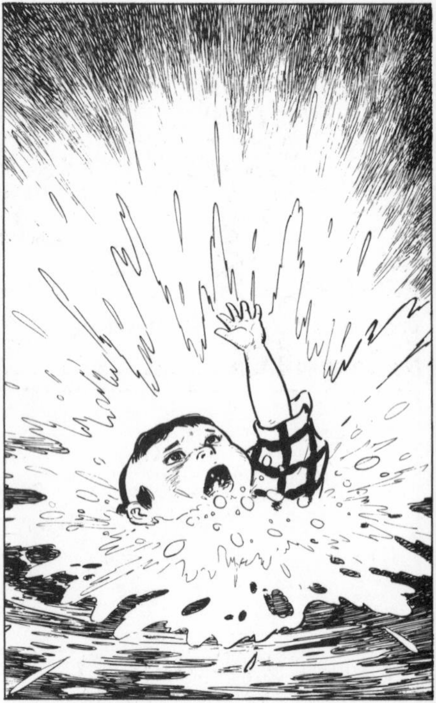

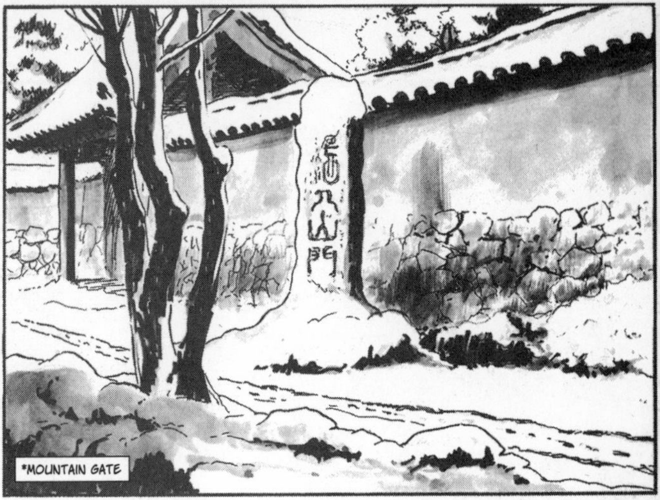
*MOUNTAIN GATE
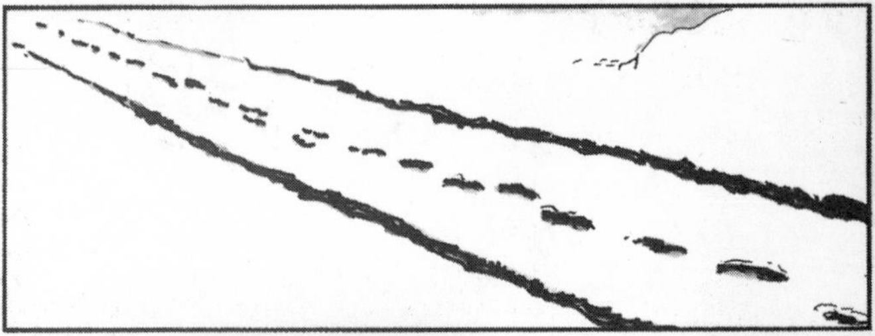
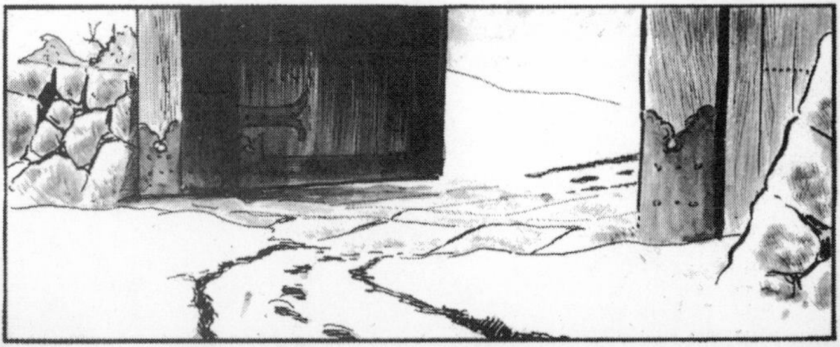

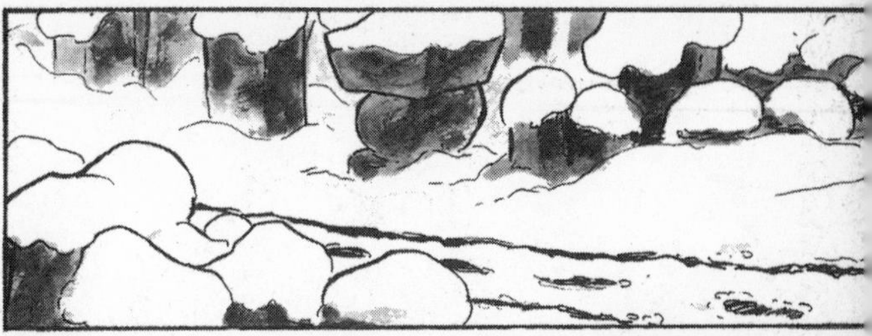
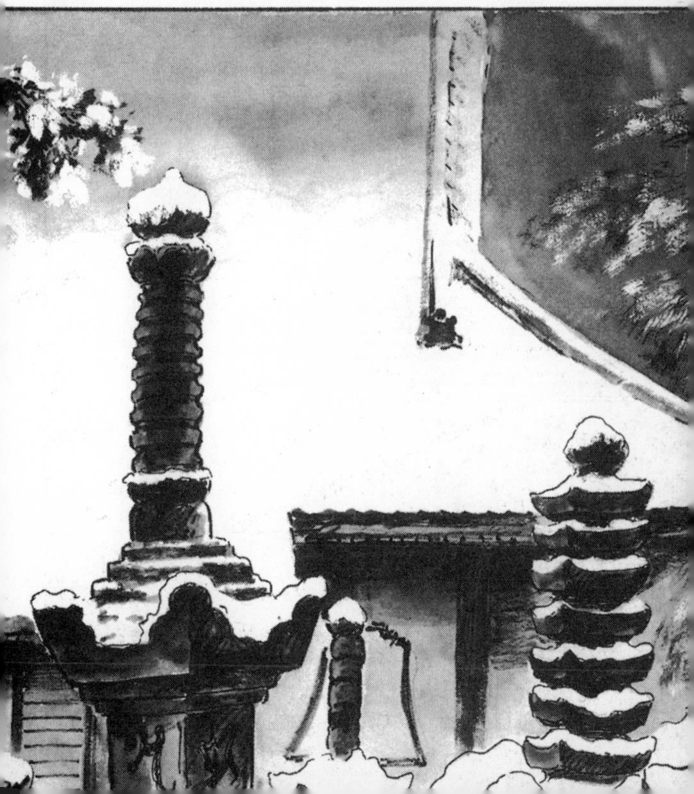

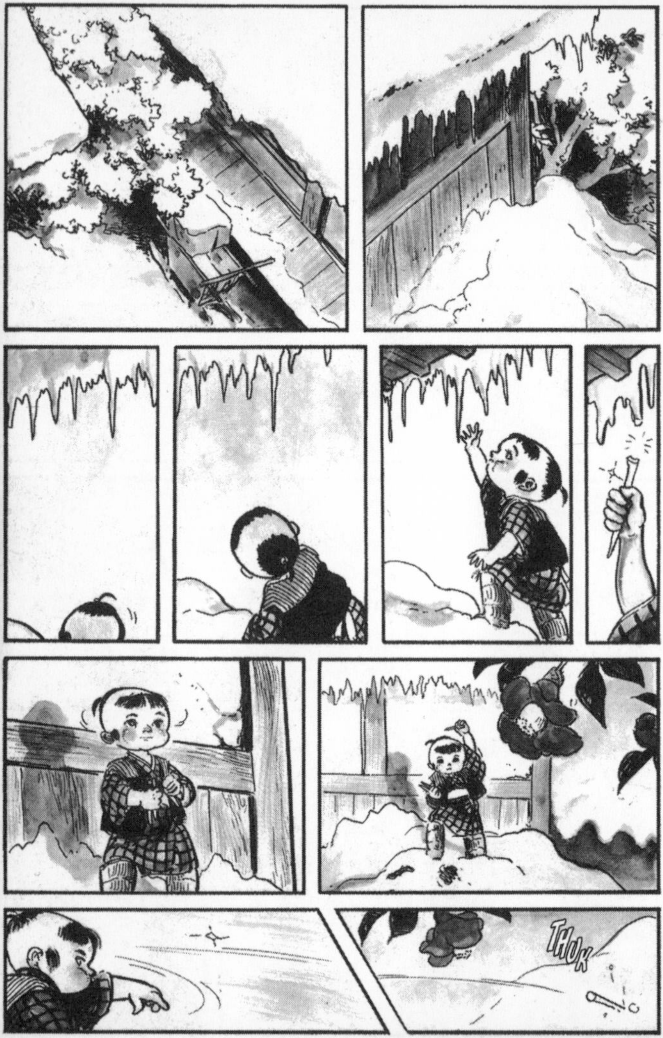
THUK

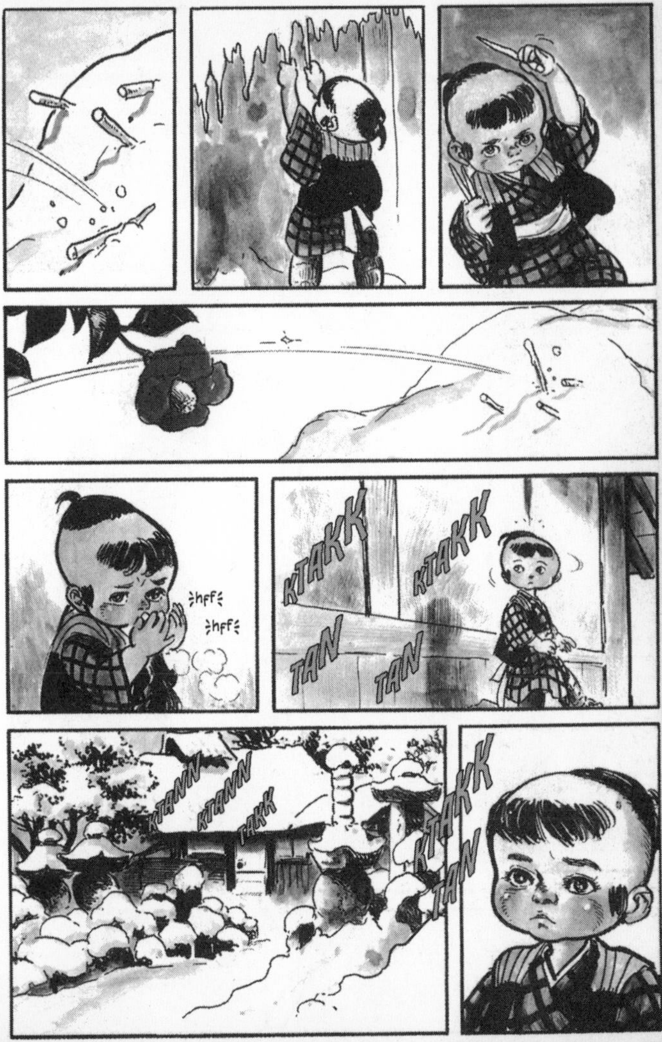
KTAKK
KTAKK
TAN
TAN
hff
hff
KTAKK
KTAKK
TAN
KTANN
KTANN
TAKK

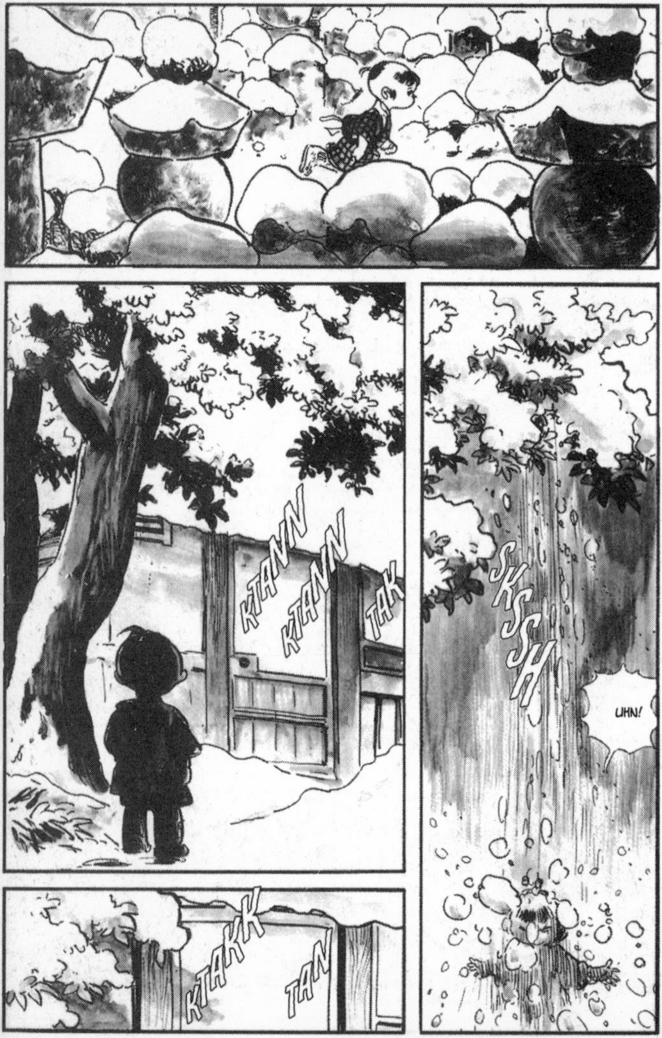
KTANN
KTANN
TAK
KTAKK
TAN
SKSSH
UHN!

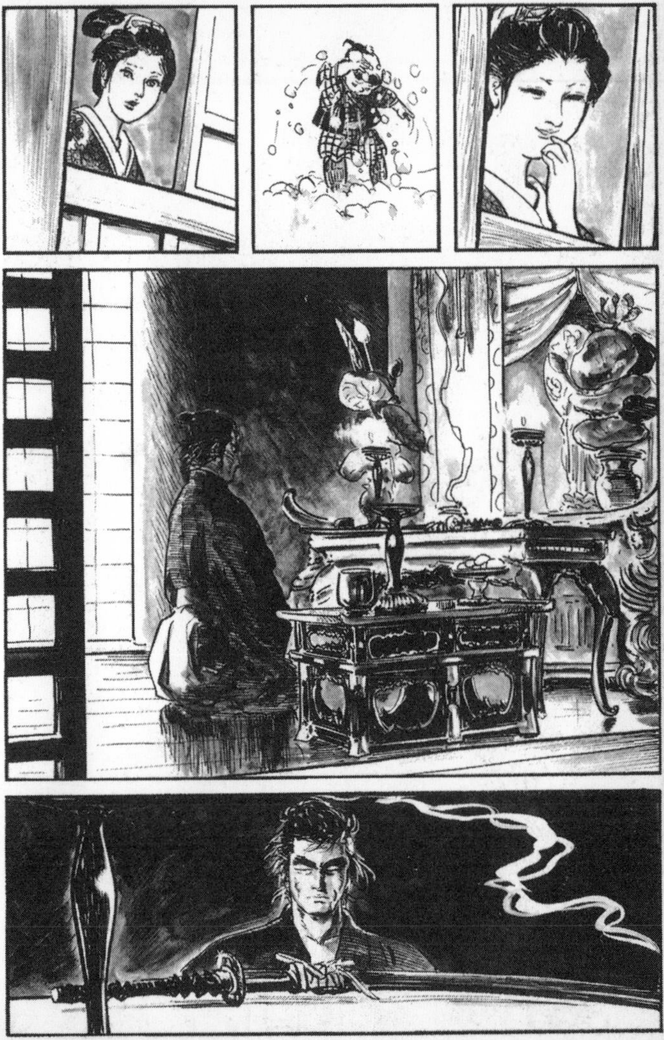

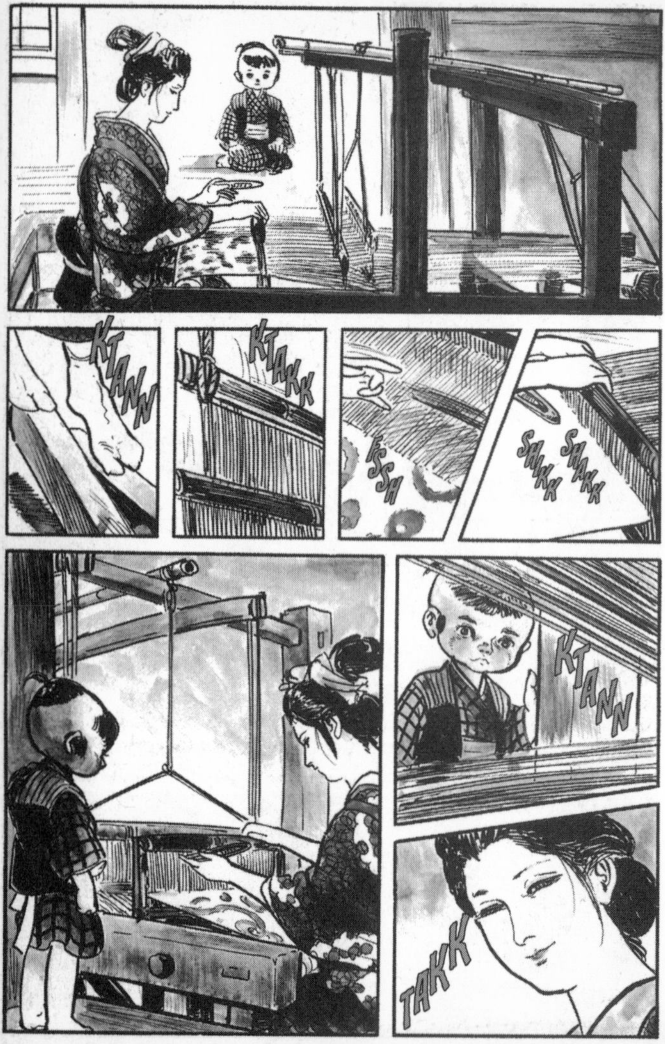
SHAKK
SHIKK
FSSH
KTAKK
KTANN
KTANN
TAKK

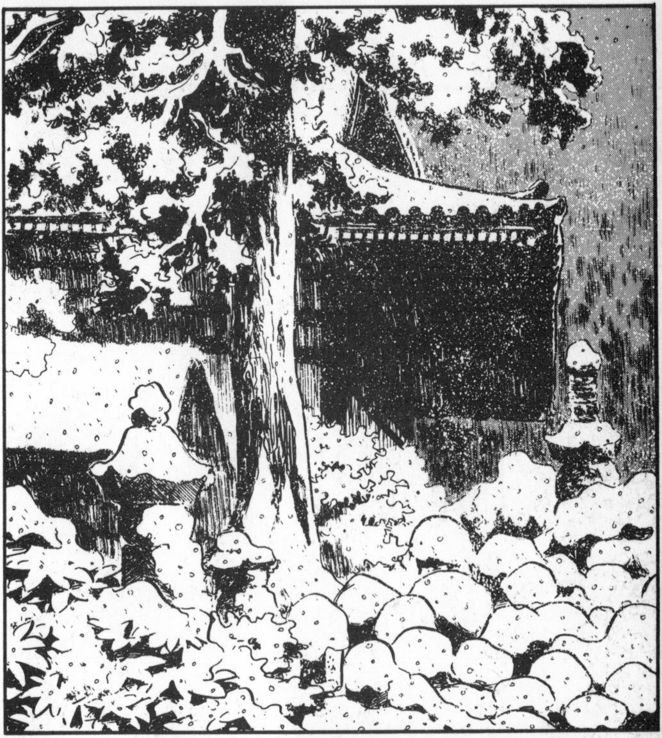
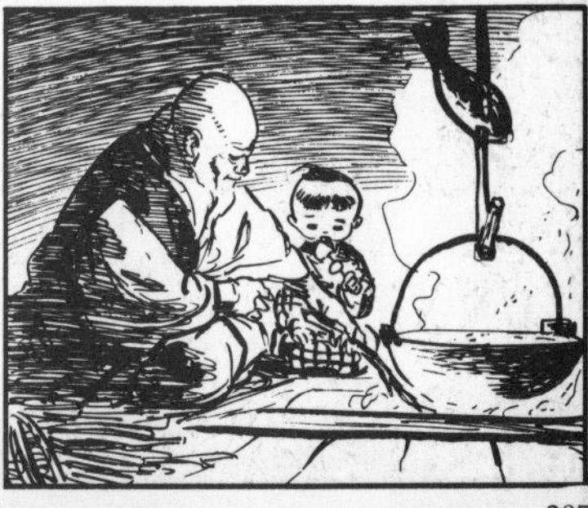
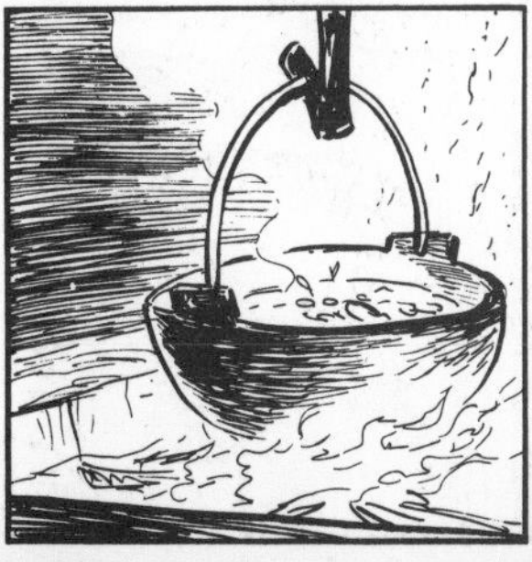

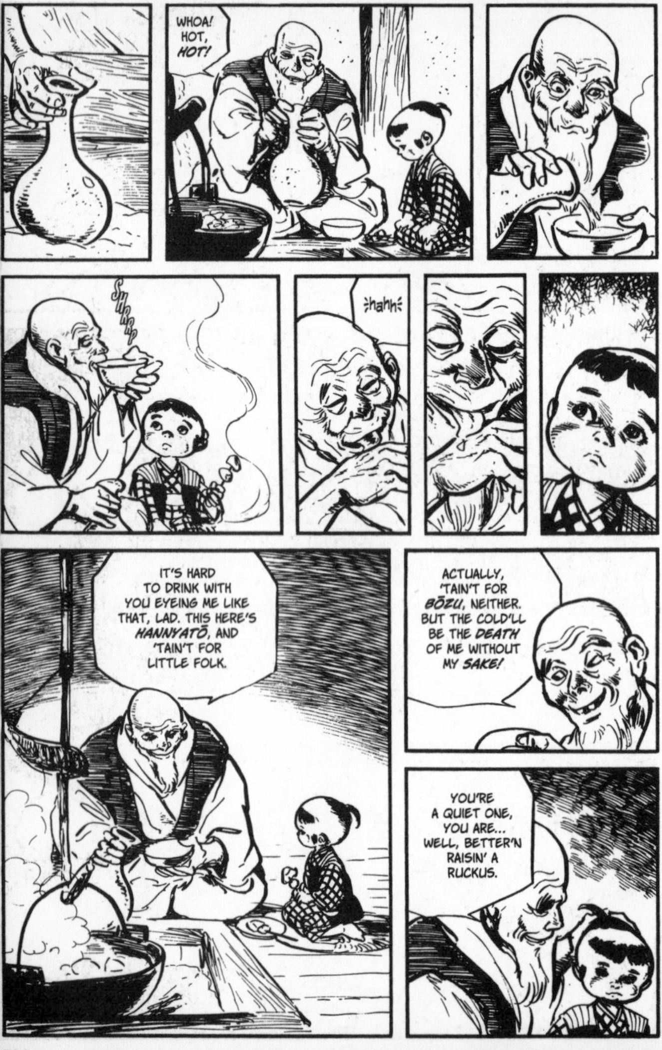
WHOA! HOT, *HOT!*
SHRRP
hahh
IT'S HARD TO DRINK WITH YOU EYEING ME LIKE THAT, LAD. THIS HERE'S *HANNYATŌ*, AND 'TAIN'T FOR LITTLE FOLK.
ACTUALLY, 'TAIN'T FOR *BŌZU*, NEITHER. BUT THE COLD'LL BE THE *DEATH* OF ME WITHOUT MY *SAKE!*
YOU'RE A QUIET ONE, YOU ARE... WELL, BETTER'N RAISIN' A RUCKUS.

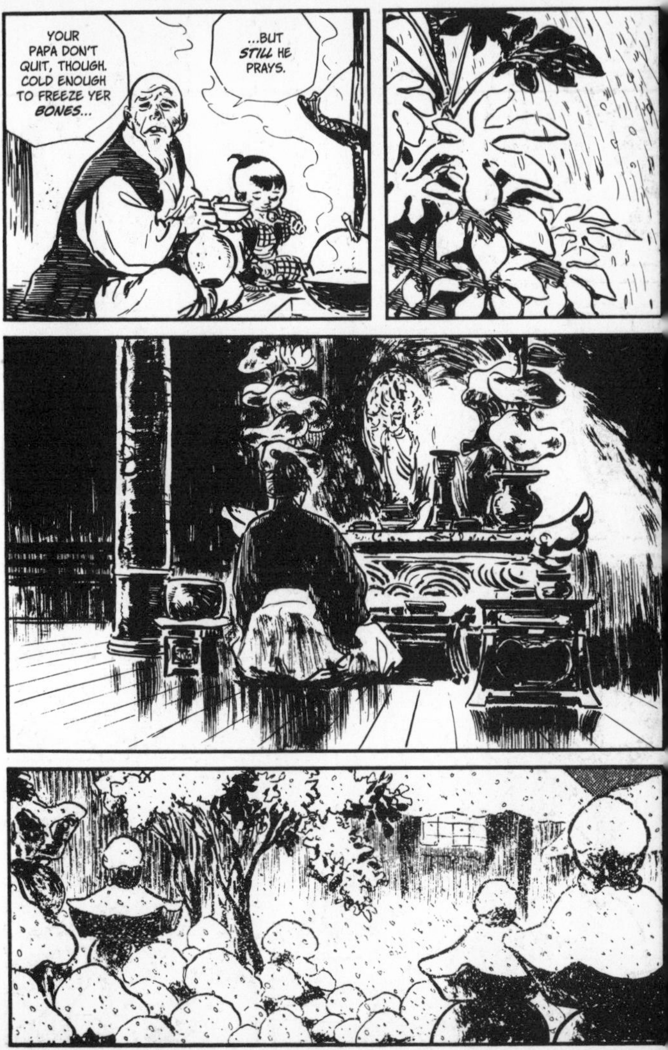
YOUR PAPA DON'T QUIT, THOUGH. COLD ENOUGH TO FREEZE YER BONES...
...BUT STILL HE PRAYS.

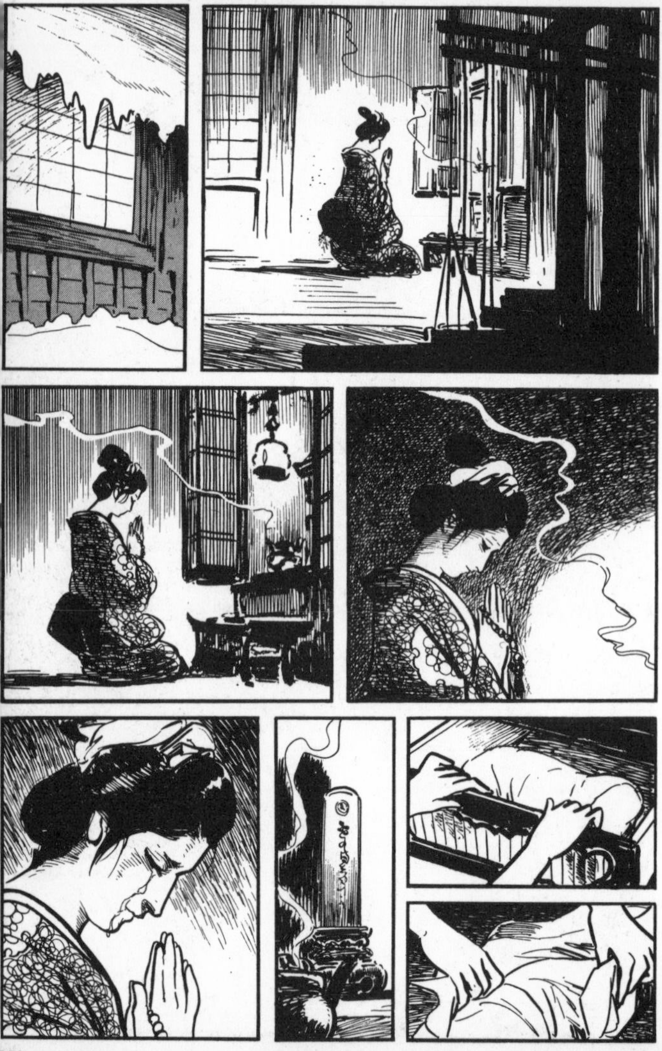

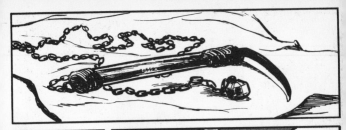

I WILL *NEVER* FORGET, MY LOVE...
. . . .

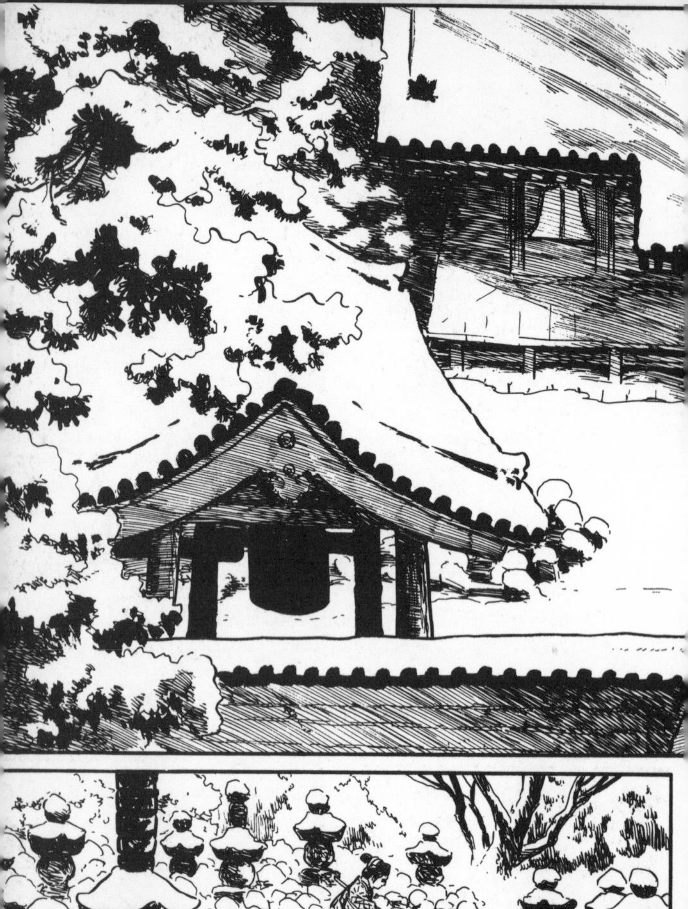
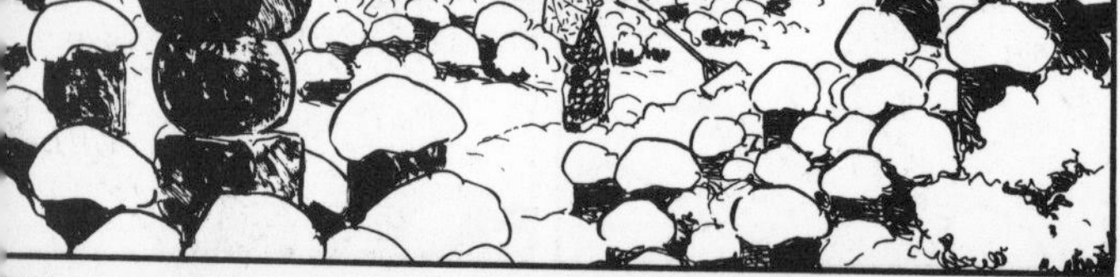

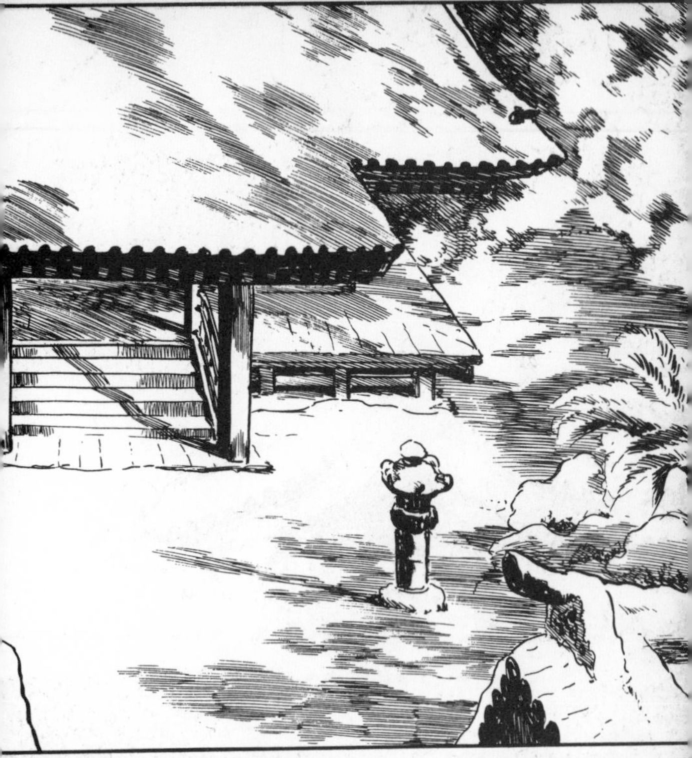
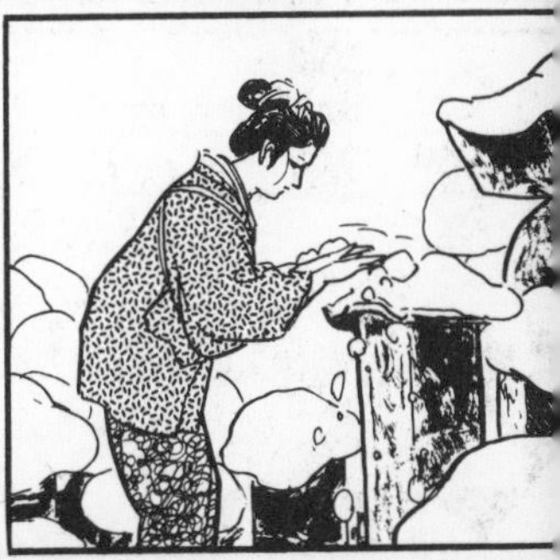
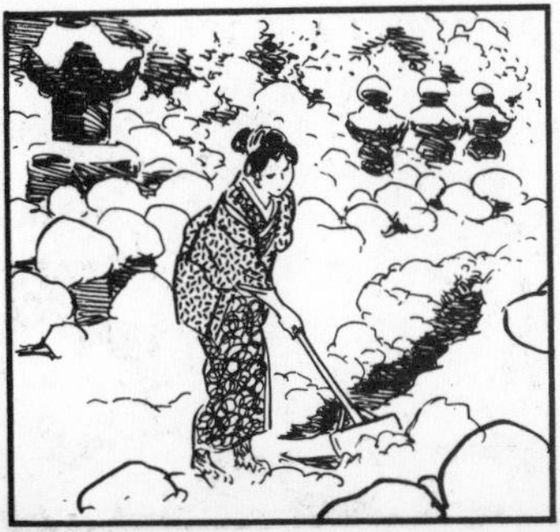

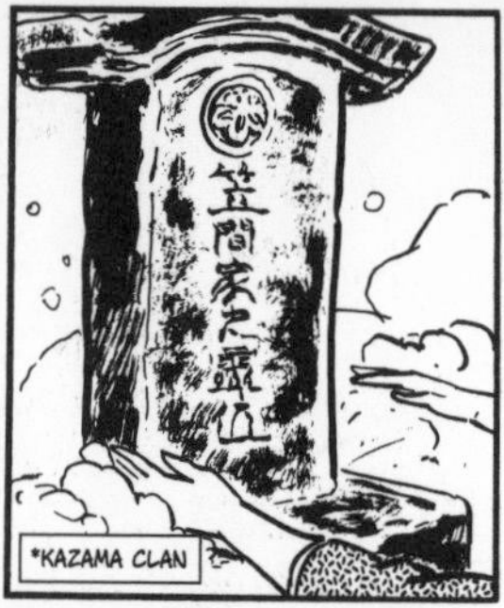
*KAZAMA CLAN

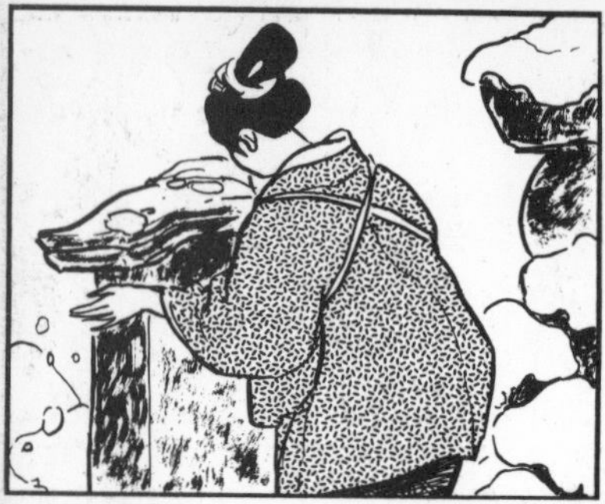

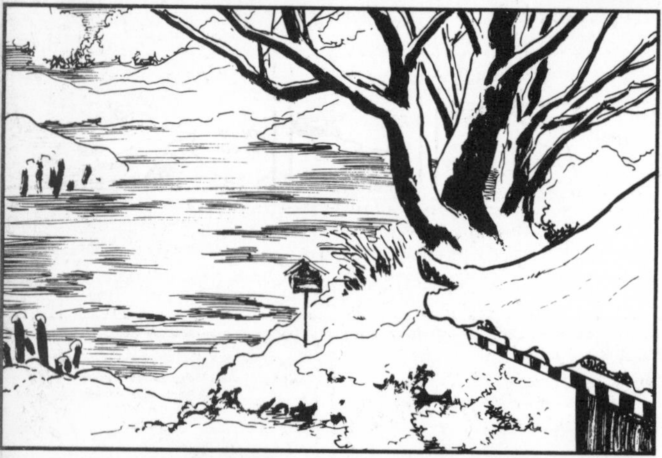

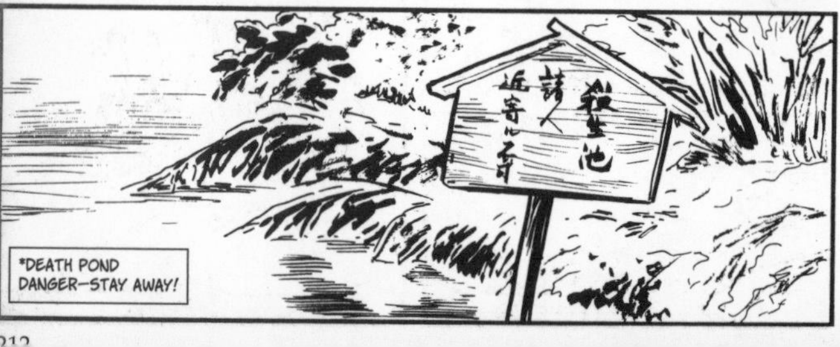
*DEATH POND
DANGER—STAY AWAY!

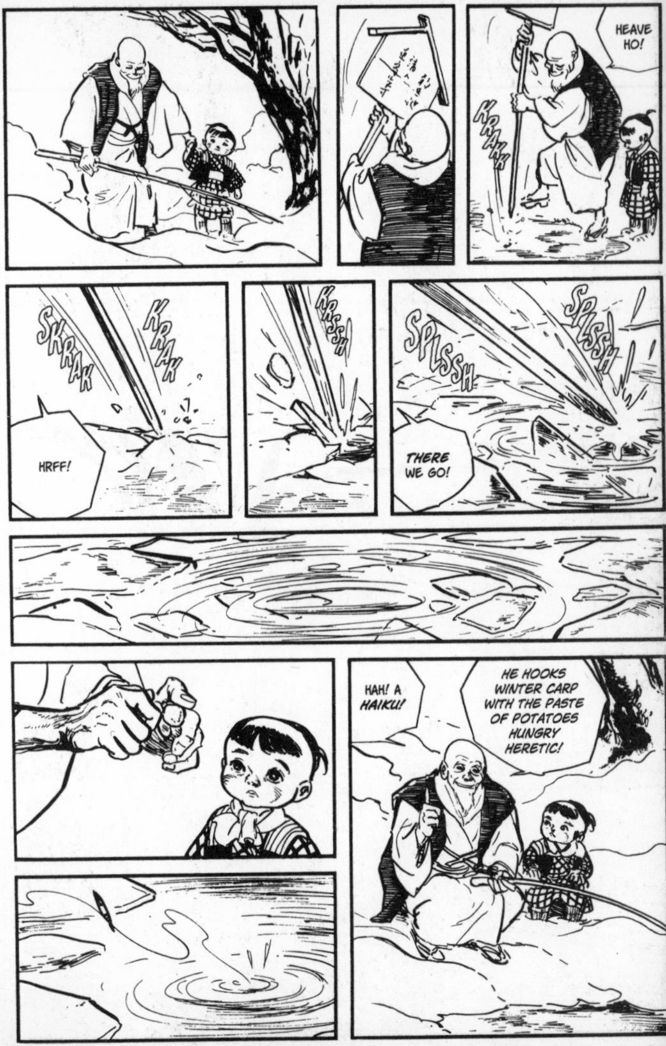
HEAVE HO!
KRAK
SKRAK
KRAK
HRFF!
KRSSH
SPLSSH
SPLSSH
THERE WE GO!
HAH! A HAIKU!
HE HOOKS WINTER CARP WITH THE PASTE OF POTATOES HUNGRY HERETIC!

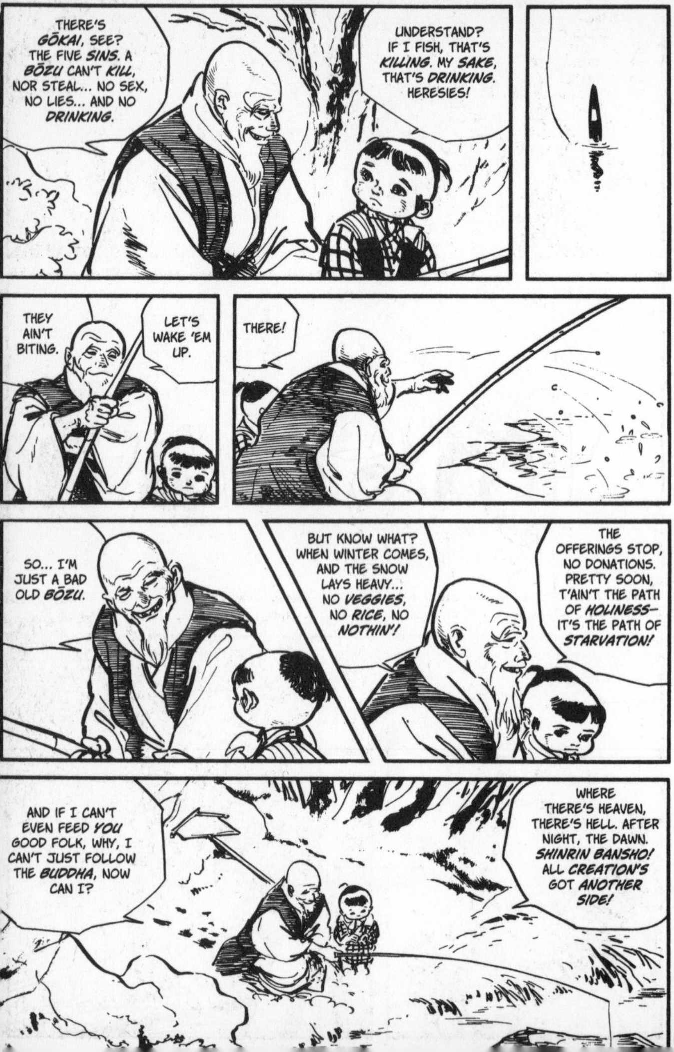
THERE'S GŌKAI, SEE? THE FIVE SINS. A BŌZU CAN'T KILL, NOR STEAL... NO SEX, NO LIES... AND NO DRINKING.
UNDERSTAND? IF I FISH, THAT'S KILLING. MY SAKE, THAT'S DRINKING. HERESIES!
THEY AIN'T BITING.
LET'S WAKE 'EM UP.
THERE!
SO... I'M JUST A BAD OLD BŌZU.
BUT KNOW WHAT? WHEN WINTER COMES, AND THE SNOW LAYS HEAVY... NO VEGGIES, NO RICE, NO NOTHIN'!
THE OFFERINGS STOP, NO DONATIONS. PRETTY SOON, T'AIN'T THE PATH OF HOLINESS— IT'S THE PATH OF STARVATION!
AND IF I CAN'T EVEN FEED YOU GOOD FOLK, WHY, I CAN'T JUST FOLLOW THE BUDDHA, NOW CAN I?
WHERE THERE'S HEAVEN, THERE'S HELL. AFTER NIGHT, THE DAWN. SHINRIN BANSHO! ALL CREATION'S GOT ANOTHER SIDE!

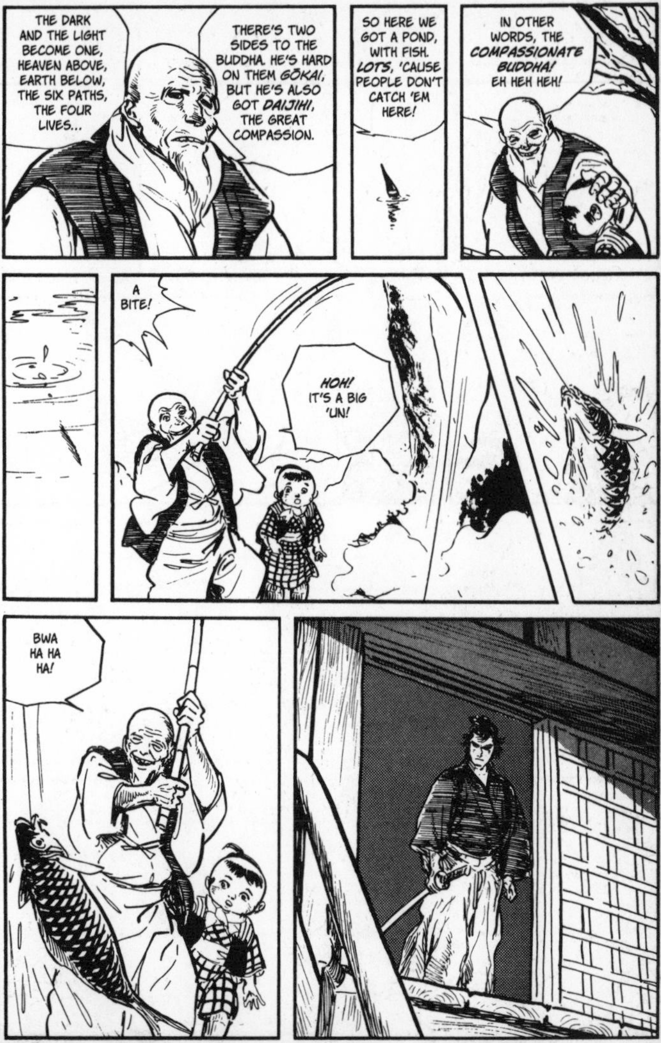
THE DARK AND THE LIGHT BECOME ONE, HEAVEN ABOVE, EARTH BELOW, THE SIX PATHS, THE FOUR LIVES...
THERE'S TWO SIDES TO THE BUDDHA. HE'S HARD ON THEM *GŌKAI*, BUT HE'S ALSO GOT *DAIJIHI*, THE GREAT COMPASSION.
SO HERE WE GOT A POND, WITH FISH. *LOTS*, 'CAUSE PEOPLE DON'T CATCH 'EM HERE!
IN OTHER WORDS, THE *COMPASSIONATE BUDDHA!* EH HEH HEH!
A BITE!
HOH! IT'S A BIG 'UN!
BWA HA HA HA!

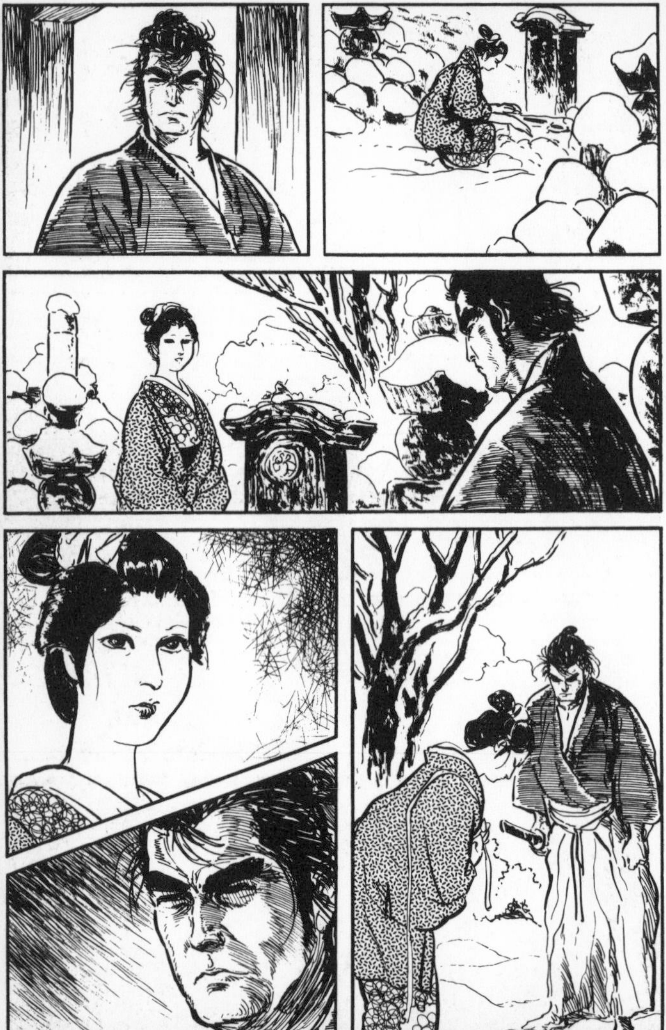

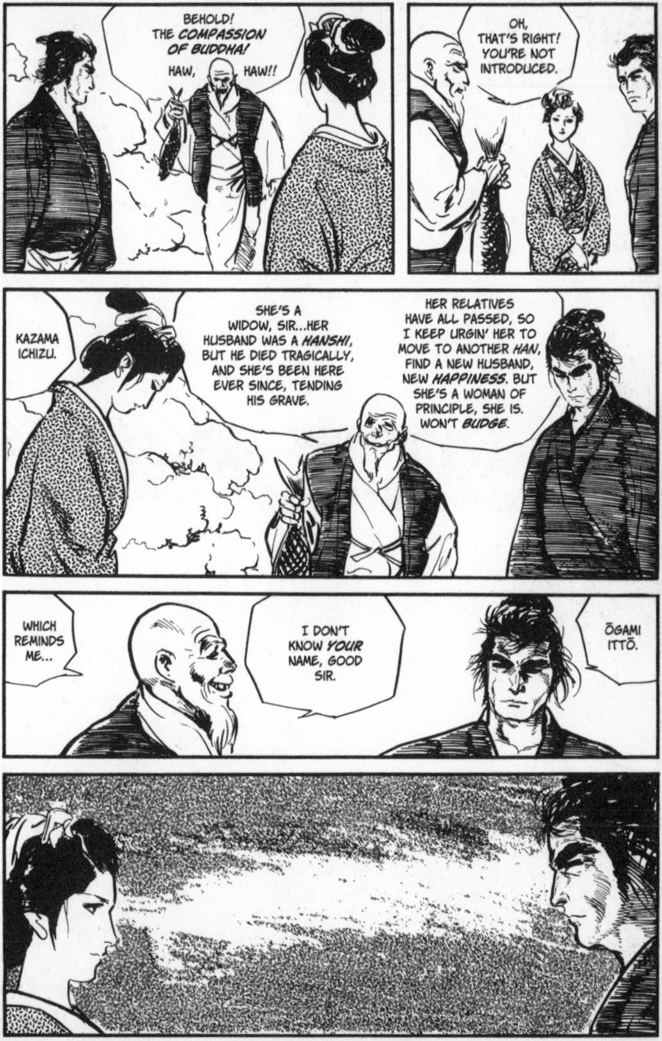
BEHOLD! THE COMPASSION OF BUDDHA!
HAW, HAW!!
OH, THAT'S RIGHT! YOU'RE NOT INTRODUCED.
KAZAMA ICHIZU.
SHE'S A WIDOW, SIR...HER HUSBAND WAS A HANSHI, BUT HE DIED TRAGICALLY, AND SHE'S BEEN HERE EVER SINCE, TENDING HIS GRAVE.
HER RELATIVES HAVE ALL PASSED, SO I KEEP URGIN' HER TO MOVE TO ANOTHER HAN, FIND A NEW HUSBAND, NEW HAPPINESS. BUT SHE'S A WOMAN OF PRINCIPLE, SHE IS. WON'T BUDGE.
WHICH REMINDS ME...
I DON'T KNOW YOUR NAME, GOOD SIR.
ŌGAMI ITTŌ.

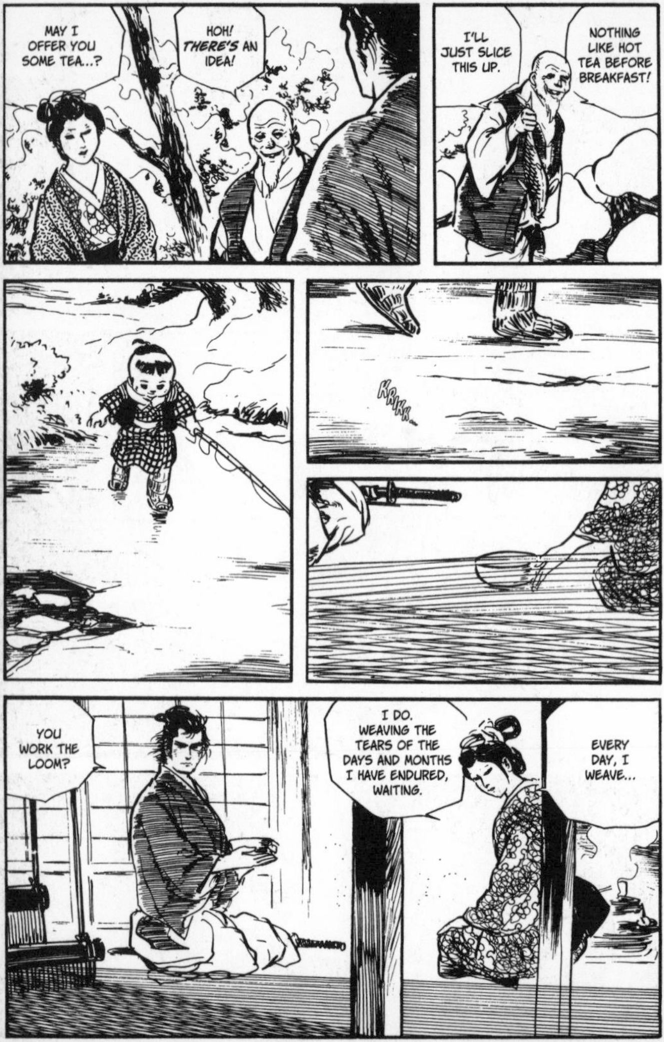
MAY I OFFER YOU SOME TEA...?
HOH! *THERE'S* AN IDEA!
I'LL JUST SLICE THIS UP.
NOTHING LIKE HOT TEA BEFORE BREAKFAST!
KRIKK...
YOU WORK THE LOOM?
I DO. WEAVING THE TEARS OF THE DAYS AND MONTHS I HAVE ENDURED, WAITING.
EVERY DAY, I WEAVE...

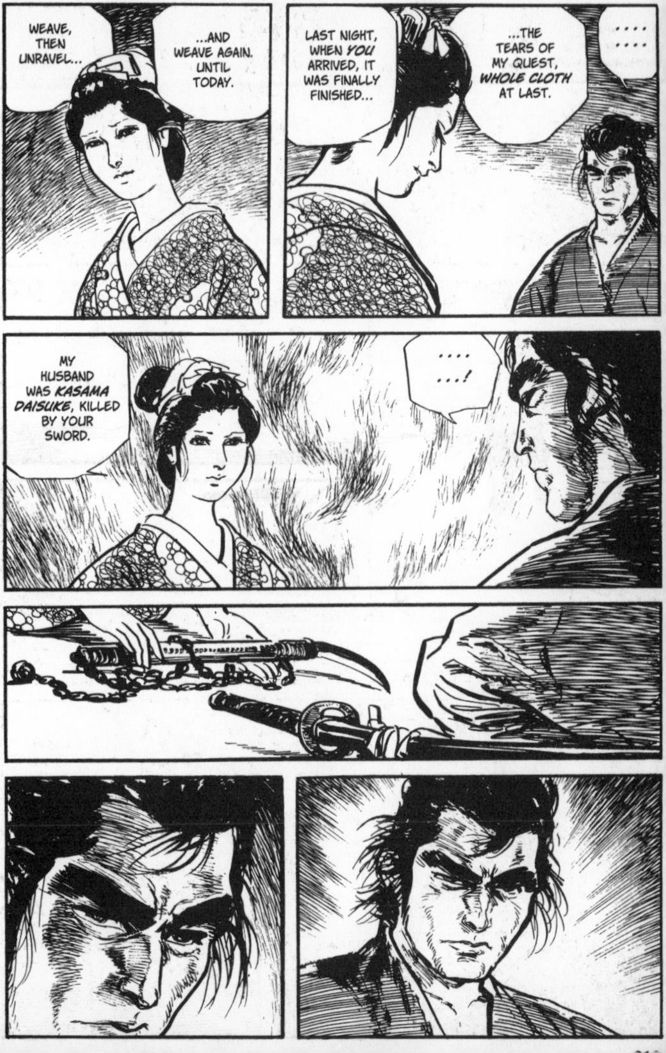
WEAVE, THEN UNRAVEL...
...AND WEAVE AGAIN. UNTIL TODAY.
LAST NIGHT, WHEN YOU ARRIVED, IT WAS FINALLY FINISHED...
...THE TEARS OF MY QUEST, WHOLE CLOTH AT LAST.
....
MY HUSBAND WAS KASAMA DAISUKE, KILLED BY YOUR SWORD.
....!

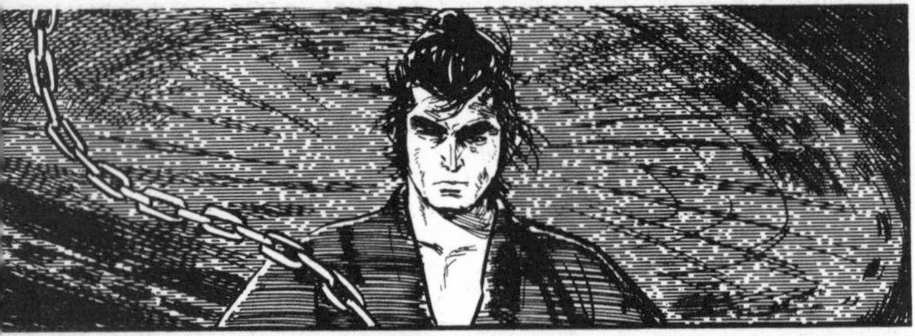
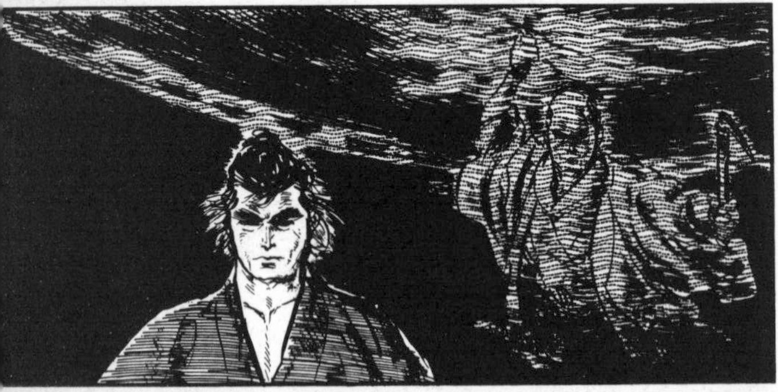
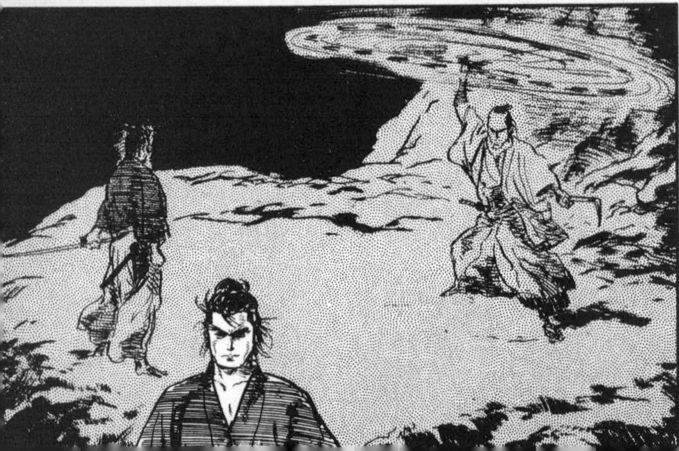

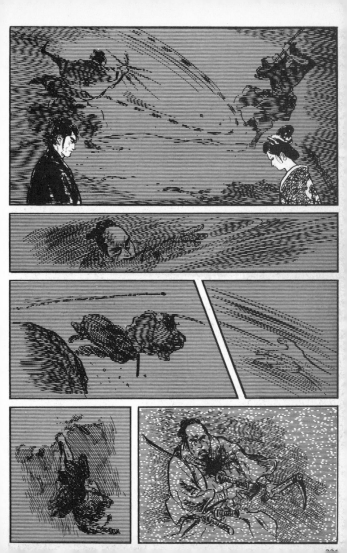

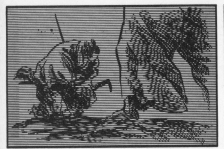

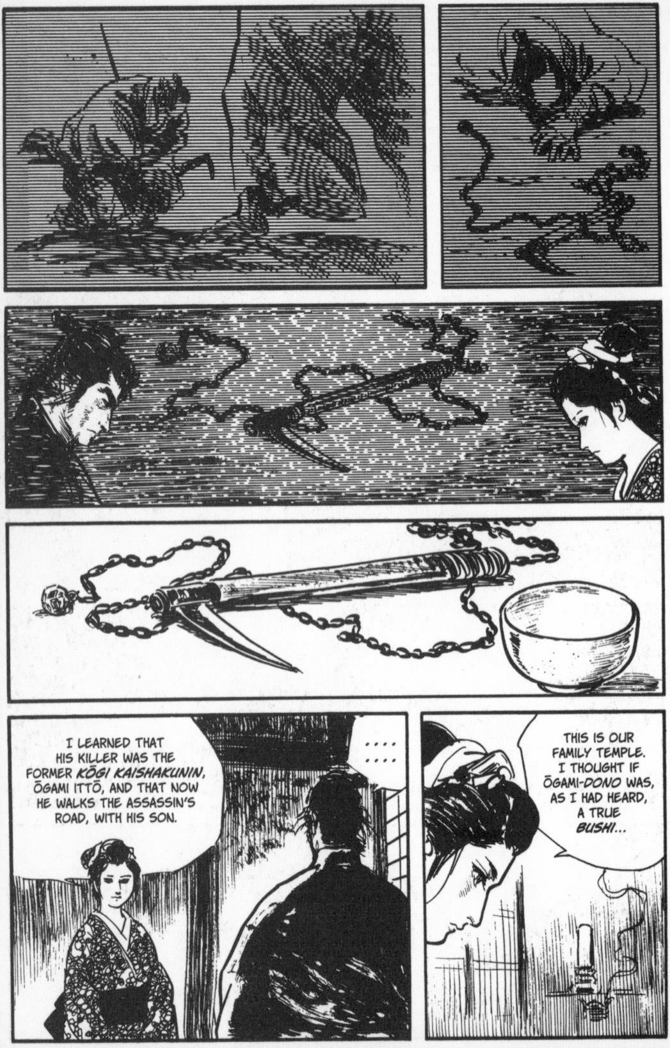
I LEARNED THAT HIS KILLER WAS THE FORMER *KŌGI KAISHAKUNIN*, ŌGAMI ITTŌ, AND THAT NOW HE WALKS THE ASSASSIN'S ROAD, WITH HIS SON.
....
....
THIS IS OUR FAMILY TEMPLE. I THOUGHT IF ŌGAMI-*DONO* WAS, AS I HAD HEARD, A TRUE *BUSHI*...

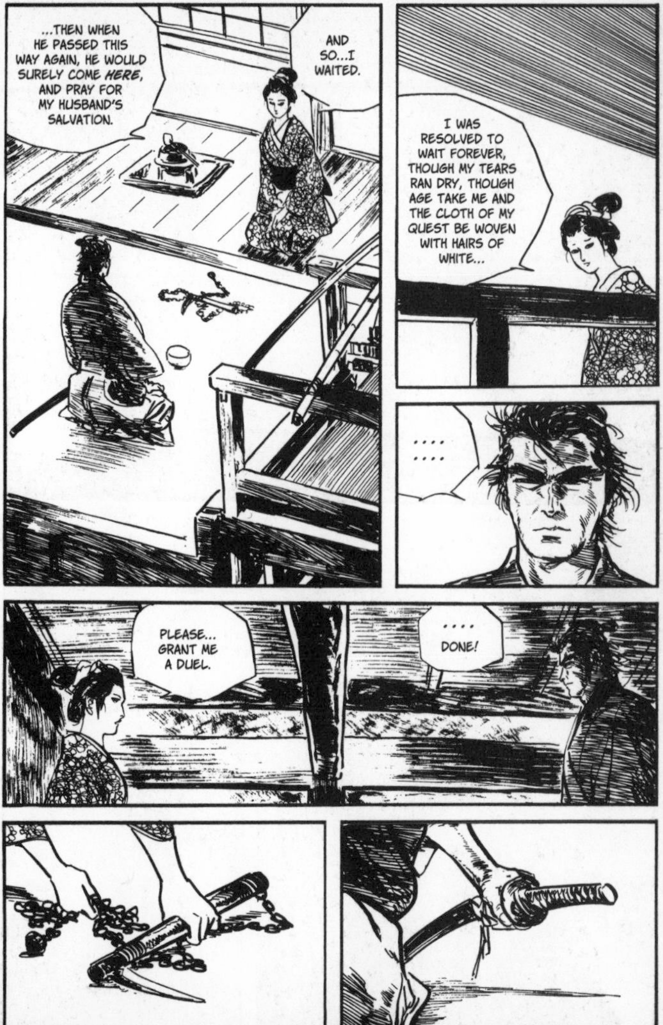

...THEN WHEN HE PASSED THIS WAY AGAIN, HE WOULD SURELY COME *HERE*, AND PRAY FOR MY HUSBAND'S SALVATION.
AND SO...I WAITED.
I WAS RESOLVED TO WAIT FOREVER, THOUGH MY TEARS RAN DRY, THOUGH AGE TAKE ME AND THE CLOTH OF MY QUEST BE WOVEN WITH HAIRS OF WHITE...
....
PLEASE... GRANT ME A DUEL.
.... DONE!

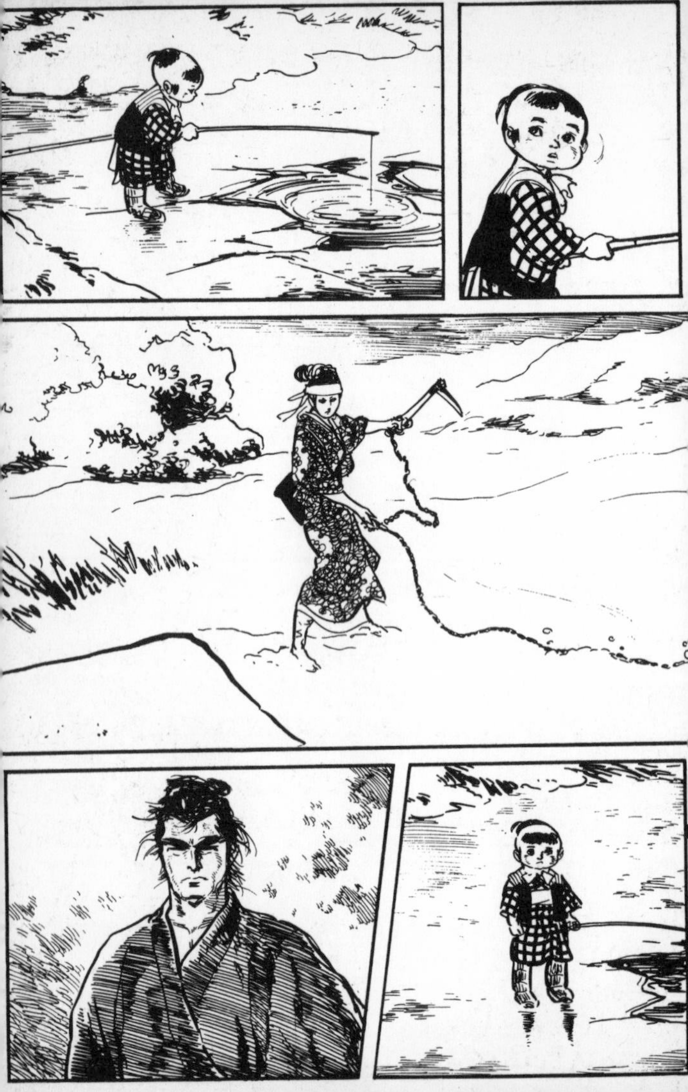

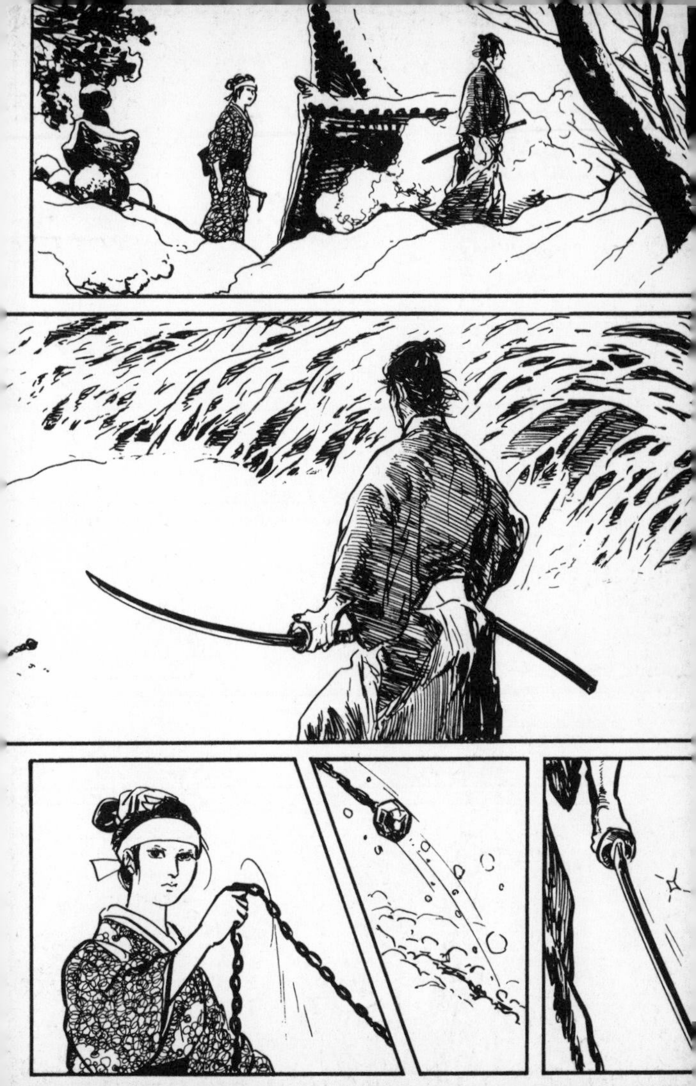

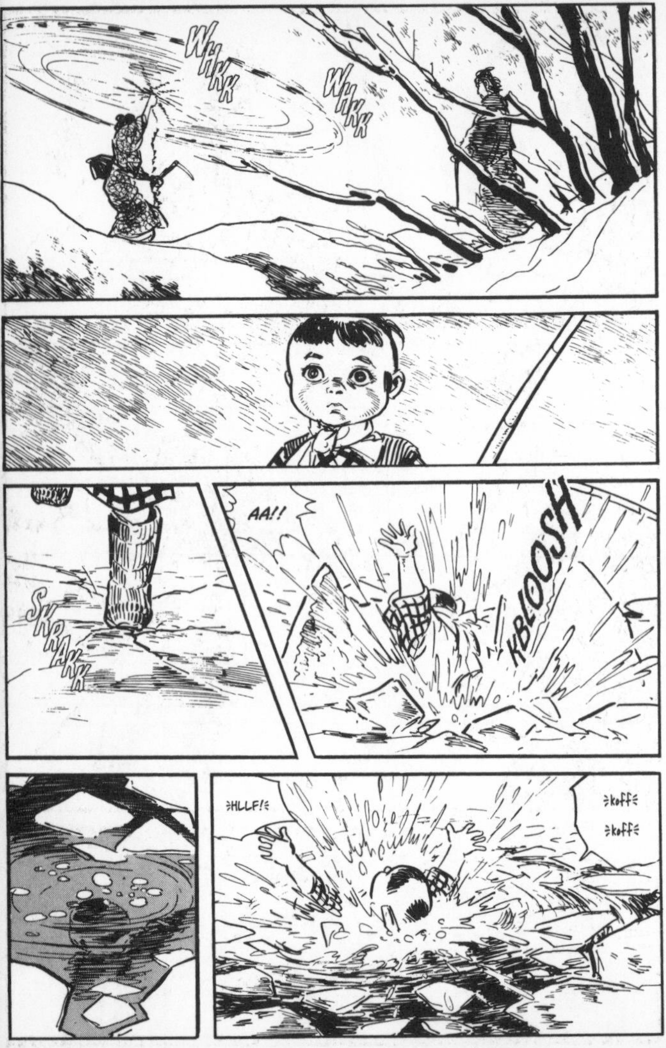
WHKK
WHKK
AA!!
KBLOOSH
SKRAKK
koff
koff
HLLF!

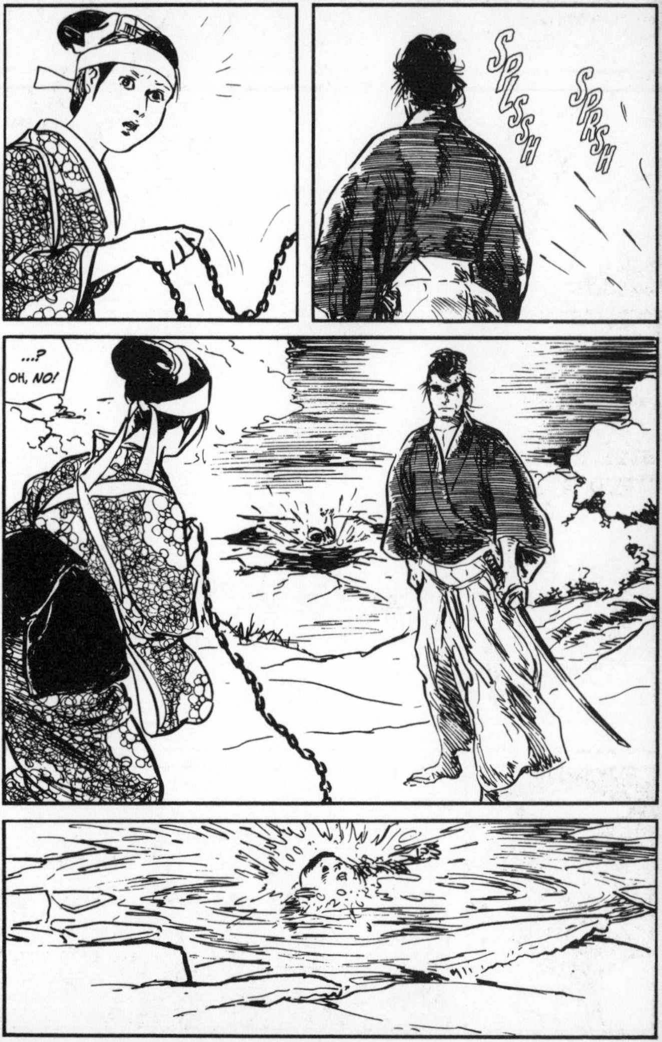
SPLSSH
SPRSH
...?
OH, NO!

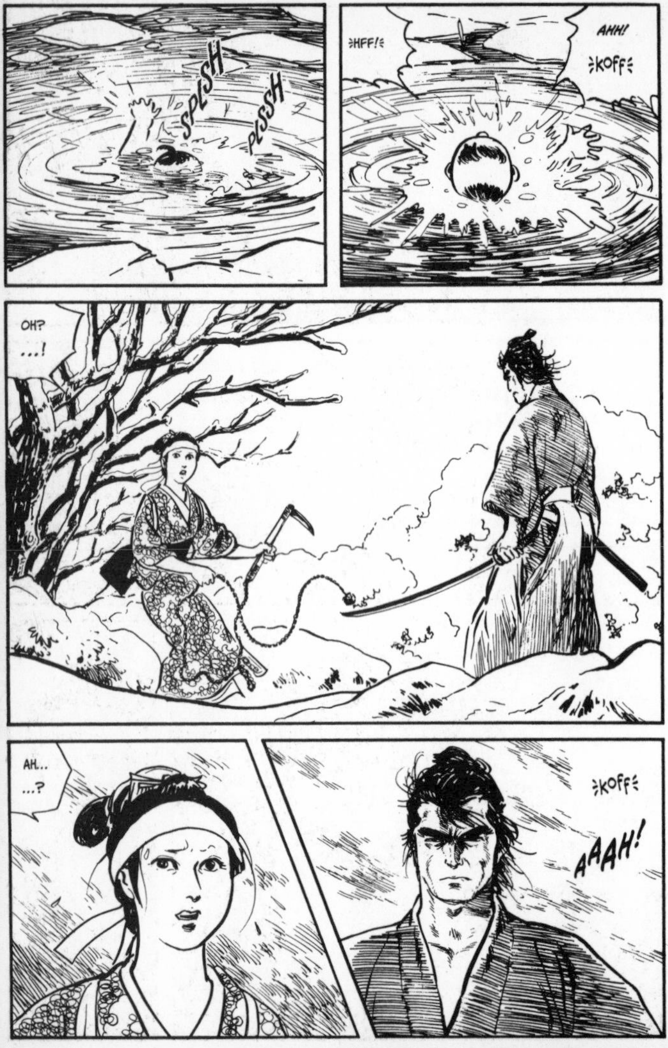
AHH!
KOFF
HFF!
SPLSH
PLSSH
OH?
...!
KOFF
AAAH!
AH...
...?

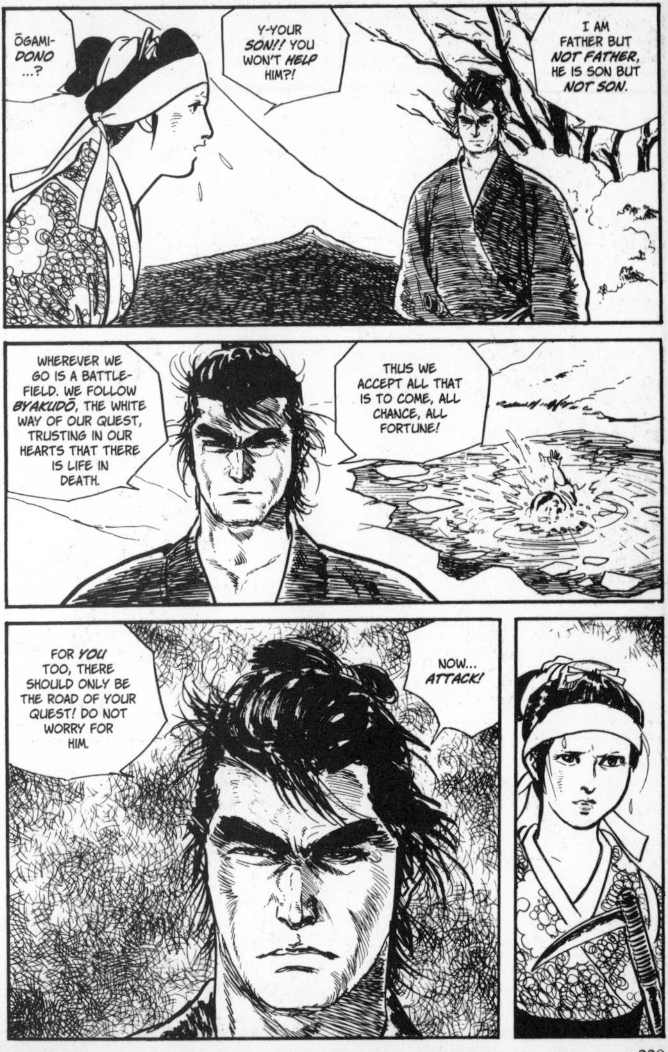
ŌGAMI-DONO ...?
Y-YOUR SON!! YOU WON'T HELP HIM?!
I AM FATHER BUT NOT FATHER, HE IS SON BUT NOT SON.
WHEREVER WE GO IS A BATTLE-FIELD. WE FOLLOW BYAKUDŌ, THE WHITE WAY OF OUR QUEST, TRUSTING IN OUR HEARTS THAT THERE IS LIFE IN DEATH.
THUS WE ACCEPT ALL THAT IS TO COME, ALL CHANCE, ALL FORTUNE!
FOR YOU TOO, THERE SHOULD ONLY BE THE ROAD OF YOUR QUEST! DO NOT WORRY FOR HIM.
NOW... ATTACK!

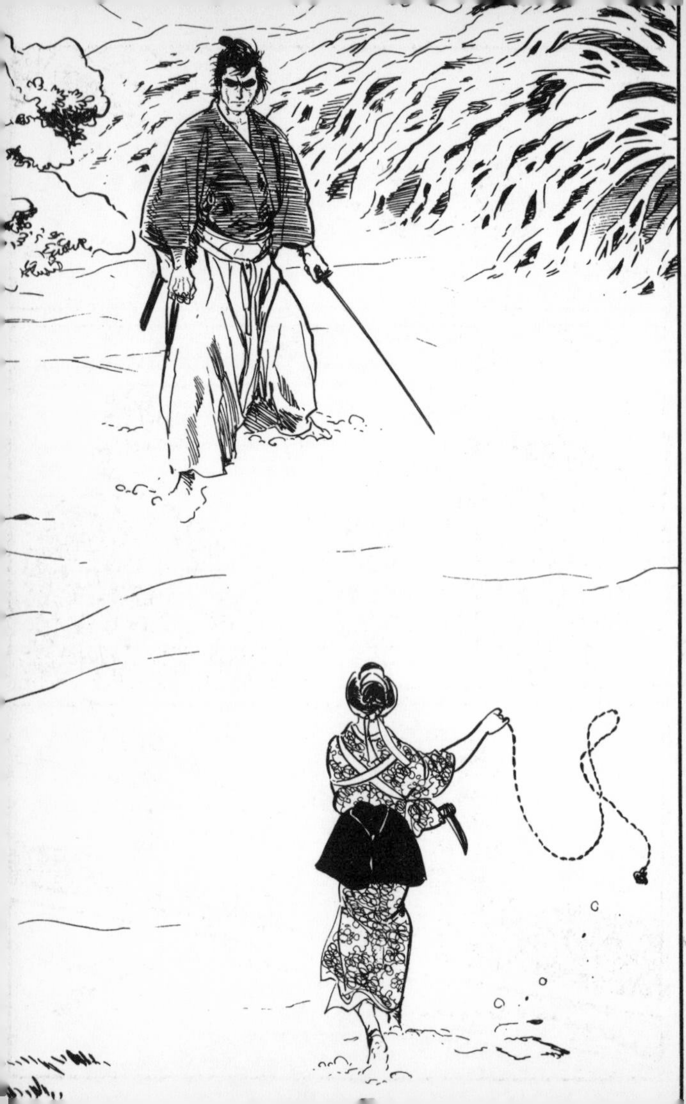

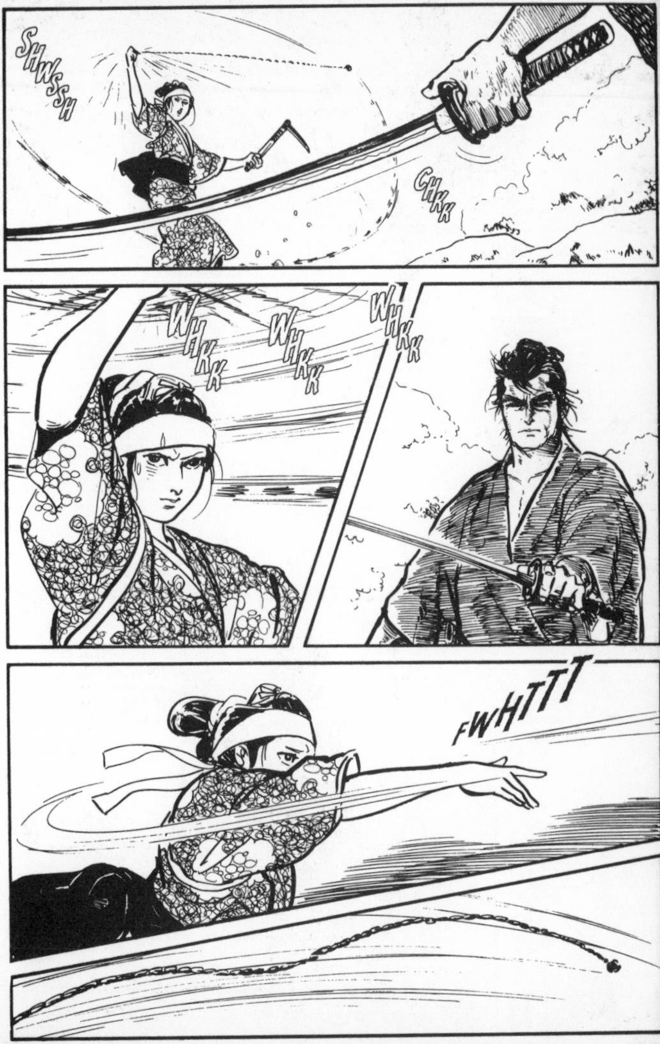
SHWSSH
CHKK
WHKK
WHKK
WHKK
FWHTTT

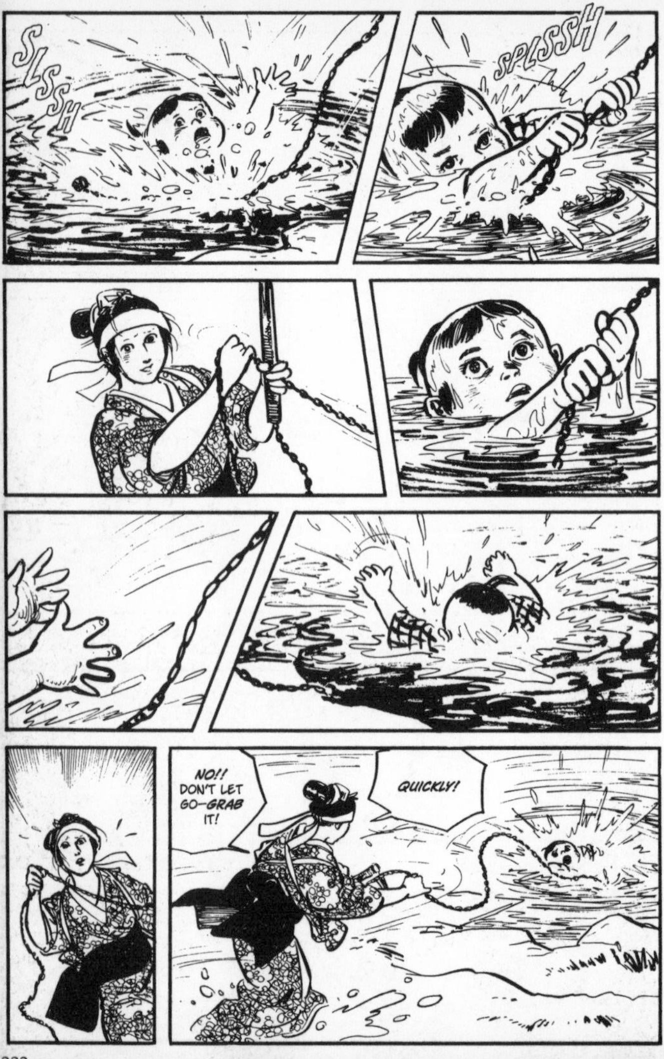
SLSSH
SPLSSSH
NO!! DON'T LET GO—GRAB IT!
QUICKLY!

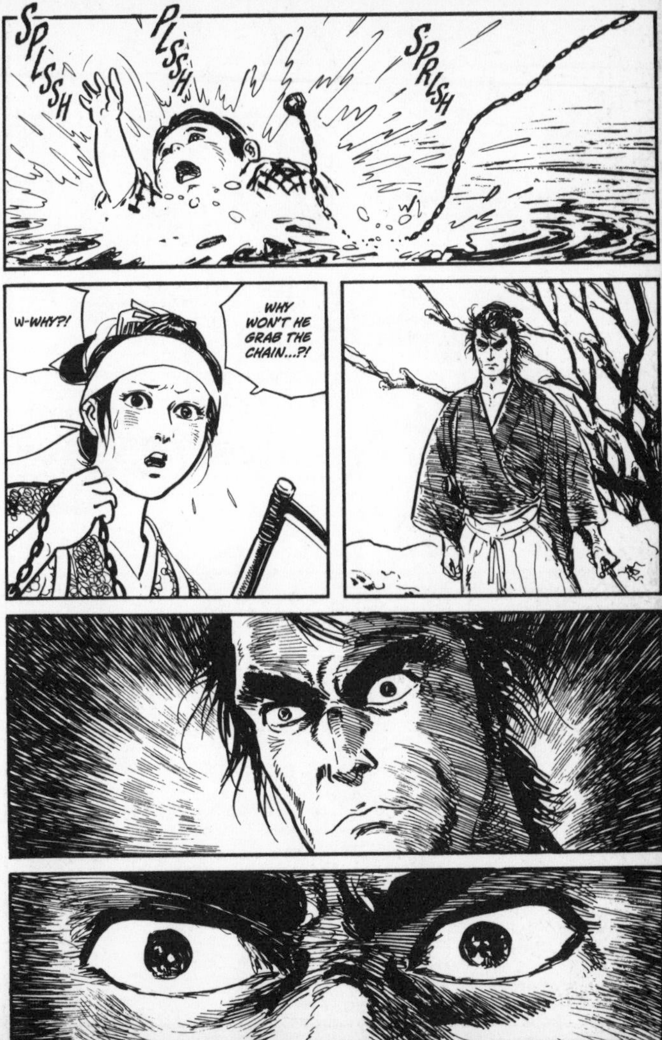
SPLSSH
PLSSH
SPRLSH
WHY WON'T HE GRAB THE CHAIN...?!
W-WHY?!

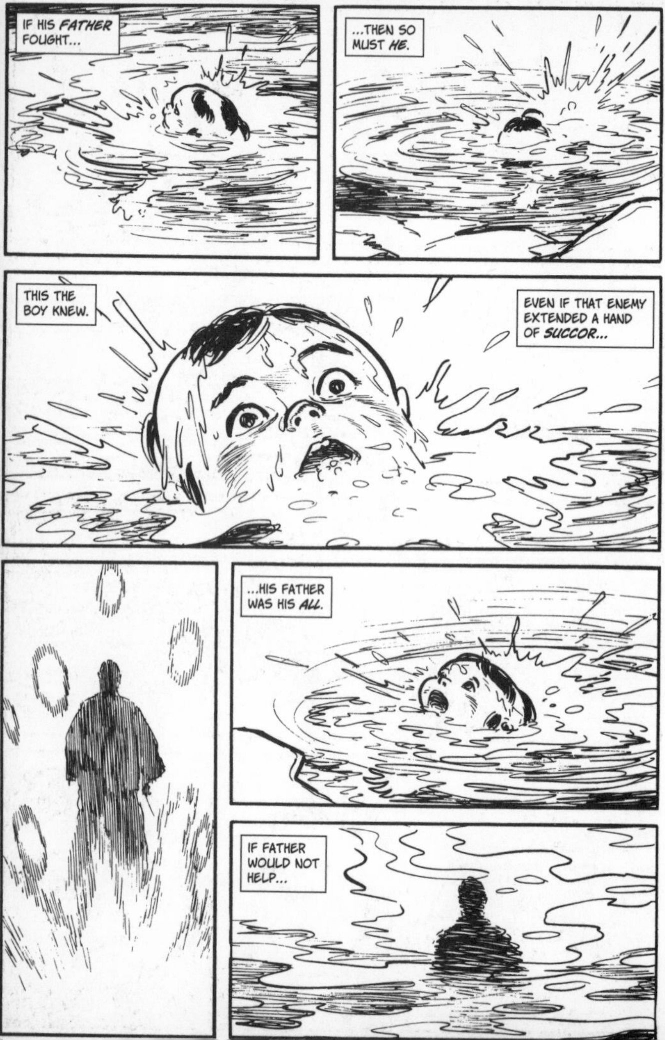
IF HIS FATHER FOUGHT...
...THEN SO MUST HE.
THIS THE BOY KNEW.
EVEN IF THAT ENEMY EXTENDED A HAND OF SUCCOR...
...HIS FATHER WAS HIS ALL.
IF FATHER WOULD NOT HELP...

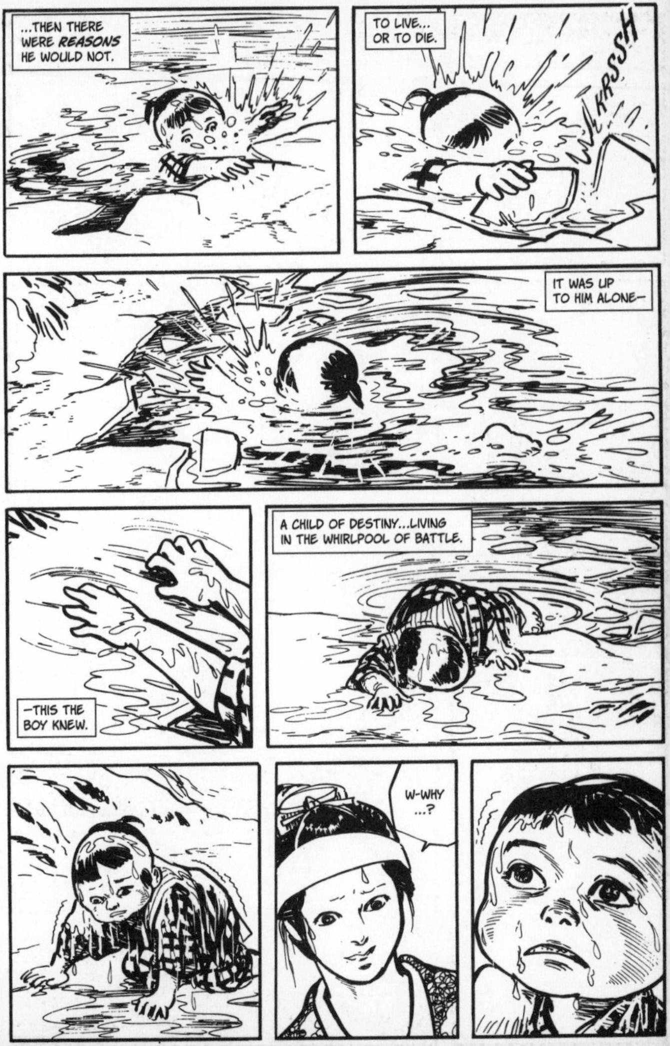
...THEN THERE WERE REASONS HE WOULD NOT.
TO LIVE... OR TO DIE.
KRSSH
IT WAS UP TO HIM ALONE—
—THIS THE BOY KNEW.
A CHILD OF DESTINY...LIVING IN THE WHIRLPOOL OF BATTLE.
W-WHY ...?

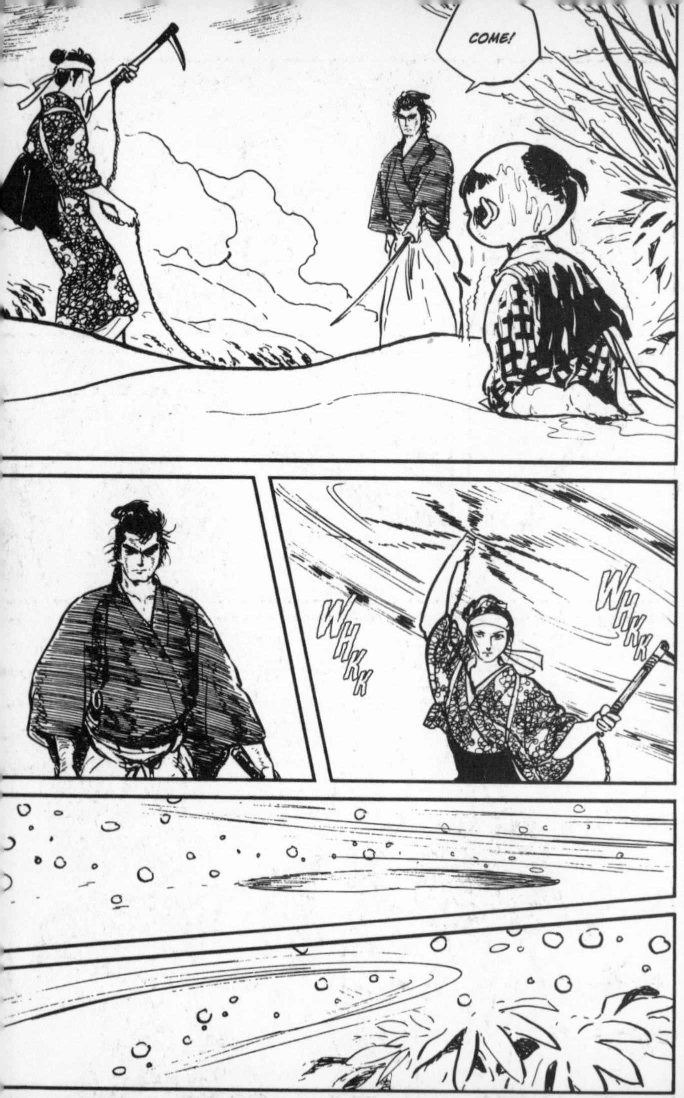
COME!
WHKK
WHKK

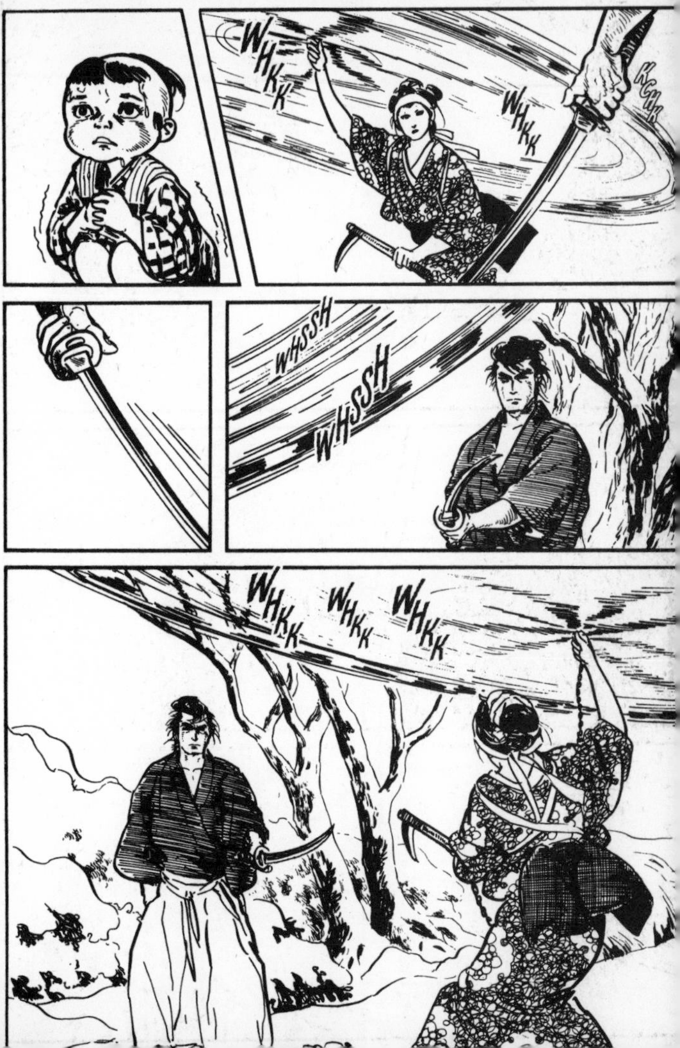
WHKK
WHKK
KCHK
WHSSH
WHSSH
WHKK
WHKK
WHKK

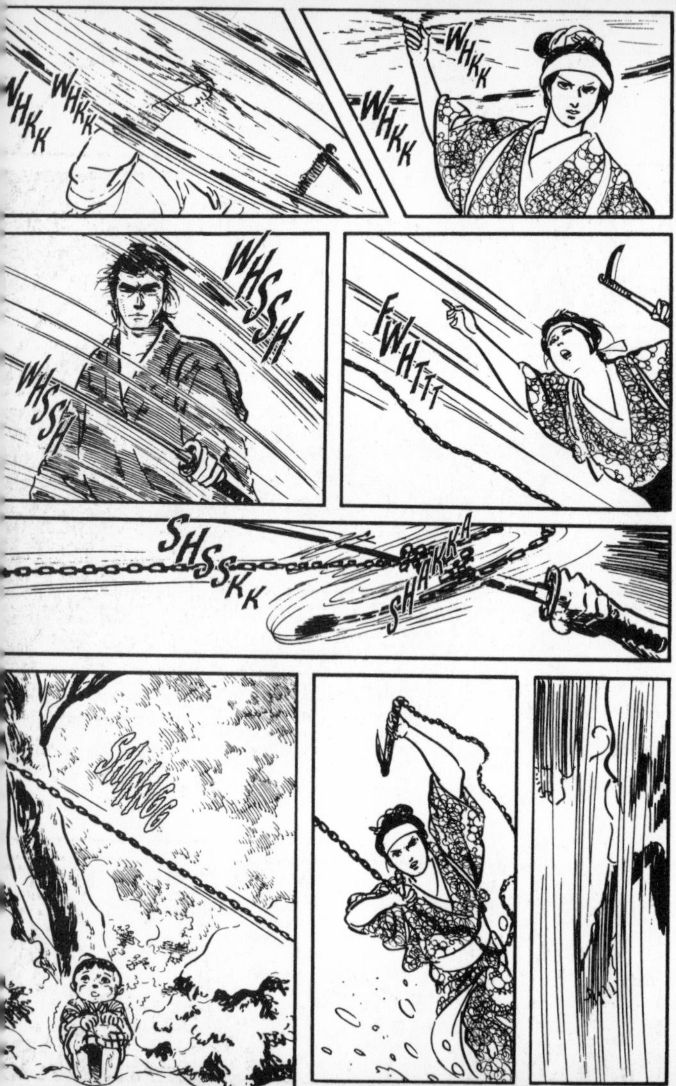
WHKK
WHKK
WHKK
WHKK
FWHTTT
WHSSH
WHSSH
SHAKKA
SHSSKK

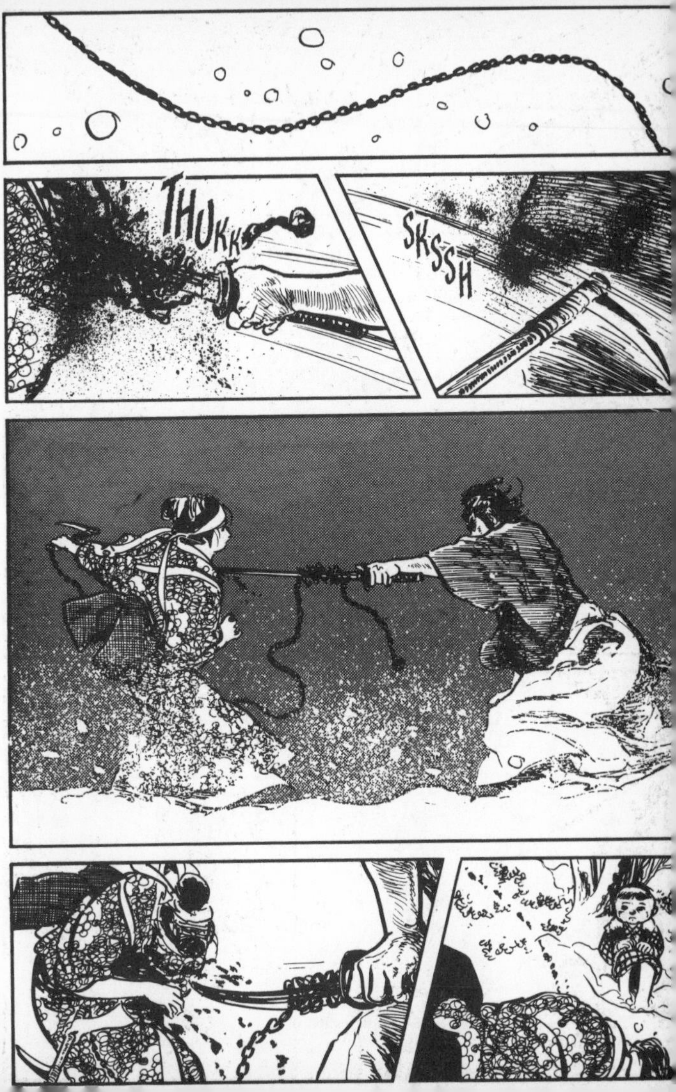
SKSSH
THUKK

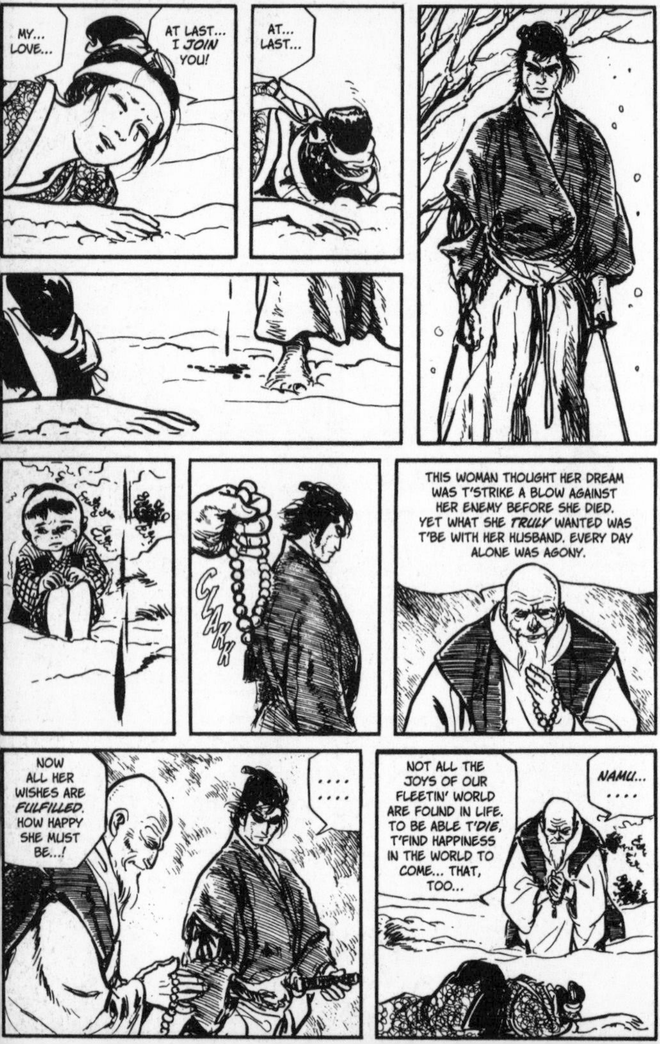
MY... LOVE...
AT LAST... I *JOIN* YOU!
AT... LAST...
CLAKK
THIS WOMAN THOUGHT HER DREAM WAS T'STRIKE A BLOW AGAINST HER ENEMY BEFORE SHE DIED. YET WHAT SHE *TRULY* WANTED WAS T'BE WITH HER HUSBAND. EVERY DAY ALONE WAS AGONY.
NOW ALL HER WISHES ARE *FULFILLED*. HOW HAPPY SHE MUST BE...!
....
NOT ALL THE JOYS OF OUR FLEETIN' WORLD ARE FOUND IN LIFE. TO BE ABLE T'*DIE*, T'FIND HAPPINESS IN THE WORLD TO COME... THAT, TOO...
NAMU... ....

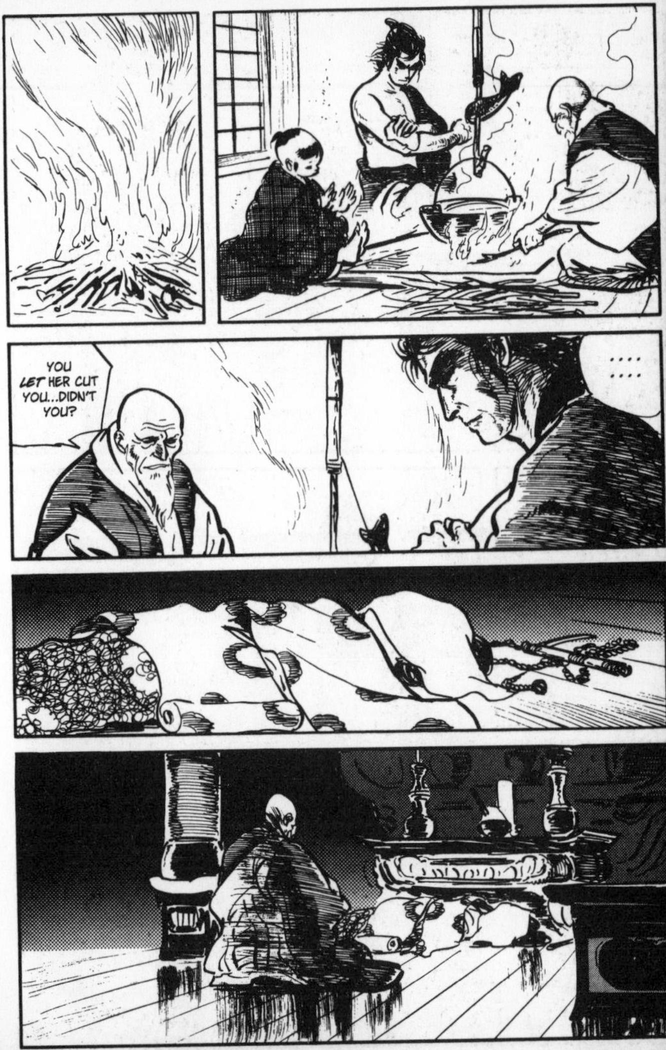
....
....
YOU LET HER CUT YOU...DIDN'T YOU?

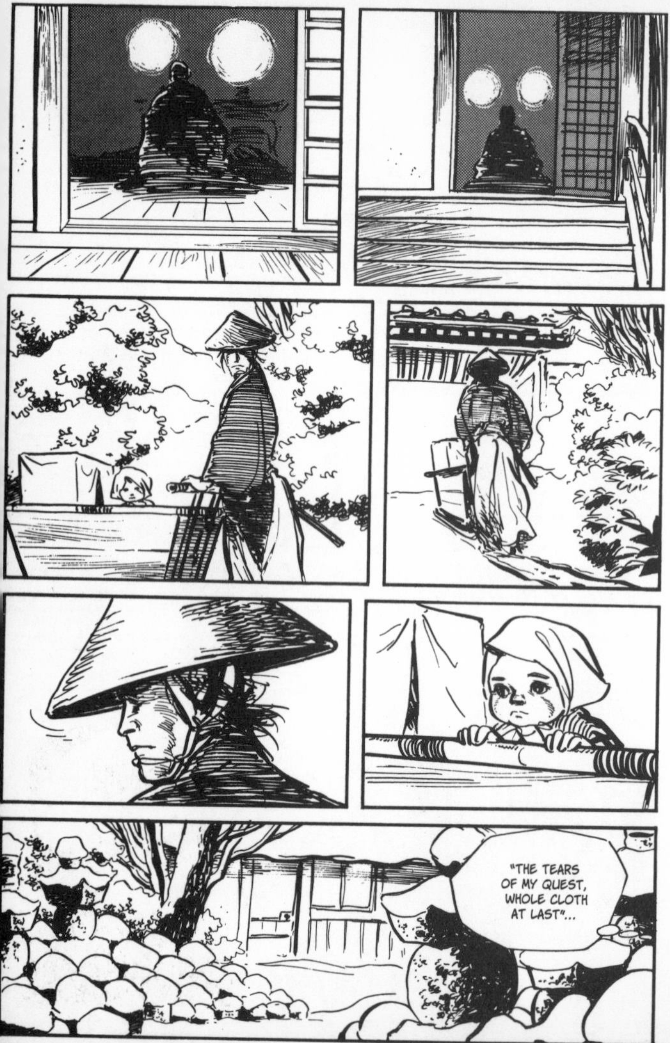
"THE TEARS OF MY QUEST, WHOLE CLOTH AT LAST"...

the forty-fourth

Beku-no-Ji

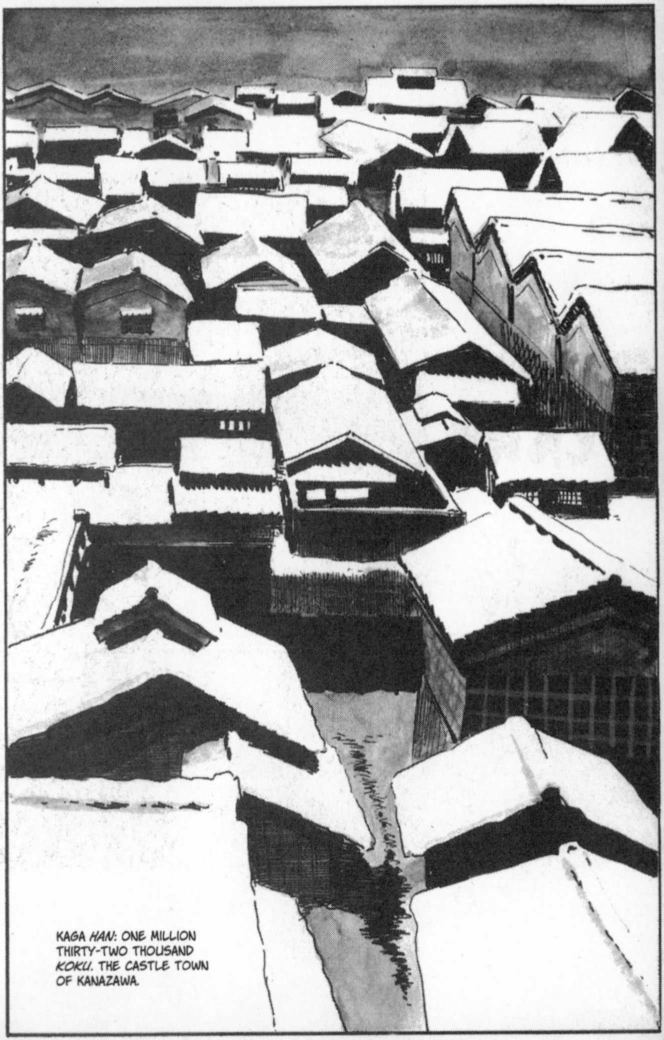
KAGA *HAN*: ONE MILLION THIRTY-TWO THOUSAND *KOKU*. THE CASTLE TOWN OF KANAZAWA.

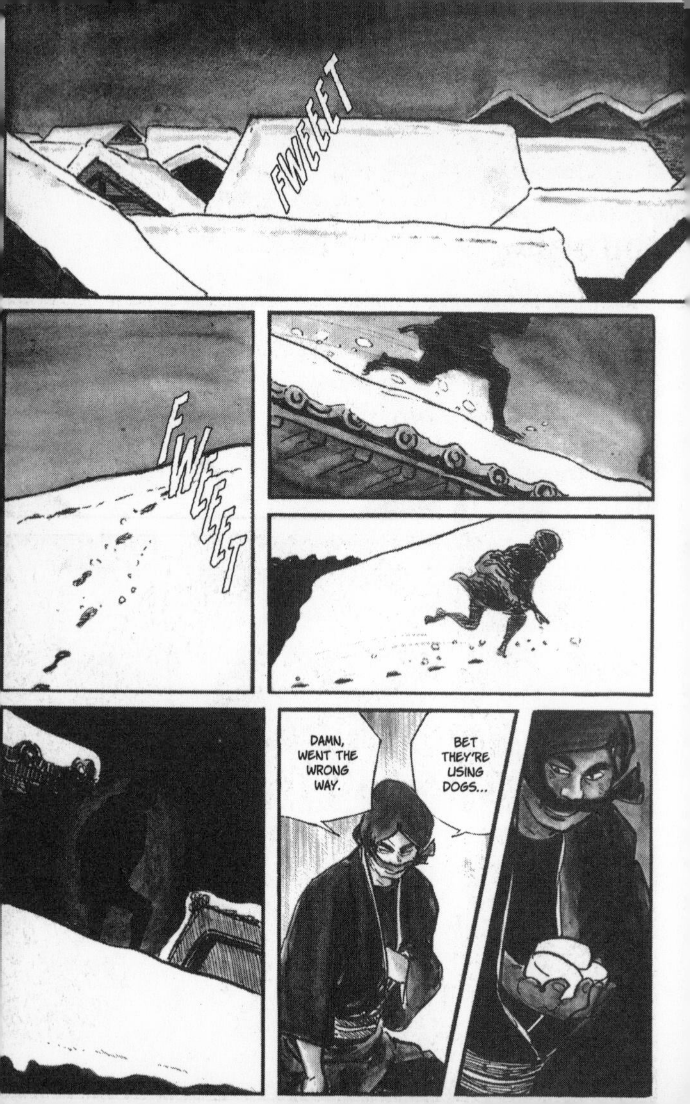
FWEEET
FWEEET
BET THEY'RE USING DOGS...
DAMN, WENT THE WRONG WAY.

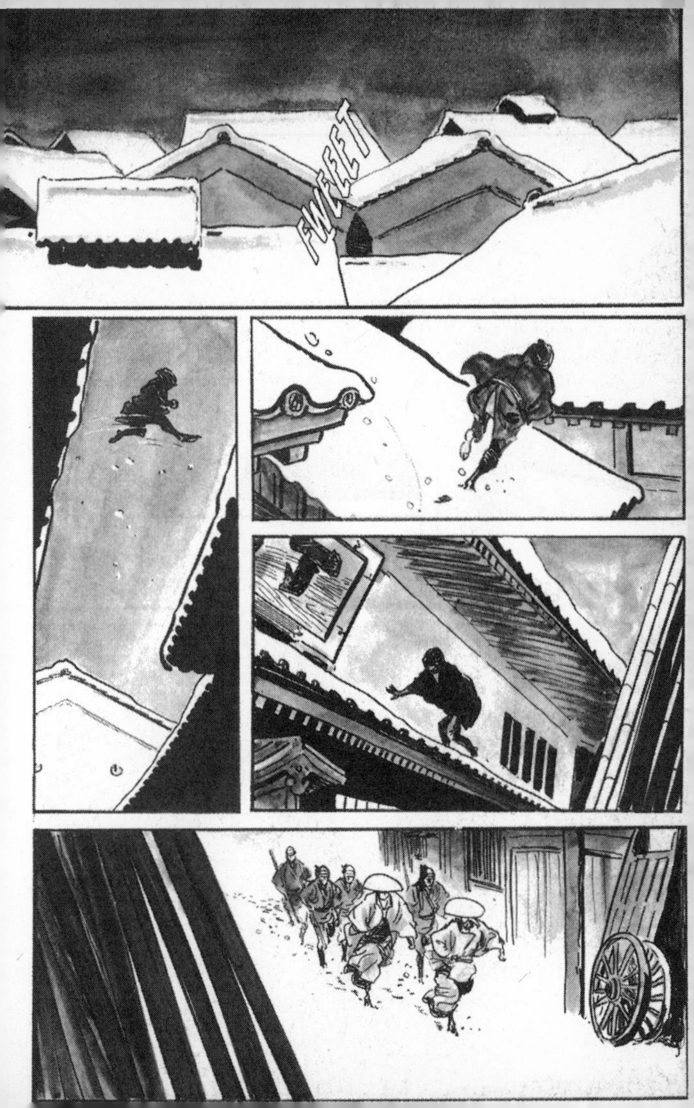
FWEET

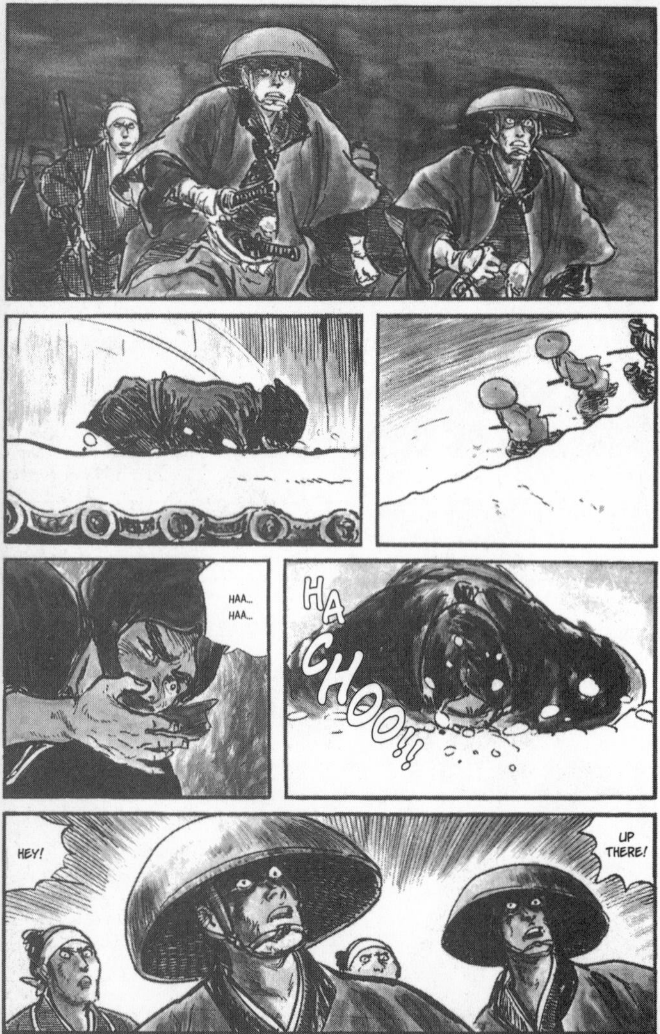
HA CHOO!!
HAA..
HAA..
UP THERE!
HEY!

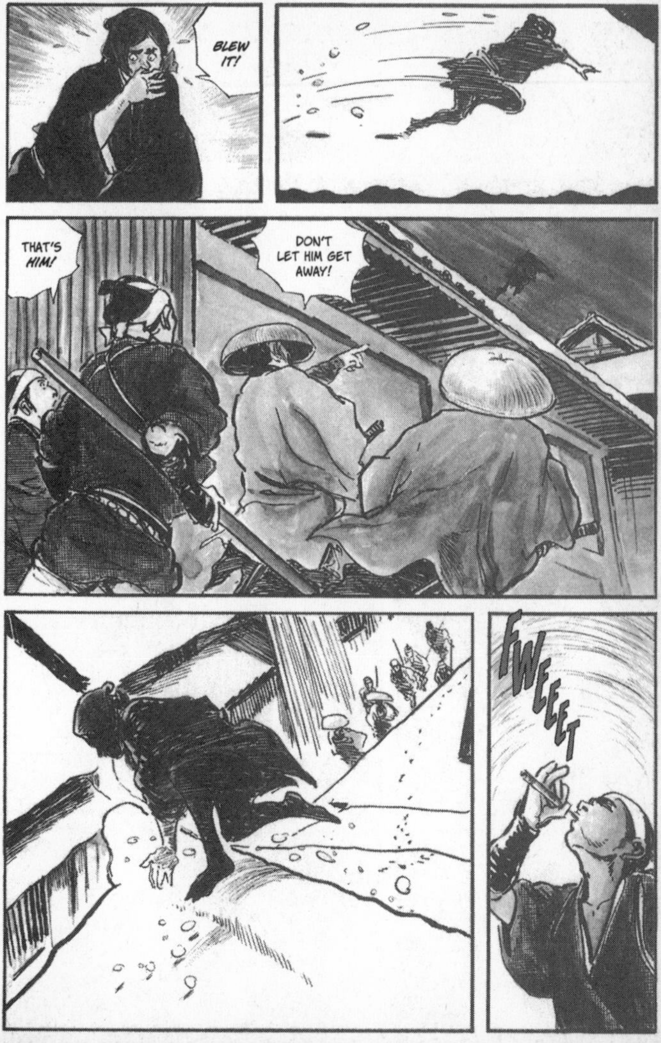
BLEW IT!
THAT'S HIM!
DON'T LET HIM GET AWAY!
FWEEEET

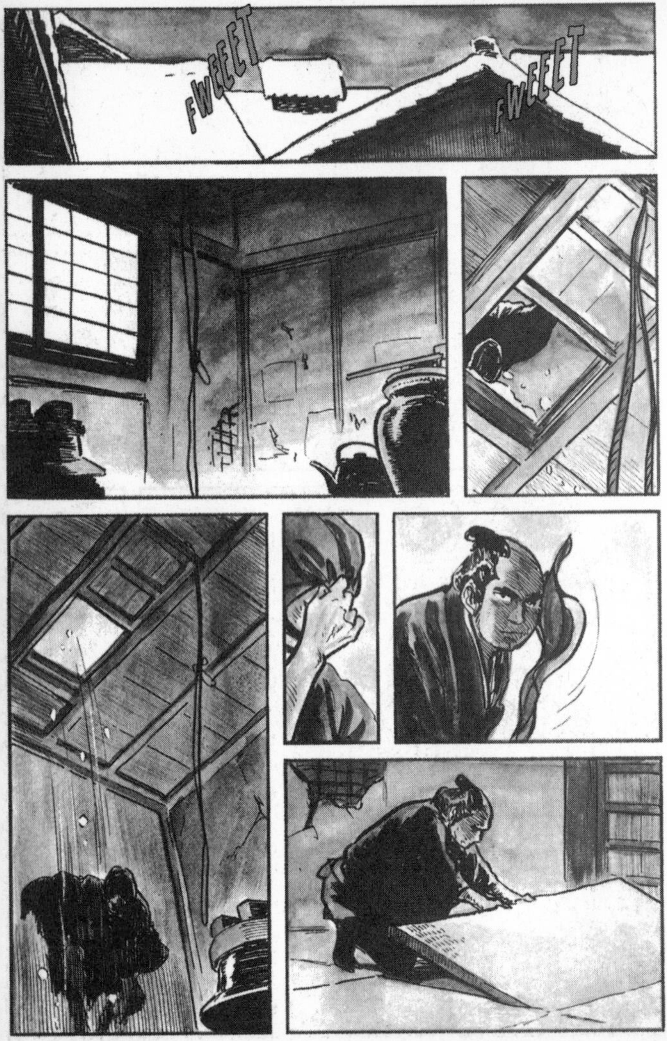
FWEEET
FWEEET

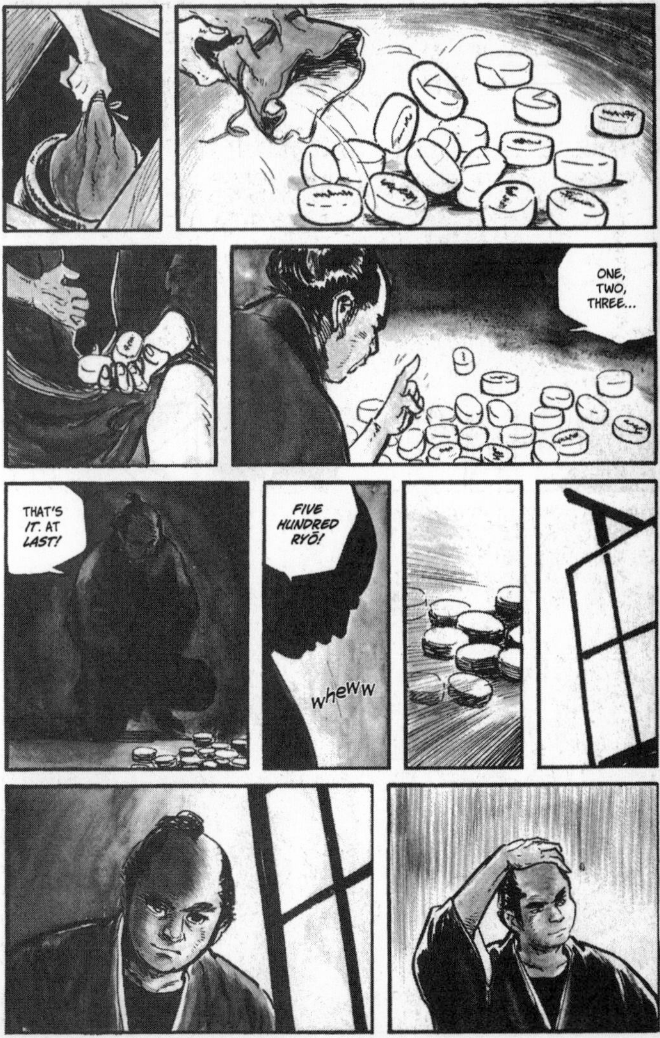
ONE, TWO, THREE...
FIVE HUNDRED RYŌ!
whewww
THAT'S IT. AT LAST!

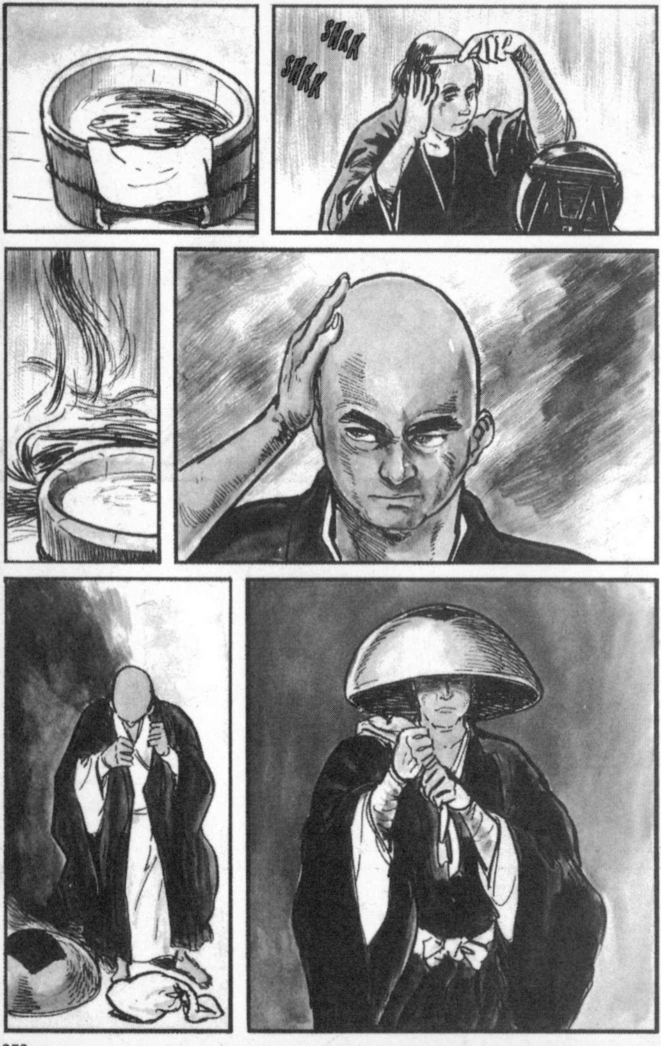
SHKK
SHKK

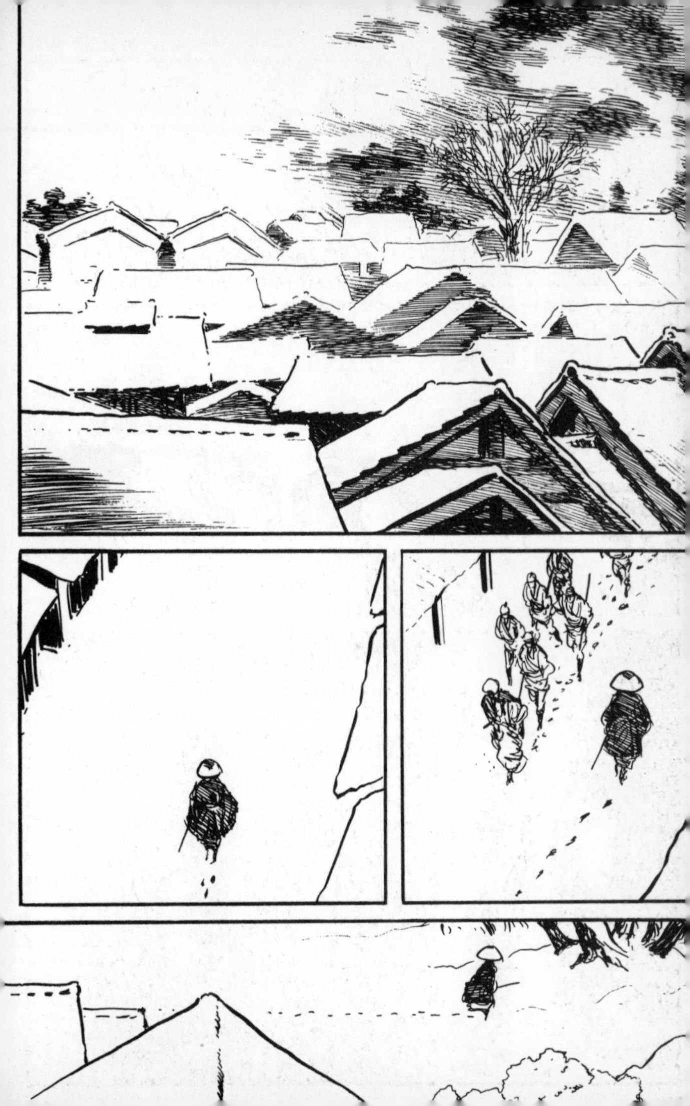

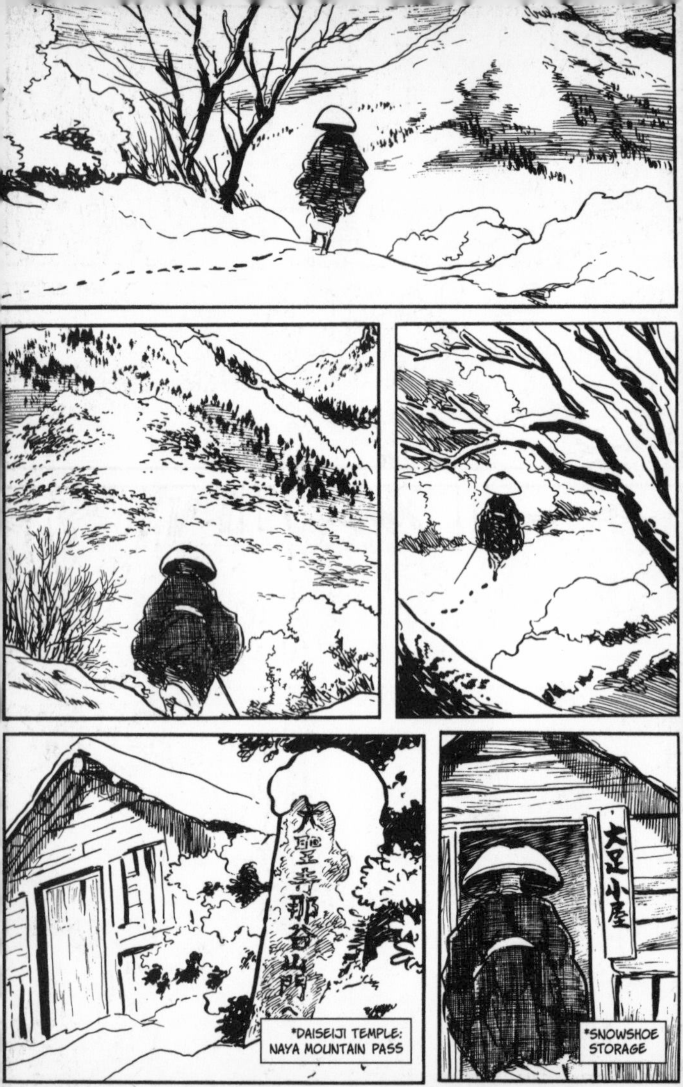
大足小屋
*SNOWSHOE STORAGE
大聖寺那谷山門へ
*DAISEIJI TEMPLE: NAYA MOUNTAIN PASS

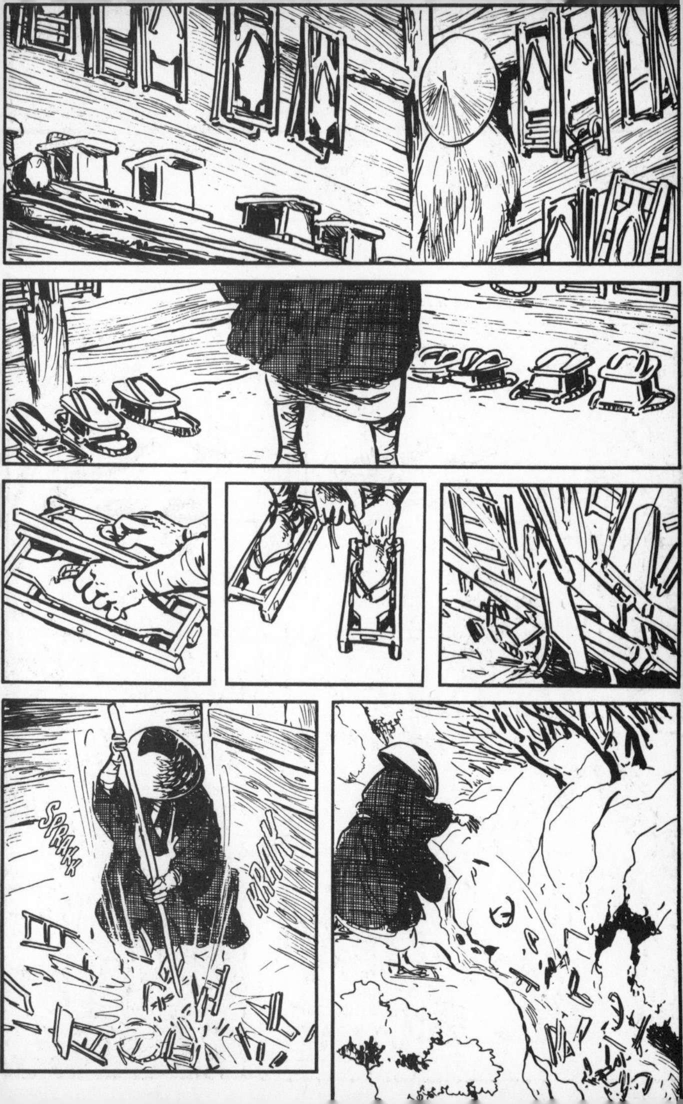
SPRAK
KRAK

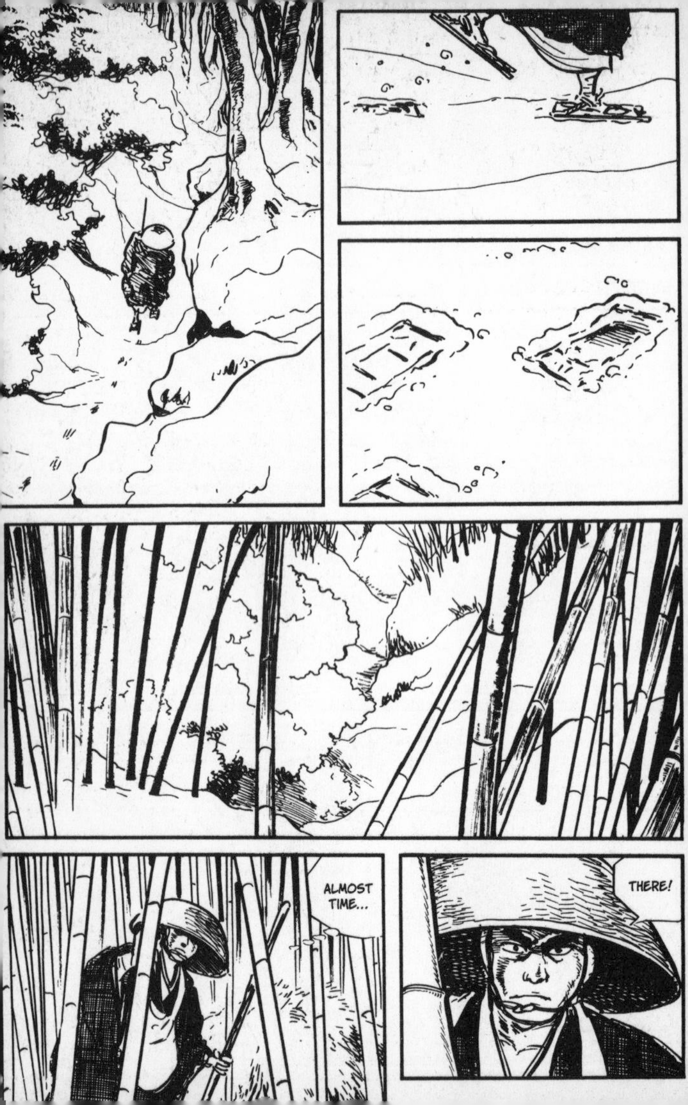
ALMOST TIME...
THERE!

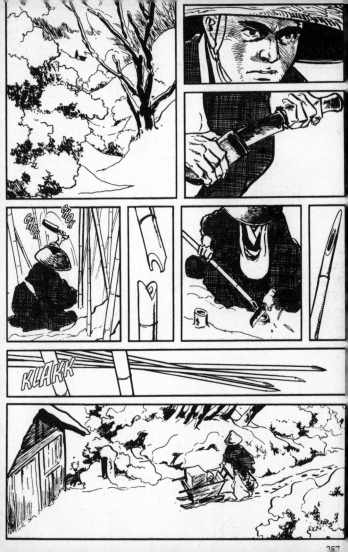

CHOK CHOK

KLAKK

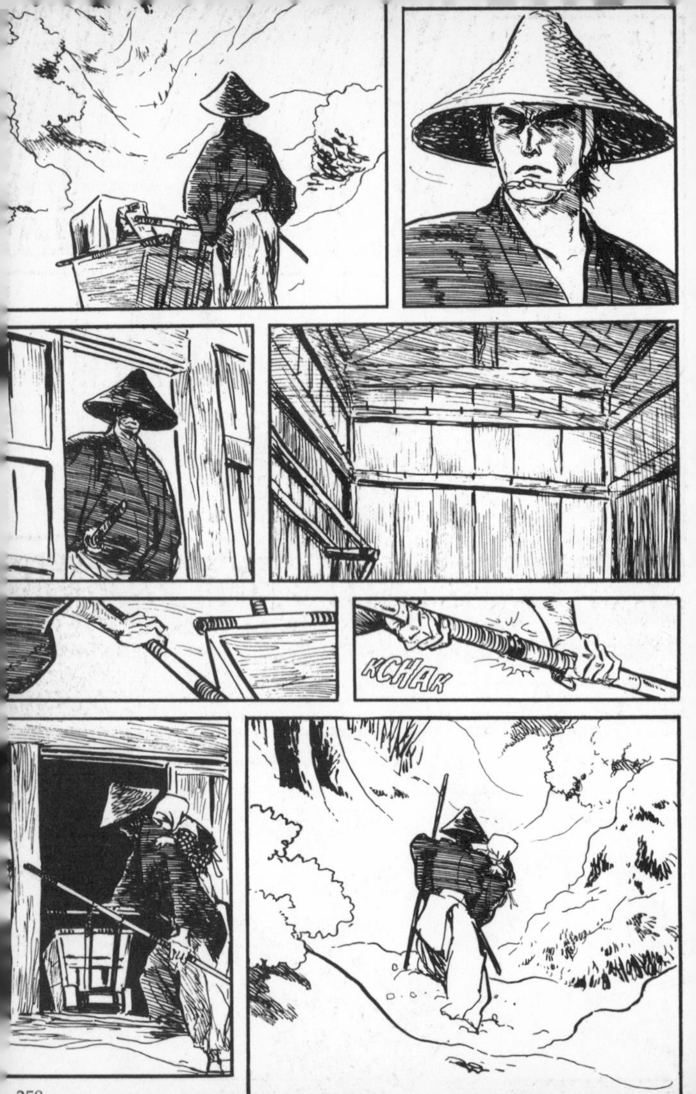
KCHAK

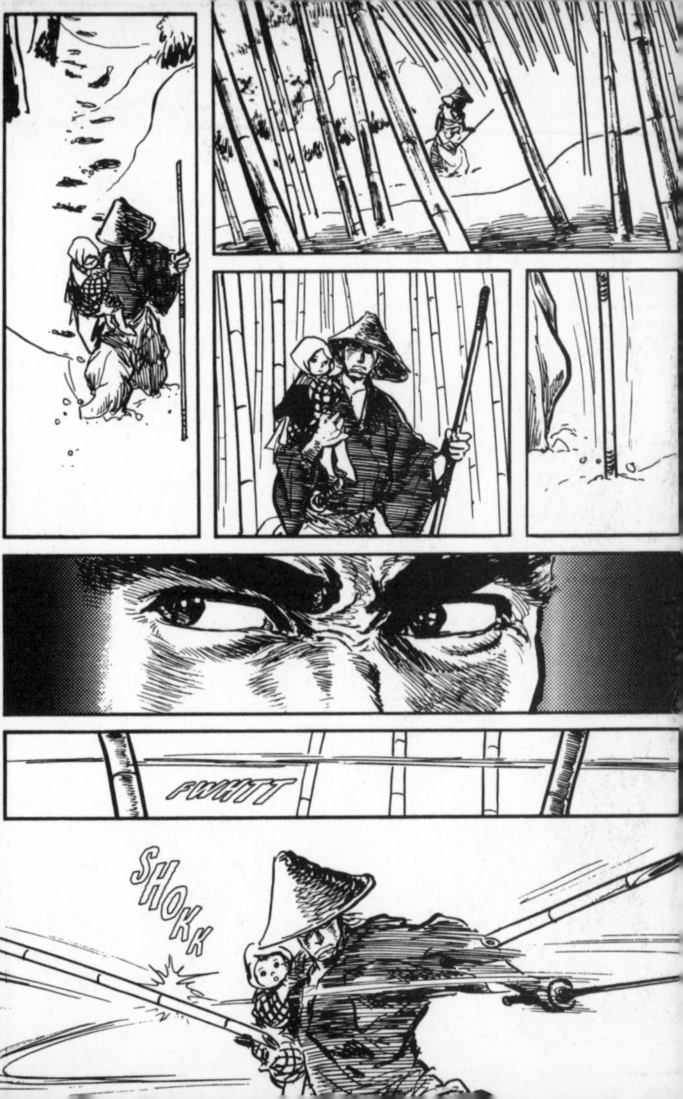
FWHITT
SHOKK

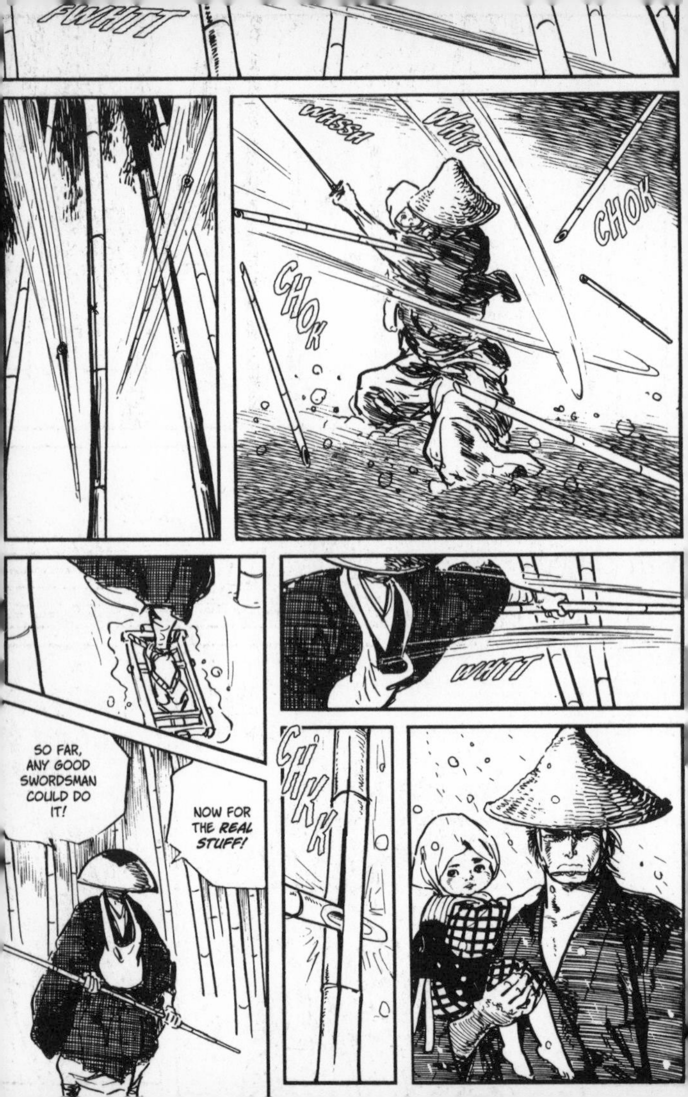
FWHITT
WHSSH
WHITT
CHOK
CHOK
WHITT
CHKK
SO FAR, ANY GOOD SWORDSMAN COULD DO IT!
NOW FOR THE *REAL STUFF!*

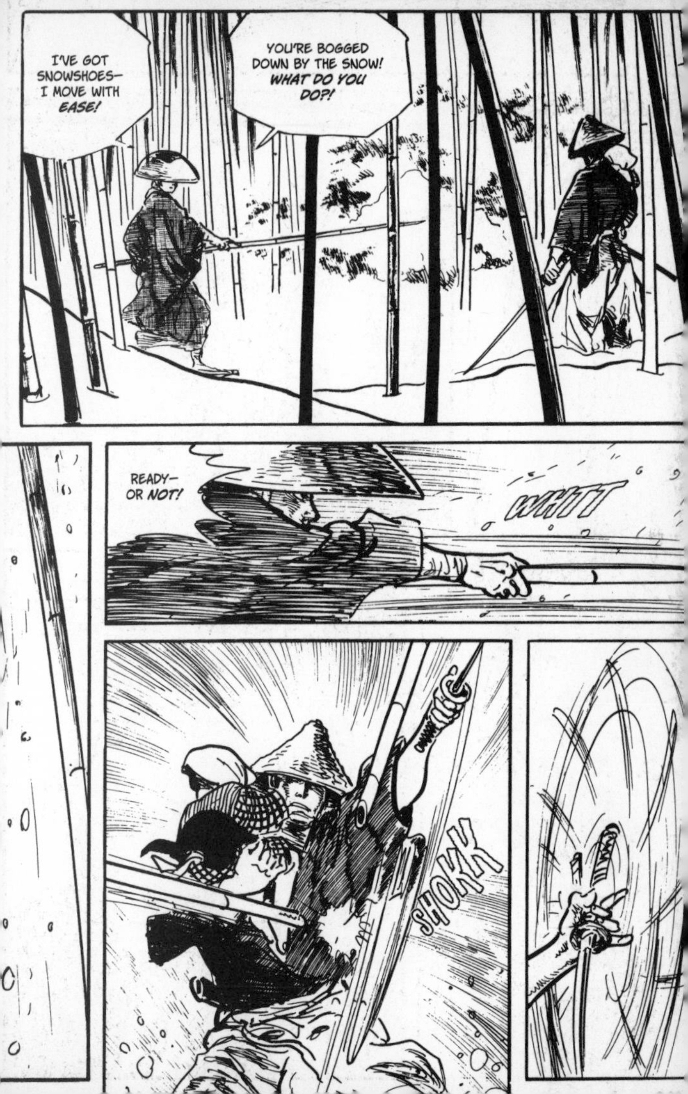

I'VE GOT SNOWSHOES— I MOVE WITH EASE!
YOU'RE BOGGED DOWN BY THE SNOW! WHAT DO YOU DO?!
READY— OR NOT!
WHTT
SHOKK

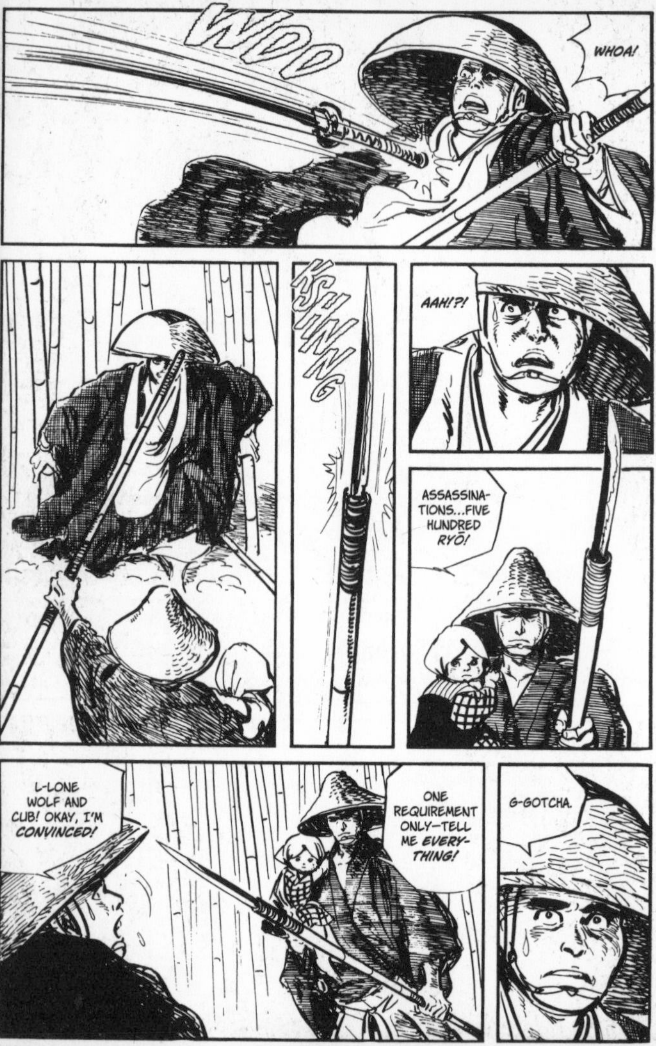
WOO
WHOA!
KSHING
AAH!?!
ASSASSINA-TIONS...FIVE HUNDRED *RYŌ!*
L-LONE WOLF AND CUB! OKAY, I'M *CONVINCED!*
ONE REQUIREMENT ONLY—TELL ME *EVERY-THING!*
G-GOTCHA.

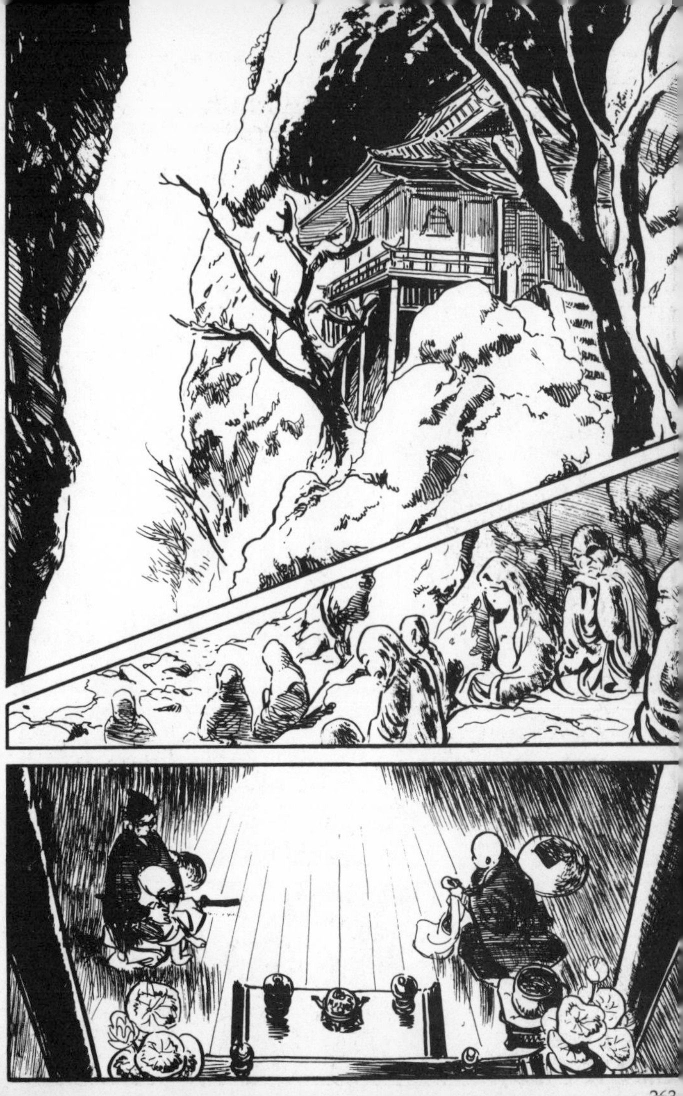

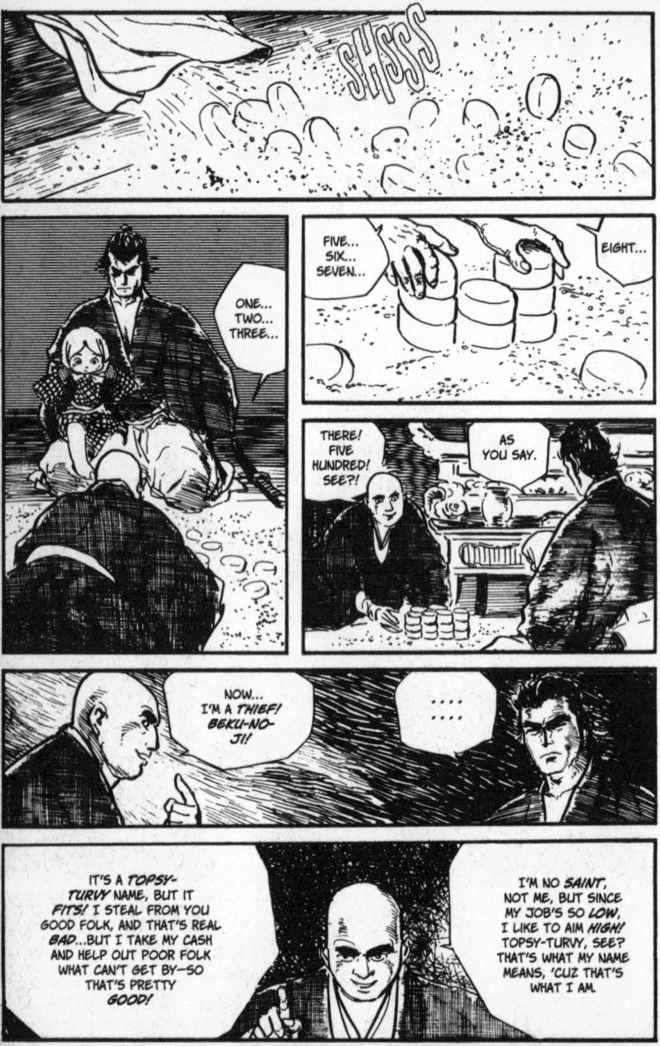
SHSSS
ONE... TWO... THREE...
FIVE... SIX... SEVEN...
EIGHT...
THERE! FIVE HUNDRED! SEE?!
AS YOU SAY.
NOW... I'M A *THIEF!* *BEKU-NO-JI!*
....
IT'S A *TOPSY-TURVY* NAME, BUT IT *FITS!* I STEAL FROM YOU GOOD FOLK, AND THAT'S REAL *BAD*...BUT I TAKE MY CASH AND HELP OUT POOR FOLK WHAT CAN'T GET BY—SO THAT'S PRETTY *GOOD!*
I'M NO *SAINT*, NOT ME, BUT SINCE MY JOB'S SO *LOW*, I LIKE TO AIM *HIGH!* TOPSY-TURVY, SEE? THAT'S WHAT MY NAME MEANS, 'CUZ THAT'S WHAT I AM.

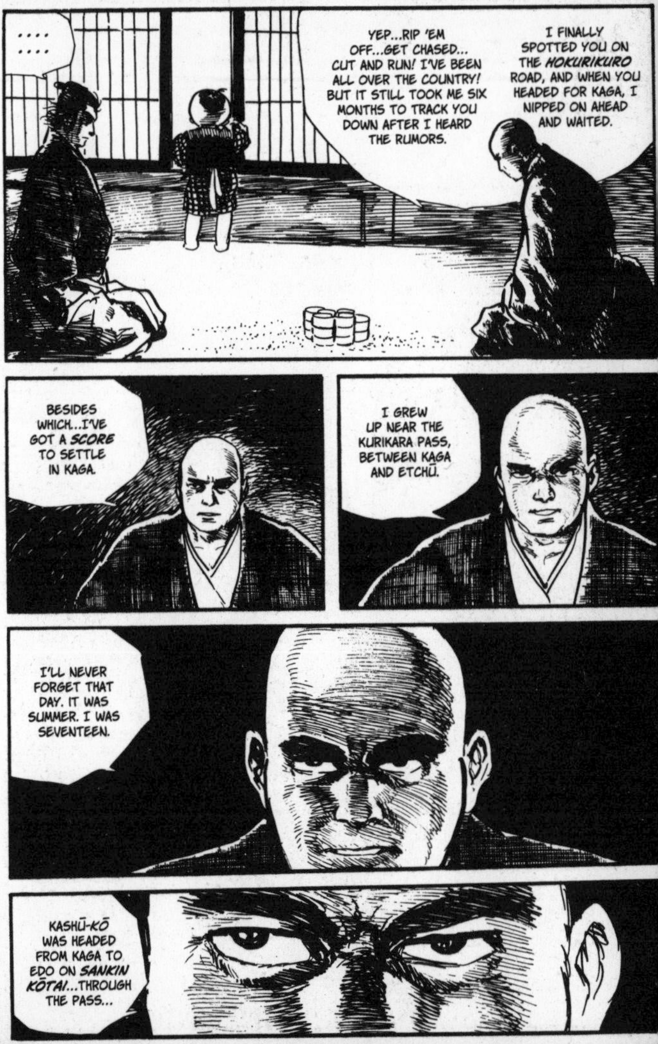
....
....
YEP...RIP 'EM OFF...GET CHASED... CUT AND RUN! I'VE BEEN ALL OVER THE COUNTRY! BUT IT STILL TOOK ME SIX MONTHS TO TRACK YOU DOWN AFTER I HEARD THE RUMORS.
I FINALLY SPOTTED YOU ON THE *HOKURIKURO* ROAD, AND WHEN YOU HEADED FOR KAGA, I NIPPED ON AHEAD AND WAITED.
BESIDES WHICH...I'VE GOT A *SCORE* TO SETTLE IN KAGA.
I GREW UP NEAR THE KURIKARA PASS, BETWEEN KAGA AND ETCHŪ.
I'LL NEVER FORGET THAT DAY. IT WAS SUMMER. I WAS SEVENTEEN.
KASHŪ-*KŌ* WAS HEADED FROM KAGA TO EDO ON *SANKIN KŌTAI*...THROUGH THE PASS...

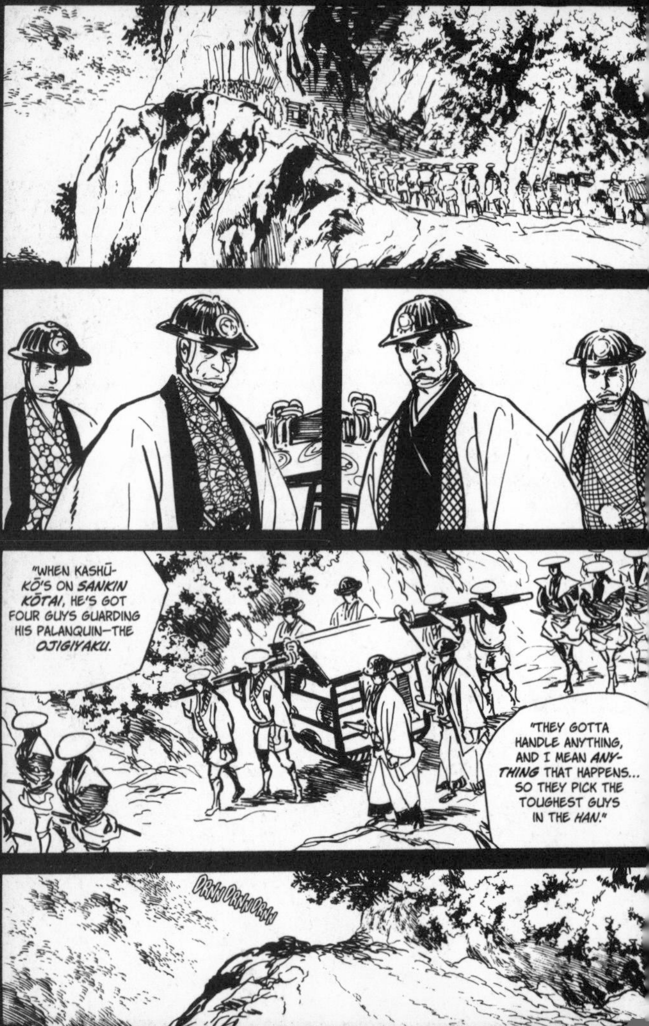
"WHEN KASHŪ-KŌ'S ON *SANKIN KŌTAI*, HE'S GOT FOUR GUYS GUARDING HIS PALANQUIN—THE *OJIGIYAKU*.
"THEY GOTTA HANDLE ANYTHING, AND I MEAN *ANYTHING* THAT HAPPENS... SO THEY PICK THE TOUGHEST GUYS IN THE *HAN*."
DRNN DRNN DRNN

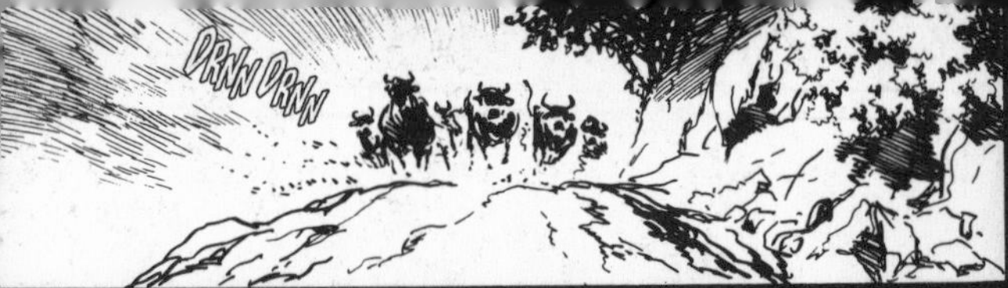
DRNN DRNN
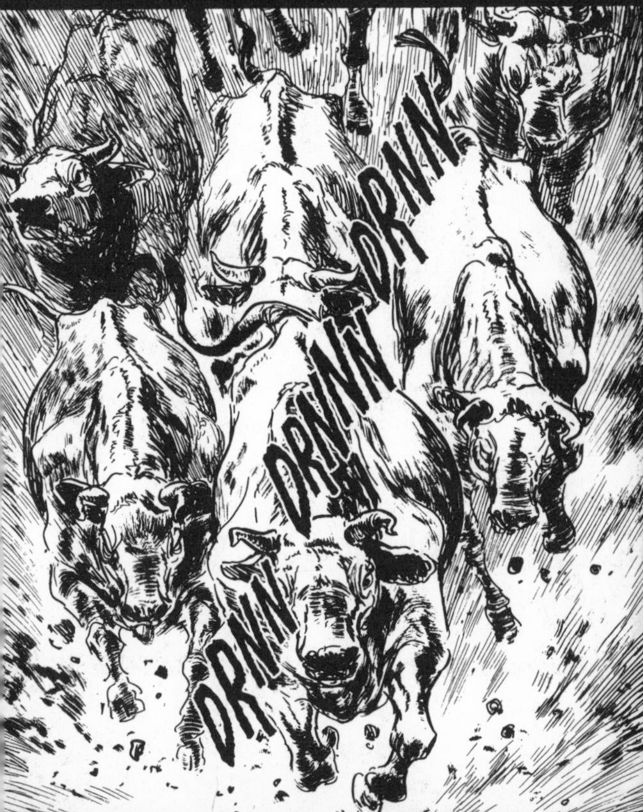
DRNN
DRNNN
DRNN!

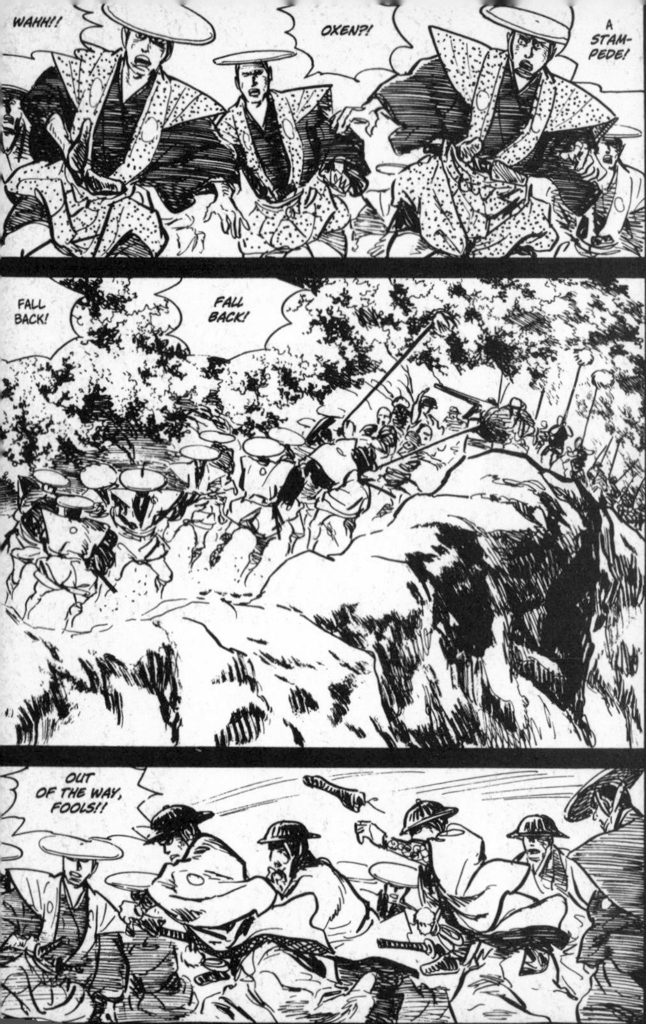
A STAMPEDE!
OXEN?!
WAHH!!
FALL BACK!
FALL BACK!
OUT OF THE WAY, FOOLS!!

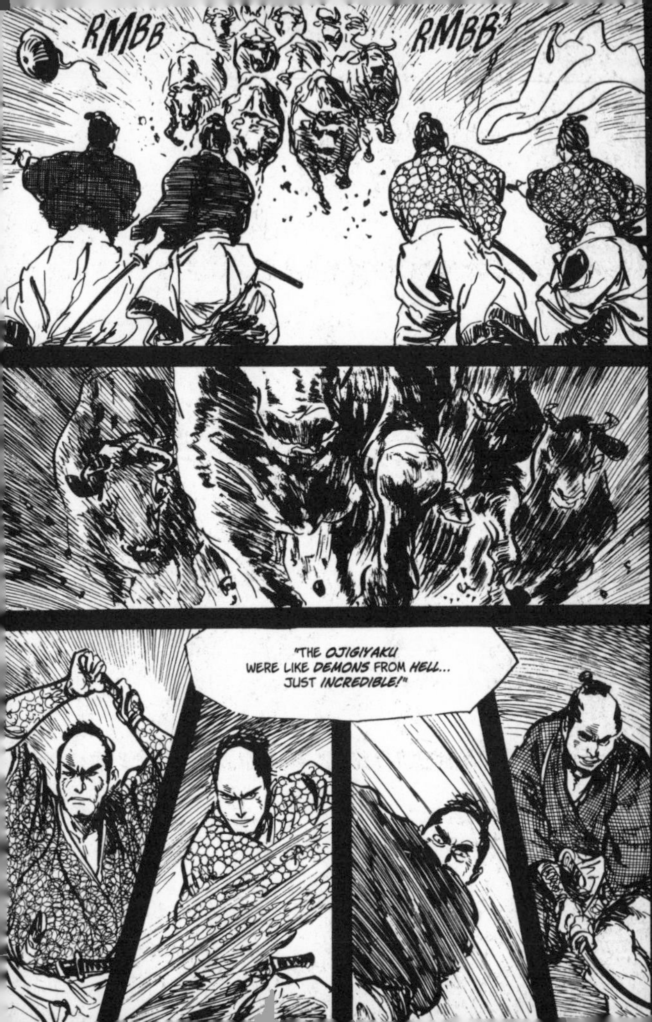
RMBB
RMBB
"THE OJIGIYAKU WERE LIKE DEMONS FROM HELL... JUST INCREDIBLE!"

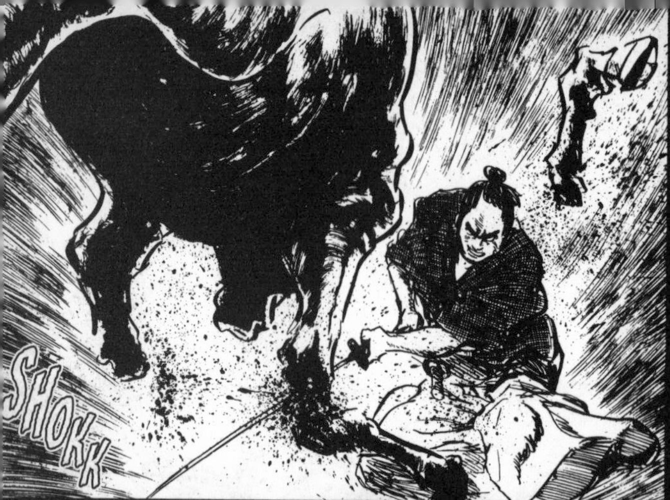
SHOKK
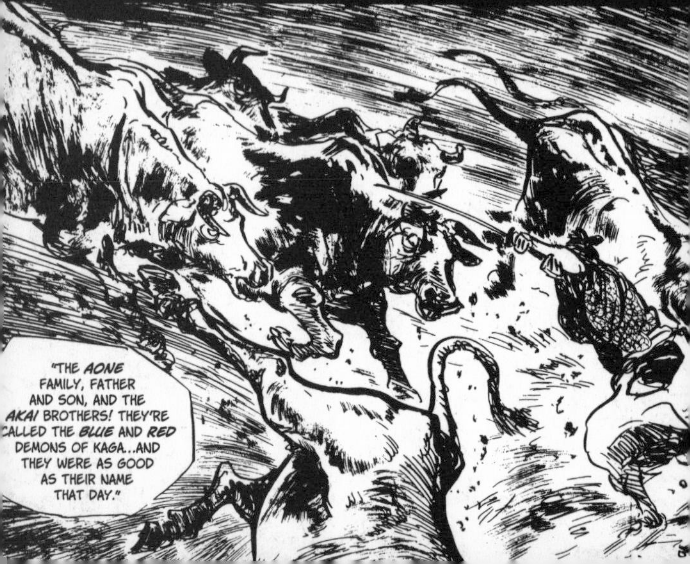
"THE *AONE* FAMILY, FATHER AND SON, AND THE *AKAI* BROTHERS! THEY'RE CALLED THE *BLUE* AND *RED* DEMONS OF KAGA...AND THEY WERE AS GOOD AS THEIR NAME THAT DAY."

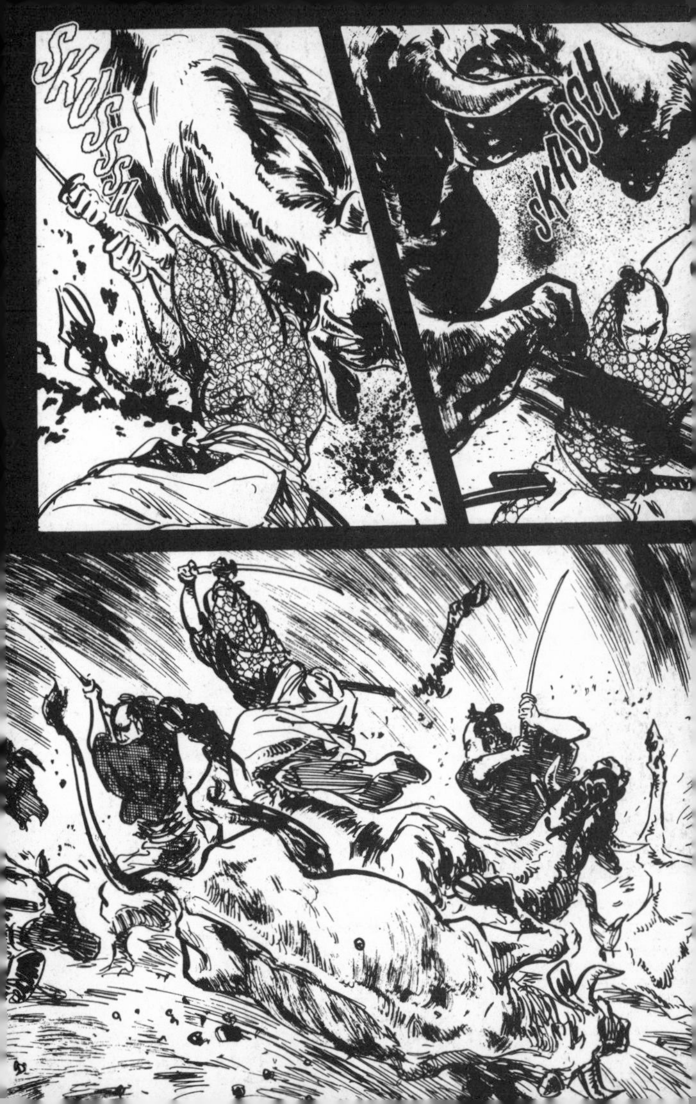
SKASSH
SKUSSSH

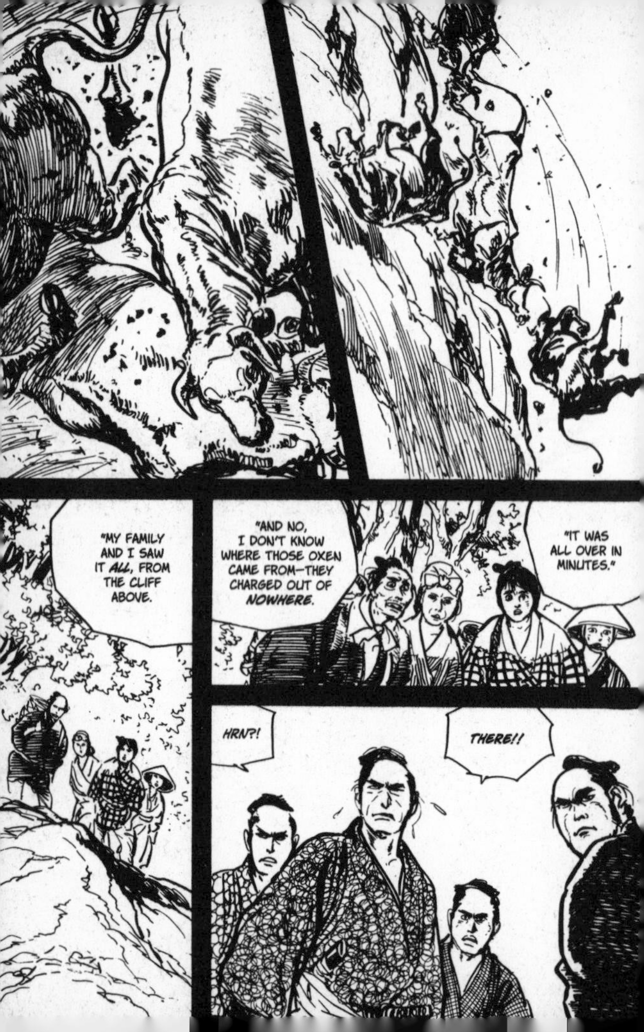
"MY FAMILY AND I SAW IT ALL, FROM THE CLIFF ABOVE.
"AND NO, I DON'T KNOW WHERE THOSE OXEN CAME FROM—THEY CHARGED OUT OF NOWHERE.
"IT WAS ALL OVER IN MINUTES."
HRN?!
THERE!!

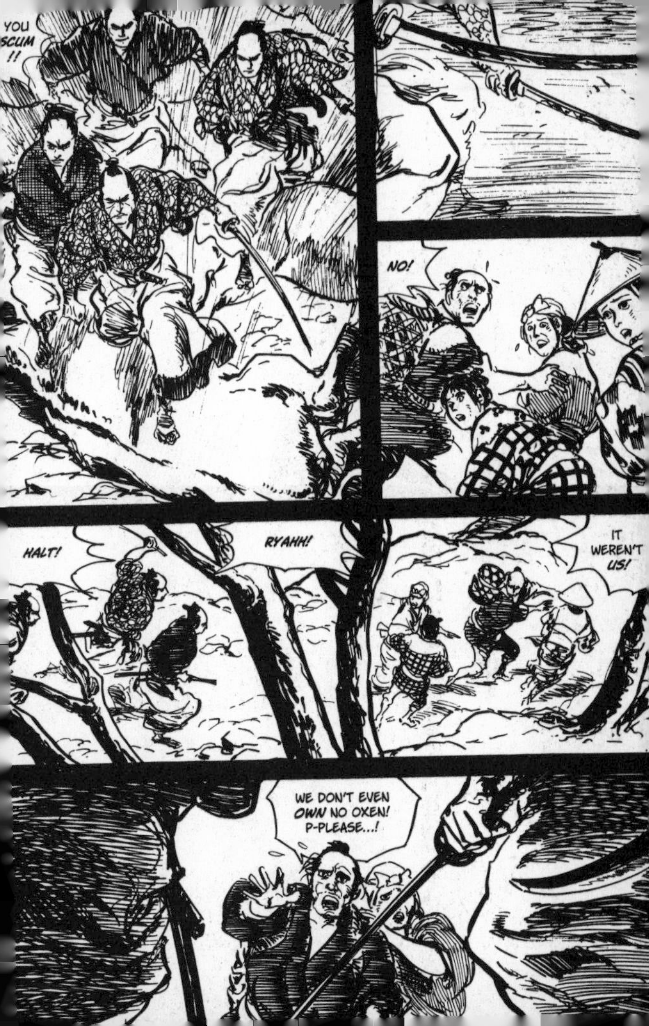
NO!
YOU SCUM !!
IT WEREN'T *US!*
RYAHH!
HALT!
WE DON'T EVEN *OWN* NO OXEN! P-PLEASE...!

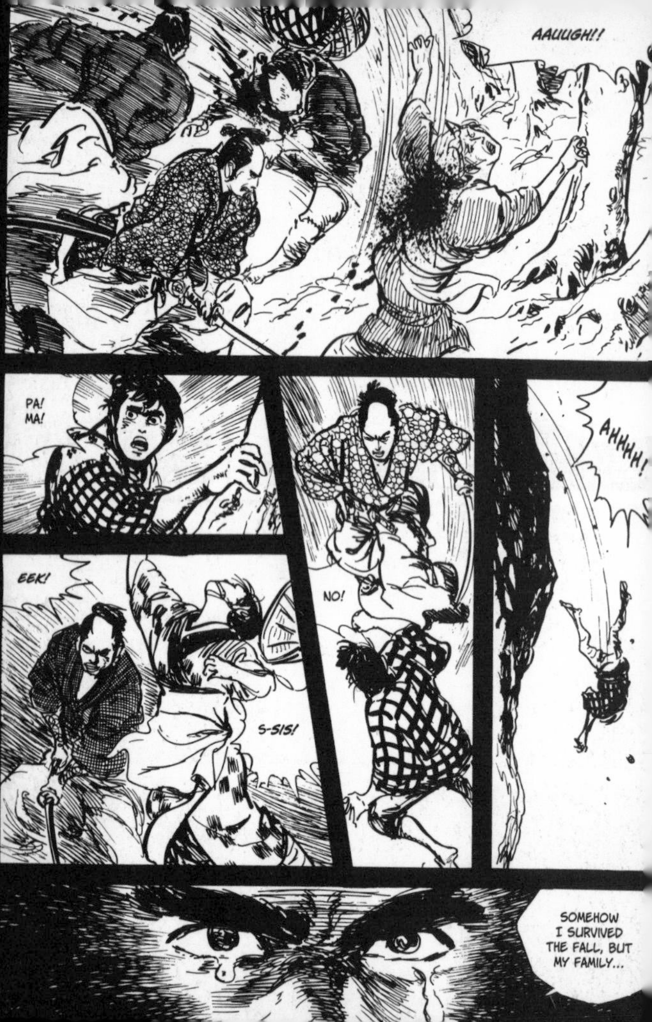
AAUUGH!!
PA! MA!
EEK!
S-SIS!
NO!
AHHHH!
SOMEHOW I SURVIVED THE FALL, BUT MY FAMILY...

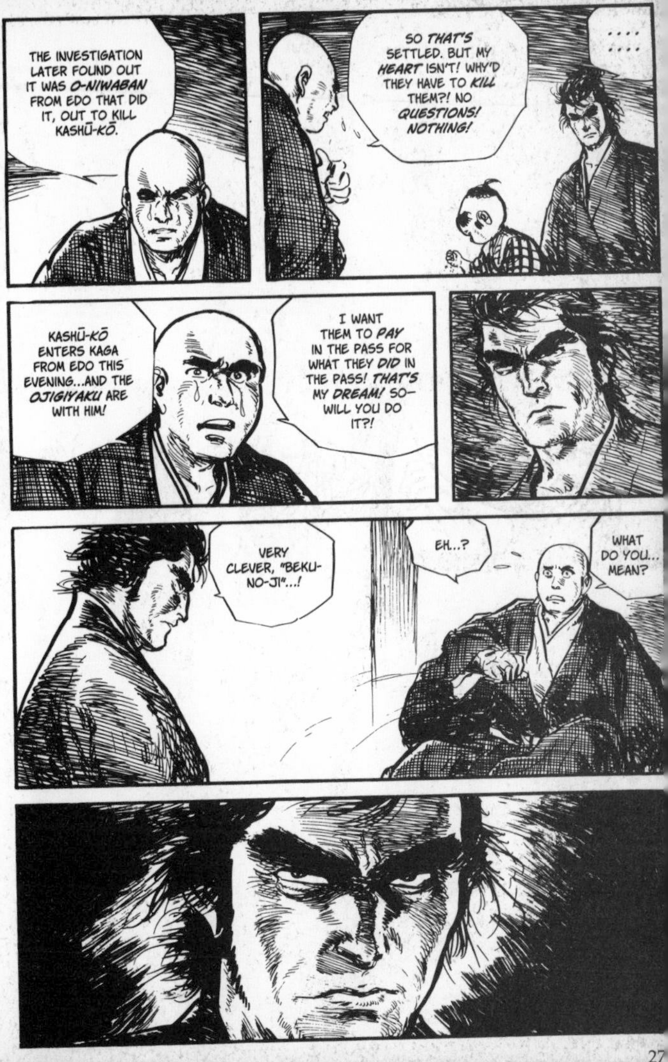
THE INVESTIGATION LATER FOUND OUT IT WAS *O-NIWABAN* FROM EDO THAT DID IT, OUT TO KILL KASHŪ-*KŌ*.
SO *THAT'S* SETTLED. BUT MY *HEART* ISN'T! WHY'D THEY HAVE TO *KILL* THEM?! NO *QUESTIONS! NOTHING!*
....
KASHŪ-*KŌ* ENTERS KAGA FROM EDO THIS EVENING...AND THE *OJIGIYAKU* ARE WITH HIM!
I WANT THEM TO *PAY* IN THE PASS FOR WHAT THEY *DID* IN THE PASS! *THAT'S* MY *DREAM!* SO— WILL YOU DO IT?!
VERY CLEVER, "BEKU-NO-JI"...!
EH...?
WHAT DO YOU... MEAN?

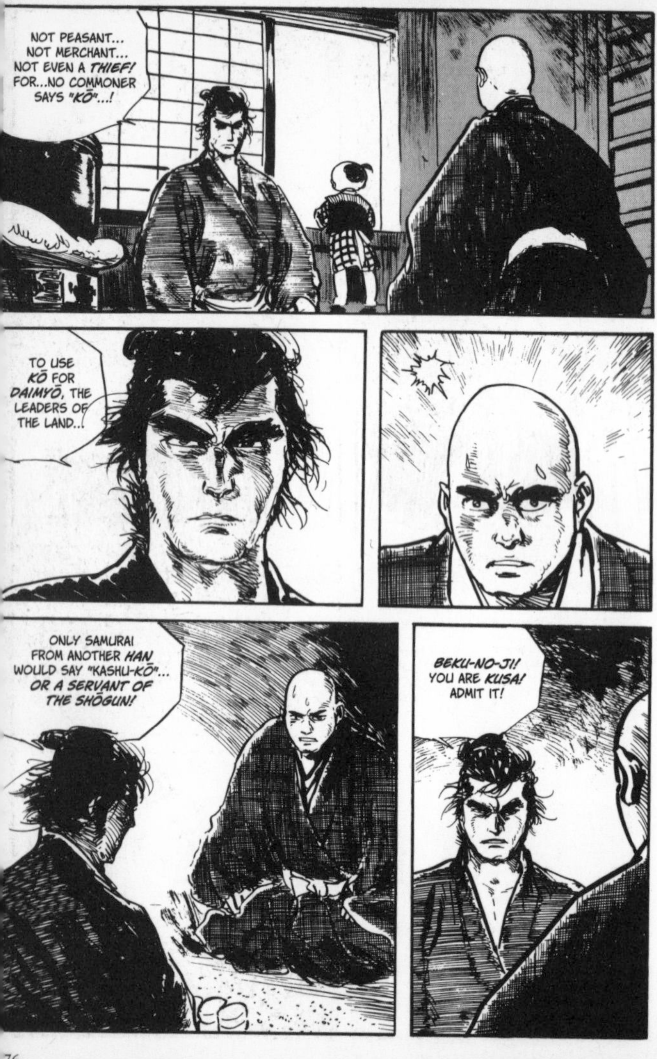
NOT PEASANT... NOT MERCHANT... NOT EVEN A *THIEF!* FOR...NO COMMONER SAYS "*KŌ*"...!
TO USE *KŌ* FOR *DAIMYŌ*, THE LEADERS OF THE LAND...
ONLY SAMURAI FROM ANOTHER *HAN* WOULD SAY "KASHU-KŌ"... *OR A SERVANT OF THE SHŌGUN!*
BEKU-NO-JI! YOU ARE *KUSA!* ADMIT IT!

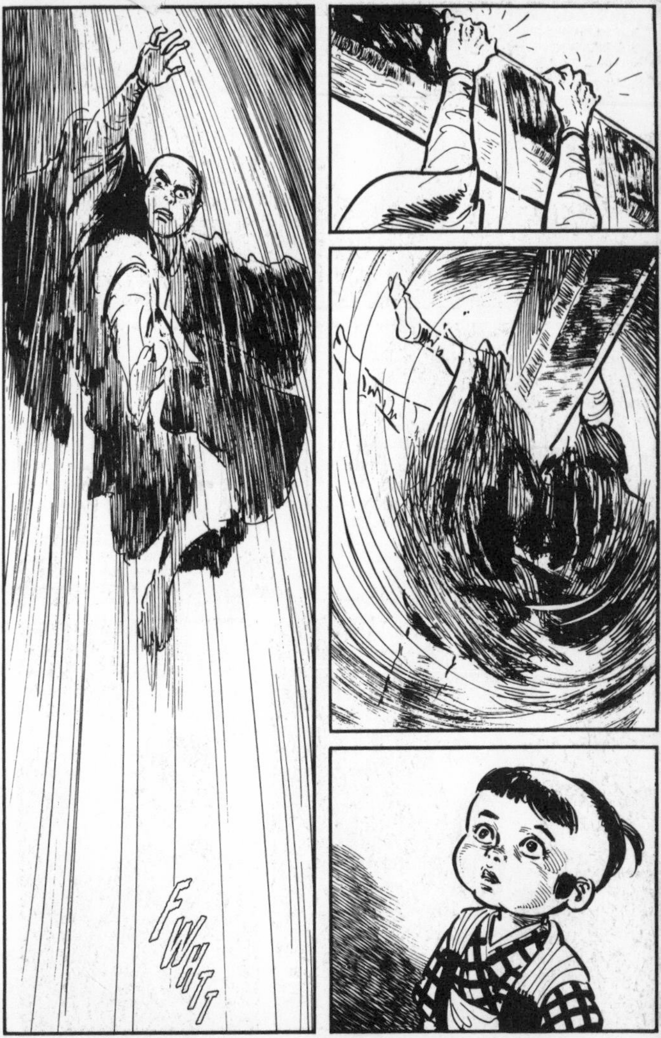
FWHTT

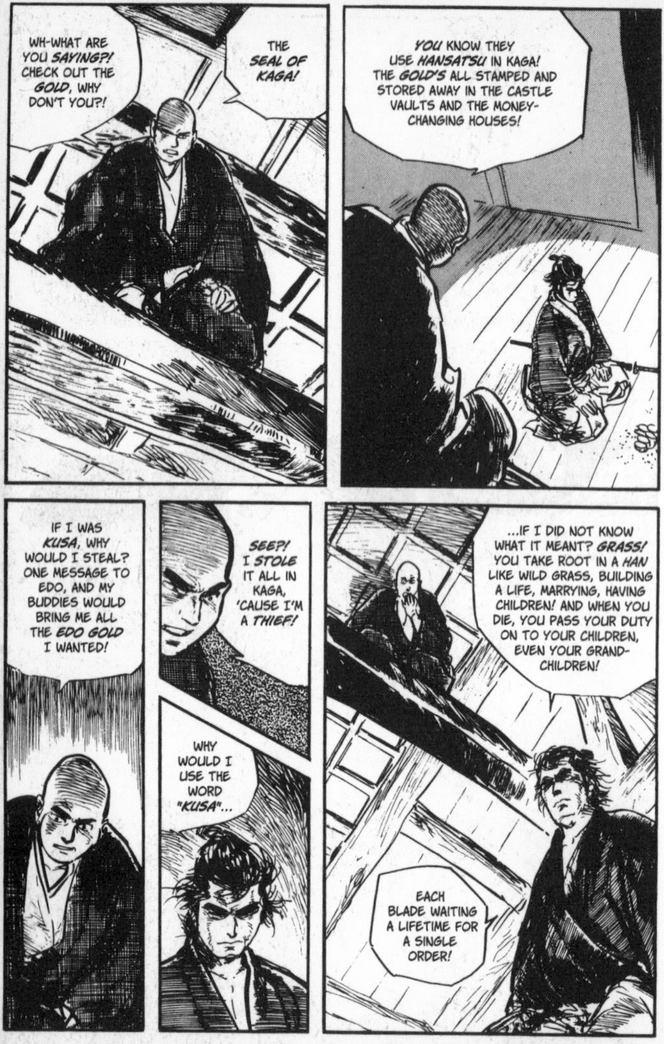
WH-WHAT ARE YOU SAYING?! CHECK OUT THE GOLD, WHY DON'T YOU?!
THE SEAL OF KAGA!
YOU KNOW THEY USE HANSATSU IN KAGA! THE GOLD'S ALL STAMPED AND STORED AWAY IN THE CASTLE VAULTS AND THE MONEY-CHANGING HOUSES!
IF I WAS KUSA, WHY WOULD I STEAL? ONE MESSAGE TO EDO, AND MY BUDDIES WOULD BRING ME ALL THE EDO GOLD I WANTED!
SEE?! I STOLE IT ALL IN KAGA, 'CAUSE I'M A THIEF!
WHY WOULD I USE THE WORD "KUSA"...
...IF I DID NOT KNOW WHAT IT MEANT? GRASS! YOU TAKE ROOT IN A HAN LIKE WILD GRASS, BUILDING A LIFE, MARRYING, HAVING CHILDREN! AND WHEN YOU DIE, YOU PASS YOUR DUTY ON TO YOUR CHILDREN, EVEN YOUR GRAND-CHILDREN!
EACH BLADE WAITING A LIFETIME FOR A SINGLE ORDER!

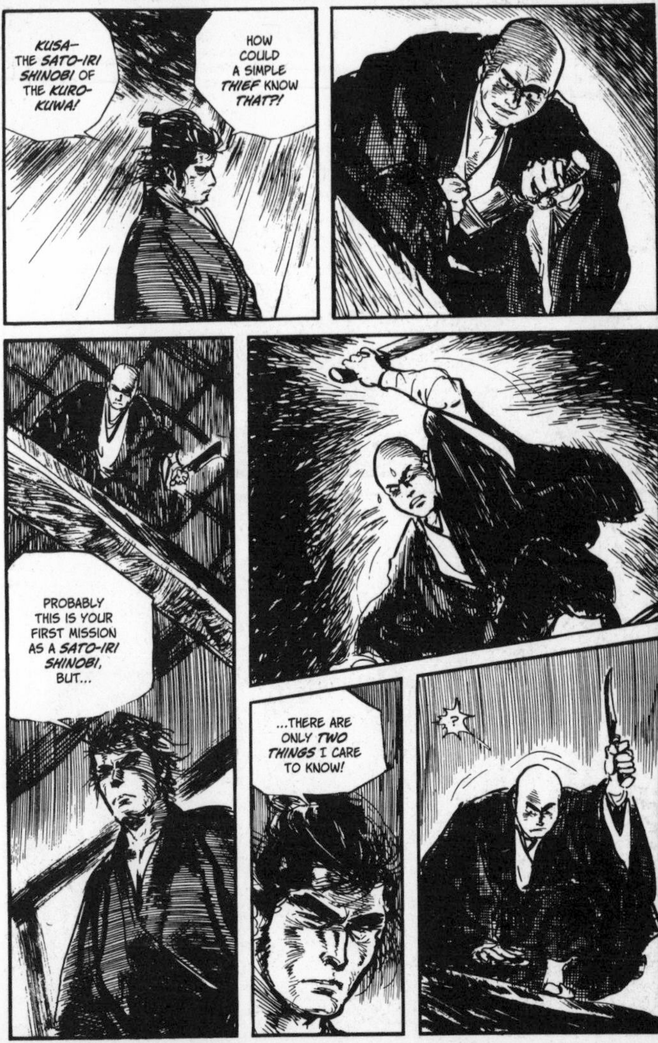
KUSA— THE SATO-IRI SHINOBI OF THE KURO-KUWA!
HOW COULD A SIMPLE THIEF KNOW THAT?!
PROBABLY THIS IS YOUR FIRST MISSION AS A SATO-IRI SHINOBI, BUT...
...THERE ARE ONLY TWO THINGS I CARE TO KNOW!
?

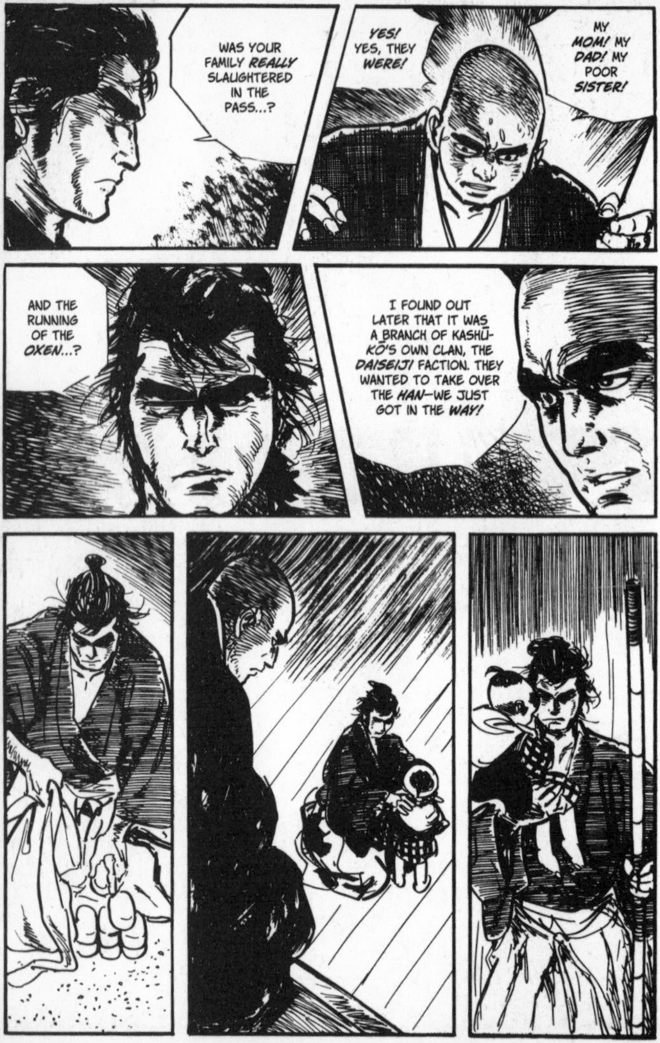
WAS YOUR FAMILY *REALLY* SLAUGHTERED IN THE PASS...?
YES! YES, THEY *WERE!*
MY *MOM!* MY *DAD!* MY POOR *SISTER!*
AND THE RUNNING OF THE *OXEN*...?
I FOUND OUT LATER THAT IT WAS A BRANCH OF KASHŪ-KŌ'S OWN CLAN, THE *DAISEIJI* FACTION. THEY WANTED TO TAKE OVER THE *HAN*—WE JUST GOT IN THE *WAY!*

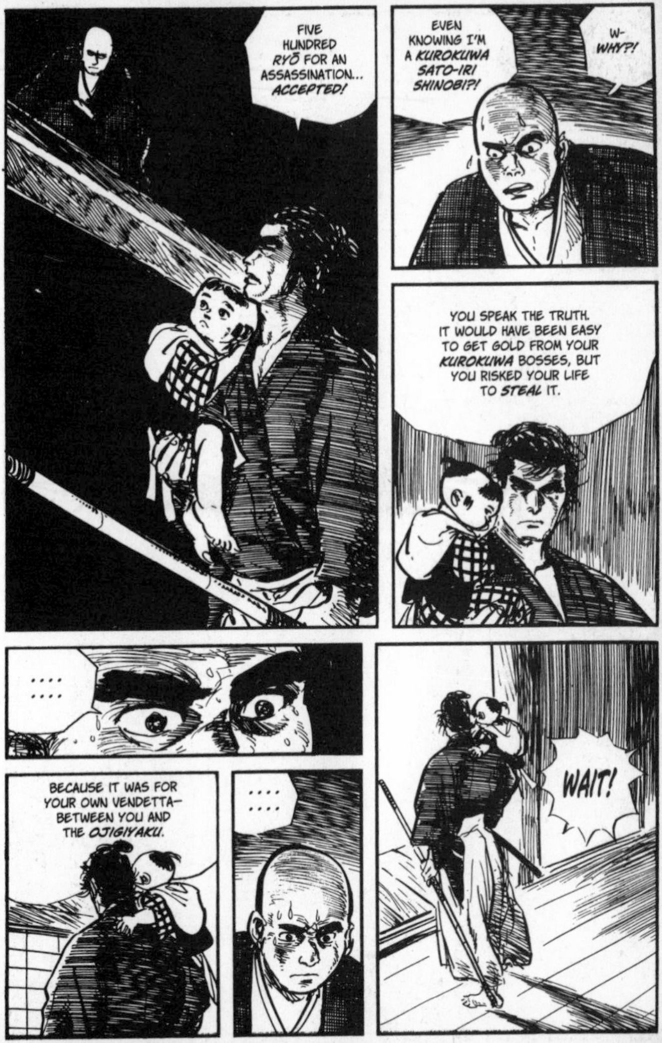
FIVE HUNDRED RYŌ FOR AN ASSASSINATION... ACCEPTED!
W- WHY?!
EVEN KNOWING I'M A KUROKUWA SATO-IRI SHINOBI?!
YOU SPEAK THE TRUTH. IT WOULD HAVE BEEN EASY TO GET GOLD FROM YOUR KUROKUWA BOSSES, BUT YOU RISKED YOUR LIFE TO STEAL IT.
....
BECAUSE IT WAS FOR YOUR OWN VENDETTA- BETWEEN YOU AND THE OJIGIYAKU.
....
WAIT!

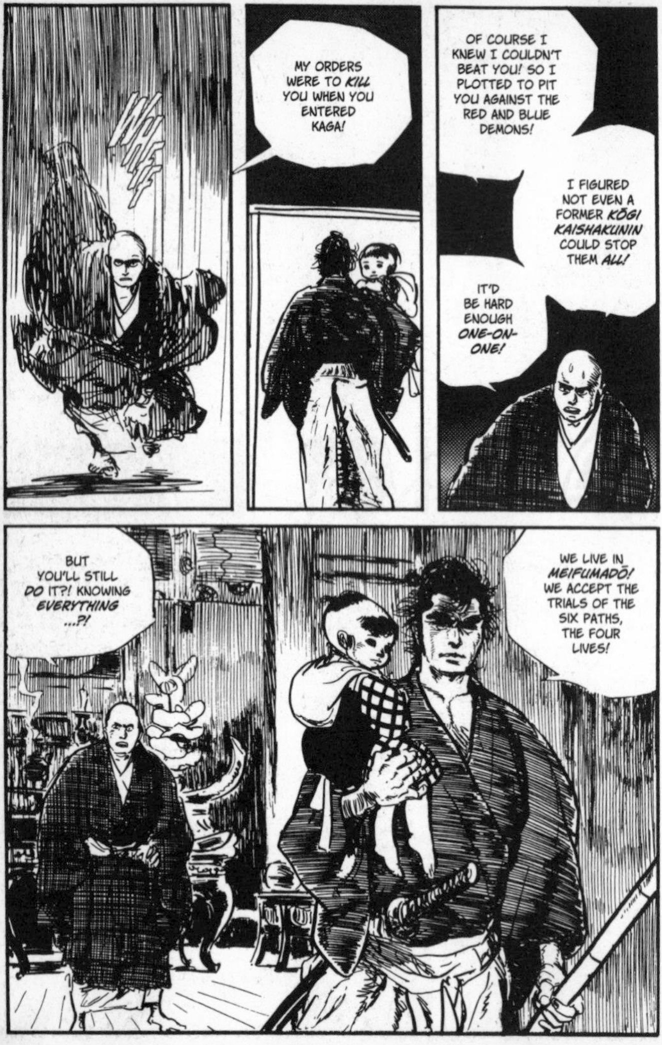
MY ORDERS WERE TO *KILL* YOU WHEN YOU ENTERED KAGA!
OF COURSE I KNEW I COULDN'T BEAT YOU! SO I PLOTTED TO PIT YOU AGAINST THE RED AND BLUE DEMONS!
I FIGURED NOT EVEN A FORMER *KŌGI KAISHAKUNIN* COULD STOP THEM *ALL!*
IT'D BE HARD ENOUGH *ONE-ON-ONE!*
BUT YOU'LL STILL *DO* IT?! KNOWING *EVERYTHING* ...?!
WE LIVE IN *MEIFUMADŌ!* WE ACCEPT THE TRIALS OF THE SIX PATHS, THE FOUR LIVES!

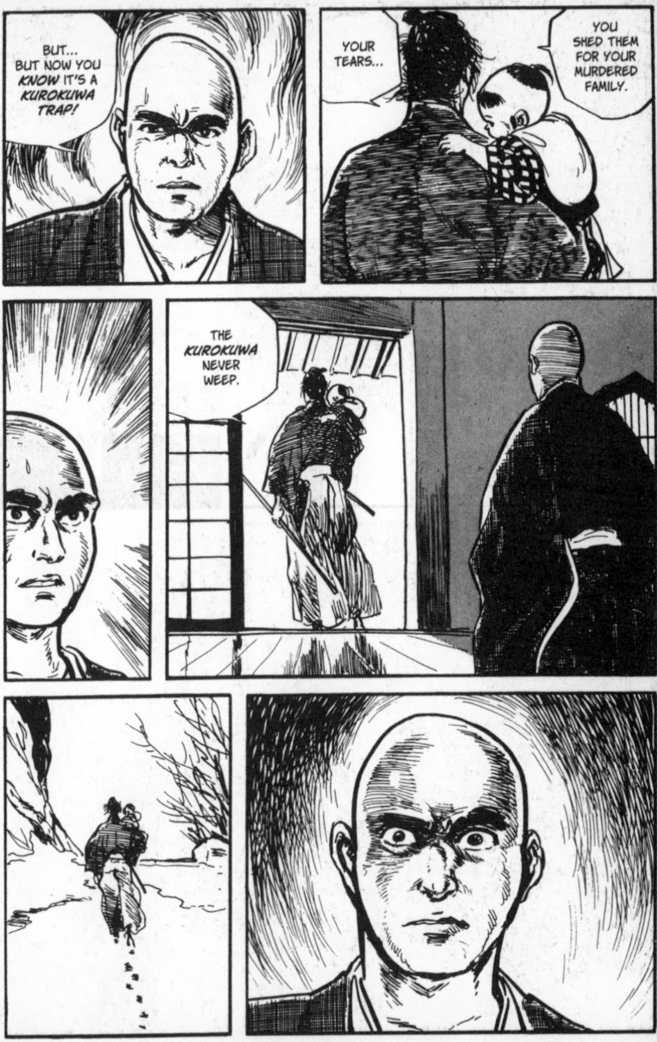
BUT... BUT NOW YOU KNOW IT'S A KUROKUWA TRAP!
YOUR TEARS...
YOU SHED THEM FOR YOUR MURDERED FAMILY.
THE KUROKUWA NEVER WEEP.

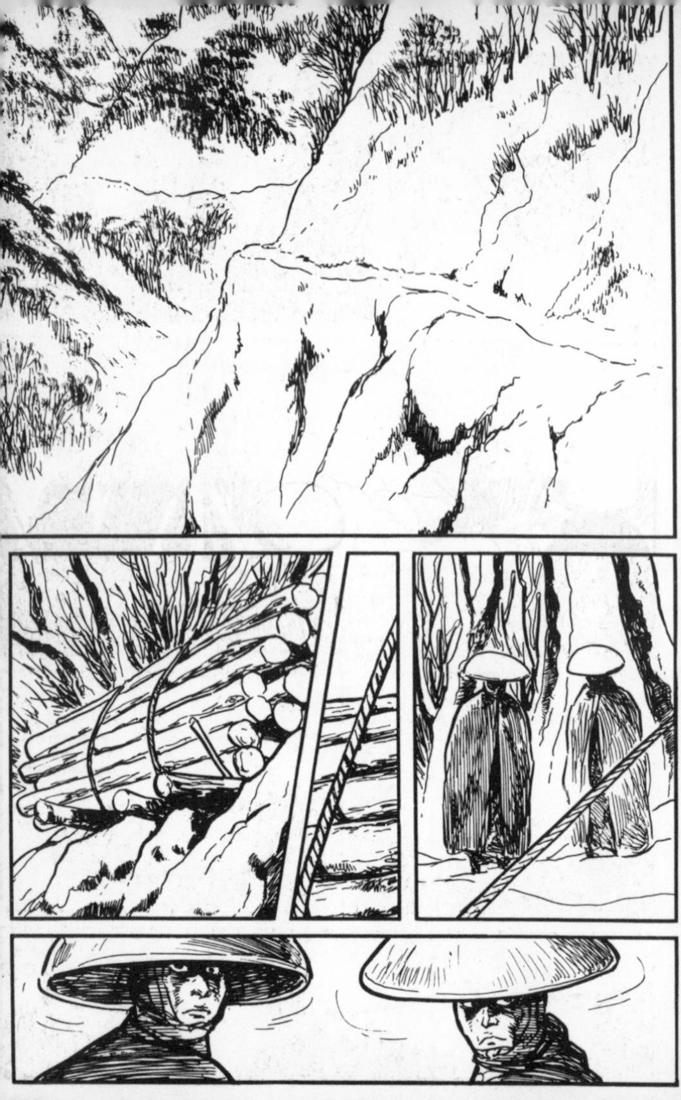

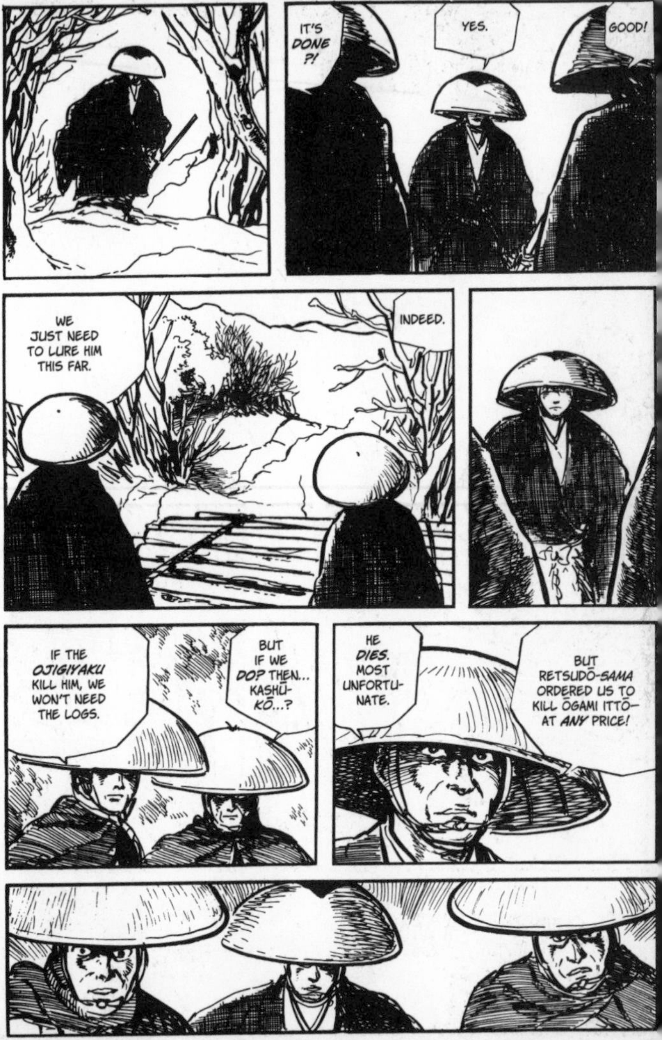
IT'S DONE?!
YES.
GOOD!
WE JUST NEED TO LURE HIM THIS FAR.
INDEED.
IF THE OJIGIYAKU KILL HIM, WE WON'T NEED THE LOGS.
BUT IF WE DO? THEN... KASHŪ-KŌ...?
HE DIES. MOST UNFORTU-NATE.
BUT RETSUDŌ-SAMA ORDERED US TO KILL ŌGAMI ITTŌ-AT ANY PRICE!

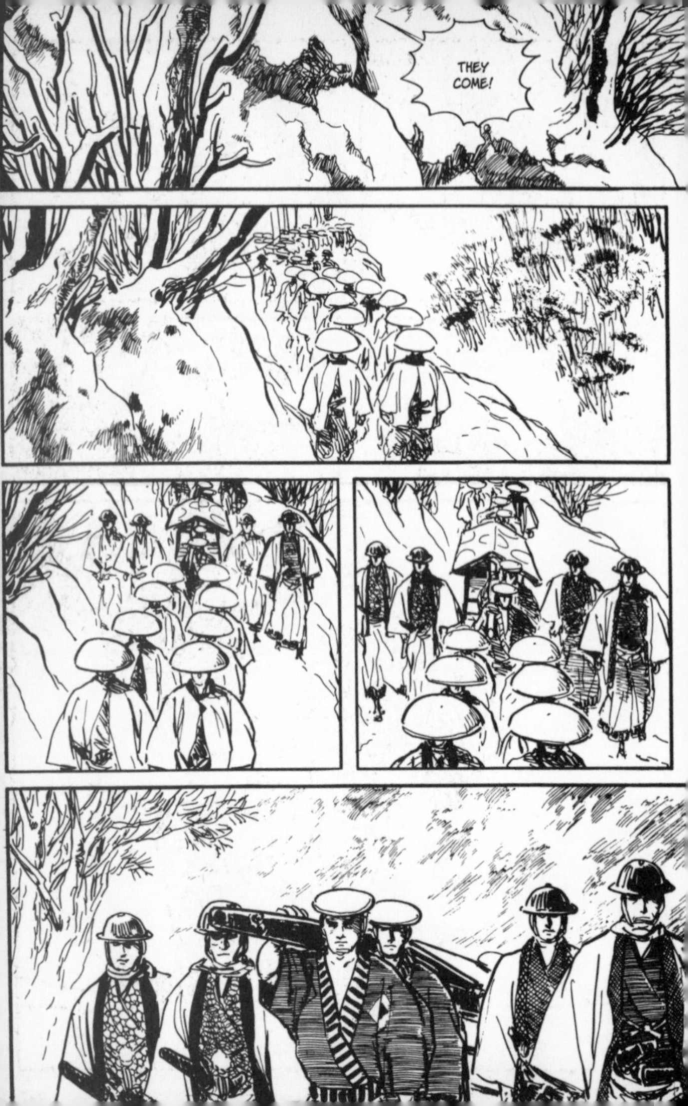
THEY COME!

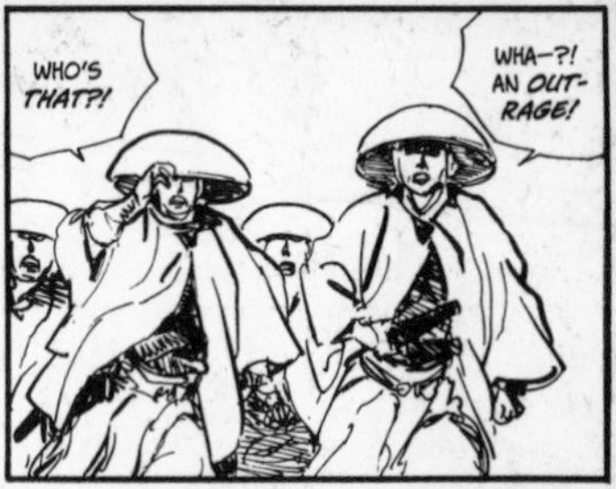
WHA–?! AN OUT-RAGE!
WHO'S THAT?!

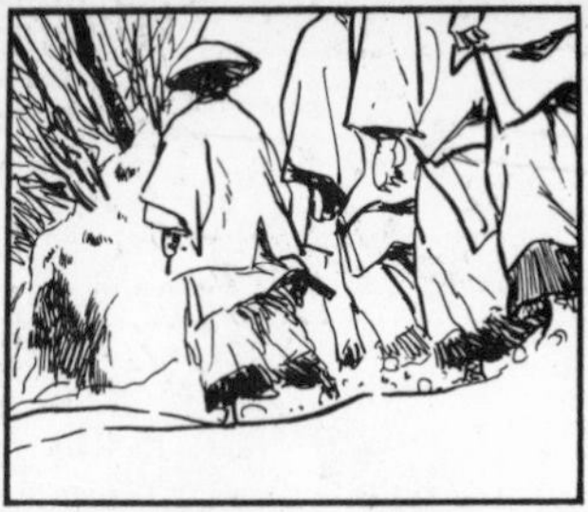

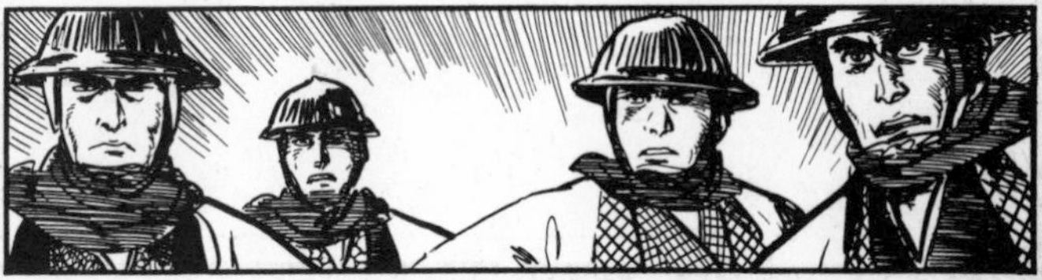

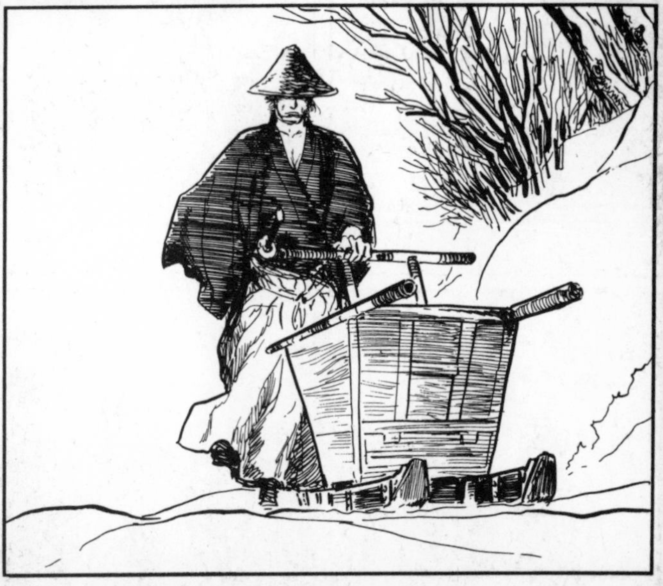

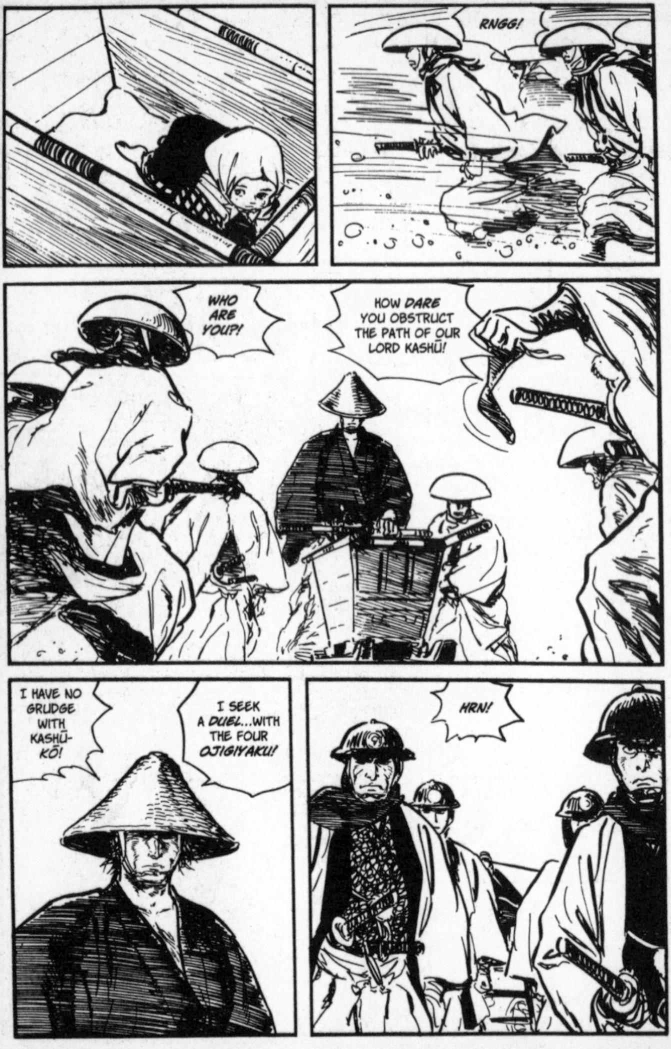
RNGG!
WHO ARE YOU?!
HOW DARE YOU OBSTRUCT THE PATH OF OUR LORD KASHŪ!
I HAVE NO GRUDGE WITH KASHŪ-KŌ!
I SEEK A DUEL...WITH THE FOUR OJIGIYAKU!
HRN!

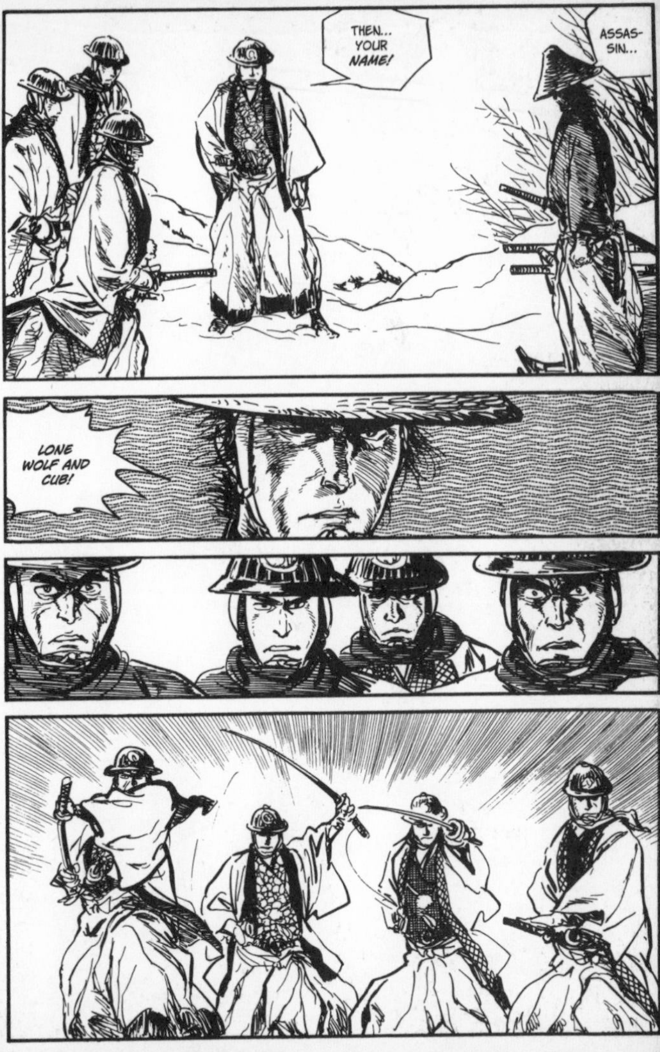
ASSAS-SIN...
THEN... YOUR NAME!
LONE WOLF AND CUB!

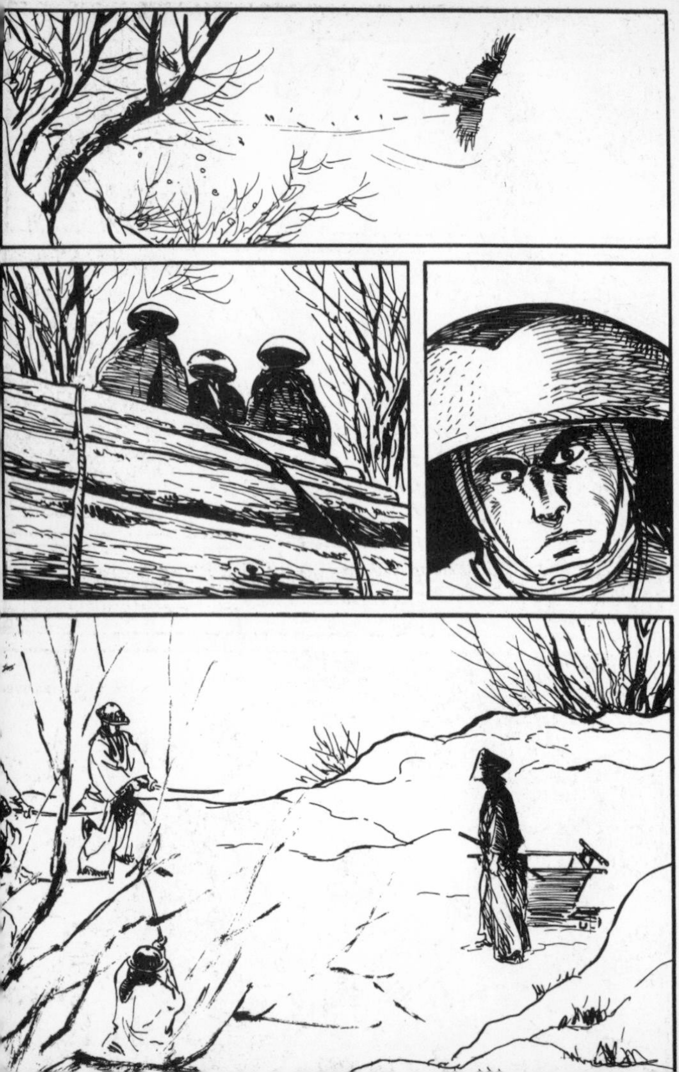

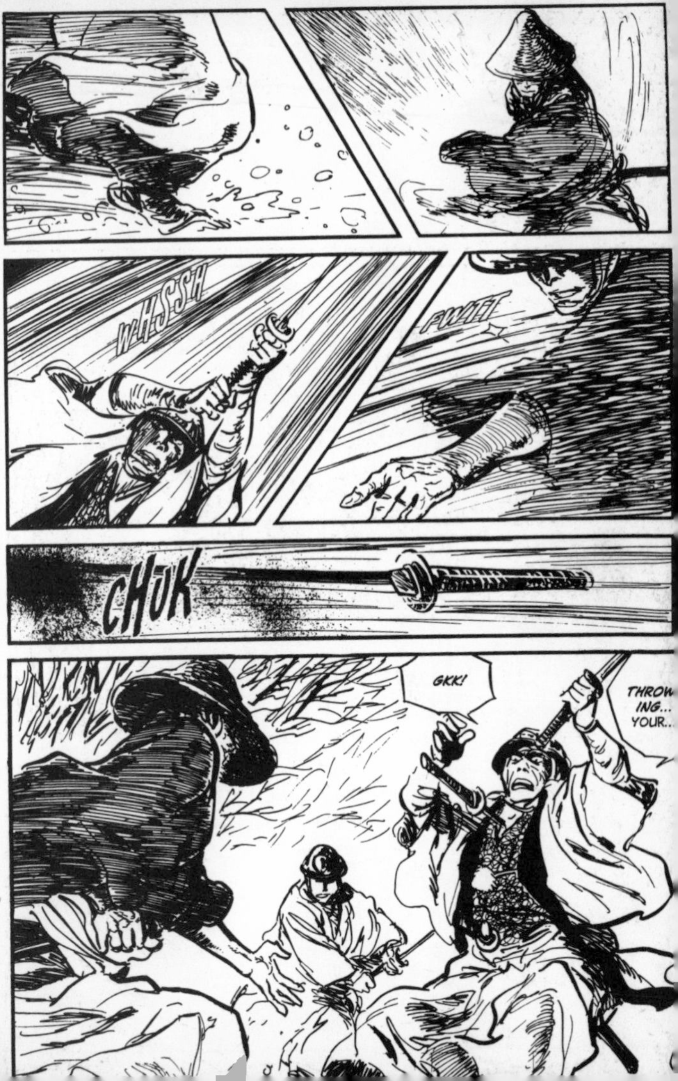
FWITT
WHSSH
CHUK
THROW
ING...
YOUR...
GKK!

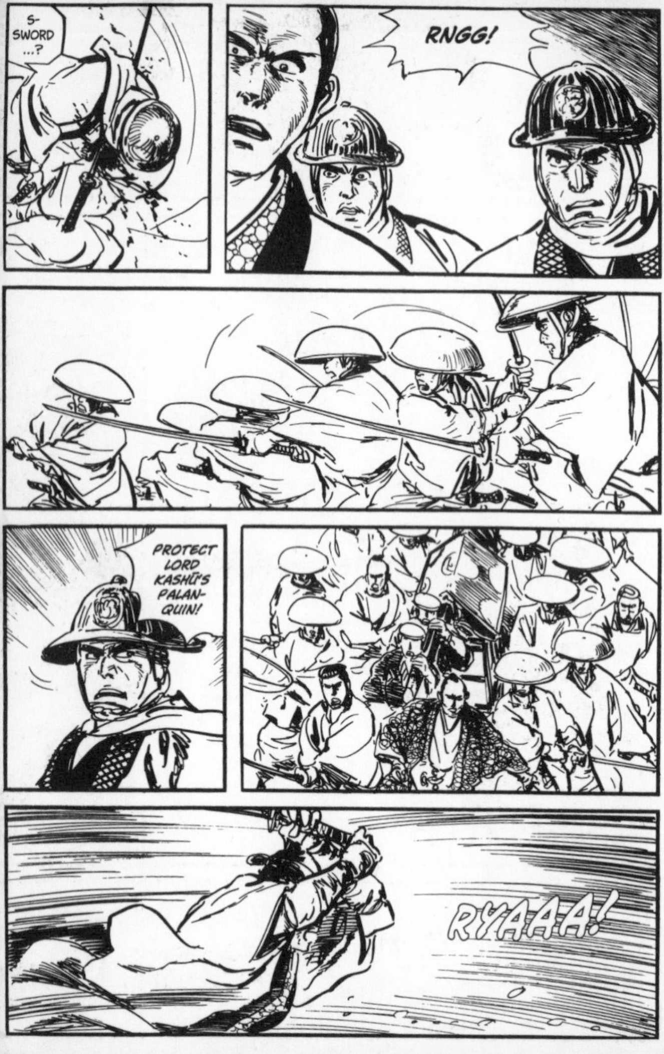
S-SWORD ...?
RNGG!
PROTECT LORD KASHŪ'S PALANQUIN!
RYAAA!

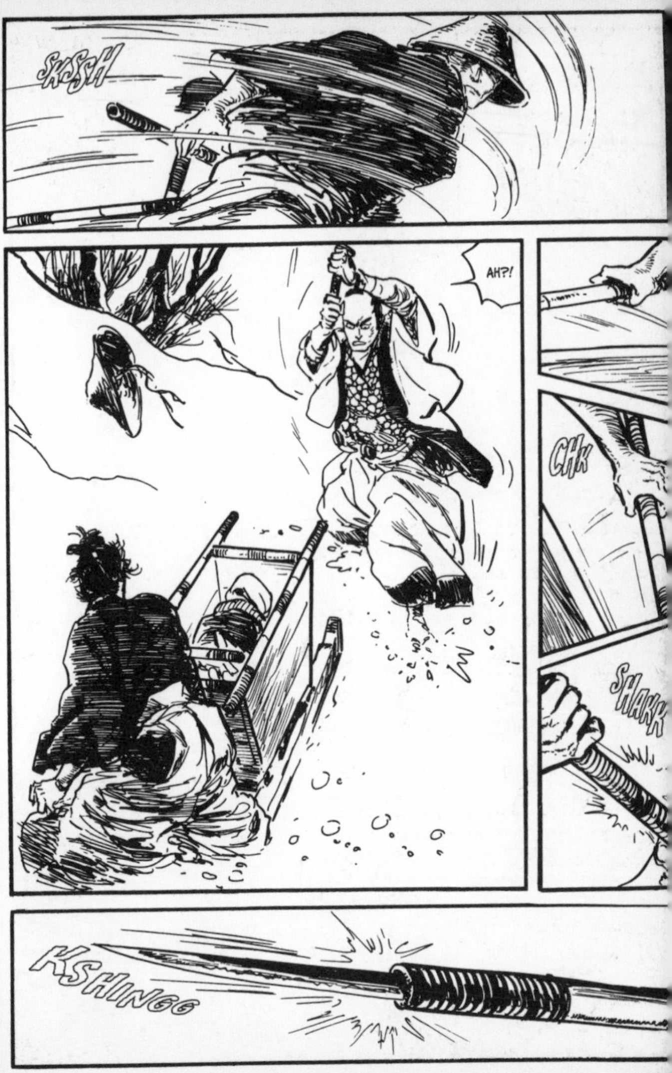
SKSSH
CHK
SHAKK
AH?!
KSHINGG

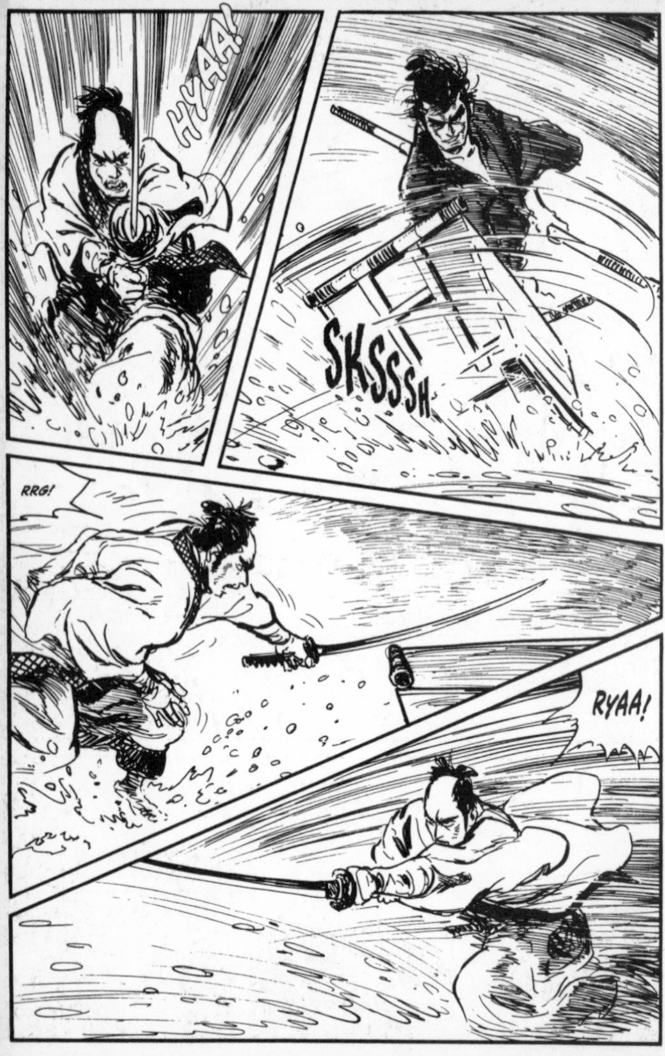
SKSSSH
HYAA!
RRG!
RYAA!

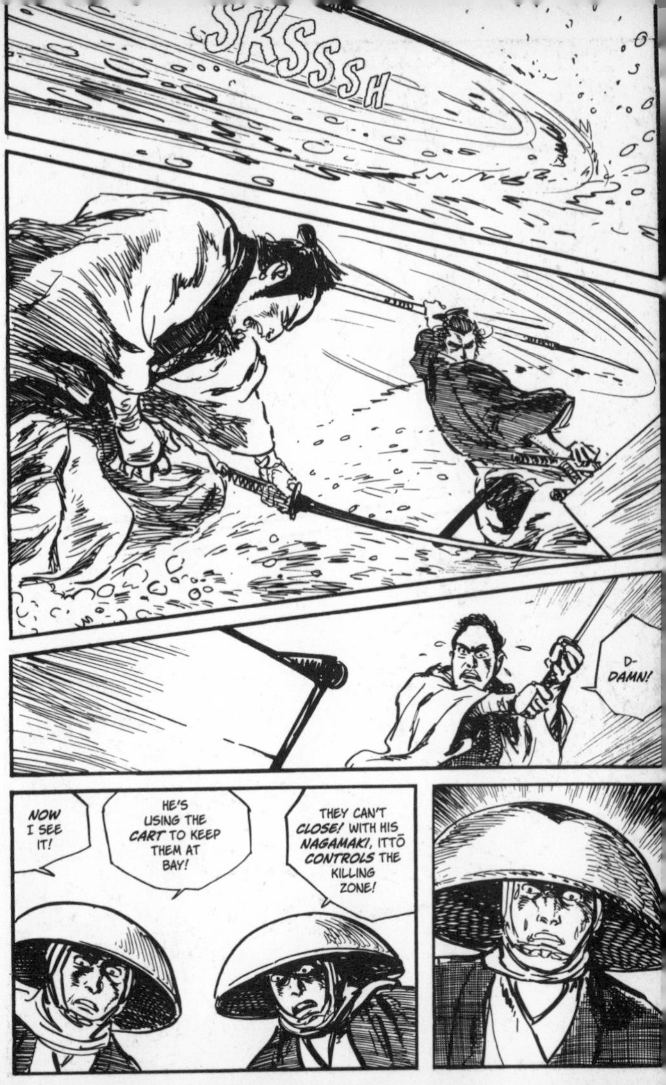
SKSSSH
D-DAMN!
NOW I SEE IT!
HE'S USING THE CART TO KEEP THEM AT BAY!
THEY CAN'T CLOSE! WITH HIS NAGAMAKI, ITTŌ CONTROLS THE KILLING ZONE!

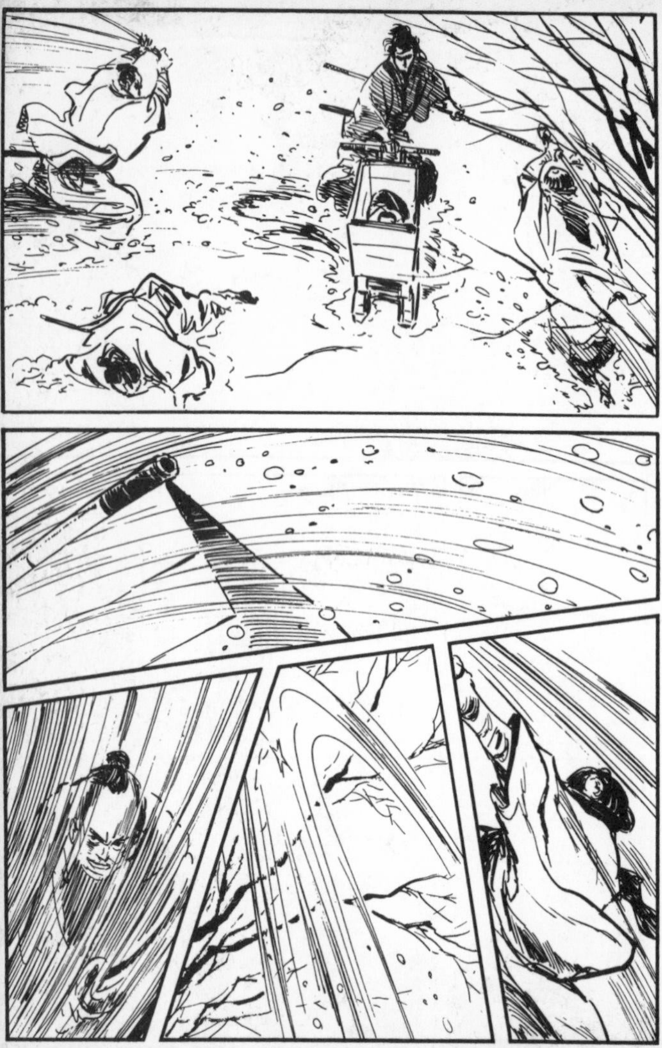

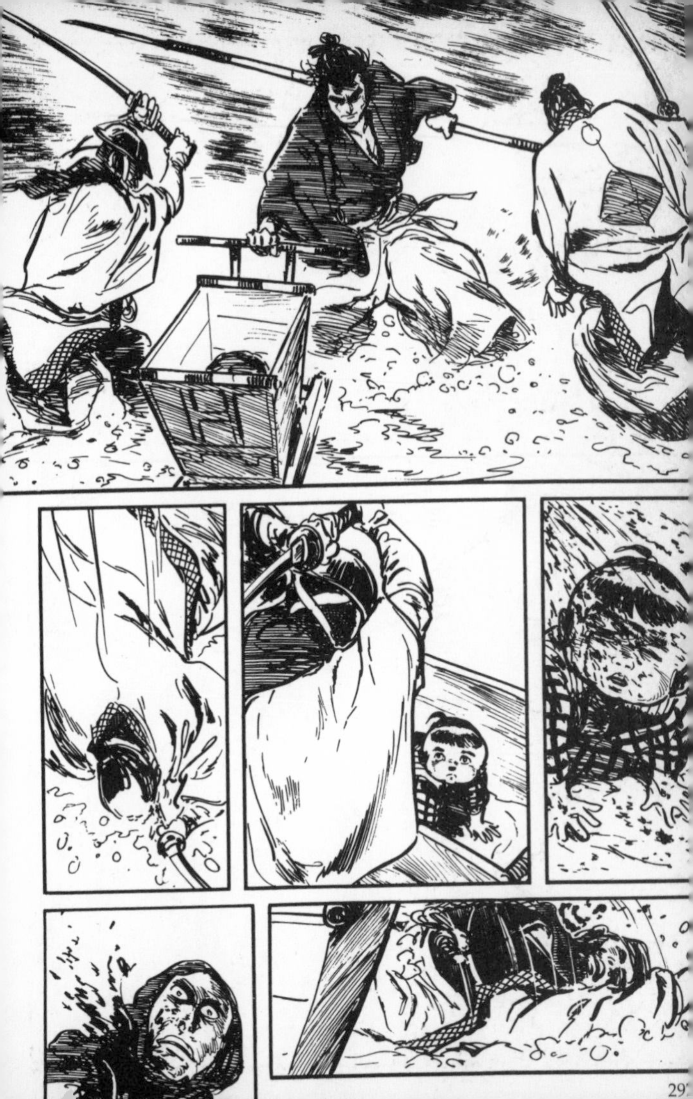

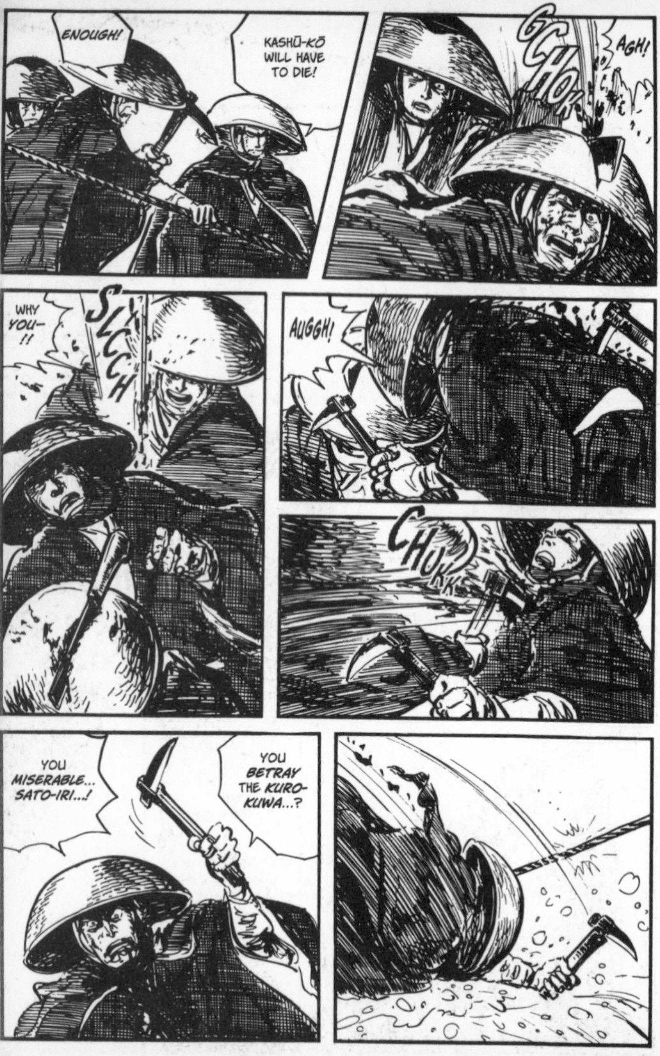
ENOUGH!
KASHŪ-KŌ WILL HAVE TO DIE!
GCHOK
AGH!
WHY YOU—!!
SLCCH
AUGGH!
CHUKK
YOU MISERABLE... SATO-IRI...!
YOU BETRAY THE KURO-KUWA...?

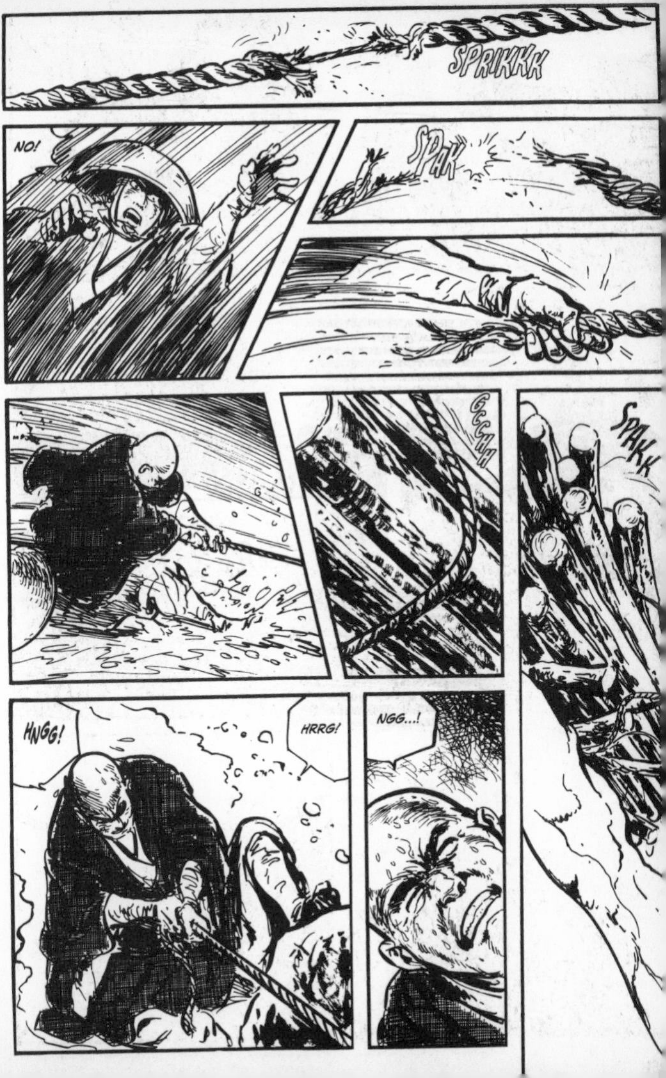
SPRIKKK
SPAK
NO!
SPAKK
GCCHH
NGG...!
HRRG!
HNGG!

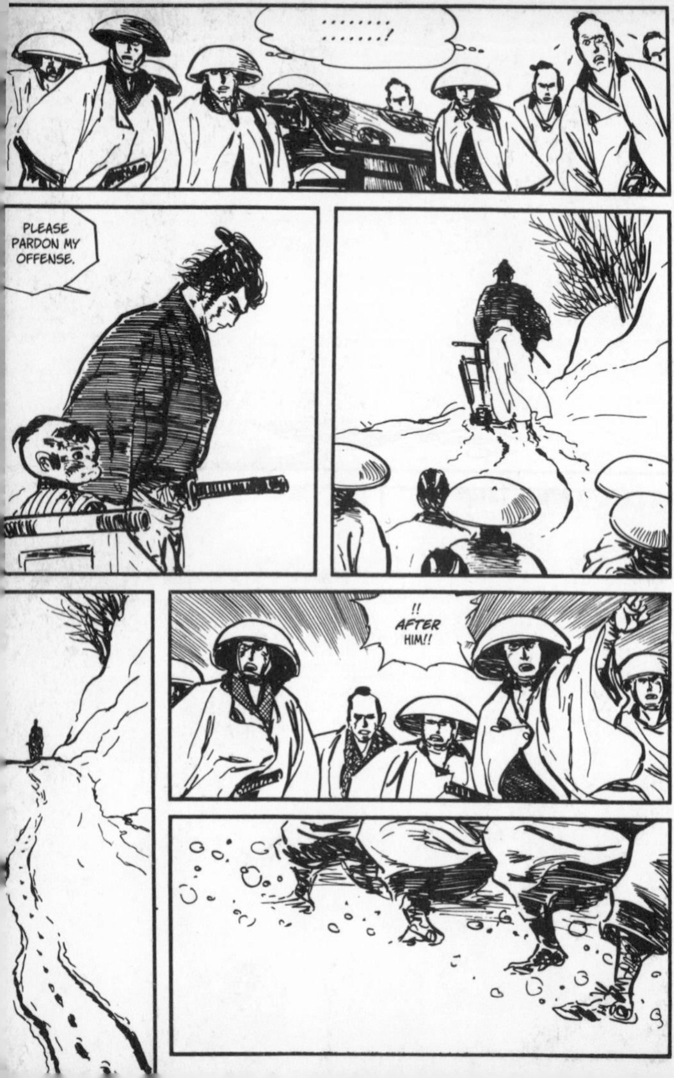
....
........!
PLEASE PARDON MY OFFENSE.
!! AFTER HIM!!

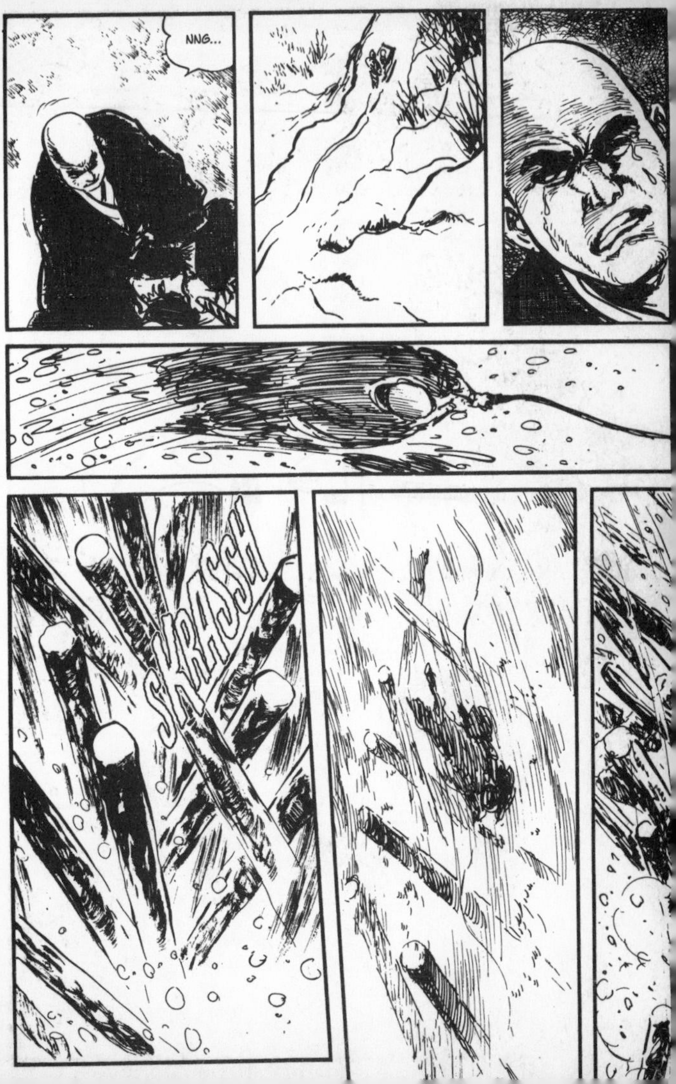
NNG...
SKRASSH

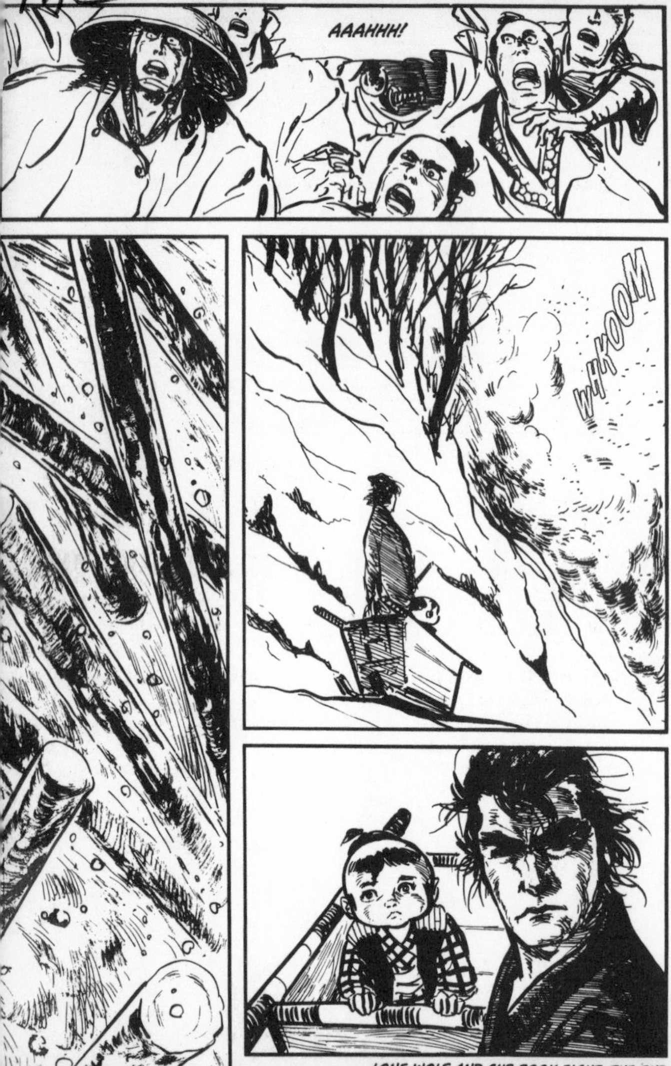
AAAHHH!
WHKOOOM

LONE WOLF AND CUB BOOK EIGHT: THE END

adauchi shamenjō

A pardon. *Adauchi* (revenge killings) were permitted by the government for family members. When a petition of *adauchi* was approved, the supplicants received an official pardon to prove they acted legally.

bakkaku

The government. The shōgun, his councilors, and his senior officials.

bōzu

A Buddhist monk.

daikan

The primary local representative of the shōgunate in territories outside of the capital of Edo. The *daikan* and his staff collected taxes owed to Edo and oversaw public works, agriculture, and other projects administered by the central government.

dōtanuki

A battle sword. Literally, "sword that cuts through torsos."

Edo

The capital of medieval Japan and the seat of the shōgunate. The site of modern-day Tokyo.

fudai

The inner circle of clans pledging allegiance to the Tokugawa. The *fudai* clans were Tokugawa allies even before the decisive battle of Sekigahara that assured Tokugawa dominance for the next two hundred years.

haiku

Traditional short verse, with a 5-7-5 syllable pattern.

han

A feudal domain.

hannyatō

"Wisdom's water." A euphemism among Buddhist monks for *sake*.

hansatsu

Paper currency, issued by individual *han* and used only within their borders.

hanshi

Samurai in the service of a *han*.

hikyaku

Runners. An Edo version of the Pony Express, delivery of mail and money by horse and by foot.

Hokurikuro

The main route into northern Japan.

honjin

The lodgings for *daimyō* and senior shōgunate officials.

honorifics

Japan is a class and status society, and proper forms of address are critical. Common markers of respect are the prefixes *o* and *go*, and a wide range of suffixes. Some of the suffixes you will encounter in *Lone Wolf and Cub*:

chan – for children, young women, and close friends

dono – archaic; used for higher-ranked or highly respected figures

sama – used for superiors

san – the most common, used among equals or near-equals

sensei – used for teachers, masters, respected entertainers, and politicians

kansho

A petition admonishing a superior, always fraught with personal risk in feudal Japan. The *kansho* in Chapter 39 is a *jiji-kansho*, addressed directly to the shōgun himself.

kenkyaku

Swordsman, *kenshi*.

kō

A *daimyō* (feudal lord).

kōgi kaishakunin

The shōgun's own second, who performed executions ordered by the shōgun.

koku

A bale of rice. The traditional measure of a *han*'s wealth, a measure of its agricultural land and productivity.

kubi

A severed head. The *kubi* had great significance, be it the head of a wanted criminal presented to claim a bounty; or the head of a samurai, proof in death of his resolute will.

meifumadō

The Buddhist Hell. The way of demons and damnation.

nagamaki

A two-handed weapon taller than a man, with a long, curved blade.

namu

From the Sanskrit *namas*: "take refuge in the Buddha." A common prayer for the dead.

o-niwaban

A ninja. Literally, "one in the garden." (See *shinobi*.)

rōjū

Senior councilors. The inner circle of councilors directly advising the shōgun. The *rōjū* were the ultimate advisory body to the Tokugawa shōgunate's national government.

ryō

A gold piece, worth 60 *monme* or 4 *kan*.